A FREEDOM TO ROAM
THE
BRIGHTON DOWNS
FROM SHOREHAM TO NEWHAVEN AND BEEDING TO LEWES

DAVE BANGS

To Jane Erin, my best ally and constant companion on Downland walks.

Book design by Andrew Jamison
andrew230@hotmail.com

Printed August 2008 by Bishops Printers, Farlington, Portsmouth
ISBN 0-9548638-1-X

CONTENTS

Page

4   Acknowledgements
5   Picture & Poem Credits
6   Maps & Diagrams
7   Preface
9   Introduction

PART ONE — THE BACK STORY

15   Public Space & Freedom
27   Down Pasture's History
37   Down Pasture's Natural History
73   Woodland and Scrub
89   The Geology & Landforms of the Downs
103   Patterns Made by People
127   Buildings on the Downs
133   Downland Connections
141   Brighton — A Downland City
155   The Urban Fringe
171   Threats to our Downland
181   Fightback
191   What Should the Future Look Like?

PART TWO — SITE BY SITE GUIDE

197   The Beeding Downs
203   The Shoreham Downs
209   From Southwick Hill to Truleigh Hill
219   From Portslade to Fulking
223   The Hangleton & West Blatchington Downs
229   The Devil's Dyke & Newtimber Hill
237   The Waterhall & Saddlescombe Valley
243   From Patcham to Pyecombe — The London Road Valley
247   Wolstonbury Hill & Clayton Windmills

Page

255   From Patcham's Ladies Mile to Ditchling Beacon
263   From Stanmer to Westmeston & Streat
269   From Balmer to Plumpton
277   Blackcap, Mount Harry & Ashcombe
283   Old Lewes Racecourse, the Chalk Pits & Offham Down
289   Hollingbury Hill & the Moulsecoomb Wild Park
293   The Bevendean & Falmer Downs
299   From Whitehawk Hill to Rottingdean
307   The Kingston Hill & Castle Hill Downs
315   The Rottingdean & Saltdean Downs
319   The Iford & Rodmell Downs
325   From Telscombe Cliffs to Southease
331   The Newhaven & Peacehaven Cliffs and Downs

343   Appendix 1: The Legal Position on Access to the Countryside in England
347   Appendix 2: Who Farms What?
349   Appendix 3: Threatened Down Pasture Sites
351   Appendix 4: Things I Take When Exploring the Downs
353   Appendix 5: A Freedom to Roam Countryside Code
355   Appendix 6: Place Names Tell Stories
363   Contacts
364   Recommended Books
365   Glossary

ACKNOWLEDGEMENTS

To the officers of the Toads Hole Valleyside Wildlife Group, Keith Bassant and Jane Erin, for their donation of funds for this book, upon the winding up of their organization.

To the past activists of Keep our Downs Public, The Land Is Ours, Earth First! and Red Rope, who have been the most eager to respond when we campaigned against the privatization of our Downland, for the freedom to roam, and against the destruction of our ancient Down pasture heritage.

To all those lay experts who have been friendly and open in passing on their knowledge. Folk like Keith Dodman (birder), Paul Harmes and Tony Spiers (botanists), John Funnell (archaeologist), Peter Hodge (beetles and bugs expert) and many more.

To Paul Millmore, Chris Smith, Paula Blackledge, Chris Stevenson and Jane Erin who critically read the book's draft.

PICTURE AND POEM CREDITS

THE poems are mine, with two exceptions. Michael Kelly's poem 'Lift Up Your Eyes', on page 14, appeared in the periodical *Countrygoer* (1946) and the *Sheffield Clarion Ramblers Handbook* (1951-2, pages 36-7). The poem quoted at the head of the Geology chapter, page 89, is from 'A Letter to an Old Sweetheart' by Charles Dalmon, verses of which appeared in *The Sussex Bedside Anthology*, collected by Margaret Galsworthy, and published by The Arundel Press (1950). I cannot find Michael or Charles's executors, but I thank them.

THE photos, maps and diagrams are mine, with the following exceptions. Inside cover and pages 42-43, 46, 47, 65, Flowers and insects: Paul Harmes, with special thanks. Inside cover and page 44, Grizzled Skipper; page 57, Adder and young: Sussex Biodiversity Record Centre. Page 30, RAF aerial photo of Portslade Downs (1946): photo provided by Department of Geography, University of Sussex. Page 33, Moulsecoomb Wild Park, old and new: Dave Larkin, Ranger, and Brighton and Hove City Council. Pages 55-57, Bird pictures: Thomas Bewick, from *Land Birds* (1797). Page 61, Young Hare: Albrecht Durer (1502), in the Albertina, Vienna. Page 62, Harvest mice: Arthur R. Thompson, *Nature by Night*, Fig. 21 (Ivor Nicholson and Watson Ltd. 1931). Page 96, Section of the strata at Castle Hill near Newhaven Harbour: Gideon Mantell, *Geology of the South East of England*, pages 54-56 (1833). Pages 109, 212, 272, 274, 320, Five maps from 'The Celtic Field System in South Britain: a survey of the Brighton District' by G.A. Holleyman, in *Antiquity* (1935), Vol. 9, No. 36, pages 443-454, published by permission of Antiquity Publications Ltd, the place of first publication. (www. antiquity.ac.uk). Page 110, Neolithic axe: David McOmish. Page 175, 'Sussex Downs Tranquil Areas Map, 1997': Map courtesy of the South Downs Joint Committee. Page 207, Old Shoreham: Mary Bangs (1983). Page 228, The Black Burgh Cup: from Plate XII of *The Archaeology of Sussex*, by E. Cecil Curwen (Methuen & Co. Ltd. 1937). Page 258, Ditchling Beacon: by Ruth Dollman, illustrator to Richard Jefferies (c.1882). Page 296, Newmarket Hill and Plantation: Fred Netley. Page 332, Raven: H. Gronvold. Plate 99 of *Birds of Great Britain and Ireland (Order Passeres)*, Volume 2, by A. G. Butler, Illustrated by H. Gronvold and F.W. Frohawk (Brumby & Clarke Ltd. c.1910). I cannot find Mr Arthur R. Thompson, Mr E. Cecil Curwen, or Mr H. Gronvold's executors, but I thank them. If I have unwittingly omitted any acknowledgements please accept my sincere apologies.

MAPS AND DIAGRAMS

Page

17 Common Land Enclosure in the 19th Century
21 Beeding Manor: Medieval Land Use
25 Public and Quasi-Publicly Owned Land on the Brighton Downs
28 Erringham Farm, Shoreham: Extent of Down Pasture 1687 and 2007
29 Unimproved Down Pasture, circa 1840
29 Unimproved Down Pasture, 1873
30 1946 Aerial Photo of the Portslade Downs
32 Unimproved Down Pasture, 1956
32 Unimproved Down Pasture and Scrub, 2007
51 The Distribution of Some Scarce and Threatened Species
75 Old Woodland Around 'The Promontories' (Wolstonbury, Newtimber Hill, and the Dyke)
78 Some Veteran Trees
92 Schematic Downland Section Between the Devil's Dyke and Hove Beach
95 The Newhaven Tertiary Deposits
98 The Sarsen Landscape
100 Downland Landforms
105 Prehistoric Barrows (Burial Mounds)
108 Hillforts, Castles, Rings and Enclosures
109 Prehistoric Field Systems Mapped
111 Whitehawk Boundary Stones
111 Hangleton Parish Boundary Features
112 Medieval Parish Boundaries
115 Some Ancient Roads
117 Patcham's Drove Roads
123 Quarries and Pits
128 Kingston Buci's Origins
134 Stanmer's Swine Pastures
136 Saxon Swine Pasture Drove Roads
138 The Domesday Book Villages, 1086AD
144 Public and Private House Building on the Downs
147 Benfield Valley Development to c. 1990
147 Benfield Valley Development, 1990 to 2008
149 Stanmer Park, c. 1870
149 Stanmer Park, 2008
151 Viewshed of Brighton High-Rise Development
152 Portslade Motor Racing Track Plans, c. 1935

156 The 'Access Sandwich'
160 New Cultural Landscapes: Golf Courses and Race Courses
163 New Cultural Landscapes: Allotments and Horseyculture
172 Protected Downland Sites
175 Tranquil Areas Map of the Sussex Downs, 1997
178 Shooting Enterprises
186 Not-so-Free-to-Roam
189 Proposed National Park Boundary
194 Sub-Landscapes of the Brighton Downs
196 The Beeding Downs
202 The Shoreham Downs
208 From Southwick Hill to Truleigh Hill
212 Thundersbarrow's Prehistoric Landscape
218 From Portslade to Fulking
225 The Hangleton and West Blatchington Downs
231 The Devil's Dyke and Newtimber Hill
239 The Waterhall and Saddlescombe Valley
242 From Patcham to Pyecombe: The London Road Valley
249 Wolstonbury and Clayton Windmills
254 From Patcham Ladies Mile to Ditchling Beacon
262 From Stanmer to Westmeston and Streat
271 From Balmer to Plumpton
272 Buckland Bank's Prehistoric Landscape
274 Plumpton Plain's Prehistoric Landscape
276 Blackcap, Mount Harry and Ashcombe
282 From Old Lewes Racecourse to Offham Down
288 Hollingbury Hill and Moulsecoomb Wild Park
295 The Bevendean and Falmer Downs
298 From Whitehawk to Rottingdean
300 Whitehawk Hill's Neolithic Causewayed Camp
306 Kingston Hill and Castle Hill
314 The Rottingdean and Saltdean Downs
320 Highdole Hill's Prehistoric Landscape
321 The Iford and Rodmell Downs
327 From Telscombe Cliffs to Southease
333 Newhaven and Peacehaven Cliffs and Down
335 Black Rock to Newhaven Chalk Cliffs
346 Who Farms What?

PREFACE

Most countryside guides just provide general information on chosen landscapes, or they may describe public 'trails', like the South Downs Way, or suggest 'pub walks', or circular walks on rights of way. Some wildlife guides give information on important nature reserves.

This guide breaks those limited patterns and describes **all** the interesting landscape sites on the Brighton Downs, whether there's a right of access or not. **It focuses particularly on the traditional old Down pasture sites, because these form the most important local habitat.** They are as characteristic of the Brighton Downs as heather moorland is of Exmoor or Dartmoor, or lakes and tarns are of the Lake District.

The book is divided into two parts, which can be read independently.

Part Two is the 'Site by Site Guide'. This is where you look if you just want to glean some information on good local Downland to visit. I have divided the Brighton Downs into 22 sub-landscapes for descriptive purposes. These sub-landscapes link urban areas to the remote areas of the Downs, to help encourage wider use and a sense of public ownership of all our local Downs.

Appendix 1 also has a short **guide to the legal position on access.** We need to know our rights in the countryside, if we are to be confident there.

All sites described in Part Two have six figure map references attached. If you do not know how to read a map reference, you can find out from your Ordnance Survey Explorer map, which has a simple guide as part of its key.

Part One is 'The Backstory'. This extended section has some landscape history, some natural history, some geology and archaeology, and quite a lot about the way the growth of the Brighton conurbation has altered our Downs. I hope readers will see the Downs differently after reading this section.

I have been influenced by the famous series of guides by Nairn and Pevsner called 'The Buildings of England', published on a county by county basis in the 1960s and still in print. That series attempted to describe all significant local buildings (exteriors and interiors) **quite irrespective of whether they were accessible to the public.** In doing so the authors provided a great public service and helped inform the cultural conservation movement.

Like Nairn and Pevsner I leave it up to readers to make their own arrangements for access.

To get the most out of this book you will need a copy of the Ordnance Survey Explorer Map 122, which covers the whole of the Brighton Downs. It marks all public rights of way and most statutory Access Land, although much other land open to public access is not marked, at present.

INTRODUCTION

THIS book has its basis in an idea. It is that that the Brighton Downs are a **public landscape** best managed democratically in public hands, with restored open permanent pasturelands forming the majority land use, around the core surviving fragments of ancient wildlife-rich pasture.

This book celebrates the pampas-like / steppe-like / prairie-like qualities of these Downs. It celebrates their roadlessness, treelessness, buildinglessness, hedgelessness, waterlessness, clutterlessness.

It celebrates their greenness and peacefulness, their tiny busy-ness of living things, memoryfullness of ancient things, abundance of useful things: sheep, corn, cattle, thyme, dung beetles, chalk, sun, grass, rain, flint, wind, orchids, butterflies, snails.

It celebrates the Downs because they bring you close to the sky and the horizon and to silence and the sea and the earth and to living wild things.

The Downs became famous for two big clusters of reasons.

One set of reasons had to do with their 'big landscape' qualities. The Downs are high, with wide, unstopped dramatic views and all the exhilaration which height and distance gives you. They have curved, smooth forms, like mushrooms or whale-backs, or fruit, or smooth bodies, or ocean waves. They are largely empty of settlements and roads (when you get away from the coastal towns). They are unenclosed by hedges or walls (and their wire fences, being largely invisible, do not detract from this visual truth). All these characteristics are emblematic of freedom — to explore, to wander, and to be unconfined.

The other set of landscape qualities had to do with the intimate, close-up qualities of Downland. They had to do with the Downland at your feet. That meant the mantle of short, scented, soft, close-cropped, sheep-grazed turf of the old Downs. The softness of this mantle meant that you could walk for miles and never tire. Your walking would be accompanied by silence and by the sky song of myriad larks. The scent was the scent of thyme and all those other tiny flowers that grew as thickly in the turf as the short, wiry grasses. And their protecting mantle cloaked the marks and bones of all the long-gone peoples who had inhabited these hills: their barrows, camps and field banks exposed by the long shadows cast at summer dawn and dusk.

I am sad that so much — most — of this Downland fabric is damaged and lost. It's a myth — an empty mantra — that the Downs are a wonderful natural landscape.

They are not. They are a wretched mess. The old pastures and the signs of the ancient peoples have been trashed. Over-development has damaged our Brighton Downs more than any other section of this 80 mile-long chain of chalk hills. Noise and light pollution, built development and the barrenness of agri-business intrude deep into these uplands.

They *were* a wonderful natural landscape, and they *could* be again. The Downs are like a loved one badly injured in an accident. They're helpless and hardly alive. Some might argue that they'd be better off dead. But *we* know that if they get the care and nurture they need they can be as beautiful and perfect as we knew them before. It's that faith that keeps people fighting for them.

It didn't have to be like that. We have had chances before. But the deal was fixed by the inequalities of capitalist power, property ownership, and market-based production. When imperialism opened up the western lands of America and the southern lands of Australasia to high tech food production the owning class just let the British countryside go hang. The ancient sheep walks of the Downs were left derelict and semi-derelict. When inter-imperialist rivalry and ambivalence towards fascism drove Britain into two world wars, the Downs were ploughed up and used as artillery ranges. And when the cold war succeeded the hot war, the Downs were ploughed up wall to wall to bolster an imperialist food policy seeking to dominate third world food economies and bully the Stalinist bloc. And the landowners and farmers played the cards which were dealt them — mostly with great enthusiasm — at the expense of their farm workers, small farmer colleagues and the Down landscape which the urban public loved.

We need a policy towards Downland which is free of the comings and goings and uncertainties of international commodity markets and local business opportunities. We need a policy which recognizes the broad public's right to determine the management of their Downland. The basis is already there, for two thirds of our Brighton Downs are already in various forms of public ownership. We need to democratize and extend this ownership so that people can really be involved in all the choices and opportunities which the countryside offers.

————————————

I N southern England the Countryside and Rights of Way Act of 2000 (the 'CROW' Act) which introduced a 'right to roam', gave walkers very little, compared to the huge expanses of mountain and moor opened to the right to roam in the Peaks, the Lake District and other uplands.

Downland walkers gained the right to roam only on some of the surviving shreds of the shattered old Down pasture fabric.

Local activists argued with all our strength for a legal right of access to all open Downland that was not under crops. We lost that case for now. But the right to usage of our countryside is common to all people. It is our natural right — a *birth-right*.

Our Downland must — *in every way* — become a public landscape.

————————————

W E cannot love what we are not allowed to know. What the eye cannot see, the heart cannot grieve over. To reclaim this heritage we must first get to know it…

The Downs are not just a backdrop to our towns, a kind of City wallpaper. And they'll keep most of their secrets if we just walk the footpaths, or view them from a distance.

Try stepping inside them instead. Take some small risks. Bash through the bushes. Get tripped up in grass tussocks. Get too hot. Get tired.

Come on! Walk through the back of that wardrobe and check out these new worlds. You won't be disappointed.

Then join in the fight to save them!

PART ONE
THE BACK STORY

The men that live in Manchester they have not far to go
To walk upon the ridges where the shouting breezes blow,
And all amongst the frowning stones are keepers lying low.
    Lord help us!

The souls that live in Sheffield town have heaven at their gate
Curlew call and lark-song and streams like ale in spate,
And there, among the heather hid, the keepers lie in wait.
    Lord help us!

The cheery ones of Chesterfield see moors not far away
Tired of streets and a drunken spire they hie them there to play,
But the keeper, with his dog and gun, is there to say them nay
    Lord help us!

The folk who live in Sussex shire they stride along their down
And scorn all walls and scorn all guns and fools who live in town
And revel in their liberty and think of us as clowns.
    Lord help us!

And since I live in the North country where liberty is dead
And a gibbering bird means more than Man and nought is done or said,
I think I must go to the South country where a man may raise his head.
    Lord help us!

Michael Kelly, *Countrygoer*, 1946

PUBLIC SPACE
AND FREEDOM

WHAT a passionate call Michael's poem was for the freedom to roam!

Yet how strangely have the fortunes of walkers from the northern mill towns and those of us in the south country reversed. Sixty years after he wrote, huge tracts of his keepered northern grouse moors were opened to all under New Labour's 'Countryside and Rights of Way Act'. Yet here, on southern Downlands and heaths, we have had to make do with the creation of a few pathetic fragments of new Access Land.

Indeed, even as Michael wrote, the last of the great plateau Down pastures were disappearing under the plough and transforming an open, free landscape into a sterile, privatized cereals monoculture.

A while ago I chatted to an elderly man who had been brought up in a village under the scarp of the Brighton Downs, before World War Two. We were talking about the controversy over the new freedom to roam proposals, which were then going through Parliament. He told me that he had spent many, many days wandering his local Downs as a boy, and had always assumed that the whole of the pasture Downs were open and free to all. So ingrained was his assumption that he did not even realize there were such things

as 'rights of way'. Since all the grassland Downs were open and free, how could it matter what path or direction he chose?

My mother, too, always used to say "There were never any fences, then. You could walk for miles on the soft turf, with only the smell of the thyme, and the skylarks singing overhead". She came from a Sussex family and had spent many happy holidays walking the Downs before that last world war.

Of course, these memories give only a partial picture. Even by the 1920s and '30s large stretches of the open Downs were being fenced with barbed wire for dairy and beef cattle. Major tracts were disappearing under scrub thickets. But their memories were wholly truthful in the way that they represented the broad public perception of the Sussex Downs as a landscape of freedom: a landscape where people could wander without let or hindrance, provided they did no harm to others.

As is so often the case, public perception lagged behind reality. By the time of their childhoods the old public spaces — the Downland commons — were almost extinct, eliminated by centuries of privatizing enclosure by rich farmers and landowners. These enclosures rarely resulted in the immediate ploughing up or fencing of all, or even most, of the enclosed land (as they often did on more fertile soils) and so wanderers could still imagine that relatively little change had taken place.

In the interwar 1920s and '30s very active campaigns were being carried on to halt the process of attrition of the old, free, Downs by fencing and built development. The cornerstone of these campaigns was the public acquisition of Downland. Their parents thought that their campaigns were creating a system of new commons, built on urban people's recreational needs, to replace the old commons, based on the economic needs of the rural poor.

The Old Commons of the Brighton Downs

THERE are still some relics of the ancient commons of the Brighton Downs to be seen, giving faint testimony to a time when the peasantry had some real, though limited, collective control over the countryside. These relics give testimony, too, of a time when the community of the poor struggled to maintain a harmony with nature against the encroaching powers of the lords. The **Old Steine, The Level, The Race Hill** and **Telscombe Tye**, all owe their continued existence as open spaces to the long survival of this ancient form of collective tenure.

Peasant Collectivism

DOWNLAND commons, in medieval times, were places which were subject to the *collective* management of the tenants, under the hegemony of the lords of the manors. They were public spaces. The lords' sheep and cattle would have been shepherded together with the tenants' stock. They would all have been subject to the collective management of 'the homage' — the body of the tenantry or their chosen jury — and their chosen shepherds and cowherds. The cutting of turf, wood, furze (the old name for gorse), and bracken would also have been communally

regulated. The tenants and the lord's bailiff would have regulated ('stinted') the numbers and type of animals grazed, and watched closely over the health of the sward (grassy turf).

Tenantry Downs and 'Sheep and Corn' Farming

BECAUSE of the central role of the lords' tenants these commons were called 'tenantry downs' and many place names still survive on the open Downs to commemorate them. Brighton has **Tenantry Down Road** and had an electoral district called Tenantry Ward. There are **Tenants Hills** north of Mile Oak and Saltdean and **Tenants' Laine** where Sussex University sits. On the eastern slope of Newtimber Hill sits the **Cow Down**, a now-gone common of Pyecombe parish, and Portslade's **Foredown Hill and Road** commemorate another vanished tenants' 'cow down'.

These commons were part of the vigorous and rational 'sheep and corn' Downland farming system. This system held sway from Saxon times right up until the late Victorian farming depression and the two world wars — over a thousand years. Under the sheep and corn system the tenants tilled the fertile valley bottom fields mostly for grain crops, and pastured their great flocks of sheep on the less fertile higher ground of the ridges and high plateau. At night the sheep were brought down to an uncropped, resting field called the 'fallow' field and 'folded' on a couple of strips of the tenants' land overnight to drop their dung. (The sheep 'fold' was an enclosure of moveable wattle hazel hurdles). Thus, over time, the sheep gradually transferred nutrients from the high sheep pastures to the corn fields. That was the sheep's most important function. This was a workable way of regularly fertilizing the rich corn lands and getting an abundance of wool and mutton as additional products.

The Modern Enclosure of Common Land on The Brighton Downs

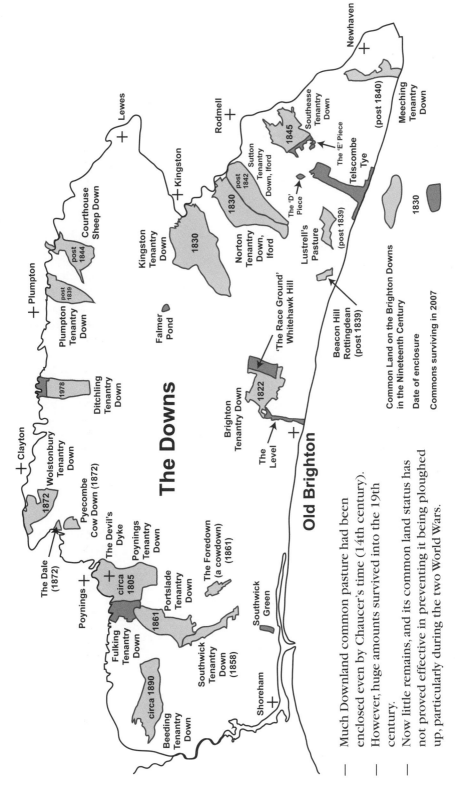

The Downs

Old Brighton

Newhaven

Lewes

Rodmell

Southease Tenantry Down

(post 1840)

Meeching Tenantry Down

The 'E' Piece

1845

Telscombe Tye

Kingston

Sutton Tenantry Down, Iford

post 1842

1830

The 'D' Piece

Norton Tenantry Down, Iford

Kingston Tenantry Down

1830

Lustrell's Pasture

(post 1839)

1830

'The Race Ground' Whitehawk Hill

Plumpton

Courthouse Sheep Down

post 1844

Plumpton Tenantry Down

post 1839

Falmer Pond

Beacon Hill Rottingdean (post 1839)

Ditchling Tenantry Down

1978

Brighton Tenantry Down

1822

Common Land on the Brighton Downs in the Nineteenth Century

Date of enclosure

Commons surviving in 2007

Clayton

Wolstonbury Tenantry Down

1872

Pyecombe Cow Down (1872)

The Level

The Dale (1872)

The Devil's Dyke

Poynings Tenantry Down

The Foredown (a cowdown) (1861)

Poynings

circa 1805

Portslade Tenantry Down

Fulking Tenantry Down

1861

Southwick Tenantry Down (1858)

Southwick Green

circa 1890

Beeding Tenantry Down

Shoreham

— Much Downland common pasture had been enclosed even by Chaucer's time (14th century).
  However, huge amounts survived into the 19th century.

— Now little remains, and its common land status has not proved effective in preventing it being ploughed up, particularly during the two World Wars.

Reproduced from the 1940 Ordnance Survey map bases with the kind permission of the Ordnance Survey.

In early medieval times it is likely that all or most of the Down pastures were managed as commons, but already by Chaucer's time, in the late 14th century, many lords had inclosed parts of the sheep walks for private 'home farm' pastures, called 'desmesne' pastures. By the time of the Wars of the Roses, in the 15th century, at least half of the East Sussex Downland was probably inclosed.[1] **Anchor Bottom**, high up on Beeding Hill by the South Downs Way was an early desmesne pasture of the lord of Beeding manor (based below Anchor Bottom at Beeding Court Farm. It is named 'Court' Farm because the manorial court, or assembly, met there). For centuries it lay next to the Beeding Tenantry Down, from which it had been cut out.

Fossil Landscapes

F R O M 16th century Tudor times onwards the numbers of tenant farmer-peasants fell, so that by about 1800 the great majority of the Brighton Downs was farmed by a small number of large capitalist tenant farmers and owner-occupiers. Strangely, though, the bones of the organization of the Downland landscape often did not substantially change throughout these centuries of 'engrossment' of the small tenants holdings. The old landscape of communally organised strip-cultivated open fields and high — often common — sheep pastures survived in fossil form, whilst its original rational meaning had been lost.

Eighteenth century Brighton itself was an excellent example of such a fossil landscape. It retained the full medieval array of four giant open fields (plus a recent one) organized in a dense tapestry of 1489 separate peasant strip 'paulpieces'. The fishermen's common of the Old Steine and the damp meadow and drove-way of The Level lined the central valley floor northwards to the great 400 acre tenantry sheep Down stretching all the way to the edge of modern Whitehawk. The sheep flock was still 1,100 strong at the time of

enclosure in 1822. Yet, by then, just three proprietors had gained control of 86% of the common rights and there were in total only eight proprietors left, of the once-numerous open field farming community.

Remarkably, in three other parishes the entire Down pastures remained as common tenantry downs right up till the final nineteenth century enclosure. Kingston by Lewes's Tenantry Down covered the huge area from the Falmer Road at Woodingdean to Kingston village. Southease Tenantry Down stretched all over the Downs between the village fields and Telscombe, and Poynings' Tenantry Down covered the whole of the Devil's Dyke and the modern Devils Dyke Farm.

Getting Through the Bottleneck

I N the eighteenth and nineteenth centuries many of these areas finally lost their status as commons. In other parts of the country where small peasant-type farmers were more numerous the enclosures were vigorously resisted, but on the South Downs the big farmers had already largely triumphed. Elsewhere in Britain the new urban-based countryside movement saw the development of big nineteenth century struggles, which brought together the economic interests of the poor commoners with the recreational interests of townsfolk. Epping Forest and Berkhamstead Common were dramatically saved from enclosure, as were many of the London commons, like Streatham, Tooting, Wandsworth, Clapham, Hampstead, and Hackney Marshes.

On the Brighton Downs this urban movement was too late, however, and almost all our commons were lost in the Victorian bottleneck of unchecked capitalist farming before the conservation movement gathered sufficient strength to become any kind of real check.

Beeding Common simply vanished. Its last commoner was admitted into his common rights in 1886, but by the 1890s the lord of the manor was developing a large Rabbit warren surrounded by iron fencing at the heart of the common and building Freshcombe Lodge on Truleigh Hill to preside over his new enterprise. Courthouse Sheep Down, covering Ashcombe Bottom, vanished too, being simply divided between the two remaining rights holders. The Devil's Dyke, part of Poynings Tenantry Down, was privatized around 1805 into the hands of an entrepreneurial common rights holder wanting to build a Devil's Dyke Hotel.

Parliamentary procedures were used to enclose the huge commons of Kingston, Iford and Southease in the Ouse valley. The common fields of Telscombe were similarly enclosed, though the common pastures of the Tye were thankfully left out of the arrangements.

It is especially sad that the commons of Portslade and Pyecombe, including Wolstonbury Hill, were lost, for they were very late enclosures. Indeed, the 1872 invocation of the Enclosure Acts to enclose the Pyecombe commons was probably the very last usage of this legal mechanism in Sussex.

Survivors

ONLY two big tenantry downs have survived into the present: at Fulking and Telscombe Tye. Part of Ditchling Tenantry Down survives on the steep scarp slope of the Ditchling Beacon, but the majority of the Down was de-registered as a common in 1977 by its consortium of farmer-commoners, prior to its sale.

The Brighton Race Ground and The Level should have been registered by the Council as commons under the Commons Registration Act in 1965, but the sixties were the nadir of Whitehawk Hill's fortunes, and no such registration was made.

And that's pretty much all there is that's left of this ancient commoning system on our local Downs apart from fragments of

village green at Kingston Buci, Southwick, Falmer, and Rottingdean.

Desolation

IN any case, their status as commons did nothing to save these survivors from the ploughing up of their aboriginal sheep walks. A large part of Telscombe Tye and all the flatter land of Ditchling Tenantry Down were ploughed up in the Second World War 'dig for victory' campaigns, and Fulking Down's flatter ground was ploughed out in the years after the last war.

Their desolation is only exceeded by those areas which had earlier lost their commons status. Beeding Hill, Tenant and Cockroost Hills Portslade, Pickers Hill north of Saltdean, Falmer Hill and Newmarket Hill are now empty deserts of arable and re-seeded pasture. Their prehistoric barrows and field systems are long ploughed out, and only tiny fragments of their ancient flowery grasslands have survived on steep unploughable slopes.

Even the new statutory right of access to all commons under the CROW Act doesn't really make that much difference to our local surviving Downland commons. Telscombe Tye was already safeguarded as open space by the Telscombe Town Council. Fulking Common had been recently acquired, restored and opened by the National Trust, and what's left of

Ditchling Tenantry Down was already open to the public as a nature reserve of the Sussex Wildlife Trust.

Bits and Pieces to Notice

A lovely atmospheric place on the Brighton Downs to get some sense of the workings of the medieval commoning and open field economy is on the **north west face of Beeding Hill**. Go there on a summers' evening when the golden shadows are long and sharply define the creases and furrows of the landscape. Sit yourself down on the steep slope north of the road up to the Youth Hostel (about TQ215 101). This slope is statutory access land and is a rich chalk grassland site with all sorts of special wildlife. It was part of Beeding Tenantry Down till about 110 years ago.

Below you the whole of the valley as far as Castle Town and all of Windmill Hill was strip-cultivated open field right up till the eighteenth and early nineteenth century. Even the steep slope of Windmill Hill was covered in cultivation strips.

Every dusk the tenantry shepherd, his assistant and their woolly Sussex sheep dogs would drive the flock from the Hill down the bostal track and fold them on the fallows of the open field below.

Just over half a mile to your west, south of Castle Town, you can see a series of bushy banks along the contour of the hillside below the South Downs Way. They're marked as cultivation terraces on the OS Explorer map. These medieval open field strip lynchets must have encroached onto the steep hillside in the high medieval days of population growth and land hunger in the twelfth and thirteenth centuries. Other strip lynchets are still faintly visible on Windmill Hill and on the slope in front of Golding Barn quarry.

Just along the slope to your north are the grassy 'hills and holes' of the old common chalk pit, which commoners of the manor would have had the use of for building stone, for agricultural liming of their wealden fields, and for slaked lime for mortar. The edges of the quarry are still covered with a fine flowery Sheep's Fescue sward which was the preferred turf of the shepherds, providing the optimum bite for their hardy sheep.

Just over the other side of Windmill Hill were the common brookland pastures of the manor, where the lambs would be taken in spring for a rich feed of early meadow grass. Later in the summer these brookland meadows would have been cut for hay for winter feed.

Like Beeding, the **west slope of Fulking Hill** still has medieval open field strip lynchets cutting into the edge of the tenantry down, TQ 246 103.

If you **look down over Poynings, westwards, from the slope of Newtimber Hill**, you can see faint open field 'ridge and furrow' surviving in the field just east of the springs (which are marked on the Explorer map at TQ 264 124).

On **Whitehawk Hill the 102 acre Race Ground** is still surrounded by 18 metal plaques defining the boundaries of the recreational common which was set up in 1822 out of the ruins of the enclosure of the tenantry down.

Notice the unfenced nature of Warren Road, Bear Road and Manor Hill crossing **The Race Ground**. The **Ditchling Road** north of Stanmer Park woods is also unfenced. Their unfenced condition is a relic of the days when they were part of unenclosed common pastures.

Until recently van dwellers in their old and modern camper vans lived around Brighton's grassy **Level**. They are still on **Freshfield Road** between the hospital and the racecourse. And the fair still comes to The Level twice a year. Those van dwellers and fairground folk are staying on old common land which must have been camped on by gypsies and itinerants for many hundreds of years. New discriminatory parking measures are now driving them away from these traditional stopping places.

Manorial Lords and Tenants, Beeding Manor circa 1750

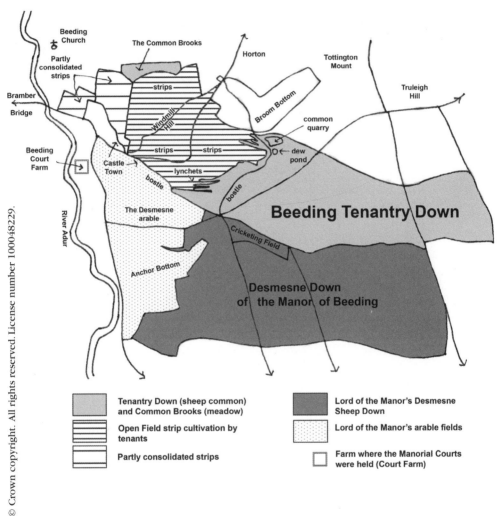

	Tenantry Down (sheep common) and Common Brooks (meadow)		Lord of the Manor's Desmesne Sheep Down
	Open Field strip cultivation by tenants		Lord of the Manor's arable fields
	Partly consolidated strips		Farm where the Manorial Courts were held (Court Farm)

How Beeding Manor's Downland was Organised

— The lower ground was managed by strip cultivation within giant open fields in medieval times. Each peasant, together with the lord, had strips scattered through the open fields.

— The higher ground was sheep and cattle pasturage under the collective control of the manorial jury of peasants and the lord's steward.

— However, early on, the lord consolidated his 'desmesne' arable and Down pasture around his own farm, Beeding Court Farm (where the manorial court was held).

— The common Tenantry Down and open fields remained in a recognizable form, though, till the end of the nineteenth century — a remarkable survival.

The New Commons?

As Victorian Brighton grew at the expense of Downland, and as British farming collapsed under the new conditions of global food markets, people began to be seriously concerned for the survival of the old Down landscape. They also began to be concerned that the unregulated growth of the town would leave residents without ready access to recreational land of any kind — or even clean water.

Parks and Play Spaces

THE population of Brighton was solidly opposed to the process of enclosure and cultivation that had been taking place all around their town. In 1822 the great 400 acre Brighton Tenantry Down had been enclosed, though the presence of the Race Course there and the popularity of Whitehawk Hill for picnics, walks and riding obliged the owners to make a large concession. The 105 acre Race Ground was preserved with new rights attached to it in perpetuity for the public to use it for racing, "exercise and diversion". It was agreed that it should remain uncultivated and "never be broken up or sub-divided". In effect, a new, recreational common was created out of the ruins of the old economic common.

This was followed by new municipal acquisitions:

— In 1883 pasture totalling 67 acres in front of Preston Manor and church was purchased by the Corporation to form the new Preston Park.
— In 1891 the Race Ground trustees, controlled by the Corporation, were able to use their huge profits to purchase and donate the 15.3 acre Queens Park to the town,
— And in 1901 and '09 part of the slopes of Hollingbury, at Varndean Farm, were purchased by the corporation Education Committee for new school use, and later, the new Hollingbury council estate.

Water Conservation

THE first large-scale moves to purchase Downland in the public interest, however, were focussed on the preservation of Brighton's water supplies, pumped up from the deep chalk aquifer. The Corporation had purchased the Constant Service Water Company in 1872 at the beginning of a 25 year process of municipalisation. With increasing concerns over the contamination of the water supply Mile Oak and New Barn Farms, north of Portslade were acquired in the 1880s. After the closure of the polluted Saunders Park pumping station in 1903, bye-laws were passed which eventually extended to over 30,000 acres of the Brighton Downs. The purchase of Downland was thought essential to prevent the ploughing up of the turf or further development over the water works headings.[2]

Brighton Buys the Downs

No real planning law existed to regulate the development of land. Prior to 1947, land purchase was the only strong tool available to local authorities which wished to intervene. The collapse of rural land values with the onset of the long farming depression in the 1880s did mean, however, that local councils could sometimes compete with developers for cheap land purchase.

The period from 1900 to 1939 thus saw a race between developers and Downland local authorities, mostly in alliance with conservationists, to acquire Downland on a massive scale.

In 1913 the crucial purchase took place of 1065 acres of Downland to the east of Brighton, including Whitehawk Bottom, Sheepcote Valley and Ovingdean Grange farm. This ground provided the Corporation with opportunities for a big slum relief housing development, as well as for the new East Brighton Park, Britain's first municipal caravan site and a major refuse tip.

— Between 1920 and '35 the Moulsecoomb Place estate and Hodshrove Farm were bought, to form the site of the large Moulsecoomb council estate.

— In 1924 the 737 acre Waterhall Estate, encompassing Sweet Hill, was compulsorily purchased to remove a big new plotlands colony, which had grown there, close to the Patcham pumping station, in response to the post-war housing crisis.

— In 1925 the 792 acre Balsdean Manor was bought.

— In 1925 the 733 acre Patcham Court Farm was bought, though land to the south that had also been sold by the Abergavenny estate went to private developers.

— In 1926 the 573 acre Saddlescombe Farm was bought.

— In 1928 Sir Herbert Carden used his financial clout and audacity to privately purchase both the 190 acre Devil's Dyke estate and part of the Ditchling Beacon landscape, consisting of the 387 acre High Park Farm. He then sold them on to the Corporation at cost. These two purchases secured the highest, most dramatic viewing points on the Brighton Downs for public ownership.

In the same year the political boundaries of Brighton were drastically expanded to take in Ovingdean, Rottingdean, part of Falmer, and Patcham parishes. Thus was consummated the dream of 'Greater Brighton', celebrated by a visit of the Duke and Duchess of York (the future king and queen) to open the tall stone boundary 'pylons' — sort of gateway columns — on either side of the London Road in the middle of the Downs a mile north of Patcham. Thus did Brighton's leaders celebrate their grandiose dreams with a great marker, like a dog spraying a tree to warn others off its territory.

— Then, in 1929 Beacon Hill, Rottingdean was purchased.

— From 1928 to '35 much of the Roedean clifftop followed.

— In 1933 Herbert Carden intervened again to secure the purchase of the landscaped farmland of Withdean, threatened by housing development. After the Second World War it became the present beautiful Withdean Park, the least 'municipal' in character of Brighton's urban Downland parks.

— In 1936 the West Blatchington estate was bought, enabling the construction of the present Waterhall Golf Course.

— In the same year the remote Standean Farm, west of Stanmer Park, was bought to prevent another housing development.

After the war the heavy death duties on the Stanmer Park Estate brought it onto the market and Brighton made by far its biggest acquisition — almost 5000 acres of let farms, parkland and a stately home. It was almost the last Downland acquisition and brought the area of the Brighton Council Downland estate to more than 14,000 acres.

Other Councils do the Same

A T the same time Brighton's neighbouring councils were making big land purchases. The old Shoreham Urban District Council bought large areas of farmland and Thundersbarrow. In the 1920s Eastbourne Council purchased all the Downland within its newly-extended borough boundaries "for public enjoyment and recreation", and even Worthing made big purchases. In recent years Lewes District Council bought Downland between the town and the old Lewes Race Course.

The National Trust, Too

T H E councils did not just intervene on their own behalf. In 1945 the West Sussex County Council gave 600 acres of Downland on the Shoreham and Southwick Downs to the National Trust. This included all the Downland between Truleigh Hill, Freshcombe and Beeding Hill, as well as Southwick Hill and Whitelot Bottom.

In more recent times the Trust has made dramatic further acquisitions including Blackcap, Mount Harry and Ashcombe Bottom in 1993, and most of the scarp still in private hands between Edburton Hill and Wolstonbury in the 1990s.

A Socially Owned Countryside

I N the space of 100 years the old patterns of landownership on our Brighton Downs have been completely broken. Gone are most of the old parasitic landowning families — the Bridgers of Buckingham Place, the Gorringes of Kingston Buci, the Sackvilles of Knole (owning Hangleton), the Nevilles of Eridge Castle (owning West Blatchington and Patcham and much of the land of the Vale of Brooks villages), the Marquesses of Bristol, the Pelhams of Stanmer Park, the Tillstones of Moulsecoombe Place, the Beards of Rottingdean, the Shiffners of Offham, the Campions of Danny, and the rest.

In effect, the social sector is in control of our Downs, and most of it is in the control of our elected local councils. The combined ownership of these public and conservation authorities on the open Brighton Downs now encompasses around two thirds of their entire area.

A new 'commons' could have been born… but it was not to be so.

A Stalled Potential

T H O U G H our Downs were now largely in public ownership, this did not ensure that they remained a free and open landscape.

After the Second World War a furious campaign to bulldoze and plough up the old sheep pastures began, encouraged both by the central state and, enthusiastically, by the local councils. British food politics were dominated by the twin insanities of

an imperialist food policy, (which had as its objective the penetration and domination of the food markets of the third world) and the Cold War (which wanted to continue the competitive productivism of the Second World War against the communist block, after the defeat of fascism). Around 3000 acres of ancient grassland and scrub were removed by Brighton Council's farm tenants, with the approval and consent of the Council, and ploughed up for cereal crops.

The great gift of the Beeding Hill/ Truleigh Hill Downs to the National Trust was entirely negated by the County Council's preceding grant of 999 year leases to the property's tenant farmers. Within a few years these businesses had bulldozed this entire landscape, with its 4000 year old clusters of bronze age burial mounds, its chalk heath, and its flaming gorse, into a barren emptiness.

Though the Councils may have understood the need to conserve the *landscape-scale* characteristics of the Downs — broad, smooth, whale-backed hills — they utterly failed to understand the need to conserve the *intimate, human-scale* richness of the Downs — the world of tiny flowers, ant hills, grasses, mosses, stone-age barrows, camps and lynchets, coconut-scented yellow gorse blooms, lichens, fungi, butterflies, glow-worms, orchids, beetles, bees, grasshoppers, lizards, pipits, linnets, furze-wrens — which had made them such a loved landscape.

Very few, even at national level, understood the dreadful implications for nature of the coming capitalist industrialization of farming. Private farmers were seen as the countryside's guardians and not as the agents of the destruction of nature and the elimination of land-based labour.

Furthermore, in 1947 and 1977 two Agriculture Acts gave security of tenure to farm tenants, first for their lifetime, and then for two further successive

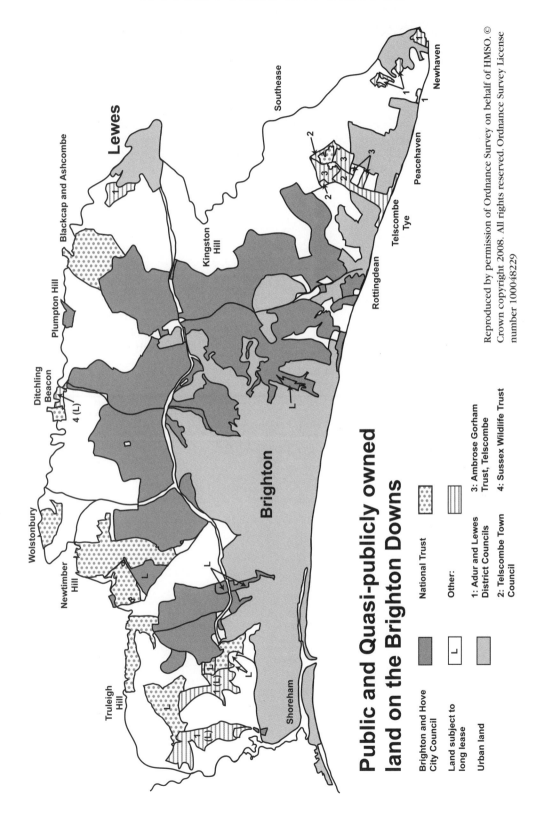

Public and Quasi-publicly owned land on the Brighton Downs

Lewes

Blackcap and Ashcombe

Plumpton Hill

Ditchling Beacon

4 (L)

Wolstonbury

Newtimber Hill

Truleigh Hill

Brighton

Kingston Hill

Southease

Rottingdean

Telscombe Tye

Peacehaven

Newhaven

Shoreham

Brighton and Hove City Council

Land subject to long lease L

Urban land

National Trust

Other:

1: Adur and Lewes District Councils

2: Telscombe Town Council

3: Ambrose Gorham Trust, Telscombe

4: Sussex Wildlife Trust

generations. This was a great victory for justice in the long campaign against the evils of landlordism, but it made no distinction between the tenants of private landlords and public landlords, such as local councils. For landowning local councils like Brighton the legislation severely damaged their democratic right to manage the land in the public interest.

To read the minutes of the old Brighton Council Farmlands Committee is a depressing business. Time after time in the 1950s and 60s the Committee consents to the destruction of ancient grassland and scrub on land not ploughed for many hundreds of years — at High Park, at Lower Paythorne, at Waterhall, at Balsdean, at Castle Hill, The Bostle, Upper Bevendean, Bullock Hill, both New Barn Farms, Housedean, St Mary's Farm, Cockroost Hill and Mount Zion, Patcham Court Farm, Plumpton Hill and Standean.

Sad notes of despair seep through the pages. In June 1960 a Mr Fell protests[3] against the clearance of scrub, especially the recent clearing on the Saddlescombe Road where nightingales sang. The Committee re-affirm that "it is in the interests of the Corporation and their tenant farmers that downland scrub land which is capable of being utilised should be cleared and cultivated, but that the Committee would be prepared to take into account any area which is considered to be of special natural history value"... *They never did!!*

Thus, much of the great work done by Herbert Carden and the pre-war Brighton Council in securing the Downs was un-ravelled by their successors. The Council's Downland estate became little more than a second-rate source of rental income to fund urban projects that would otherwise have not easily attracted finance. By 1993 the council spent only 4% of the rent roll (17,000 pounds) from the farmed estate on conservation management plans.

Few people growing up in Brighton in the 1960s even realized that the majority of the Downs they walked were in public ownership. No signs existed telling them so. (They still don't). Public access was confined to footpaths and to designated open spaces, mostly not managed agriculturally, like the Dyke and Whitehawk Hill, Moulsecoomb Wild Park or the woods of Stanmer Park. The old vision of a free, open Down landscape where nature, people and sustainable farming would co-exist, was replaced by a system of honey-pot open spaces and a desert of agri-business grain crops.

Things reached a nadir with the sale in 1977 of remote Mary Farm, high up on the Downs between Stanmer and Plumpton Plain. The sale was supposed to part-finance the building of the Prince Regent Swimming Complex, though it was later admitted that the money was not needed for that purpose and could have been found elsewhere. The result was the steep ratchetting-up of the destruction of that farm's ancient landscape.

In 1994 the Labour administration sold the Devils's Dyke and Saddlescombe Farm to the National Trust. Secret proposals were made to sell off the rest of the farmland estate. The Council had lost all sense of its responsibilities for the Downs.

Some of the new battles for the Brighton commons that had to be fought are described in the 'Fightback' chapter.

Footnotes

1 *The Common Lands and Wastes of Sussex* — Peter F. Brandon, Unpublished PhD thesis (University of London, 1963), page 200-210. This is a superb source.

2 *The Encyclopaedia of Brighton* — Timothy Carder (East Sussex County Libraries, 1990), Item 200.

3 Brighton Corporation Farmlands Committee Minutes 1957-60. Item 241 (9/6/60). Held at East Sussex Record Office.

DOWN PASTURE'S
HISTORY

The Growth of Down Pasture

THE peoples of the Neolithic[1] Age, around 5 or 6000 years ago, created the great Down pastures, using their flint axes and their grazing animals to push back the wildwood. Previous to their forest clearances the open grassland species from the earlier tundra had survived only in natural glades created by wild grazing animals, windfall, ageing and erosion (as on the river and coastal cliffs), though these openings may often have been quite large.

The peoples of the Bronze Age, around 3 or 4000 BP (Before the Present), massively expanded this open ground, bringing settled farming communities and a patchwork of fields and pastures. By the time of the Roman colonization our Brighton Downs were already an open landscape with only residual woodland.

Our hills remained dotted with settlements and enclosures right through the period of Saxon colonization and up till around 800AD. Then the high ground was finally abandoned to grazing pastures and the farmers regrouped in valley, scarp foot and coastal plain villages and hamlets. From this period and for over a thousand years the high Downs were claimed by the shepherd and traveller, and by Bustard, Wheatear, Hare, Linnet and Lark.

Waxing and Waning

THE huge sheep walks have advanced and retreated in several long pulses over the last millennia, but never — till the last 60 years — so drastically as to alter this pattern of high, lonely pastures and valley bottom cornlands.

As the medieval population[2] expanded peasants were driven to extend the common fields onto higher ground and even to re-start settlements on the high plateau. Thus Perching Manor in Fulking developed a Downland hamlet, whose strip-cultivated open field survived until Victorian times. West Blatchington and probably Hangleton extended their fields onto the high ground north of the settlements. And the peasants of Beeding, Newtimber and Piddinghoe extended their fields, whose lynchets can still be seen on the northwest slopes of Beeding Hill, around the crown of Newtimber Hill, and on the Ouse valleyside.

With the Black Death the medieval population crashed and the newly tilled high ground reverted to sheep pastures.

In the late seventeenth century new legumes and grass mixes encouraged farmers to break up old Down pasture to grow fodder crops for sheep. We have a manorial survey map of 1687 from Erringham, Shoreham, showing exactly

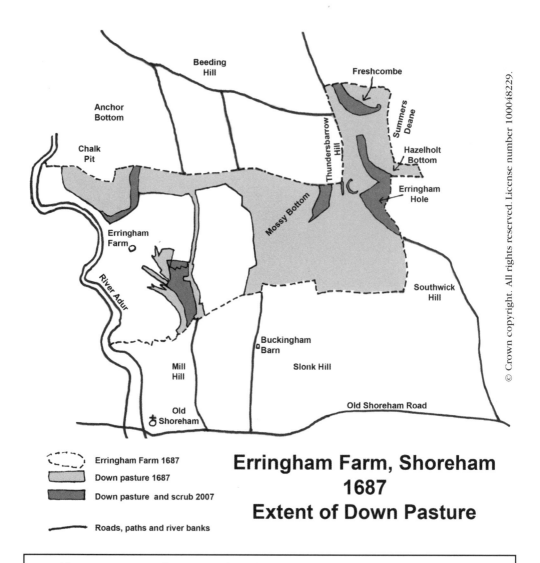

**Erringham Farm, Shoreham
1687
Extent of Down Pasture**

Legend:
- Erringham Farm 1687
- Down pasture 1687
- Down pasture and scrub 2007
- Roads, paths and river banks

— The pastures were huge, stretching from the edge of the River Adur's saltings and brooks to just west of the present Mile Oak Farm.

what land use looked like at that time. Despite all the new innovations more than two thirds of the Downland farm was pasture — including some wet riverside pasture and 'gratton' (land returned to pasture after a period of tillage). Well over half was Down pasture. A shepherd could walk for two and a quarter miles, from the riverside to Hazelholt Bottom, without once leaving Down pasture.

In the eighteenth and early nineteenth century some pastures were encroached upon. Brighton's Church Hill was ploughed up, as was Round Hill, Black Rock Down and Scabies Castle Farm (where Woodvale Cemetery is now), to be followed by a general enclosure of the huge Tenantry Down in 1822. Preston saw its Down pastures at Hollingdean and Race Hill ploughed up. Falmer saw encroachments around Housedean. There were more plough ups in the Napoleonic wars to grow corn in the times of the French blockade, though much of this reverted to

Unimproved Down Pasture in 1840

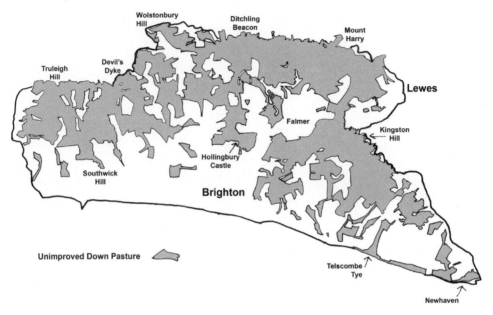

Unimproved Down Pasture in 1873

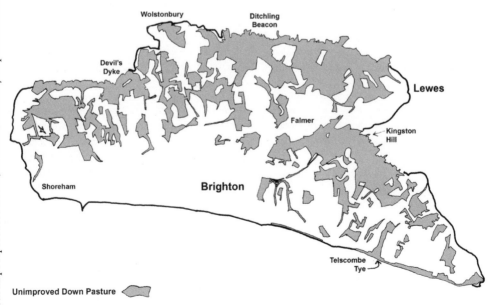

Both maps reproduced from 1940 Ordnance Survey map bases with the kind permission of the Ordnance Survey.

grassland when peace came in 1815.

The Tithe Commutation Act Survey Maps of Circa 1840

THIS comprehensive survey shows that almost the whole of the high Downs were still sheep walk around 1840 and arable tillage was largely confined to the valley lands. Some plough ups of the higher ground had taken place, for instance at Truleigh Hill and the Dyke Farm, Ashcombe and New England, north of Mill Hill, Rodmell, but the great blocks of Downland north and north east of Brighton were still undivided.

The First Edition Ordnance Survey Map of 1873

THE decades of high Victorian farming in the middle of the nineteenth century brought new plough ups, particularly near to Brighton and on the better soils, as entrepreneurial farmers cashed in on the new food markets for the expanding urban population created by the industrial revolution.

Despite all the new farming innovation, however, the basic pattern remained unaltered. The high ground was the land of the sheep walk and the low ground was cultivated.

The Long Agricultural Depression

FROM around 1880 there began a long agricultural depression. It was brought about by the perverse effects of imperialist expansion, technical innovation and free trade, with competition from the new North American prairie cornlands and the huge new livestock industries of the southern hemisphere. This farming slump was to last for 60 long years, broken only by the interlude of the First World War. The sheep flocks on the Downs shrank to a

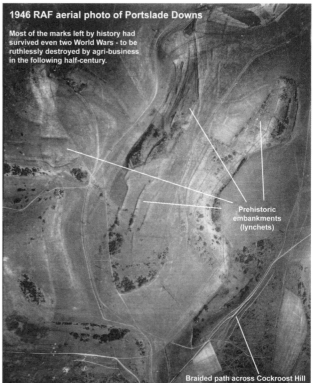

1946 RAF aerial photo of Portslade Downs

Most of the marks left by history had survived even two World Wars - to be ruthlessly destroyed by agri-business in the following half-century.

Prehistoric embankments (lynchets)

Braided path across Cockroost Hill

quarter of their earlier numbers. Previously hard grazed Sheep's Fescue pastures became tall and rank, and thorn scrub spread widely, coalescing into sometimes gigantic thickets.

There were no more big plough ups, though. Even the food growing campaign of the First World War made little impact overall, having to take in large areas of ex-arable land which had reverted to pasture before it tackled the ancient sheep walks.

Remarkably, the footprint of semi-natural pasture and scrub in 1939 was not qualitatively different from the pattern of 1880. The main difference was the huge rise of scrub as a component of those pastures.

Dig For Victory

IT is often thought that the 'Dig For Victory' food production campaign of the Second World War marked the death knell of the Down pastures. It is not so. A great part of the eastern, open Downs was taken over for military training. The buildings of the Downs suffered terribly, being used for target practice. The ancient pastures, however, were preserved 'in aspic' by this military occupation. They were churned up, battled over and shelled, but they were not destroyed, merely continuing their long succession to scrub, and rank grassland.

The RAF's aerial photo survey of the Downs done in 1946, shows that, still, the basic millennia-old pattern of sheep pastures and low-ground arable was recognizable. All the old components were still there: sprawling braided trackways, clumps of old gorse and thorn, barrows, lynchets and dew ponds, scattered across the wide pastures.

Agri-business Does its Work

THE trauma that hit the Downs from 1947 onwards, when the military left, made all the previous attrition and dereliction seem like pin-pricks. In the next 50 years the Brighton Downs was hit by a whirlwind of bulldozing, ploughing, and drenching with fertilizers, pesticides, and herbicides. By 1990 the only Down pasture that survived where farming was the dominant land use was on slopes too steep for cultivation. Only on areas managed for recreation, mostly in public ownership, did any Down pasture survive on the old high plateau lands which had previously been the core of the sheep walks.

The behaviour of this new generation of capitalist farmers was as thorough and universal as a law of physics. *On any Downland accessible to machine cultivation and under the control of private farming old Down pasture will have been destroyed.*

The result has been the trashing and splintering of the old Downscape.

It took a while to get underway, however, and the mapping exercise undertaken by the East and West Sussex County Councils in the early 1950s to chart the resource of surviving 'open country'[3] showed that

even at so late a stage the large unitary blocs of Down pasture and scrub centred on Kingston Hill and Blackcap were still recognizable, though tatty.

By the end of the century the dirty deed was done. On the Brighton Downs the total area of old Down pasture and associated scrub had been reduced to around 9% of the open chalk outcrop (from the historical average of around 40-50%). What was left was shattered into 180 scattered fragments, varying in size from the three mile long scarp between Truleigh Hill and Devil's Dyke to isolated sites of a few acres or less.

Seeing What We've Lost

Continuity

IF you want to sense what Down pasture was like 500 years ago, at its peak, then you still can. Go to **Anchor Bottom** south of Beeding. It is a superb ancient valley. Or go to the **Underhill Lane between Poynings and Edburton**. The scarp you look up at is still largely a wiry Sheep's Fescue pasture, almost bare of scrub. **Iford Hill's** scarp slope similarly has an ancient cover of Sheep's Fescue. **Wolstonbury Hill**, especially on its western top, still has this same bare, soft and bony feel, though the pasture has much tussocky Tor Grass these days. **Kingston Hill and Cold Coombes**, too, are still covered with a mantle of Down pasture, though with a richer soil and much Tor Grass and Upright Brome. On the dip slope north east of Woodingdean, the valleysides of **Castle Hill and Falmer, Newmarket and Standean Bottoms**, all share that same feel of the old sheep walks: the smells of sheep and herbs, the sound of bees and grasshoppers, larks and pipits, and the flitting of butterflies.

The Victorian Decline

IF you want to sense what Down pasture was like during late Victorian and Edwardian times through to 1940,

Unimproved Down Pasture in 1956

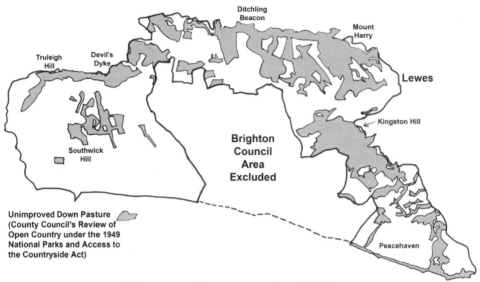

Unimproved Down Pasture
(County Council's Review of
Open Country under the 1949
National Parks and Access to
the Countryside Act)

Unimproved Down Pasture in 2007

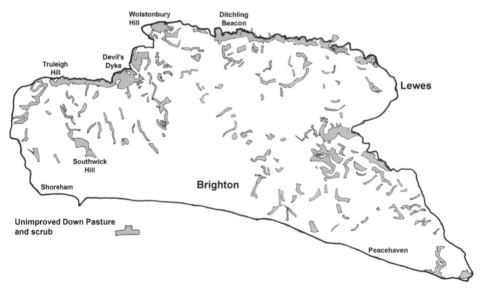

Unimproved Down Pasture
and scrub

Both maps reproduced from 1940 Ordnance Survey map bases with the kind permission of the Ordnance Survey.

Unimproved Down Pasture 2007

There was a great continuity in the footprint of old Down pasture right into the late
1950s, despite the need to feed the Industrial Revolution's rising population, and
despite the ravages of plough-up campaigns in the Napoleonic Wars, and the First and
Second World Wars. It was modern agribusiness — operating in the political context of
imperialist food policy — which finally smashed and fragmented the last of the great
plateau Down pastures

then go to **Southwick Hill**. With its mixture of close-grazed turf and scrub thickets, sometimes mature enough to harbour small maiden oaks, it's the best representative of that period. Its scrub and grassland are in a never-ending fight, back and forth, for advantage. **Newtimber Hill's** matrix of grassland, scrub and incipient woodland also captures that sense of the Downs at the time of the long agricultural depression. **Dencher Bottom**, south of Keymer Post, sadly, is acquiring that character too, as hawthorn scrub scattered across its slopes grows unchecked.

Full-on Dereliction

THERE are still many places which exemplify the nadir of the Downs in the 1950s and '60s when the introduced disease myxomatosis eliminated the rabbits as the last grazing agent and scrub coalesced into giant thickets, eliminating any residual pasturage. **Ewe Bottom, south of the Devil's Dyke** — and once part of that landscape — is an excellent example. If you're on the run from the law and want somewhere to hide out, then Ewe Bottom would be good for a while. Its thickets will claw and scrape you as you battle through. You can walk the valley bottom, but on parts of the valley sides you need to be about badger height. **Moulsecoomb Wild Park** is another tragic example, its ancient scrubby grasslands grown over to Sycamore woodland and dense, impenetrable thickets. **Newhaven's Downland at Castle Hill, Rushy Hill and Hoddern** (next to the Peacehaven Golf Course) too, marks an especially sad loss, for

its wall-to-wall thorn thickets sprawl over a lost heathland which was both strange and unique on the Brighton Downs. Oh well!

Ashcombe Bottom, south of Blackcap, strikes a more hopeful note, for the National Trust are defending the residual grasslands, and even reintroducing grazing to the woods.

Improvement

BEEDING **Hill and the Downs south of the Truleigh Hill Youth Hostel** also exemplify the Downscape of the 1950s, but display the other side of the coin from dereliction: the 'improved' Downs of the bulldozer and the plough. For over two kilometres north to south and east to west this high plateau is a desert of improved

Moulsecoomb Wild Park circa 1930 — open flowery grasslands with a few bushes.

Moulsecoomb Wild Park circa 2000 — flowery grassland reduced to tiny glades in huge scrub thickets.

grassland. The cluster of bronze-age barrows, the gorse thickets, the chalk heath and acid grassland and the flowery valleys are all long gone under the bulldozer. **Cuckoo Bottom on Houndean Farm**, within the embrace of Lewes's old racecourse, shows both sides of the coin at once, its rich pastures lost to scrub thickets and one gigantic sweep of ploughland. Soon the last rich grasslands of this landscape — between the old grandstand and the prison — will be lost, also, if the residents of Lewes do not get their finger out and campaign for their restoration.

Public Use Versus Private Gain

The Separation of Public Use From Economic Value

THE close match, historically, between rights of way and old Down pasture is now gone, except on the north scarp of the Downs. To travel across the Downs in the old days was to walk in freedom across these sheep walks. Nowadays farmers have succeeded in thoroughly separating the traveller from an intimate association with the wildlife that inhabits the land across which they travel.

From prehistory roads of both inter-parish and wider importance followed the long Down pasture ridges in preference to the soggy and difficult river valleys. Thus, the main highway from Shoreham mounted Mill Hill and passed up over Beeding Hill before descending to Bramber Bridge. The Juggs Road tracked from Brighton up over Race Hill, then along the ridge to Newmarket and down Kingston Hill to Lewes. The ancient Port Road from Portslade towards London, tracked through Hangleton and across Round Hill, up the line of the Dyke Road and across Summer Down before descending around the edge of the Dyke to Poynings and the Weald. It was reported to be used by coaches right up until the 17th century.

For large stretches these routes were braided trackways, taking whichever line was easiest travelling across open pastures which were free of fence and hedge, and with boundaries simply marked by features such as stones, old thorn bushes, lynchets, barrows and furrow edges.

Now, you may walk for many miles along these Downland ridges and never touch any part of these ancient Down pastures. Urban walkers enjoying a 'Downland' experience may get an entirely false impression of a poverty of wildlife in this landscape. Walkers mostly have to be content with barbed wire and rank grassland along a pathside, offering nothing specifically about Downland's place identity, and nothing different from thousands of pathways on improved or derelict land the length and breadth of Britain.

There are about 58 rights of way crossing the plateau of the Brighton Downs from the urban edge to the high scarp. Of these, 41 (71%) either do not touch any old Down pasture fragments or touch them only momentarily. Along the 17 public paths which do either cross ancient Down pasture or pass alongside it there are only 12 sections where the paths cross Down pasture in a way which provides the walker with a real, satisfying experience of that ecosystem. On all the rest the walker is either screened from the pasture by fences and bushes or the pasture is damaged or of poor quality, or there is no means of public access. And the best sections mostly constitute together a tiny proportion of the total length of the paths of which they form a part.

Occasionally, rights of way have a rich flora of their own. The roadside of the Saddlescombe Road, north of Varncombe Barn, bears colourful displays of vetches, particularly the scarce blood-red Grass Vetchling. Mostly, though, these Downland pathways across arable and improved grassland have long lost their special flora under the influence of crop sprays, by ploughing out, or by dereliction. For a mile along Benfield ridge, northwards towards the Dyke, the bridleway — once decorated with Sainfoin, Broomrape, Knapweed and Wild Strawberry — was entirely ploughed out and re-fenced. The banksides of the Stanmer Park bridleways have lost their colourful displays of cowslips and dainty flowers under the effects of crop spray drift.

The Disappointment of the South Downs Way

22 miles of the South Downs Way cross the Brighton Downs. For much of this length it follows the high scarp top of the Downs, passing such delights as the Devil's Dyke, Saddlescombe, Blackcap, and Kingston Hill. You can see immense stretches of coast and Weald — from the chalk cliffs near Beachy Head around to the Isle of Wight and across to Blackdown and Leith Hill in the Surrey Hills. The grand scale is magnificent.

Yet the walker will not be rewarded by any of Downland's renowned beauty at the close scale of the turf around her feet. The Trail barely touches those areas of scented flowery turf and gorse which gave the Downs such a strong place identity. For the most part walkers will be passing over fertilized and improved pastures and arable fields. On an intimate scale much of the Trail route is a non-event.

Out of this 22 mile stretch only one mile (that is 4.4%) passes across Down pasture which is arguably of reasonable quality. A further 2.7 miles (or 12.3%) crosses semi-improved Down pasture, which may provide a soft springy grass turf, but will be floristically very poor. Its affinities will be closer to recreation ground turf than alpine flower meadow.

At the best spots — on Perching Hill or Summer Down — it will be possible to see lovely and special displays right by the trackside, though intermingled with improved grassland and rank, derelict

grassland and scrub. And on Kingston Hill the open, unfenced path will bring us happily near rich areas of acidic and chalk grassland.

At worst, however, the Trail will offer us barbed wire fencing on one or both sides, as at Plumpton Plain, and will direct the walker away from what remains of flower-rich scarp top turf, as at Blackcap and Mount Harry.

Yet for much of its length, a long continuous area of rich Down pasture lies just to the north of the Trail. This northern slope is too steep for many walkers, and lies at sufficient remove from the Trail that walkers who aren't wildlifers (the vast majority) never know what they are missing.

Footnotes

1   Neo=New; Lithic=Stone
2   The Medieval period stretched from around 800 AD to around 1500AD. Before that the 'Dark Age' stretched from about 450 AD to 800 AD. The Dark Age was a period of steep economic and population decline and population movement, in the wake of the collapse of the Roman Empire. The Medieval period gradually reversed those trends and laid the basis for the birth of capitalism.
3   East and West Sussex County Councils were unusual in undertaking the mapping of 'open country' under the permissive terms of the National Parks and Access to the Countryside Act of 1949. Only six councils submitted open country maps. The definition of open country encompassed 'mountain, moor, heath, down and common'. Without a doubt, this was a very coarse survey, and many smaller sites were omitted from the map, whilst some areas were erroneously included.

DOWN PASTURE'S
NATURAL HISTORY

CLASSIC Down pasture is a short turf. It's made up of an intimate mixture of tiny herbs and grasses co-existing and made stable by the continual nibbling action of sheep, rabbits, and other grazing animals. In old, grazed chalk grassland you may find thirty and more — even up to 50 — species of grasses, flowers, mosses, liverworts and lichen (not to speak of fungi) in just one square metre of ground. More than 90% of these species are perennials. The turf is mostly closed, tight, and springy. The low and wiry **Sheep's Fescue**, *Festuca ovina*, grass is the bond that ties much of the sward together, though other grasses, like the Oat-grasses, are also very important.

That is the classic Downland turf that you can walk tirelessly for hours.[1]

On our local Downs a quite remarkable proportion of the surviving Down pasture is still of that classical type — much greater than you'd find in neighbouring Surrey or Kent, or outside London. In fact, our Downs are quite a stronghold for that nationally rare grassland type.[2]

Nowadays, however, distressingly large areas of surviving Down pasture are under-grazed or un-grazed, and have turned into tall grassland. In such grasslands the sward will be dominated by varying amounts of **Upright Brome**, *Bromus erectus*. If the process hasn't gone very far then the grassland may remain very rich in flowers, other grasses and old meadow fungi. The little mosses and lichen will be vastly reduced, though, and may have been eliminated altogether.

Later, after years of neglect without grazing, this tall grassland enriches the soil, the dainty little flowers disappear, and the sward is taken over by another tall grass called **False Oat-grass**, *Arrhenatherum elatius*. Sometimes taller chalk-loving flowers will survive, but it's just as likely to be Nettles, Brambles and scrub which accompany this rank grassland.

On the urban fringe the neglect by the Council and local farmers means that much of the surviving chalk grassland is of these two tall grassland types.

Another very aggressive and competitive species, **Tor Grass**, *Brachypodium pinnatum*, has become a great problem over the past century. It forms dense patches, with a deep leaf litter, and its tissues accumulate silica, which makes it very unpalatable except in springtime. It's thought that air pollution, particularly by 'nox's' — Nitrogen oxide pollutants largely from cars — encourages this species, as does the relaxation of grazing. When Tor Grass gets a hold other species are mostly eliminated.[3]

Paradox

OLD, herb-rich Down pasture is a paradoxical ecosystem. Its *richness* for wildlife depends on the *poverty* of its soils. Fertilisers will kill it. It is a very *ancient* plant community, yet it is inherently *unstable*. If we take our grazing animals away, it will soon-enough turn to poor quality woodland.

Many plants love the calcium-rich soils of the Downs, yet this substrate is also lacking in key nutrients, so many of our old chalk grassland species have evolved adaptations to enable them to cope with this low-productivity habitat. They have a low growth rate.[4] They've developed storage organs, such as rhizomes, to uptake extra nutrients when these occasionally become available. They have lots of roots (compared to their above ground presence) which are long-lived, and they have highly developed mycorrhizal associations (that is, their roots have joined up with fungus 'roots') to enable them to efficiently take up nutrients.

International Affinities

OUR ancient Down pastures have many affinities with the great range-grazed pastures of the steppes that stretched from Hungary eastwards all the way to Mongolia, or with the American prairies and pampas. They have affinities, too, with the wild, high pastures of our limestone mountain ranges both below and above the tree line. Many of the characteristic plants and animals of our Downs — or their close cousins — can be found right across these distant places.

But there is one key difference between our chalk grasslands and those naturally open ranges. Our grasslands were created by the human activity of clearing the forest. If grazing ceases for too long, the woods will return. Chalk grassland, then, is a *semi*-natural system — made up largely of naturally occurring wild species, but kept in place by human agency.

Where is it?

ABOUT 9% of the open chalk outcrop of the Brighton Downs is surviving old

Paythorne Down, north of Southwick. A postage stamp of bushes and ancient pasture within much larger new pastures.

Down pasture and associated scrub. That's made up of 180 fragments scattered thinly across the Downland plateau. Only on the plateau's northern scarp does chalk grassland still dominate the landscape, as on the five mile long steep, north facing slopes between Keymer Post and Offham Hill.

What Kind of Fragments are They?

T H E example of the dip slope of the Hove and Shoreham Downs[5] will tell the story for the whole Brighton Downs. 29 of its 58 old Down pasture fragments are less than 10 acres in size, and only two major clusters survive — around Southwick Hill and around Waterhall and Varncombe Hill. The mean distance between these fragments (measured at the narrowest points between them) is 150m — a very daunting prospect to cross for any mini-beast or tiny plant that finds travel difficult.

All but seven of these dip slope sites are on very steep slopes, often at 20 degrees or more, so you don't stand much of a chance on them if you're a person with mobility difficulties. The only surviving sites on level ground are managed for public recreation — at Southwick and Benfield Hills and on the Waterhall Golf Course roughs.

The South Downs Don't Face South

O N L Y six of these fragments on the Hove Downs are south facing. That might seem weird, seeing as we're talking about the *South* Downs, but, in fact, a combination of geography and agribusiness has left a remarkable shortage of south facing sites along the entire Downland chain. If you want to bask in the full sun from the south you'd do better to live near the North Downs, where the long scarp is entirely south facing. This shortage means that those plants and insects dependant on the hottest, continental-type conditions — like Adonis Blue and Silver-spotted Skipper butterflies — are at quite a disadvantage.

Perhaps the hottest of these few south facing sites is the Newhaven undercliff.

Its boulders, rough grassland and scrub bake in the summer sun, to the delight of many sun-loving creatures. Several other grasslands on the urban fringe, like Bevendean Down, Moulsecoomb Pit, the Newmarket Hill to Castle Hill slope, and Hog Plantation have full southern aspects. On the high Downs the Devil's Dyke, Anchor Bottom, Tottington Mount, Newtimber Hill, Dencher Bottom, Big Bottom, Kingston Hill and some others have good south facing slopes. The list is short, though.

The greater part of our dip slope Down pasture sites face easterly, with a large westerly minority. You'd think that because most of our dry valleys run southwards there would be a rough symmetry in the number of old pasture sites surviving on their east and west flanks, but this is not so. In fact, most of our dry valleys have an asymmetrical profile. On the Hove Downs this means that the valleys mostly have steep western slopes and gentler eastern slopes. There, two thirds of the dip slope old Down pasture sites face broadly easterly.

On the Patcham-Lewes Downs there's a broken sub-scarp between Holt Hill and Ashcombe Bottom, which gives a number of sites a somewhat northerly aspect, and on the Falmer-Saltdean Downs a similar broken sub-scarp gives many sites a north easterly aspect, complemented by a suite of south westerly facing slopes.

So, all in all, a lot of our Downs are a bit shady for large parts of the time and face away from the south. That means that they have places excellent for tiny mosses and liverworts and more damp-loving things, as well as for the creatures of sunny conditions.

Small Plants and Small Creatures

IN fact, most of the special things on our Down pastures are small or even tiny. It really is a miniature world. You have to get down on your hands and knees a lot to see things. Big **Bloody-nosed Beetles**, *Timarcha goettingensis*, and big multi-coloured stripey snails are all very well, but the *average* size of beetles in Britain is 2mm, and many of the really special snails of the Downs are also of that order of smallness. Children are best at adjusting to that scale, so get them tuned in and then follow their lead. They have more stamina, too.

You'll all need magnifying hand lenses to enjoy the beauties of those tiny things. You'll miss most of the good stuff if you don't have one.

Indicators of Specialness

C E R T A I N plants and mini-beasts occur only on our old Down pastures. You won't find them on newer grasslands, even if these are undamaged by agro-chemicals. When you find them you know you're in a special place.

Look out for **Horseshoe Vetch**, *Hippocrepis comosa*. It's a low growing plant with a head of clustered flowers. Old pastures, like Mill Hill and Whitehawk Hill's slopes, flush yellow with it in May and early June. This little plant is the host for the caterpillars of our two most beautiful Blue butterflies, the **Chalkhill Blue**, *Lysandra coridon*, and the **Adonis Blue**, *Lysandra bellargus*. They are shepherded by two species of Downland ants, which milk them for their honeydew and protect them at night and when they turn into chrysalids.

Both Chalkhill and Adonis like the hotter slopes and the shorter turf. Chalkhill Blue will tolerate turf of 2-6cm in height, but Adonis females will only lay their eggs in the hottest turf, between a half and one cm tall (though global warming seems to be making both species less fussy). Chalkhill Blue adults can be seen throughout the school summer holiday time and a bit beyond. Their large silvery blue males make a delightful dance on old path sides in hot weather. The Adonis males beat them for sheer dazzling beauty, though.

They look like tiny fragments of the vault of the purest blue summer heavens, broken off and brought to earth. They glitter and shine as they catch the sun. When I surveyed the Hove and Shoreham Downs for these two species thirteen years ago I found Adonis at 13 out of 98 possible sites. It was clustered at all three of the sites facing the Adur Valley and on the three promontories of the Dyke, Newtimber Hill and Wolstonbury. Chalkhill Blue was scattered right across the dip slope and on the bostal sides of the northern scarp.

Rockrose, *Helianthemum nummularium*, too, is entirely confined to these old pastures. Its flower looks like a miniature yellow Cistus, and it is a cousin of those hot Mediterranean beauties, but, in form, it looks just like another small Down pasture herb. It isn't, though. It's actually a sub-shrub, with a thick woody stock and a long vertical woody taproot. Very occasionally you can find a bit that actually looks like a little bush (such as in the valley north of North Heath Barn, on Waterhall Farm).

Rockrose has a whole range of special beasties dependent on it. The most obvious is the **Brown Argus** butterfly, *Aricia agestis*, which is actually a 'Blue', *Lycaenid*, butterfly that doesn't have any blue on it. It looks like a daintier, quicker version of the female **Common Blue**, *Polyommatus icarus*. I found it at one in six of the Hove and Shoreham sites, but it is probably commoner, now. Last summer I came across a roosting gang of 17 Brown Argus all on one clump of Tor Grass. A lot of the Blue butterflies sleep in 'dormitories', like that.

There are at least four Leaf Beetle and three Weevil species dependent on Rockrose in Sussex, including the scarce *Bruchidius cisti*.

Rockrose and 'Ghost Woods'

R O C K R O S E has a much more obvious group of associates, though, than these tiny beetles…

…In July, three summer's ago, I kept finding what I thought were woodland fungi growing out on the limestone pastures of the Yorkshire Dales, always where there were carpets of Rockrose. There were lots of Boletes, Web Caps (*Cortinarius species*), and **Grisette**, *Amanita vaginata*.

At the same time I found out that fungus experts were puzzling about the same paradox. Some people have even thought they were finding the sites of *ghost woods* out on the pastures and have delved into the archives looking for past evidence of woodland. So, afterwards, I kept a sharp eye for the same phenomenon on the Brighton Downs.

Lots of fungi have a mycorrhizal mode of life — that is, their sort-of-rootlets fix on to the rootlets of trees and shrubs and exchange food products to their mutual benefit. And some of them are able to live happily away from their normal woodland habitat by fixing onto Rockrose rootlets out on the bare Downs. They are exiles from the woods living in a mutual aid society with Rockrose — which looks like a delicate herb above the waist, but behaves like a woodland tree below!

My findings were mainly in August, for Boletes especially are often summer species. I did find good swarms in autumn, though, particularly of the Web Caps and Milk Caps, Lactarius.

On the best site I found seven species: **Panther Cap**, *Amanita pantherina*, Grisette, **Lurid Bolete**, *Boletus luridus*, two Web Cap species, **Poison Pie**, *Hebeloma crustuliforme*, and **Oak Milk Cap**, *Lactarius quietus*. That site is also an excellent place for Waxcap fungi, **Striped Grasshopper**, *Stenobothrus lineatus*, and **Mottled Grasshopper**, *Myrmeleotettix maculatus*, (Downland rarities), and cloud-fulls of Adonis and Chalkhill Blue.

The commonest species in my survey was the Lurid Bolete, which I found on eight sites. It occurs often in little troops, a

The Lurid Bolete, *Boletus Luridus*. Found in July/August cohabiting with Rockrose, with which it intermingles its roots.

bit the colour of shammy leather. Its lemon yellow flesh turns dark blue on cutting. Its stem has a reddish net over it, like a fish-net stocking. It's long been known that this species commonly associates with Rockrose.

I found Web Cap species on five sites. They are a difficult group and I didn't have the time or knowledge for the microscope work. The only one I could get near identifying was a beautiful little chestnut brown silky-fibrillose species, which I guesstimated to be *Cortinarius cinnamomeobadius*. (Did I say that right?).

I found an interesting cluster of four sites around Pangdean on the A23 London Road, with high cover of Rockrose and the same two Boletes — all four with Lurid Bolete and two of them with *Boletus queletii*. Maybe a sort of meta-population?

I had hoped to find some rare and powerfully folkloric species, like the goblinesque **Satan's Bolete**, *Boletus satanus*. This deadly poisonous (but handsome) jobbie does occur in chalk grassland, for instance at Twyford Down. It has occurred on the Brighton Downs. Fruiting of all these species is probably sporadic, though, and there's no end of sites still to visit.

'White-Outs'

M Y mum used to tell me that when she was a girl (in the 1920s) she'd go mushrooming very early in the morning on the Downs, and find places sometimes as white as snow with mushrooms. I've learnt since that mycologists (fungi experts) call this phenomenon a *'white-out'*. You don't see that nowadays. There are many places, though, where our Down pastures still bear good crops of **Field Mushrooms**, *Agaricus campestris*, as well as **Horse Mushrooms**, *A. arvensis*, and several other species. In fact a good old Down pasture site may well have four or five species of *Agaricus* mushroom upon it. You have to be a bit careful, for some of these may well be poisonous, and, anyway, mushrooms are now so scarce that it's best not to do systematic picking. Just take one or two to taste.

Dropwort, *Filipendula Vulgaris*. A herb reliably found on ancient Down pastures.

Pride of Sussex

T H E R E are even more visible chalk grassland indicator species than Rockrose and Horseshoe Vetch. The best of these is **Round-headed Rampion**, *Phyteuma tenerum* — known as the 'Pride of Sussex'. It is found on 80% of all our old chalk grassland sites. It's an adaptable species and can survive well in tall grassland. That makes it one of the last good species to cling on when old Down pasture is left long derelict. You can still see good displays of it on the steep slope at Whitehawk Hill and on Waterhall's old grasslands even after 60 years or more of neglect. Sussex has the vast bulk of the species, which elsewhere occurs only on the Surrey, Hampshire and Wiltshire Downs, though never with the same abundance as in Sussex. Late summer Downsides can be blue-tinted with its gorgeous flowers, which harmonise with the purple, red, and blue tints of the two **Knapweeds**, *Centaurea nigra* and *C. scabiosa*, **Greater** and **Lesser Scabious**, *Knautia arvensis* and *Scabiosa columbaria*, and **Devil's-bit Scabious**, *Succisa pratensis*.

Dropwort, *Filipendula vulgaris*, too, with its snowy midsummer flowerheads — like a miniature Meadowsweet — is a faithful indicator of the antiquity of chalk pasture. Like Pride of Sussex it will be one of the last species to go when these pastures are damaged and neglected. On the damaged slopes of Bushy Bottom on the lost Beeding Hill Common, Dropwort clings on with **Basil**, *Clinopodium vulgare*, and some other survivors.

Squinancywort, *Asperula cyanchica* will be found in very many ancient short-cropped pastures. It's a kind of low-growing bedstraw and its flowers make little scatters of white dots in the turf. The name's an adaptation of 'quinsy-wort', for it is a very old medicinal herb, used to treat 'quinsy's' — inflammations of the tonsils and surrounding throat tissues. The Latin specific name 'cyanchica', comes from two

Greek words meaning 'dog-strangle'!

'Eggs and Bacon'

THAT'S only one of over 70 local names[6] for **Bird's-foot Trefoil**, *Lotus corniculatus*, along with Fingers and Thumbs, Hen and Chickens, Ham and Eggs, and Granny's Toenails! You can't really count Bird's-foot Trefoil as an 'indicator of specialness' on the Downs in the same way as 'Pride of Sussex', Horseshoe Vetch and Rockrose, for it occurs just about everywhere on and off the chalk. It doesn't even have a dot map of its own in the Sussex Plant Atlas,[7] because it's so ubiquitous. Yet it *is* especially important.

Small Elephant Hawkmoth, *Deilephila porcellus*. A lovely pink and ochre Downland moth not seen half as frequently as it should be. Seems to be much commoner across the English Channel.

Its little bacon-orange and egg yolk-yellow flowers and vaguely trifoliate leaves are food plants for so many creatures. The Common Blue butterfly, largely depends upon them as caterpillar food. I've found it on nearly half of the Hove and Shoreham Down pasture sites, and it's probably present on many more. The caterpillar of the **Dingy Skipper** butterfly, *Erynnis tages*, lives on Bird's-foot Trefoil, though it also uses Horseshoe Vetch. At the same time as Dingy Skipper is flying you are quite likely to see a couple of day-flying moths: the **Mother Shipton**, *Callistege mi*, and the **Burnet Companion**, *Euclidia glyphica*. They're all three about the same size and all three are dainty little things, but well disguised amongst browning grass stems. Burnet Companion and Mother Shipton both use Bird's-foot Trefoil, as well as other flowers in the Pea family — vetches and clovers. There's a couple of weevil species dependent on 'eggs and bacon', too.

That's not all. Some very familiar Downland moths feed on it. They are the Burnet moths, all cousins: the **Six-spot Burnet**, *Zygaena filipendulae*, the **Five-spot**, *Z. trifolii*, and the **Narrow-bordered Five-spot Burnet**, *Z. lonicerae*. Telling the Five and Six-spot's apart is obvious, but telling the Narrow-bordered Five-spot from the Five-spot is a bit mind-numbing. I've made no great effort, because you'd have to capture lots of each to make proper comparisons and that'd be just daft and irresponsible. Often the Five-spot has the middle two red spots fused together and its Downland race flies earlier (May and early June) than the Downland race of Narrow-bordered (June and July). That's good enough for me.

They are such laid-back and beautiful moths. You can go right up to them where they are clustered on Thistle, Knapweed and Scabious flower heads, whilst they're nectaring, resting and mating. They have good reason to be so unafraid of us, for their bodies are packed with cyanide-containing liquids, which will give any hungry bird or mouse a nasty shock. The strong black and red colouration means 'keep-off — I'm poisonous'. Burnet Moth caterpillars are yellow with black stripes and can be seen feeding in daytime quite openly. The chrysalids live in yellowy white papery cocoons, stuck on grass stems that survive long after the moths have hatched and gone.

The Five-spot Burnet is now in serious trouble, and may be zeroing down to extinction on our local Downs, in contrast to its still abundant relatives.

Chalk Carpets

THERE'S another 'eggs and bacon'-eating moth that I've long had a fancy for, and in recent summers I've been doing a bit of a special search for it. It's the day-flying **Chalk Carpet**, *Scotopteryx bipunctaria*. Forget the 'carpet' bit of the name. It doesn't look anything like one. It just has lots of cousins in the *Geometridae* family, which do have patterns a bit like Turkish carpets, and the eighteenth century moth-namers liked using names that referred to things around them in their lives (like 'wainscots', 'brocades' and 'footmen', 'lutestrings', 'daggers', 'lackeys' and so on).

The Chalk Carpet has spent aeons evolving to look just like a bit of dirty chalk rubble — white with a grey smudge across it — and it only seems to be found in

Grizzled Skipper. A springtime species occasionally to be found on Downland.

places where bare chalk remains exposed. It seems to need these hot places to bask and roost. In the old days the nibbling and trampling of great sheep flocks always ensured that there was exposed chalk available on steep hillsides. Then, our little moth, which flies weakly like a bit of thistledown in the wind, occurred in teeming thousands on our Downs. Now, I've found it mostly only in single figures on the sides of the old quarries, bostals and whiteways of the northern scarp slope. Most everywhere else the unchallenged grass has eliminated the white chalk.

So my moth doesn't show itself on otherwise excellent chalk grassland sites like Dencher Bottom, Bevendean Down, Southwick and Whitehawk Hills. Those sites have lost their ancient terracettes kept open by the action of generations of sheep. The white chalk of the Victorian quarries will disappear, too, under grass and scrub unless we can revive sheep grazing.

'Succession' and Rarities

THE great majority of the scarce and rare plants of our old Down pastures prefer the short-grazed swards of the old Downs. Within this, nearly half of the rare chalk grassland species are *strictly* short turf specialists. They include the tiny **Bastard Toadflax**, *Thesium humifusum*, cousin to the tropical sandalwood which made fragrant the flabby bodies of many a Maharajah, and perfumes Hindu, Buddhist and Muslim ceremonies. This tiny, semi-parasitic little herb is scattered across some of our oldest grasslands. **Musk, Early Spider, Green-winged** and **Burnt-tip Orchids**, (*Herminium monorchis, Ophrys sphegodes, Orchis morio, O. ustulata*) are all short-turf lovers. The now-very-rare **Early Gentian**, *Gentianella anglica*, the **Eyebright** *Euphrasia pseudokerneri* and the not-quite-so-rare **Field Fleawort**, *Tephroseris (Senecio) integrifolia* all share this same preference. The tiny **Moonwort** fern, *Botrychium lunaria* hasn't made it, being last seen on our Downs in 1965 at Castle and Newmarket Hills. Another primitive little fern, **Adder's-tongue**, *Ophioglossum vulgatum*, which looks like a miniature version of Lord's and Ladies, has recent sites in the damp grass in the cleft bottom of a couple of old bostals, as well as on a ride in Stanmer Great Wood.

Succession to rank grassland, or take-over by Tor Grass, is the enemy of all these species, and many more. Land managers do not find much profit in sheep or cattle management, and, despite the re-creation of much new permanent pasture under the ESA (Environmentally Sensitive Area) scheme and its successor, much of the new grazing is not targetted and by no means intensive enough. It is a sad and common sight to see a large sheep flock grazing a newly sown pasture and either excluded from or happily ignoring the poorer bite provided by some adjacent fragment of ancient down pasture, which desperately needs those nibbling teeth.

Grazing is useless to old Down pasture conservation unless it is targetted at the older, threatened swards. The public subsidy spent on it is simply a waste of our money.

Of course, there are some rare herbs that are happier in the taller, less grazed swards, or at least in places which allow their taller habit to express itself. Apart from Pride of Sussex there are rarities like **Man Orchis**, *Aceras anthropophorum*, **Meadow Clary**, *Salvia pratensis*, **Nottingham Catchfly**, *Silene nutans*, **Slender Bedstraw**, *Galium pumilum*, or the **Fragrant Orchid's** (*Gymnadenia conopsea*) *densiflora* subspecies (though that form is not so tall). The colourful displays of tall Knapweeds, Scabious, **Hogweed**, *Heracleum sphondylium*, **Carrot**, *Daucus carota*, and **Hedge Parsley**, *Torilis japonica* help make late summer delightful and are alive with multitudes of bees, flies and plant bugs. They provide homes and winter sustenance for birds, small mammals and many over-wintering mini-beasts.

For all that, the balance of farming and conservation attention has to be vigorously re-adjusted towards the healthy survival of the important earlier successional stages of chalk grasslands, from bare chalk, to moss and lichen-rich cover, to sparse thin grasslands (more bare ground and tiny flowers than grasses, really) and the springy, short turf of the old sheep walks. And even the taller swards must be regularly grazed or cut or they will lose their interest and eventually be lost.

Orchids

ORCHIDS vie with Pride of Sussex in their emblematic importance for the Downs. They're so fleshy and exotic, with connotations of tropical forests, millionaires' hothouses and extravagant love gifts. I can remember the first time I found each orchid kind, though that is forty years ago for most of them.

May and June is the optimum time to see the orchids of our Down pastures, though some are later and a couple start earlier.

The first time I saw **Early Purple Orchis**, *Orchis mascula*, in the spring of 1962, it was growing amongst scrub on the upper slope east of Mount Zion. There was a new Brighton Council farm tenant at New Barn Farm and he was proving his worth by bulldozing large areas of gorse, thorn and ancient Down pasture for cereal crops. My Orchids were blooming forlorn at the very edge of the bulldozer's path. When I went back later they were gone. Scrub edge and shady grassland are familiar sites for this Orchis, though it is just as happy deep in woodland. Its biggest claim to fame was its long usage for the making of the beverage known as 'salep', which was only replaced in importance by the importation of coffee. You can still buy salep in the middle-east, but it's just a sugary drink like any other, no longer made from orchid roots.

Bee Orchid
Ophrys apifera

There are scattered sites on the Brighton Downs for the Early Purple's sister species, the Green-winged Orchis, though it is far less common. Its classic location is in old meadows, so look for it in grasslands with that lusher feel of richer soils. Its best site on our Downs is on the grassed-over roof of a Southern Water reservoir, where it flowers in gorgeous profusion.

The species' that make the big displays on our Downs are the **Common Spotted**, *Dactylorhiza fuchsii*, Fragrant, and **Pyramidal Orchids**, *Anacamptis pyramidalis*. They can swarm in hundreds. They are a lot more adaptable than perhaps they are given credit for, and can re-colonise old sites and new ones fairly readily. Fragrant Orchis reappeared at Whitehawk Hill recently after a gap of many years.

Burnt-tip or Dwarf Orchis, is much more common to the east, on the Downs beyond the River Ouse, but we do have a couple of sites for it.

Man Orchis is oddly rare in Sussex, only appearing at a scatter of sites around Wolstonbury. In contrast, **Autumn Ladies Tresses Orchis**, *Spiranthes spiralis*, can turn up anywhere in short turf. It appeared on the lawn of a church in South Portslade and had a huge swarm on the cliff top turf above the Brighton Marina, next to the pitch and put course.

Undoubtedly the orchids which most capture people's hearts are the insect orchids, of which our Down pastures have **Bee**, *Ophrys apifera*, Early Spider, and **Fly**, *O. insectifera*. They've evolved to mimic the females of various species of bee and wasp. It's not just a visual mimicry, either, for the flower also mimics the pheromonal smell of the female insect. The males come along and attempt to mate with the flower, and, in the attempt, get the pollen bundles attached to themselves, achieving cross-fertilisation of the Orchid when they attempt copulation with other flowers. Thus the flower gets 'pregnant', but the bee has a frustrating time![8]

Bee Orchis is almost as adaptable as one of those weedy species you find on building sites. It appeared in thousands along the side of the new roadworks at the Blue Circle Chalk Pit, Upper Beeding. Tony Spiers, who recently surveyed for Brighton Council the plants of the restored Sheepcote Valley, which was long a municipal rubbish dump, said that the displays of Bee Orchis there were the biggest in Sussex!

Early Spider Orchis has less mobility, though, like the Green-winged Orchis, it's nipped up onto the slopes of a covered reservoir near Brighton. Its most famous site is at Castle Hill, of course, where it is now found in thousands. Whilst sitting there having a picnic one blustery spring day I told my partner the story of how the orchis attracted a particular male solitary bee to 'mate' with it. No sooner had I spoken than a large male Mining Bee of that species, *Andrena nigroaenea*, landed on the orchis flower in front of us and gave a demonstration!

Musk Orchis and **Frog Orchis**, *Coeloglossum viride*, both like similar

Early Spider Orchid
Ophrys sphegodes

places along the top break of slope of the high scarp, and on the thin turf of old quarries and other chalk workings. They're both very low and insignificant plants, and you could be quite forgiven for walking back and forth over a Musk Orchis site and never seeing it. It's totally green and could be a bit of grass, or plantain or something.

Prehistoric Fleas

FIELD Fleawort is a plant with some tales to tell. It's a small plant usually, though it can grow tall. It's covered in white fluff, like Eidelweiss or one of those other woolly alpine flowers. In fact, you often see it, or one of its cousins, growing out of lichen-covered rocks when you are scrambling the high Alps. It's a rare plant, growing only on the South Downs, the Wessex Downs and along the Ridgeway up to the East Anglian border.

It's very faithful to the oldest Down pastures, but it also seems to particularly like areas of ancient disturbance. You can find it around the oldest chalk pits, Iron Age camps like Cissbury or Uffington Castle, and around ancient trackways and areas with Iron Age field systems. It doesn't seem to occur in the prehistoric record before the Iron Age, though that doesn't mean it wasn't here, hanging on amongst all the wildwood on some sea-cliff top or river-cliff refugia. It doesn't occur, either, in northern France, which suggests that people might have brought it in from more easterly places.

It doesn't appear in my few herbals, but its name would imply it was valued as a vermifuge. Perhaps that's the key

Fly Orchid *Ophrys insectifera*

to its distribution — it was used to keep the prehistoric fleas away from our ancestors.

On our Downs it occurs near the line of the ancient Port Way over Round Hill Hangleton, and Summer Down, as well as around the South Downs Way and its descending bostals. It occurs on fragments of ancient Down pasture at Tenant Hill and Cockroost Hill north of Portslade, where there was extensive Iron Age Activity, and also near the Juggs Road and the ancient pastures around Castle Hill.

Blasted Heaths

IN Victorian times our Downs would have been as purple with Heather as any moorside in the Scottish Highlands. Way back in 1864 Mrs Merrifield wrote of our Downs[9] that, although **Bell Heather**, *Erica cinerea*, and **Ling**, *Calluna vulgaris* "are extremely abundant… yet I can hardly forebear a passing tribute to the beauty which the dense masses of flowers of the Bell Heather… give to our hills". Indeed, in those times the people of Lewes called Offham Down 'Little Scotland' for its purple heathery display.

You won't see that now. Bell Heather has been reduced to one tiny site on the Peacehaven Golf Course and Ling Heather chiefly survives only as a few senescent bushes and tiny low tufts, largely unnoticed in otherwise grassy swards. Till recent years one old Ling bush survived in Loose Bottom, east of the Falmer Road. It was surrounded, foolishly, with a protective paling fence, for it did not need protection from grazing. To the contrary, the lack of grazing was the cause of its demise, and when I returned to the site last year it had disappeared and the rotten fence was collapsed upon its grave.

Thus, in a century, a whole sub-landscape of our Downs has passed into entire extinction. Only a scattering of place names commemorates its passing, though some of those are old indeed. On East Moulsecoomb's slope were the lands of 'Hodshrove' Farm, running over Falmer Hill. The name derives from the Saxon 'Hoth schorf', meaning 'heathy slope'. 'Hoth' was a common name for heath, still surviving in local names like Hoddern ('heath down') Farm, near Peacehaven, and East and West Hoathly. Overlooking Bevendean from the south lies the bluff of 'Heath Hill' and there are 'Heathy Brows' at both Peacehaven and the high ridge south of Ditchling Beacon. On Varncombe Hill, east of the Saddlescombe Road, is the site of North Heath Barn, built, no doubt, on the new corn lands which had replaced the old heath. The names 'Varncombe' and nearby 'Braypool' also commemorate heathy vegetation, for 'varn' is a local development of the Old English 'fearn' (fern), meaning Bracken, which is also the meaning of the 'bray' element of Braypool.

This heathy landscape had been the product of two great developments. Firstly, there had been the results of the millions of years of deposition of Tertiary sands, gravels and clays on top of the chalk and their subsequent erosion. This has left a series of relatively well-structured acidic deposits on the higher Downs at Newhaven, Peacehaven and Falmer, as well as under the built-up coastal area from Brighton to Shoreham. During the last two million year Ice Age further erosion and fierce winds had left highly mixed, largely windborne ('aeolian') deposits on the hilltops, which we call Clay with Flints. Secondly, the results of rainfall and several millennia of cultivation have leached out and washed away the richness of our Downtop soils. Many centuries of sheep grazing transferred further nutrients from the hills to the valleys.

These developments left a mosaic of both acid and calcium-rich soils, often with soil gradients through acid topsoils to chalky sub-soils. Heathy and chalk-loving species were able to survive together in the most unusual combinations: Heather and **Wood Sage**, *Teucrium scorodonia*, alongside Squinancywort and Rockrose. It is this mixture of chalkland and heathland species which was named 'chalk heath'.

Chalk Heath

THERE'S really only one small chalk heath site surviving on our Brighton Downs: at Pyecombe Golf Course, on Middle Brow, three quarters of a mile south of the Jack and Jill windmills at Clayton. There's a small deposit of Clay with Flints on the Brow. The golf course was created in 1894 on ancient Down pastures, and the mowing of fairways and roughs has preserved this relic plant community, though the encroachment of scrub has reduced it to tiny islands. It still has **Heath Bedstraw**, *Galium saxatile*, **Slender St John's-wort**, *Hypericum pulchrum*, Ling Heather, **Heath Speedwell**, *Veronica officinalis*, **Dyer's Greenweed**, *Genista tinctoria*, **Dwarf Gorse**, *Ulex minor*, and **Tormentil**, *Potentilla erecta*. Some of the

A fence put around the last surviving Ling Heather bush at Loose Bottom, Falmer. The fence just hastened its extinction.

Ling is mown, and survives well, but other clumps are left to grow in rank grassland and several old clumps on the golf course have been lost in the last ten years. **Heath moth**, *Ematurga atomaria* atomaria, is still here, and its food plant may be the heather, though elsewhere on the Downs it must rely only on Clovers and Trefoils. Alongside these acid-loving species you can find classic plants of the chalk, like Fragrant Orchis, Bastard Toadflax, **Betony**, *Betonica officinalis*, Dropwort, **Crested Hair-grass**, *Koeleria cristata*, Horseshoe Vetch and **Stemless Thistle**, *Cirsium acaulon*. And in the autumn, the Waxcap fungi can put on a great display in the mossy turf, with little Fairy Clubs and Earth Tongues, too.

If you want to know what this lost landscape looked like then go to Lullington Heath on the Eastbourne Downs. It's the largest chalk heath site in the country, and in recent years English Nature have done fantastic work in hauling the long-derelict site back towards pristine condition. Sheets of purple Heather vie with the ghostly green-white plumes of Wood Sage, and there are mats of heathy mosses and hoary lichens.

Acid Grassland

T H O U G H chalk heath is extinct as a local landscape and reduced to one site, there are a scatter of places where acid grassland survives as a kind of transitional community between classic chalk grassland and chalk heath.

Southwick Hill has quite a large area of acid grassland (good for Waxcaps), where in one place tiny sprigs of Ling heather survived alongside Bastard Toadflax ten years ago (perhaps they still do) in a soft rabbit-grazed 'lawn'. The interiors of the prehistoric camps at Hollingbury and Wolstonbury both have top-knots of acidic grassland on Clay with Flints, and there's a large area of acidic grassland on the promontory of the Devil's Dyke. Look out in these places for species like

Common Bent-grass, *Agrostis capillaris*, Tormentil, Heath Speedwell, **Field Wood-rush**, *Luzula campestris*, the two Sorrels, *Rumex*, and the long haired moss *Dicranum scoparium*.

There are minute bits of Heather surviving on these acid grassland fragments at Blackcap, Ashcombe Bottom, Hogtrough Bottom south of Ditchling Beacon, part of Castle Hill, near Woodingdean, and probably elsewhere, too.

Offham Down and Castle Hill near Woodingdean still had the very rare **Heath Dog-violet**, *Viola canina*, till recent years. Maybe it still hangs on there.

There are good fragments of acid grassland on Keymer Post Down and above adjacent Burnhouse Bostall. Newtimber Hill has lots of acid grassland on its top where there used to be rich chalk heath 150 years ago. Much of it is poor quality now, but the summit of North Hill, where the round barrows sit, is still excellent. High Hill, Kingston Hill, Hog Plantation Moulsecoomb, Fulking Hill scarp, Varncombe Hill, and other places still hold fragments, and there are many places which have not been properly recognized yet.

Often the little Tormentil flower will be the give-away species that strikes your eye. It nearly always has just four yellow petals. That's the thing to look for.

The True Heaths of Newhaven

T H E R E ' S one area of the Brighton Downs which breaks all the rules, and that's the district west and south of Newhaven, bounded by Peacehaven, and the open cliffs. Here, a north/south ridge between Bollen's Bush and Chene Gap on the clifftop dominates the landscape. Rushy Hill forms its highest point.

The old name for this ridge is 'Hoathdown' and that's a good name to revive (rather than the nonsense name 'Friar's Bay' three quarters of a mile from the sea), for it accurately describes the area as 'heathy down'.

This was an area of *true* heath, not 'chalk heath', for it has very little exposed chalk at all. This whole area has a different geology, and consequently a different historical vegetation, than most of the Brighton Downs. Its deep and relatively intact deposits of sand, gravels and clays give its soils an acidic chemistry, and areas of poor drainage cause streamlets and marshy conditions to form.

Most of this old heathland has disappeared under the welter of thorn scrub that is now such a feature of this area, but enough survives on Peacehaven Golf Course, amongst the gorse to its west, and on the cliffs and undercliff of Castle Hill to tell a very different story than the rest of our Downs.

When I looked at the results of my own impressionistic survey of these Downs a while back I found that nearly a third of the plants I had recorded were species of acid, neutral and wet ground! Out of the 29 such species I'd noted, 20 more or less preferred acidic soils, five liked roughly neutral soils, and four preferred wet conditions.

This district has a real heathland rarity like **Upright Chickweed**, *Moenchia erecta*, as well as the Downland-averse **Heath Spotted Orchis**, *Dactylorhiza maculata*. It has Bell Heather, Heath Bedstraw, **Heath Milkwort**, *Polygala serpyllifolia*, **Heath Groundsel**, *Senecio sylvaticus*, and Wood Sage. The classic flowers of old meadows, **Pepper Saxifrage**, *Silaum silaus*, and Green-winged Orchis, have strong populations here, and **Fleabane**, *Pulicaria dysenterica*, **Field Horsetail**, *Equisetum arvense*, and Rushes line some of the marshier tracks.

Southwards, its only on the cliff edge and undercliff at Newhaven's Castle Hill that you can still see a smidgeon of the old heathy vegetation, and here it mingles with gorgeous splashes of pink, white, and yellow from the cliff face Stonecrops,

Sedum, **Thrift**, *Armeria maritima*, and Bird's-foot Trefoil.

On the trampled and salty turf here, you can find a little community of Clovers, more reminiscent of old village greens and commons. There's **Strawberry Clover**, *Trifolium fragiferum*, **Shamrock**, *T. dubium*, **Rough Clover**, *T. scabrum*, and the tiny **Fenugreek**, *T. ornithopodioides*, as well as the very common **White Clover**, *T. repens*, and **Hop Trefoil**, *T. campestre*. And down on the undercliff there are patches of the dainty and rare **Sea Clover**, *T. squamosum*.

Seeing a Second Summer
Waxcap Grasslands

THOSE already familiar with old Down pasture know that summer is the prime time to be there. In winter the Downs are a bleak place. It is the summer when the grass is starred with the yellows, blues, wine red and white of tiny flowers, and the blues, whites and russets of little butterflies.

I never imagined that there was a second summer on our Downs. I didn't realise that the turf could shine again in autumn as bright as in June or August. Bright scatters of scarlet, blobs of warm brick orange, glistening sovereigns of egg yellow and lemon yellow, and dark humps of crimson cluster in the mossy grass as colourful as pastures in children's story books.

It's odd that these so-colourful **Waxcap fungi** have had so little recognition on our Downs. Recently this has been changing, though, and a four autumns ago Peter Russell and I set out to rectify our ignorance. We walked 33 of our 180 old chalk grassland sites. Since then we've looked at more. The results have been startlingly good and show that we have sites that are of regional and probably national importance.

These Waxcaps are the fungal 'flowers' of old pastures and other grasslands. Experts

What You Can Find If You Look!

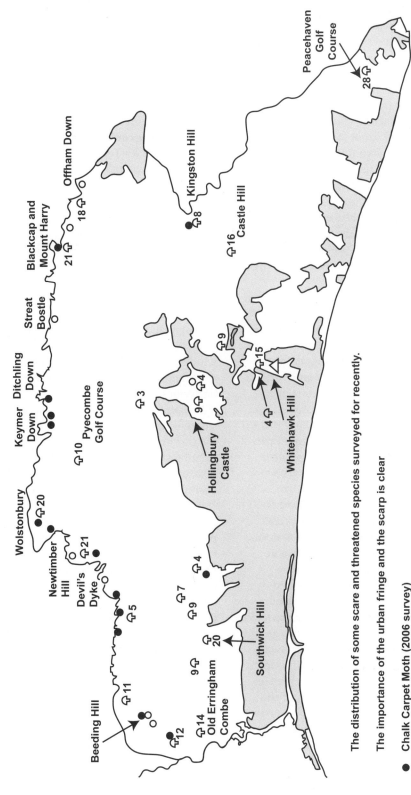

The distribution of some scare and threatened species surveyed for recently.

The importance of the urban fringe and the scarp is clear

- ●   Chalk Carpet Moth (2006 survey)
- ○   Orange-Tailed Clearwing Moth (2005)
- △   Six-Belted Clearwing Moth (2005)
- ♀   Old meadow fungi: Waxcaps, Fairy Clubs, Earthtongues and Pink Gills (2004).
      The number adjacent is the total species seen.

don't seem to know why they've evolved such bright colours. Perhaps to reflect the sunlight and stop them drying up, says one theory. Perhaps to make them attractive to eat and thus to spread their spores through dung, said my theory. But sheep and cows are *colour-blind*, and anyway the fungal spores would be dark — melanised, like the colour of Field Mushroom gills — if they had to travel through animals' guts. Their caps often shine and glisten because of an outer waxy coating and also because they are often glutinous and moist, which are probably features for surviving in the higher temperatures found in open grassland. The Latin name for Waxcaps — *Hygrocybe* — means 'moist head'.

Waxcap fungi are now recognized as special indicators of old, undisturbed grasslands. They are intolerant of disturbance, of fertilizers, ploughing, mulch or herbicides. They need a long, long time for a flora to establish anew. And they are easily recognised, so ordinary folk can monitor them easily.

They're also a bit like invisible ink. You can't see them when you usually try to 'read' the Downs — in spring and summer. And you can tell things from them you can't tell from the richness of ordinary flowers. The Waxcaps will be hit by fertilizer application *before* the flowering plants, so a poor Waxcap flora may indicate damage to a site which the flowers don't show. And they may occur in different places than the best flower displays. A place with a poor herbaceous plant flora may still have a good Waxcap display.

They especially like areas with mossy grassland and deeper soils, and on the Downs these tend to be on flatter areas, such as the plateau tops where clay-with-flints or other Tertiary deposits enrich the soils. Yet these are the very places that farmers have most assiduously destroyed in the great plough-ups of modern capitalist agriculture.

Perhaps that's why the Waxcap grasslands of our Downs have been neglected for so long. The most obvious plateau areas where people walk (such as around the South Downs Way) have largely had their ancient grasslands ploughed out or 'improved'.

Fairy Clubs, Earth Tongues, and Pink Gills

SEVERAL other groups of fungi seem to share the same indicative value in old grasslands and to operate in similar ecological ways to Waxcaps. They're often a bit less obvious and often much smaller, but they're just as charming. The (mostly yellow) Fairy Clubs, *Clavulinopsis*, and (mostly black) Earth Tongues, *Geoglossum*, have little wavy arms that poke up amongst the short mossy Fescue turf in late autumn. The Pink Gills, *Entoloma*, are ordinary gilled 'Toadstools' and can be big or small, but several of them are extremely beautiful. The species in these three groups are more difficult to identify, but the numbers of species can still be roughly counted and thus used to work out the quality of a site.

The 'Second Summer' Sites

SEVERAL sites put on displays that were as good as a second summer. Newtimber Hill, Southwick Hill, Offham Down and Mount Harry/Blackcap produced areas with great cornucopias of **Meadow Waxcap**, *H. pratensis*, **Crimson Waxcap**, *H. punicea* and **Scarlet Hood**, *H. coccinea*, together with *H. aurantiosplendens, H. quieta, H. irrigata* and many of the smaller species. Scatters of Earth Tongues and clumps of five or six Fairy Club species were all around.

Other sites had very high species counts, but didn't put on such dazzling visual displays. Wolstonbury Hill had a count of 20 of these old grassland species, including 16 Waxcaps. Peacehaven Golf Course scored even higher with 28 species, including five Fairy Clubs and nine Pink Gills. Dencher Bottom had eighteen species. I only visited Castle Hill,

Woodingdean and Pyecombe Golf Course after frosts had hit, but both sites produced great results. Other delightful suprises were to find colourful groups of species on Bevendean Down and Hollingbury Hill Fort.

Things 'Ain't What They Seem

I LEARNT an important lesson from all this Waxcap hunting : that you should never give up on a site.

I had always thought that the Devil's Dyke Golf Course had lost all its old pasture interest. Massive scrub invasion and golf course management have clearly taken a heavy toll. The flowering plant flora is very uninteresting. Yet, in two visits, I have recorded seven Waxcap species, three Fairy Clubs and three or four Pink Gills, including the dainty little **Green Pink Gill**, *Entoloma incanum*, with its green stem and funny mousey smell.

The biggest surprise, though, has been on my own site, Whitehawk Hill. My first season's looking resulted in finding only four Waxcap species, all at the base of the steep slope. In the second season I started looking at the grassland at the top of Bear Road and next to Warren Road. I'd never rated this area as important for plants, given its partial improvement and its history as a Racecourse coach park. Yet, in several visits, I've found 12 old grassland fungi there, and a couple of new ones elsewhere, bringing the Whitehawk Hill total up to 14 or 15 species. That makes it the best Waxcap site on Brighton and Hove City's urban fringe, at the moment!

There were other lessons to learn. Some golf courses proved to be important refuges for Waxcaps. Unmown and ungrazed chalk grassland, which is so common on the urban fringe, proved depressingly poor in those species. Yet, when an urban fringe site is traditionally grazed, like Southwick Hill, this second summer can really bloom!

The Lowest of the Low

I F , like Alice, you shrink so small you could walk down a rabbit hole, you will start noticing all sorts of tiny plants that otherwise you are very likely to miss. Flints and lumps of chalk in chalk pits and tracksides are mosaic'd with tiny 'volcanoes', or minute lawns of moss, or crusts of grey or white, or occasionally yellow. Bits of bare ground and earth have little bristly bushes, like the trees put around to decorate track layouts on toy train sets (and these plants are used for that). Indeed, once you "get your eye in", some of these little assemblages of miniature plants can be like tiny gardens, with five, six, ten and more species jostling for space.

The community of mosses, liverworts and lichen on our chalk grasslands is distinctive from that found elsewhere. Many species love alkaline ground and are found only there. Some species have varieties that specialize in chalky soils (like the *lacunosum* variety of the moss *Hypnum cupressiforme*). Many species have become much rarer over the last century, and the community of rare 'hepatics' (Latin for liverworts) that you get on ancient chalk grassland is now almost extinct on our local Downs.

The best places to look for these tiny gardens are on the northern scarp of the Downs, where the shady and damper conditions are perfect for these little plants. Look especially at the sides of bostals and sheep walked terracettes, and any chalk workings and quarrysides — anywhere where bits of bare chalk are exposed in fairly stable conditions. These are plants which can only cope in such places, where they are free of the competition of more evolved, 'higher' plants.

In one or two places we have the very rare little lichen *Petractis clausa*. If your eye has wandered over the fancy puff pastries and tartlets in the windows of delicatessens, then you will know what the fruits of this little job look like. They are like an apricot tart which was made only for the tiniest pygmy fairies — little orange centres with a puffy crust round it. The body of the lichen is growing inside the rock (endolithic) and the little tartlets are actually semi-immersed in the rock, too, like tarts in a baking tray. How about that! Actually, quite a lot of Downland lichen, like the *Verrucarias*, have fruits partly immersed in the rock. When they die the rock surface is left with lots of little empty pock-marks all over it, like the pits you get left on your skin from a bad bout of acne!

The most obvious non-crustose lichens are those little *Cladonia* bushes that sit amongst the dry stems of the Sheep's Fescue grass. Be careful not to tread on them, for they are so brittle that they just break up into pieces. There are two more frequent species that you may

come across, *Cladonia rangiformis* and *Cladonia furcata, ssp rangiformis*. They are very alike. Lichenologists use chemicals to tell species apart. They carry round little bottles of powders and liquids with cocktail sticks to dab them onto bits of the lichen. The bit of the plant that's been dabbed will then change colour (or not) and this will be a big clue to telling what the species is. Both of these *Cladonias* stain yellow when touched with potassium hydroxide, so that's not a lot of use, but *rangiformis* stains red with Paraphenylenediamine. (Try saying that five times quickly!)

Pseudoscleropodium purum makes up for being the commonest Down pasture moss by its fancy name. It's got fat little branches and is a bit shiny. You can find mats of it anywhere on old Downland pastures. Because it doesn't get eaten by rabbits it's able to grow at the expense of other plants. You'll often find the mosses *Homalothecium lutescens* and *Calliergon*

Sheep and cattle walk regular paths on Downland slopes which create mini-terraces — terracettes — over time. Each terracette has its own tiny ecosystem.

cuspidatum growing with it. The name *lutescens* means yellowish, and this plant can really add significant colour to the turf, especially when big mats of it are scuffed up and scattered by rabbits and sheep.

Under the edge of sheep terracettes and hanging from over-hanging grass clumps, you will often find big mats of a robust moss called *Neckera crispa*, together with its biggest pal the moss *Ctenidium molluscum*. (How can anyone resist these names — they're like poetry!) They form a characteristic community with other mosses, like *H. cupressiforme ssp lacunosum*. *Neckera crispa* really does have a lovely crinkly, crispy feel to it, a bit like rubbing bubble wrap between your fingers. It's almost wholly found on the north escarpment and seems to be a good indicator species.

Underneath the *Neckera* mats, where the bare chalk is exposed, you may find the tiniest little liverworts, like *Leiocolea turbinata* and the minute moss *Seligeria calcarea*.

Anything much smaller than those little things would be invisible to the naked eye.

Sometimes in these moss communities you may find the rare moss *Ditrichum flexicaule*, looking like little tufts of dyed green hair. And — just as rarely — you may find the pretty *Bryum pallens*. It's a give-away because of its pink, or even rose reddish colour. Very nice.

The real prize on our Downs has eluded me, despite hunting and hunting for it. This is the moss *Rhodobryum roseum*. It's big (as mosses go), from 2-10cm tall, with a little rosette of leaves at its top. It seems to particularly like the tops of anthills, where there are lots of other little rosettes of leaves to confuse you. I've clambered up and down numerous steep slopes, zigzagging backwards and forwards, eyes to the ground, inspecting ant hills where ever they appear, but never found it. It's been pointed out to me growing in a sandy wood many miles away, but that's not the same as seeing it on my own Downs. The trouble is, *rabbits* love anthills as much as mosses and other little plants do and rabbit numbers are very high at the moment. Every anthill you see (or so it seems) has been piddled on by rabbits, who love to use these thrones! The anthills are urine stained and their characteristic vegetation is yellow and half dead. Hey ho…

The Birds of Desert Places

G R O W I N G up with open Downland stretching beyond your suburb you're most likely to focus in on the wild flowers and the summer butterflies if you're interested in natural history. They are so obviously varied and colourful. But birds? — well, the birding is very lean on the Downs. The first time birds really struck my consciousness big-time was during the great winter of 1962-3, when **Curlew** flew over Hangleton Valley and the bodies of colourful **Linnets, Goldfinch** and **Greenfinch** were preserved deep-frozen in the snow, to emerge one by one as the melt progressed.

There is, however, a fascinating suite of steppeland, prairie birds that are special to the Downs, though some of them are now extinct, and some now occur only as passage migrants or occasional visitors. That older community of birds of the high desert places on the Downs is very, very threadbare these days. **Great Bustard** is now extinct (though being

THE GRASSHOPPER WARBLER,

reintroduced on Salisbury Plain) and **Stone Curlew** nearly so. Small groups of Great Bustard clung on between the Dyke and Thundersbarrow and north of Patcham till 200 years ago, and the last one seems to have lived north of West Blatchington around 1825.

At Sheepcote Valley in 2005 quite a list of these 'prairie' loving birds was recorded: **Kestrel, Short-eared Owl, Skylark, Meadow Pipit, Whinchat, Stonechat, Wheatear, Grasshopper Warbler,** Linnet and **Yellowhammer**. To that list we should add **Quail, Corn Bunting** (for which the Brighton Downs were a stronghold), **Dartford Warbler**, the two **Whitethroats, Grey Partridge, Merlin** and **Hen Harrier** as being characteristic of that assemblage.

Sheepcote is an excellent place to watch **Short-eared Owl** in the winter and early spring. It is a large, dramatic bird, with long narrow wings, and is surprisingly tolerant of viewers, providing we stay at a respectful distance.

There are **Buzzards** now breeding again on the Brighton Downs, nearly two centuries after they were expirpated here.

Autumn and spring are the most abundant times for Downland bird watching, as many migrants spend time on our Downs recovering or preparing for their long overseas journeys. As well as Sheepcote, favourite birding places are Mill Hill Shoreham, Hollingbury Hill, and Newhaven cliffs.

THE SWALLOW.

My own childhood notebooks record winter flocks of **Lapwing** mixed with **Black-headed Gull** on the Hove Downs, but, for me, Lapwing are a rare sight on these Downs nowadays.

Twice in June 2006 I heard Quail calling at evening time from the wide corn lands below Cold Coombes, west of Kingston. It is a tiny partridge-like bird, the size of a small pheasant chick. Its song — the unmistakeable three note *'wet-my-lips'* — is very far-carrying and difficult to locate. It could come from anywhere around you.

Cold Coombes is also a good place to see migrating **Ring Ouzel** in September and October. The steep shadowed north facing slopes must remind them of the mountain homes they have just left. They are our mountain Blackbird, with a tell-tale white breast bib.

Back in the eighteenth century Parson Gilbert White recorded them in small parties all along the Sussex Downs from Chichester to Lewes. He also noted **Chough** from our chalk cliffs and Great Bustards "on the wide downs near Brighthelmstone".[10] As for the Bustard-like Stone Curlew — a bird now seen locally only as a very rare visitor — he tells us that "it abounds in all the champaign parts of Hampshire and Sussex and congregates in vast flocks in the autumn".[11]

By 1900, when WH Hudson wrote,[12] the Stone Curlew had been completely extirpated from our Downs.

Hudson's descriptions chronicle some birds still familiar to us at an abundance that is now far-gone. Looking down on the village of Ditchling he describes the Swallows and Martins as like "a multitude of bees or other insects, flying about a hive".[13]

Wheatear is still a frequent bird of passage on our Downs though it has gone as a breeding species. Local efforts are being made to encourage it to breed again by the provision of artificial holes in the ground, such as it needs for nesting. This time it will be free of the massive persecution by the poultry trade in which Downland shepherds greatly supplemented their wages by systematic trapping.

THE ROOK

Grasshopper Warblers can still be heard, though rarely. Even though I was no birder I knew straightaway that the long reeling churr I was hearing one spring forty years ago up at the Devil's Dyke was this bird. It was common on our Downs right up till the second world war. In 2004, birds were seen locally at Balsdean, Whitehawk Hill and Ovingdean, and it bred at Beeding Brooks.

Stonechat and Linnet can still be found frequently across the open Downs, especially in gorsey places, like the Hollingbury Castle Iron Age camp, on the gorse at the north end of Whitehawk Hill, and at Newhaven Cliffs. Dartford Warbler should always be looked for at such sites, too. It's been a familiar bird on the bushy parts of Whitehawk Hill.

Serpents

I got into the habit of tramping up to and beyond the Devil's Dyke most Saturdays when I was coming up to my 12th birthday. That spring we were exploring the rough grasslands there when we came across a beautiful **Adder** basking amongst tussocks and the occasional small Hawthorn bush. She had obviously just come out of winter hibernation and was soaking up the still-weak sun. She didn't move, and we watched her for a while before we moved away. She was a lovely yellowy-brown creature with the clearest zig-zag of black down her spine. I hiked there twice more over the next few days

to see her, and she was always to be found curled up in the same spot. She had the most beautiful ruby eyes with a black slash of pupil down the middle. Her little black tongue flicked in and out.

My family always called Benfield Hill 'The Adder Patch', and we found a beautiful sloughed Adder skin there as recently as April 1994. They slough their old skins often in one piece, like pulling off a vest, and the skin I've kept from Benfield is absolutely perfect except for being a bit crumpled round the head. Still, if you haven't got any arms you can be forgiven for not getting it exactly right. Unfortunately, that Adder, or another of the small number found on the Reserve, was killed that May by a dog walker and left by the gate. At Whitehawk Hill we think the Adder became extinct some 15 years ago, at least.

Adders especially like old Down pastures, heaths and moors, though you can find them in open woods and rough farmed countryside, too. Finding a population of Grass Snakes in old Wealden meadows recently got me thinking about

Mrs Adder and her young family

just how often I have come across Adders over the years. I went through all my untidy records to come up with a list. My biggest cluster of sightings was when I was National Trust under-warden of Lavington Common and Durford Heath for a year. Then I saw them frequently.

What struck me forcefully, though, was how rarely I have seen them on our Brighton Downs in recent years, compared to when I was a boy.

In the four boyhood years I kept notes — from 1962 to 1966 — my Adder sightings on the Brighton Downs averaged out at one every 6.5 months. In the last eighteen years, though, my sightings on the Brighton Downs have averaged out at only one Adder seen every 3 years. That's a pretty big fall!

As a boy I found Adders on a couple of sites on the scarp slope and a couple of dip slope sites north of Hove. In the past eighteen years I've still only found them at two Hove dip slope sites and three (different) scarp slope sites. To be sure, I've spent more time on the Hove Downs than to the east, so I expect they are present much more widely. I've had recent reports of them from Ditchling Beacon, Offham Down, Lewes old racecourse, behind the Newhaven cliffs, and Waterhall, for instance.

The seasonal pattern of my sightings has two peaks. The first and strongest peak is in April, when the Adders have just come out of hibernation and are sluggish and sedentary. In that month (and it might be earlier now because of global warming) you can easily see Adders basking and go back over the next few days to see them again in the same spot. April is obviously the best month for spotting Adders. The second, weaker, peak I've noticed is in August. The Adders slough their skins in spring and again in high summer and that's when you can find the old skins. They give birth in high summer and you may see the babies then. They're pretty independent from birth.

As an adult I was primarily interested in Downland flowers for many years and they don't really put on much of a display till May and June, so it may be that the smaller numbers of Brighton Downs Adders I've found in recent years are partly due to me not venturing out on the Downs so much till after their April period of high visibility. I don't know.

The big crash in numbers seen is very worrying, though.

Most of the urban fringe must be becoming much more difficult for Adders because of the numbers of dogs walked off the lead, and the hostility Adders receive from some dog walkers and other members of the public. I once found a pregnant Adder smashed to death, with her dead babies spilling out of her split abdomen. Yet the wider, farmed plateau is mostly even more unsuitable because of habitat loss and fragmentation. Adders, I suspect, will become much more hemmed in to the less-used parts of the north-facing scarp and the larger scale and less disturbed dip slope sites.

Adders hunt lizards and small mammals deep in their burrows, and their eyes are especially adapted to give them good vision in the dark. They hibernate for up to six months of the year, usually in communal dormitories (in mammal holes and such like) which are repeatedly used. The males have a really eerie sparring dance in springtime, if they end up as rivals, when they rear up against each other and sway backwards and forwards. I'd love to see that!!

Don't harm them or let your dog do so. There's a good law imposing pretty massive fines if you're caught. Adder bites cause fewer deaths than wasp, bee or mosquito stings. They are NOT an aggressive animal and will only bite if attacked. Most bites are on dogs' and cats' heads where they've attempted to seize the Adder or been over-curious.

Grass Snakes are not frequently seen on the Downs because they like watery places, where frogs abound, but they do occur at the edge of the Downs and — rarely — on the urban fringe. I've seen one near the Castle Hill Nature Reserve, well away from water. Smooth Snakes are not found on the Downs. You have to go to the hot Hampshire and Dorset heaths to see them.

Lizards are still abundant on old Down pasture sites and across rough, uncultivated land and even gardens. They must number many thousands on a rough site like Whitehawk Hill. You'll only get **Common Lizards** and **Slow-worms** (which are a legless lizard) on our Downs, so don't believe it when someone tells you they've seen a Sand Lizard! The nearest sites for them are Midhurst-way.

All three **Newt** species can be found in some Downland dew ponds.

Toads and **Frogs** are not common on the dry Downs. Toads played a big part in the controversy 11 years ago over the proposed ploughing of Offham Marshes, for it was on behalf of the huge Toad population that the Marshes had been made into a Site of Special Scientific Interest. Much of the year they live in the chalk pits and the woods that now drape Offham Hill above the Marshes. Every spring large numbers migrate down to the Marshes. Toad numbers had declined greatly, and that had provided a rationale for the ploughing of the Marshes. Thankfully, direct action prevented the Marshes ploughing, and a major research programme was initiated into the problems of the Toads and the Marshes.

We are much more likely to see Toads in our urban gardens, nowadays. They are not free of problems there, though, for fragmentation of their back garden populations (by roads and concrete) leads to genetic bottlenecks. So scoop up some

of that Toadspawn, and take a jam jar of it round to a friend's garden pond. You'll be doing a bit of useful genetic enrichment on behalf of our warty friends!

Rabbits

"L O O K , *there's a Rabbit!*" we say enthusiastically, and we point along a hedgeline for the benefit of Jane's fifteen month old toddler grandson. He's more interested in a pebble. Nonetheless, it's Rabbits that we're most likely to see when we take our children for Downland walks. They are as familiar as Sheep, and a lot more obvious than Skylarks, or other old Downland wildlife.

Their biomass (the combined weight of all the animals) is greater than any other wild mammal in Britain, and twice as great as the next weightiest, the Red Deer (which is scarce down south, but 'as common as Rabbits' in the Scottish Highlands). Rabbits are the fourth commonest wild mammal in Britain. Only the Wood Mouse, the Common Shrew and the Field Vole have greater populations, but with a tiny fraction of the Rabbit's biomass.

They were the farmer's bane, and often still are. At various times it was estimated that from 5-25 % of our cereal crops were being eaten by them. By the First World War there were as many Rabbits as humans, and they became more common till 1954, when the imported disease, myxomatosis, killed off 99% of them. Their numbers partially recovered in the 1970s and '80s, and continue to do so, though they have not again reached the plague proportions of the time before 'myxy'.

Farmers net their fencelines against Rabbits along the edge of cereal fields, with varying success. Sometimes, too, they bulldoze their 'burys', or group tunnel systems, in banks and bushes.

They have also used 'Rabbit control' as an excuse for attacks on surviving Downscape features. In recent years I have heard 'Rabbit control' used to excuse the bulldozing of two fragments of ancient Down pasture, one with an Iron Age lynchet. About a third bushy Down pasture site the farmer was more circumspect in describing his destructive motives, though I suspect the Rabbit was the excuse he expressed in different company.

Nature conservationists have a more positive view about Rabbits. After the decline of Sheep grazing from late Victorian times onwards, Rabbits became an increasingly vital agent in maintaining the ancient Down pasture turf. So, for Down pasture the advent of myxomatosis was a disaster. After an initial glorious flowering of the turf, now untrammeled by those nibblers, the rank grasses and scrub advanced with renewed vigour. Famous butterfly sites like Mill Hill, Shoreham, disappeared in the 1960s under a waving sea of tall Brome grass, and the clouds of Adonis and Chalkhill Blue butterflies were reduced to the edge of extinction. Colin Pratt, our local butterfly and moth expert, described the effects of 'myxy' as "a triumph for farmers and their wallets, but a catastrophe for butterflies".[14]

Rabbits are vital to ancient Down pasture's survival. They are delicious to eat, too, and it would be good to see them used more systematically as a crop, to make common again the memorable taste of wild Rabbit stew, and the softness of Rabbit skin gloves.

The problem with Rabbits, though, is that they cannot be so easily controlled as sheep and cattle. When their numbers are very high they can replace the Sheep's Fescue sward with a scruffy cover of Nettles (round their burys) and unpalatable species, like Ground Ivy, Viper's-bugloss, Hound's Tongue, and Gromwell. That may be perfectly acceptable in some places. On Benfield Hill high Rabbit numbers allow good displays of Large Thyme and Autumn Gentian, but species like Green Hairstreak butterfly and Burnet moths may be disadvantaged.

Rabbits were not always so difficult to control. They were brought over to Britain first by the Normans, less than a millennium ago, as a cosseted luxury food. For many centuries they were confined to special 'warrens', with purpose built bury's (called 'pillow mounds') complete with ready-made tunnels. **Warren Road**, Woodingdean, **The Warren**, on Beeding Hill, and **The Warenne**, at Wolstonbury, all commemorate such enterprises. Even as late as Parson Gilbert White's time in the late 18th century they were easily managed, and clearly not a pest. It is likely that changes in farming and more efficient game keeping (which eliminated their predators) helped turn them into a major problem by Victorian times.

They are native only to the Iberian peninsular and neighbouring southern France, though they used to occur here, way back in the Ice Age. The Romans spread them widely, but not to Britain. Their medieval name was 'Coneys'. 'Rabbit' was the name used for the juveniles, which were a culinary delicacy till the eighteenth century.

We must watch out, for new Rabbit control horrors are being planned on behalf of farmers, such as a viral carrier of a birth control agent. Luckily, the horrible Viral Haemorrhagic disease, which has decimated Rabbit populations on the continent, seems to have had a greatly reduced efficacy after its introduction in Britain.

Mad as a March Hare

BACK in the 'sixties when I was a boy on the Downs we used to see **Brown Hares** a lot — in all seasons and situations. Often they'd be grazing quite close and show no great desire to make their escape. I'm not sure they use their frontal vision that much, judging from the times when a grazing Hare would hop towards us, only seeming to realize our presence when we were a few yards away. They have big bulging eyes on the sides of their heads and pretty-much all-round vision, so I guess they see almost too much to take in! Two thirds of those boyhood sightings were in springtime, and a third in April alone, though we saw them in winter snow, too. We saw them often on the high Downland arables (where they love those juicy spring cereal crops), but also once in the middle of a wood, and once we flushed a pair out from underneath some pondside logs.

Only once in my life (and not on our local Downs) have I seen that March madness when the Jack (male) Hares meet to box and kick and chase each other across the fields. From the cover of a wood edge we watched these breeding antics of a large gathering of Hares scattered across a wide Downland cornfield as they raced after each other, took breath, sparred and grazed. That was a special privilege to see. They'll rise up on their haunches and box vigorously with their forefeet — and even use their teeth if need be. No Queensbury Rules there.

Once in Maytime we saw eight Hares together on the Northease Downs, though this is too unseasonable to have been a gathering for some boxing madness. In fact, nearly half of those sixties sightings were of more than one hare — usually of two hares together.

All that is in stark contrast to my more recent sightings, few of which have been of more than one Hare. Just once — on the Downs south of Ditchling Beacon — have we recently seen three, possibly four, Hares together. Things don't seem good for these lovely creatures.

Beagling

WHEN we were teenagers my brother and I became for a while followers of the Brighton and Storrington Beagles. They were one of a series of packs of beagle hounds whose followers hunt Hares on foot. You didn't have to have a horse to join in. We didn't come from a hunting background, but I thought it would be a good way of seeing some old-fashioned country life and getting up close to wildlife.

It was. We saw lots of Hares. Once at Hamsey we saw ten Hares on just two or three fields. The beagles would very often start the Hares right in front of us (for their behaviour is to lie low until they're absolutely sure that they've been seen) and off they'd go, the Hare bounding out far ahead whilst the beagles doggedly followed after, baying the whole time, and making up in slower persistence for the Hares clear sprinting advantage. We'd get an exciting run, squelching across ploughed fields, barbed wire and winter cereals, by gorse thickets and rimey down pastures, adrenaline pumping and deep belly-pleasure at the winding of the horn and the baying of the hounds. On clear open Down country the Hares would tend to run in a great arc, and if the hounds did not catch the Hare first then its run would curve back on itself. It would then be running straight back at the hunt followers. Then the whippers-in and master (the hunt leaders) would order us all to stand stock still and the Hare would run straight at us,

Durer's famous picture of a Hare. He made the ears a bit big.

zig-zagging through the crowd as we froze where we were, its great eyes staring and ears flat back, surrounded by the people it always sought to avoid.

There were lots of kills. Enough to satisfy the closet sadism of us all. Often the hounds would kill immediately they'd come across the Hare. Then for just a few moments there'd be a writhing, struggling bundle of hounds, and when they separated there'd be little remaining of the Hare except the blood staining the hounds' coats and muzzles, tufts of skin and fur and maybe the torn head. At other times the Hare would be killed only after a long exhausting run, its energy finally gone and its lungs blown.

I loved it all in a perverse and sadistic way.

And what did the other hunt followers make of it? They seemed mostly friendly and kind upper class types. I was only on nodding aquaintance with them, so I never knew them well enough to ask them the nature of their pleasure. I am sure, though, that the deep atavistic stirrings that the winding horn and baying hounds, and the running of a frightened animal evoked in me must have been shared by many of the other followers. My perverse pleasure (for perverse it was) cannot have been unique to me alone. I think it was — at root — the same pleasure that the white lynch mobs of the Deep South felt when they went after their victims, torches and

lanterns blazing, and saw them hanging from those trees.

Hunt supporters could argue that those kills were quick — and that there's little suffering in a quick death, but the killing of Christians by wild beasts in the Roman Circus must also mostly have been mercifully quick. And would you want your dog or cat to die that way, leave alone yourself or a person you love?

But am I being fair to all the followers? Perhaps not. For what has struck me about many of the hunt followers I have been with (and I also followed another beagle pack and fox hounds and have worked as a beater on Pheasant shoots) is not at all their cruelty, but their indifference to the matter of the kill. They do not seem overly concerned to observe the kill or even whether there is a kill in a days hunting.

I think their motives for hunting are often genuinely un-sadistic. They enjoy the run and all its furiousness and unpredictability — the winter fields, the hedges and brooks, hills and banks to negotiate. They enjoy the dressing up, the tradition, the power of horseback riding, and all the fun of meeting your (mostly very owning class) mates. It's a very exciting freedom to roam they enjoy, with thrills and spills and fellowship. That's no justification for participating in cruelty, though. Eaters of pate de fois gras or white veal are not cruel people either and they do not enjoy sadistic thrills when they eat, but they share moral responsibility for unnecessary suffering, nonetheless.

Un-sadistic they may be, but a-moral they certainly are.

Harvest Mice. Britain's smallest mouse. Much commoner than it appears. Many areas of tall grass and bramble will hide it.

The law has now made it much more difficult for hunters with dog packs, of course, but many hunts survive and even thrive. If the Conservatives return to power we may see these cruel old practices fully revived.

Stoats and Weasels

YOU'RE more likely to see **Weasels** than **Stoats** on our Downs. Weasels prefer open rough grasslands, where the Field Vole provides their main food item. They've been seen recently on the Brighton Racecourse landscape at both Whitehawk Hill and Sheepcote. They are also more often seen around farmsteads and human habitation than the Stoat, although cats sometimes kill them.

Stoat populations tend to rise as Weasel populations fall, and vice versa, for Stoat's main food item is Rabbits, which create a short turf and thus depress the Field Vole populations of long grass that Weasels need. Stoats also prefer woodland. Certainly my Stoat sightings have mostly been in wooded countryside, whereas my Weasel sightings have mostly been on open ground, like Down pasture, corn lands, moor or dune.

I don't see Stoat or Weasel very much these days. In the past 18 years I've only seen Weasel once on the Brighton Downs — on Falmer Hill — and Stoat not at all. In Britain overall in that period I've only seen them nine times. Admittedly, my eyes are mostly stuck on the ground, or close-up on a hedgerow, or bit of grassland. That's where you tend to look if you're primarily interested in mini-beasts and plants. Even so, I used to see them in the sixties a lot more. Nowadays I've been coming-up half as likely to find Polecat or Polecat-ferret (as road-kill) as I am Stoat or Weasel!

I find it odd, however, that I do not see Stoat on our Down pastures anymore, given the huge Rabbit populations that these sites now carry. Could this be the result of the rapid spread of keepered

Pheasant and Partridge shooting on the open Downs? Back in the sixties you used to find gamekeepers' gibbets from which hung all the 'vermin' they had killed. Stoat and Weasel would often be dangling there, along with other Pheasant egg-taking victims of the landowner, like Crows, Jays and Magpies. The gibbets were a way of telling the landowner that the keeper was doing his job. I haven't seen one of those gibbets for a long time, but I'm sure that the new breed of Downland keepers shoot Stoat and Weasel whenever they get the chance.

Both Stoat and Weasel are far too curious for their own safety. They will often play and hunt right in front of you, fully aware of your presence. It's always a good idea to stand still after one of them has passed you, for you can be almost sure that they will return to check you out. If they've disappeared down a small mammal hole, they will pop their heads up again in a minute or so, perhaps from another hole close by.

Busy Bees

THE humming of bees from flower to flower is a large part of the close-up experience of summer on old Down pastures. The bees you'll mostly notice at first are Bumble-bees and Honey-bees, but as you get your eye in you'll notice many other smaller species, too, some of which could superficially be taken for little flies or wasps.

I've several times recently found colonies of **Honey-bees**, *Apis mellifera*, living in holes in older trees on the Downs, just as they did in the days of the 'wildwood', and you can find the swarms, too, in the most unusual places. Honey-bees can travel good distances — kilometers — so finding honey-bees at flowers doesn't necessarily mean hives or a wild colony is near. One late autumn recently I found a swarm in Woodvale Cemetery, and the following year another on a steep slope at the Devil's Dyke. Gerald Legg from the Booth Museum (who's a beekeeper) came out to rescue them, for no unprotected swarm would survive the winter.

Bumble-bees are far more charismatic-looking, with their dumpy bodies and thick and colourful furry coats. There's been both a steep decline in bee populations over the past decades and a more recent rise in interest in bees, so it's now possible to access several simple keys and guides to common Bumble-bee species. We have six reasonably common species on our Downs, several more local species and one or two more just clinging on. The **Buff-tailed, White-tailed** and **Early Bumble-bees**, (*Bombus terrestris, lucorum* and *pratorum* respectively) are the early risers after hibernation, their over-wintering queens quartering the ground in early spring looking for nest sites in holes and crevices. The **Small Garden Bumble-bee**, *B. hortorum*, shares their basic pattern of black and yellow stripes. The **Large Red-tailed**, *B. lapidarius*, is very distinctive, though it has a less-common 'cuckoo' species in tow called the **Hill Cuckoo-bee**, *B. rupestris*, which is a look-alike. Look for the dusky wings as a give-away that you've spotted the cuckoo species. It's fairly frequent on our Downs. The **Common Carder-bee**, *B. pascuorum*, has an all over ginger coat, so you won't mistake it. It generally emerges from hibernation later than the first three species. It's called a Carder-bee because it weaves its above ground nests from bits of grass, like a mouse nest.

The Common Carder has a much scarcer relative, the **Red-shanked Carder-bee**, *B. ruderarius*, which is another look-alike of the Large Red-tailed (except for the red shanks). I found its nest on top of a rough field bank on the Southease Downs a few years ago. A Badger had broken it open, and the disoriented workers were wandering round the chaos of little broken honey pots and nursery pots.

All these bees love large expanses of flower-rich grassland. The fragmentation and attrition of old down pasture, and the widespread elimination of weeds and opportunist flowers has done them much harm. The **Brown-banded Carder-bee**, *B. humilis*, clings on by the skin of its teeth. Steve Falk has recently rediscovered it at the Castle Hill reserve, but it would have been a much more familiar little beast on the older Downs.

We've lost many more. The **Great Yellow Bumble-bee**, *B. distinguendus*, is now largely confined to the Outer Hebrides, though it used to occur round Brighton! The **Knapweed Carder-bee**, *B. sylvarum*, the **Moss Carder-bee**, *B. muscorum*, and the **Broken-belted Bumble-bee**, *B. soroeensis*, are now gone from our Downs and you need to travel to Salisbury Plain if you want to see rare species like these in any numbers together. The **Short-haired Bumble-bee**, *B. subterraneus*, and **Cullum's Bumble-bee**, *B. cullumanus*, are now nationally extinct.

The Heath Bumble-bee, *B. jonellus*, used to be a frequent species on Brighton's high plateau chalk heathlands, but you need to travel to Chailey Common or Ashdown Forest to see it now.

There are many other local bee species which are robust and noticeable in size, though not as big as most Bumblebees. The Mining Bees, Andrena, have a good number of larger species, like the rare **Scabious Mining-bee**, *Andrena hattorfiana*, which is still at Castle Hill NNR and maybe a few other places.

The Flower Bees are often mistaken for Bumble-bees, though they are faster flying and more acrobatic than the flying fortress Bumbles. On the Brighton Downs we have both the common **Hairy-footed Flower Bee**, *Anthophora plumipes*, which is a frequent user of suburban gardens, and its extremely-rare cousin the **Potter Flower Bee**, *Anthophora pilipes*, which I've netted on the Newhaven cliffs, though its nearest nesting aggregations are probably on the other side of the River Ouse. Two Aprils ago we found a colonial nesting site of the Hairy-footed Flower Bee in a vertical clay bank, where its little nesting pots were crumbling out of the clay. Their workmanship was superb. Each little pot could have been thrown on a tiny wheel, with a perfect flat bottom and lid and what looked like glaze on the inside to stop the baby food of honey from leaking through. The returning Flower Bees were being tracked by *two* cuckoo bees[15]: a handsome black and white **Armed Melecta**, *Melecta albifrons*, (a close relation), and another, much smaller jobbie. What a life! In the old days when our countryside was much richer in wildlife the Flower Bee also had to contend with great lumbering cuckoo Oil Beetles, but nowadays, Oil Beetles are on the very brink of extinction on our eastern Downs. The most adept flyer amongst the Flower Bees is the **Green-eyed Flower Bee**, *Anthophora bimaculata*, which has a large population on the Newhaven undercliff and outliers on the Tertiary deposits around Newhaven. They buzz so fast they emit a high-pitched whine, zonking about in the hot sun. Their beautiful irridescent green eyes fade after death.

One little bee its worth making a special search for is the **Gold-tailed Cilissa** or **Bellflower Bee**, *Melitta haemorrhoidalis*. I've only found it once or twice. When it's raining you can find them curled up inside Harebell flowers, which they neatly fit, like little flower fairies. That's where I found it recently at Dencher Bottom, after a summer shower, towards evening.

Hoppers and Crickets

B A C K in olden times Swedish peasants, so they say, used to catch big fat Bush-crickets and hold their strong jaws against any warts that they wanted to remove. The Bush-crickets would oblige by biting them off — and in the process cauterize the wound with the secretion they produced

from their mouths. The favoured type of Bush-cricket used came to be called the **'Wart-biter'**, *Decticus verrucivorus*.

That cricket used to occur in scattered locations across southern England. It was probably one of the last of our crickets and grasshoppers — Orthoptera — to hop across the land bridge between the continent and Britain before we became an island. The heathland race (larger and darker) probably hopped across on the west side and the Downland race (greener and smaller) on the east side. The heathland race clung on at Middlebere Heath on Purbeck right up till a few years ago, when, I think, it finally became extinct in Britain. The Downland form still survives and has its national redoubt on the Downs between Kingston and Woodingdean. In fact, about 90% of the British population was living around Castle Hill and nearby Kingston Hill when its desperate state was finally recognized and measures implemented for its recovery. Till recent decades these two groups of survivors would have been part of the same population, but the ploughing up of the plateau of Kingston and Castle Hill separated them.

The Wart-biter is a big beast of about 3.5 cm long, so it's very vulnerable to becoming a juicy meal when it's full

Wart-Biter Bush-cricket. NOT biting a wart!

grown in high summer. Its right on the edge of its range this far north west, so its offspring need the shortest, hottest turf to thrive, but they then need much longer grass to hide in as adults to avoid predation. It thus needs a mosaic of grassland types, and that is what the experts are now providing for it. Paradoxically it has benefitted from the invasion of the tall and tussocky Tor Grass — normally a serious enemy to Down pasture wildlife — as it provides the safe refuges for the adults.

The Wart-biter occurs alongside its even bigger cousin the **Great Green Bush-cricket**, *Tettigonia viridissima*. They both hunker down in tall vegetation, and when the sun is hot, they both fill the air with their reeling songs. When I first looked for them it took me hours to distinguish the loud bicycle-wheel song of the Great Green Bush-cricket from the winding-of-a-fisherman's-reel sound of the Wart-biter and to work out where on earth these free-floating sounds were coming from. Up and down, back and forth, I tracked, with Adonis and Chalkhill Blue butterflies glinting on the slopes around and Common Green , Meadow and Field Grasshoppers jack-in-a-boxing around me wherever I stepped. A more soothing and soul-calming way of spending a hot summer afternoon I cannot imagine.

The Great Green Bush-cricket has a wide distribution along the Channel coast, with some inland stations, but it is suffering greatly from site destruction by urban development and the more intensive use of the countryside. It particularly likes rough land, such as the bramble patches, tall grass and scrub edges you get on the urban fringe and coastline. It is a famous insect in East Brighton, for many householders and workers have experienced this big beastie whirring in through their open windows, or flying up from cover like a little bird when they're taking the dog for a walk.

When you're walking our Downs almost all the grasshoppers you will meet will be either **Meadow Grasshoppers**, *Chorthippus parallelus*, or **Field Grasshoppers**, *Chorthippus brunneus*. These two occur everywhere and abundantly. They're easy to tell apart. The Meadow Grasshopper is usually very green in colour and (usually) has only small useless wings. The Field Grasshopper is mostly brownish and has long wings with which it flies readily. In fact it's the only British grasshopper which shows swarming behaviour, like locusts, although its flights only manage a few hundred metres — not kilometres!!

When you're identifying grasshoppers it's always useful to look at the back of their neck or collar. The collar (or 'pronotum', as entomologists say) of Field Grasshoppers is pinched inwards sharply and the collar of Meadow Grasshoppers is more or less straight sided. Get the children to catch some to see. They're great grasshopper catchers.

Grasshopper and cricket music fills the Downland air like bird song in high summer so its good fun to spend some time working out the different songs. The Field Grasshopper sings a series of half-second chirps. If one male starts chirping another will join in by chirping in the spaces between the first chirper (so to speak). So they'll hold a sort of grasshopper conversation of alternate chirps. It's called an 'alternation song'. If you want you can join in by imitating their chirps. You can become an honorary grasshopper for a bit! The Meadow Grasshopper makes a series of pulsing rattling sounds like: 'zrezrezrezrezre'. You'll pick it up easily. The song of the **Common Green Grasshopper**, *Omocestus viridulus*, is a rapid ticking noise which starts quietly and builds to full volume after about 10 seconds. Each burst lasts about 20 seconds.

The Common Green Grasshopper is widespread, and abundant when you find it, though I don't find it that often. It is largely confined to old grasslands — like our ancient Down pastures — and can't colonize the new wastelands and rough patches that Field and Meadow Grasshoppers are so happy on. So it's a good 'indicator species' of unimproved pasture. It's present at places like Whitehawk Hill, Moulsecoomb Wild Park, and Kingston Hill where the grass is long.

The longer swards that you get in those kind of places are home to the two native species of Cockroach found on our Downs. Cockroaches are close relatives of Grasshoppers. Don't worry, they're little dainty creatures nothing like the great monsters that used to haunt old fashioned kitchens and scare householders coming down for a midnight snack. Moulsecoomb Wild Park has **Tawny Cockroach**, *Ectobius pallidus*, and there's **Dusky Cockroach**, *Ectobius lapponicus*, on Beeding Hill. The Devil's Dyke has good numbers of both species.

Our high Downs around the crest and scarp are the best places to find the grasshoppers of classic short turf. We have two scarce species that are good indicators for this habitat. The **Stripe-winged Grasshopper**, *Stenobothrus lineatus*, is a big handsome beast with a prominent white line along the side of its fore-wing. It's happiest in chalk and limestone country — in places like Wolstonbury and Anchor Bottom. The **Mottled Grasshopper**, *Myrmeleotettix maculatus*, is a very active little thing, often fawn or brown. They 'ping' away from your trudging feet as you walk up hot, ancient trackways. It's not so fussy about being on chalk, but it must have very short hot turf.

Down on the undercliff at Newhaven we have one very special Orthopteran cousin of the hoppers: **Lesne's Earwig**, *Forficula lesnei*. It really is very rare. It's only a little thing by earwig standards, and likes rough herbage, so you're not likely to find it even if you do know the difference between it and our **Common Earwig**, *Forficula auricularia*. (Lesnei has short wing cases, no real hind wings and its forceps are a bit different). Even so, it's nice to know it's still there.

The Minotaur of the Downs

E v e r y year in ancient times (so the story goes) seven young men and seven young women would have to be sent, amidst great weeping, as tribute by the Athenians to the King of Crete. These poor so and so's would then be fed, one by one, to satisfy the appetite of a huge and fearsome monster called the Minotaur.

Each dawn one of them would be thrust into the entrance of a great labyrinth (a maze of tunnels) to await their fate. The Mediterranean heat would hit them from the white walls, and the bleached bones of previous victims lay scattered on the tunnel floor in front of them... Then they'd hear the monster coming...

If you are a grasshopper up on our Downs in the hot summer months of July and August you have to contend with a mini-Minotaur, too. Scattered across our old pastures, particularly at the scruffy edges of paths and down against low growth of bramble and gorse there are these sheet webs. At the beginning of summer they are only small, but by the height of summer they have grown up to a foot in width. Sometimes there are many of them within quite a small area of grass and bushes. They have a wide platform of densely woven silk with all sorts of guy ropes rising from it. At the rear of the platform is a deep tubular white tunnel. If you tip toe quietly up to the web and don't disturb the vegetation you may be lucky enough to see the Minotaur sitting at the entrance to her tunnel labyrinth. Scattered at the tunnel entrance will be bits and pieces of her unfortunate prey, if she's fed well. Spider lovers know her as *Agelena labyrinthica* (a nice classical name) — **The Labyrinth Spider**.

Jumping grasshoppers get entangled in the guy ropes of her web and fall onto the sheet below. The Minotaur then rushes out and bites them repeatedly till they're subdued. Then she hauls them back to the labyrinth entrance, and maybe deep inside, to consume. Later in the summer she'll build an elaborate double-walled chamber deep in the labyrinth to keep her eggs safe.

There are other grasshopper-eating specialist spiders out on our summer Downs. They all have tough orb webs to catch their athletic prey. For me, the nicest of them is the **Four-spot Orb Weaver**, *Araneus quadratus*. She is a lovely chubby job, with a big round tummy, often creamy-white, but sometimes, greeny, orange, red or reddy-brown. It has four spots arranged upon it. Her legs are pretty with black rings round them. The web is very like that of her cousin, the **Garden Spider**, *Araneus diadematus*, but it's mostly on tall grass, not bushes. She lives in a little tent at the end of one of her guy ropes, not poised in the middle of the web, like the Garden Spider. Look for her on older, taller, late summer grasslands. She carries the British weight record for the heaviest spider: 2.25 gms — 4000 times the weight of her web!

The **Wasp Spider**, *Argiope bruennichi*, is another cousin and has become very common in the last few years. She's a great big affair — all waspy-striped yellow, white and black to see-off any hungry birds. She has a big orb web, with a sort of white silken ladder down the middle — a 'stabilamentum'. You can find her old egg sacs — like big silken flasks — right through the winter and into the following spring. That's the usual way you detect her presence out of season. When I first found one, on the top of a windy cliff at Lulworth in Dorset 15 years ago, I was thrilled. I still love them, but now they're so common

(because of global warming) you can find them even in your back garden.

The most emblematic spider of our Down pastures is undoubtedly the **Purse-web Spider**, *Atypus affinis*. She's the only British representative of the dizzyingly old Mygalomorph order of spiders, which include the Bird-eating and Trap-door Spiders of the tropics. She lives very like the Trap-door spiders, only — instead of a trap door — the top of her tunnel web is a bit like the finger of a silken glove lying on the vegetation. If you look at the south-side base of ant-hills, or at the base of tussocks and bits of overhanging vegetation, you may find her webs. When you find a colony there may be quite a few webs. Close-mowing or heavy grazing may harm her. She needs light grazing and scrub control to keep going. They have a very normal family life and are quite friendly, so no need to get the creeps at the thought of her.

Here's a (bad) poem in her honour…

God, you're old! You really are.
You go back so blooming far.
I can't get my head around
Just how boggling old you are!!

When you kicked off
The dinosaurs weren't even properly invented.
There weren't no flowers; there weren't no bees,
There wasn't even proper trees.
There weren't no lions; there weren't no tigers —
Nor any human beings either!

Nope! — none of us to mess you up.

I'm always finding bits of you —
Your mown-off silkey, tubey roofs,
Your little baby spiderlings,
Your dried-up skeleton;
And once I even dug you up
(For which my conscience is uneasy
Though I took you home again).

I wish you luck, you little thing.
I'd shake your hand if you were bigger —
But if you were then I'd be dinner!

She has some enemies, apart from us. Rabbits can destroy a whole colony by their scuffing and digging (which I think may have happened at Round Hill, Hangleton). Choughs eat them. Most interestingly, there is a species of solitary wasp called *Aporus unicolor* that very bravely breaks into her silken burrow and paralyses her. She then lays her egg with the paralysed spider and the emerging wasp larva eats her and pupates amongst the remains. I netted one of these tiny wasps on Newhaven cliffs, though I've not yet found the spider there. Apparently the wasps do get around, though they are very rare and getting rarer. The wasps have specially elongated head and thorax, flattened heads and powerful front legs for taking on their formidable prey.

'Other Flying Creeping Things'[16]

Midsummer Magic

I F you go up onto any sizeable old Down pasture site around midsummer at the time when darkness has just begun you'll have a good chance of seeing tiny green lights in the grass. They look very much as though the stars have fallen down into the grass. If you're very lucky and the weather is warm and dry you could see up to several hundred of these fairy lights. At Benfield Hill in the summer of 2007 the Benfield Wildlife Group recorded 450 of these luminescing **Glow-worms**, *Lampyris noctiluca*, on one summer night. You'll never forget a sight like that.

Glow-worms are one of only two British species of the Firefly family, Lampyridae, which has over 2000 species world-wide. The other British species, *Phosphaenus hemipterus*, is teetering on the edge of extinction. Glow-worms are beetles, not worms, though the females (which are the ones we mostly see glowing) are wingless and a bit like caterpillars. The Saxons (who named some of our wildlife) called all creeping things 'worms' — from snakes and dragons to proper worms and insects.

Glow-worms need dark skies at night. They don't occur any longer at Whitehawk Hill or Sheepcote Valley, and I haven't found them at Newhaven cliffs, despite that site's extraordinarily rich insect life. They don't occur at the southerly end of Southwick Hill, where the hillside's in close-up view from Mile Oak. The artificial lights from the neighbouring urban areas must have finally done for them.

They also need older, unimproved grasslands. For that reason they are a fairly good flagship species for our old Down pasture fragments. If they're present we can be cheerful about a site. If they are lost then the site may be in trouble.

They are present on lots of our urban fringe Down pasture sites, like Southwick Hill (northern end), Benfield Hill, Ladies Mile, Waterhall and Moulsecoomb Wild Park (just). I'm not sure how well they survive on many of the small fragments of plateau Down pasture, though they are present at the Dyke Rail Trail which has only the tiniest fragment of surviving chalk grassland. They are probably most plentiful along the scarp slope, where I know populations at Beeding Hill, Fulking, the Devil's Dyke, Newtimber Hill, Blackcap and Offham Down.

You may well see Glow-worms at other times of year if you are eagle-eyed. You sometimes come across the larvae walking across paths earlier or later in the year than the period of adult luminescence. They look very like the adults. You may also be lucky enough to see a larva slurping up a meal from a snail shell. They only eat snails and slugs, which they inject with a poison and turn into a soup with a digestive enzyme. Occasionally you can find several larvae with their heads together deep in a snail shell, like Roman feasters getting drunk from a cornucopia.

More Midsummer Magic

B A C K in July a couple of summers ago we were having an evening picnic on the north west slope of Beeding Hill, looking across the Downland turf towards Castle Town. As the warm dusk drew on, first one, then a few more, then dozens of **Midsummer Chafers**, *Amphimallon solstitiale*, rose into the air about us and started flying around the top of a Hawthorn bush in whose lea we were sitting. They looked as though they weren't used to flying and weren't even sure they liked it — swinging backwards and forwards and buzzing round about the place. They're quite big rotund beetles (about 1.75 cm long) with lovely laquered brown wing cases, long legs, and wispy body hair in nooks and crannies (like us humans). As the light faded we could watch the bush and its whirring attendants in ever-sharper silhouette. We focussed our attention on a large Chafer, which landed on a nearby twig. She extended her abdomen tip and waved it about, like a church altar boy waving the incense holder. This must have been her big 'come-on', distributing her sexy smelling mating pheromones to all the lads roundabout. We soon had this interpretation confirmed, as two smaller males landed on her together and jostled to occupy her back. Eventually one of the males disappeared and for half an hour or so the remaining male rested quietly on the female. When we then shone our torch on her (how mean of us!) we could see that the male had at last started mating with the female. There were big bats circling low in the dusk as we left. I hope our pair of lovers made it through the night without being eaten.

...So all that circling around the thorn bush was a mating phenomena! You can see it often enough on our Downs if you are in the right place at the right time. Once I was out listening for Quail in the dusk on the bare Downs near Steep Down, Sompting. The only thorn bush on the whole hillside was circled with whirring chafers, accompanied by one or two equally focussed moth species (Underwings of some kind, I think).

'Driven up the Wall by Invasion of Flying Bugs'

ONCE, when we were holding a summer evening meeting of the Forum of Local Wildlife Groups at Waterhall, these Midsummer Chafers started their dusk flights around us as we sat outside and talked. You could stand up and catch them in your cap. They really are quite dozy flyers.

At Whitehawk the Midsummer Chafers congregate at the top of Bear Road around the bushes overhanging the flint boundary wall of the cemetery. They also particularly love a mature Whitebeam at the top of Queensway... and therein lies a story...

...On June 25th 2007 the *Evening Argus* carried a half page article which commenced "A family is being terrorized by a plague of flying bugs". The Queensway Midsummer Chafers were attracted into their flat through a vent opening in the living room and were giving the poor family the heeby-jeebies. They needn't have worried, for the bugs are completely harmless, sting-less, bite-less, clean-living vegetarians.

The problem is that because they fly towards profiles emergent against the horizon (like our thorn bushes and Whitebeams) they will fly around houses in urban areas and often enter rooms on summer evenings.

The Midsummer Chafer has a much-bigger (up to 4cm) cousin that we know best as the **Cockchafer** or **May Beetle**, *Melolontha melolontha*. A lot of the ones we see on our Downs or in our gardens have flown across the channel in spring. In some years they can be quite common, but generally they seem to be at much lower numbers than they were.

The word Chafer has a common Saxon and old German root and modern Germans recognize it, for their word for beetle is 'kafer'.

Footnotes

1 This type of 'typical' chalk grassland is known to plant sociologists (yes, Mrs Thatcher, even plants have communities) as the 'Sheep's Fescue-Meadow Oat-grass' community, or 'CG2', for short.

  If you're really interested you can find out all about these different plant communities, now classified in the 'National Vegetation Classification' ('NVC'), in *British Plant Communities, Volume 3, Grasslands and Montane Communities*, edited by J.S. Rodwell (Cambridge University Press).

2 *A Botanical Survey of Unimproved Grassland on the South Downs in East Sussex* — G Steven and N Muggeridge, English Nature (1992), Page 42.

3 The shorthand for Upright Brome grassland is 'CG3'. The shorthand for enriched False Oat-grass grassland is 'MG1' (the 'M' stands for 'mesotrophic'). Tor Grass swards are known as 'CG4' — or 'CG5' if they're mixed with Upright Brome.

4 *Community Dominance, an investigation into the competitive mechanisms of Brachypodium pinnatum and possible methods of reducing its dominance on ancient chalk grassland* — Audra Hurst, University of Sussex DPhil thesis (circa 1996), Page 6.

5 Taken from my thesis: *An examination of three chalk grassland sites north of Hove in the context of a review of the decline of chalk grassland on that part of the eastern South Downs* (Birkbeck College, 1995).

6 *Flora Britannica* — Richard Mabey (Sinclair-Stevenson, 1996).

7 *Sussex Plant Atlas, an atlas of the distribution of wild plants in Sussex* — P.C. Hall F.L.S. (Borough of Brighton, Booth Museum of Natural History, 1980).

8 Though Bee Orchis is unique amongst European insect orchids in being largely self-pollinating. It has evolved to do without its insect partners.

9 *A Sketch of the Natural History of Brighton and its Vicinity* — Mrs Merrifield (H & C Treacher, 1864), page 129.

10 'Letters to the Hon. Daines Barrington', Letter 7, October 8th 1770. From *The Natural History of Selborne* by Gilbert White, first published in 1788.

11 'Letters to Thomas Pennant', Letter 15. From *The Natural History of Selborne*. 'Champaign' or 'champion' countryside was the treeless, hedgerow-less landscape of the old open strip-cultivated fields. In Sussex it was characteristic of the open Downs and the coastal plain.

12 *Nature in Downland* — W.H. Hudson (1900), Chapter 5 'Wildlife'.

13 *Ibid.* Chapter 10 'Swallows and Churches'.

14 I am indebted for this account of Rabbits to two main sources. Firstly, to Colin R. Pratt for his wonderful book, entitled *A Revised History of the Butterflies and Moths of Sussex* (1999) published by Brighton and Hove's Booth Museum of Natural History as a DVD, and available from them. Secondly, to *The History of British Mammals* (1999) by Derek Yalden, published by T & A.D. Poyser Ltd.

15 Cuckoo bees and cuckoo beetles are so called because they behave like Cuckoos (the birds). That is, they lay their eggs in other species' nests. Sometimes the host species even raise their young as though they were their own.

16 From the Bible: Leviticus, chapter 11, verse 23.

WOODLAND AND SCRUB

Woodland

THERE's very little woodland on the Brighton Downs. That's fine. The neighbouring Weald is where we mostly need to go if woods are what we want.

Our local Downs do, however, hold a number of small woods and one substantial wood — Stanmer Great Wood — as well as some large scrub thickets which are gradually acquiring a woodland character.

Woods tend to be more interesting the older they are. They gather to themselves an ever-greater flora and fauna of flowers, trees, insects, fungi and other life forms as they gain in antiquity (providing they are not cripplingly isolated from other woodlands). The big displays of **Bluebells**, *Hyacinthoides non-scriptus*, are usually in ancient woods. New woods will hold few of the older woodland plants and special creatures, though more mobile life forms, like birds and the commoner fungi, will quickly move in.

Some of our woods are 'ancient'. That is, they are known to have been in continuous existence since before the year 1600. If they go back that far they may well have existed far longer, perhaps even since the end of the last Ice Age. We have other good woods that are younger than this 400 year minimum for ancient woods, but are still two or three centuries old. Other woods are more modern, and new woods are being formed by planting or natural succession right into the present.

Beech: It Comes and Goes

WE tend to think of classic Downland woods as being dominated by big **Beech**, *Fagus sylvatica*, trees. It was mostly Beech that was planted in the 18th and 19th centuries, and they grow very well on our well-drained soils. Natural Downland woods in ancient times, though, would have had Beech as only one minor player. **Ash**, *Fraxinus excelsior*, **Hazel**, *Corylus avellana*, **Large-leaved Lime**, *Tilia platyphyllos*, **Wych Elm**, *Ulmus glabra*, **Maple**, *Acer campestre*, **Oak**, *Quercus sp.*, **Whitebeam**, *Sorbus aria*, and **Holly**, *Ilex aquifolium*, would have been the main components. We selected for Beech for its wood-working qualities, as with the furniture industry in the Chilterns, and sometimes as an ornamental, as in our Brighton Downland woods.

The Great Gales of '87 and '92 demolished the majority of the mature beeches in our local woods.

Sycamore, *Acer pseudoplatanus*, and Ash dominate the re-generating woods since those gales. In 50 years time we

will look up at the maturing canopy
of Sycamore woods, not through the
translucent green of Beech.

Ancient Woods

LIKELY ancient woods on the Brighton
Downs occur in two forms.

There are firstly a series of small holts,
copses and a shaw on the upper plateau
and scarp, mostly clustered in the parishes
of Pyecombe, Newtimber and Clayton,
around the promontories of Wolstonbury
and Newtimber Hills. These are Newtimber,
Clayton and Pangdean Holts, together with
Newer Copse, Crabtree Shaw and (possibly,
but unlikely) Waydown Copse. There is
also a possible fragment of the ancient
'Bocholt' within Ashcombe Bottom.

Secondly, there is a long, linear 'rew'
wood, till modern times scarcely more
than a hedgerow in many places, running
along the base of the scarp between
Truleigh Hill in the west and Offham, in
the east. This linear wood is broken in
some places, wider in others. Sometimes it
has been relieved by the addition of early
plantations in which its woodland species
could expand (as at the Devils Dyke, Ashen
and Coombe Plantations) and sometimes
by the growth of secondary woodland
(as at Newtimber Hill, Clayton, Blackcap
and Offham). This rew woodland, seen
collectively as two long sites, respectively
east and west of the A23 London Road, is as
rich in indicator ancient woodland plants
as any of the individual more regularly
shaped surviving ancient woods. So just
because its dead skinny, don't knock it.

There isn't *any* ancient woodland and
only the titchiest fragments of woodland at
all on the whole triangle of Downs behind
the chalk cliffs — between Whitehawk
Hill, Newhaven's Castle Hill, and Kingston
Hill near Lewes.

Primary Woodland

ANCIENT woodland that goes right back
to the first return of woodland after the
retreat of the ice, 10,000 years ago, is called

primary woodland, and it's very difficult
to attest to. How can we be sure it's so
old? Much ancient woodland may well be
'ancient secondary' woodland, cleared at
some point by prehistoric folk, before it
returned. Species richness is the strongest
clue, perhaps, and particular species tend
to be markers of the oldest surviving
vegetation communities. Soil qualities,
archaeology (or lack of it) and site location
are also good clues.

Large-leaved Lime is one of the best
marker species. It is now a very rare tree
in Britain, but it was widely characteristic
of woodland from the late Boreal and
Atlantic periods onwards (at 7500 - 7000
BP). It provides very tasty browse for
farm animals, and also had a variety of
other uses, so it's not surprising it's been
munched and chopped into extreme
rarity. Steep and difficult slopes are likely
to have been cleared least (as they still
are nowadays) and the occurrence of
Large-leaved Lime in such steep, remote
woods constitutes strong evidence for
very ancient continuity. Astonishingly,
Large-leaved Lime has only recently been
recognized as a significant relict species on
the South Downs over the last 20 years.[1]

We have one old Large-leaved Lime
tree surviving, in the rew woodland at the
northern base of Wolstonbury, growing at
the junction of the east/west bridlepath
and the north/south path from Little
Danny up to the top of Wolstonbury. It is
many-stemmed and springs from an old
coppice stool. Clayton Holt had a specimen
till at least 1838 and there are still two big
old hybrid Large-leaved/Small-leaved Limes
growing at the base of slope of that wood
along with big old Beeches. Newtimber
Holt, too, has a very large old hybrid tree
right at its heart.

If any fragments of our Brighton Downs
woods are primary it's got to be those bits
of base of slope rew and holt.

There are other super-special species
clinging on there, or only recently

Old Woodland around 'The Promontories' (Wolstonbury, Newtimber Hill and The Devil's Dyke)

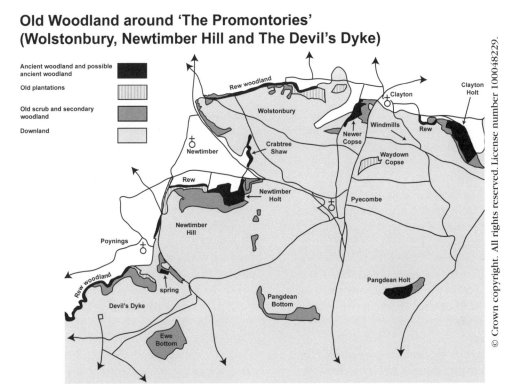

departed. The drop-dead-gorgeous **Lady Orchis**, *Orchis purpurea* — up to three feet tall — was reported as growing "on the downs near Pyecombe in 1860" (just where our ancient woods are clustered) and "near Lewes" in 1911. It's frequent in and around the woods of the eastern chalk scarp in Kent, and very common just across the Channel in France.

The funny little **Three-toothed Snail**, *Azeca goodalli* (which has 3 bony teeth in its mouth and looks like it needs some dental work), hangs on in the little Newer Copse under Wolstonbury. It's almost extinct in Sussex and is generally a scarce woodland species, with a broadly 'Atlantic' distribution, liking damp, mossy places.

Ancient Woodland Indicator Species

WHEN you look at the flowers of our ancient woods there are certain species that you'll keep on finding there, but rarely notice in our younger woods. They seem to find it very difficult to spread out beyond these old enclaves. For that reason

these species have lately been recognised as having great value collectively as indicators of the likely antiquity of a wood.

Flowers like Bluebell (the native one, not the **Spanish-English hybrid Bluebell**, *Hyacinthoides hispanica x non-scriptus*, that's spreading so vigorously in places like Coldean woods), **Moschatel**, *Adoxa moschatellina*, **Primrose**, *Primula vulgaris*, **Wood Anemone**, *Anemone nemorosa*, **Nettle-leaved Bellflower**, *Campanula trachelium*, and woody species like Maple, Wych Elm and Holly (if it's in the middle of the wood and not obviously planted) are all good indicators of ancient woodland. If you look in a wood like Coombe Plantation you'll find that Bluebell is largely confined to the slope bottom, in the ancient rew, and hasn't spread in quantity to the more recent plantation above.

On the Brighton Downs I've found an aggregate list of 45 such indicator species, and there are other species that are now extinct, or that I've not seen. If you can make a list of 20 or more of such species in a wood then there's a good likelihood that it's ancient. However, a count of less than 20 species doesn't **necessarily** mean that a wood isn't ancient, and a count of 20 or more doesn't necessarily mean it **is** ancient!

Thus, you can easily see 20 ancient woodland indicators in Newtimber Holt, but I've only found 13 species in Clayton Holt and 10 indicators in Pangdean Holt, despite their documented antiquity. Their relatively small size and lack of variation across their sites must reduce the numbers.

In contrast, my own list for Stanmer Woods stands at 23 indicator species, though the woods are certainly not ancient, being laid out in the first half of the 18th century. Some of the 'indicators' have been obviously planted in recent years.

One of the greatest surprises I found in making sense of my records of the Brighton Downs woods was that the scarp foot rew woodlands had larger totals than the more compact woods. Both the western rew between Truleigh Hill and Newtimber Hill, and the eastern rew between Wolstonbury and Offham Hills had totals of 23 indicator flowering plants within them, making them the richest woods on our Downs despite their extreme linearity.

There's a species of snail called the **Land Winkle**, *Pomatias elegans*, which pops up again and again in our older woods and scrub thickets. It occurs much more widely than in ancient woods, but its presence still has some value as a measure of a wood's antiquity. It looks just like a less dumpy version of the winkles we find in rock pools and it comes complete with the same horny trap-door protecting it when it retreats into its shell.

Orchids of the Woods

W H E N I was about 14 I found my first **Greater Butterfly Orchis**, *Platanthera chloranthera*, on Newtimber Hill's scrubby woodland edge. I was so chuffed I managed to persuade my mum to walk back up there with me from Hangleton, where we lived, the following evening, after school. We trudged up over Benfield Hill, past the Devil's Dyke, through Saddlescombe and up onto the Hill. Gradually the sunny evening faded to dusk and inky black rain clouds appeared. By the time I triumphantly showed her the orchid the first heavy drops were falling and dark was coming on. We scrambled down off the Hill to Pyecombe in darkness and torrential rain. There was no bus due. We slopped back down the London Road, cars whooshing past — my mum refusing to let us hitch — till some friendly bloke took pity on us and stopped his car. Heroic…

There's a whole group of native orchids which live their lives in our Downland woods. Most of them are nifty enough to colonise our more recent woodlands as well as the ancient fragments, and many of them are happy in scrub and woodland edge tall grassland, too. It can be completely magical, stumbling through some steep and dusty tangle of Beech, Ash and Hazel, to come across the bulbous white flowers of the **White Helleborine**, *Cephalanthera damasonium*, scarcely opened and protruding only their little yellow tongues. You'll get five gold stars, though, if you re-find the **Sword-leaved Helleborine**, *Cephalanthera longifolia*. It used to occur in Coombe Plantation, and was found by a Sussex University student in Stanmer Woods, where it certainly occurred up to 1982. **Broad-leaved Helleborine**, *Epipactis helleborine*, too, can be found flowering in woods in school summer holiday time. It's been recorded in the Stanmer woods and maybe still occurs in other woods. The **Lesser Butterfly Orchid**, *Platanthera bifolia* — much rarer than it's 'Greater' cousin — has been found in Clayton Holt as well as near Shoreham and the Devil's Dyke.

Only the **Bird's-nest Orchid**, *Neottia nidus-avis*, is wholly confined to the deep shade. It's a weird yellow thing, without any obvious leaves and no green colouring, and is wholly dependent on the nourishment it gets from the 'mycorrhizal' fungi which infect its roots. You rarely come across it on our Downs, though it has occurred in the Stanmer woods and around the Blackcap and Mount Harry woods.

Twayblade, *Listera ovata*, too, will be found in deep shade, but it's very common and you'll also find it out on the scrubby grasslands. It's all green and doesn't look at all exotic, but you get very friendly towards it as a constant companion on the Downs in spring. When we found it in our first summer of orchid hunting in 1963 we only had old Edward Step's 'Wayside and Woodland Blossoms' for identification, and managed to fool ourselves that we'd found the rare Man Orchis…don't you be so daft!

More Modern Woods

F R O M the 18th century onwards there was a whole spate of tree planting on the Downs as new landlords, like the Pelhams of Stanmer, the Roes of Withdean, and Brighton's new municipal government, responded to the new aesthetic of the 'picturesque' and rejected the treeless wilderness qualities of the Downland 'steppe'. Such modernity is now rather old, however, and numbers of the surviving Beeches in Stanmer woods are in excess of 250 years old, whilst many of Brighton's Elms are over 150 years old. That's plenty of time for these trees and woods to have acquired many special species, including 'old forest' rarities. Peter Hodge has recorded both the big longhorn beetle *Stenocorus meridianus* and the fascinating Honey-bee mimicking hoverfly *Mallotus cimbiciformis* in Stanmer woods, and you can see big red **Cardinal Beetles**, *Pyrochroa coccinea*, basking on old Beech logs there. At least two of Stanmer Woods' fallen veteran Beech giants have played

host for some years to the spectacular old forest **Bearded Tooth Fungus**, *Hericium erineus*, with its hanging mane of long white needles. Stanmer woods, too, have hosted the deadly-but-beautiful Satan's Bolete, with its white cap and blood-red pores.

Veteran Trees

S E V E R A L of these 'old modern' woods, such as Coombe and Ashen Plantations on the scarp, have huge old Beech surviving, though small woods on the chalk plateau, like Newmarket and Cranedean Plantations, lost most of their big trees in the 1987 gale. Waydown Copse, just north of Pyecombe golf course, has many fine mature **English Oak**, *Quercus robur*, 'maidens' (free-growing timber trees), and Stanmer Park, just south of the Lower Lodges, has a huge veteran **Sessile Oak**, *Q. petraea*, standing alone.

The especially old trees[2] we have on the Brighton Downs, however, are not necessarily found in woodland, and can occur on roadsides, on open Down pasture, or associated with old buildings. Thus, there used to be a whole cluster of veteran Elm pollards associated with the old manor houses round Brighton. Hangleton Manor had huge old Elms (that the farm servants hung their washing from), and Ovingdean Grange still had one old pollard till a few years ago. Now only the huge Moulsecoomb Place pollard Elm (on the grass verge of the Lewes Road) and the magnificent 'Preston Twins' survive. These two ancient Elm pollards, by the Manor House garden wall in Preston Park, are reckoned to be the oldest remaining Elms in Britain.[3] There's also one maiden Elm left in Court Farm Road, near the site of the ancient West Blatchington manor house, and Hodshrove Lane, Moulsecoomb, has just seen the last maiden Elm which graced this entrance drive to the lost medieval Hodshrove Farm cut down.

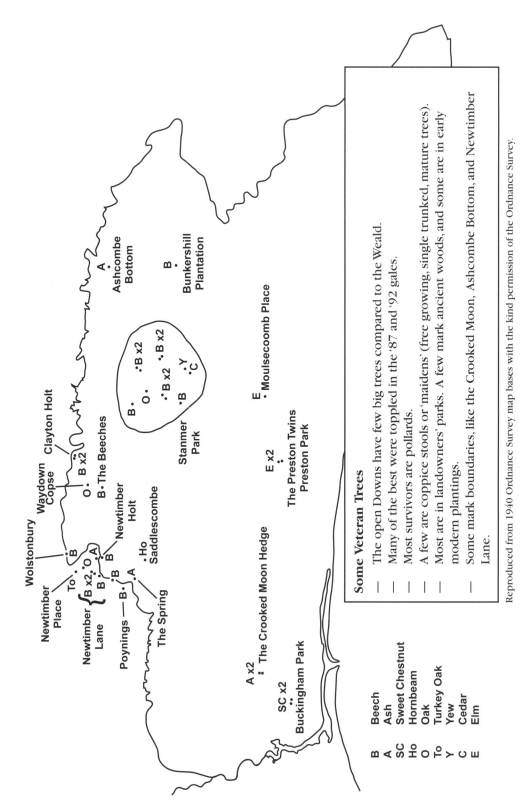

Ashcombe
Bottom
A

B
Bunkershill
Plantation

Wolstonbury

Clayton Holt
Waydown
Copse

B x2
O

B•The Beeches

Newtimber
Holt

Saddlescombe
•Ho

B x2
• B x2
B•
O•
•B x2
•B
•Y
C

Stanmer
Park

E
• Moulsecoomb Place

E x2

The Preston Twins
Preston Park

Newtimber
Place

B

To
B x2
B
B
A

O
A

B
A

Poynings

The Spring

Newtimber
Lane

The Crooked Moon Hedge

A x2

SC x2

Buckingham Park

Some Veteran Trees

— The open Downs have few big trees compared to the Weald.
— Many of the best were toppled in the '87 and '92 gales.
— Most survivors are pollards.
— A few are coppice stools or 'maidens' (free growing, single trunked, mature trees).
— Most are in landowners' parks. A few mark ancient woods, and some are in early modern plantings.
— Some mark boundaries, like the Crooked Moon, Ashcombe Bottom, and Newtimber Lane.

B   Beech
A   Ash
SC   Sweet Chestnut
Ho   Hornbeam
O   Oak
To   Turkey Oak
Y   Yew
C   Cedar
E   Elm

Reproduced from 1940 Ordnance Survey map bases with the kind permission of the Ordnance Survey.

Buckingham Park, Shoreham, still retains a cluster of gigantic veteran **Sweet Chestnuts**, *Castanea sativa*, from a now-gone avenue.

Clayton Holt, Newtimber's Holt and Beggar's Lane, Wolstonbury's Ashen Plantation, Coombe Plantation, and Stanmer Woods are the best places to see veteran Beeches. The woodland belts on the Ditchling Road north of Piddingworth, and west of Stanmer Down, still have wonderful old giants surviving. 'The Beeches', a scrubbing-up piece of old chalk grassland south of Pyecombe Golf Course, has a good group of very picturesque old trees of that species, which must now be a good 200 years old.

Big Tree

I *know* it has no consciousness,
But we cannot help respect
The brute whose arms expand and grow
For dozens of our human lives.

We cannot help respect
The tree whose leaves un-rumple green
Season on season whilst we wilt and fade,
Whose massive bulk meets all that comes —
The loss of limbs, the rot within,
The parching, soaking, gnawing, sawing,
The gales and heat and frost —
But still grows on.

Inch on inch its girth grows on,
Its heart a home and grave
To moth and lichen, bat and owl,
Long moss streak, fern and beetle.

I *know* it has no consciousness,
But consciously I contemplate
Its growing, changing timelessness,
Its living stillness,
Earth and rock enlivened,
Earthy, woody greenness,
Not-busy kindness,
Not-busy liveliness.

Dead still and dead alive.

Recent Woods

QUITE large areas of derelict Down pasture are now succeeding past the scrub stage to become woodland. Large areas in Cuckoo Bottom and around Offham Hill, west of Lewes, have reverted to woodland since the last World War. Much of Moulsecoomb Wild Park and Waterhall is now gaining a woodland character, as are the scrub thickets of Ashcombe Bottom.

Many of these new woodlands have sadly replaced areas of extraordinary richness for their grassland character. That's what's happened on parts of the humpty-dumpty old chalk workings on Offham Hill, with their fine moss

The giant Beech pollard on the Roman road under Newtimber Hill. This picture doesn't do justice to its immense bulk.

flora, orchids and **Grayling** butterfly, *Hipparchia semele*. We have allowed the replacement of locally distinct, rare and fascinating grassland wildlife with common woodland species which would appear in any garden in just a decade of neglect!

However, there are compensations. You can lose yourself in Dead Man's Wood, beyond the railway line behind Moulsecoomb Place, as though you were miles from the adjacent industrial and housing estates. We have found three species of Morel Fungus there, including the scarcely-found **Thimblecap**, *Verpa conica*. This humid, sunny new wood has **Hart's-tongue**, *Phyllitis scolopendrium*, and **Polypody ferns**, *Polypodium sp.*, **Redcurrant**, *Ribes sylvestre*, **Celandine**, *Ranunculus ficaria*, and Twayblade Orchid, and it's noisy with a varied community of Tits, Woodpeckers, Warblers, Wrens, Robins and Dunnock. It's a busy place!

Hidden Woodland Things

THERE'S layer on layer of interest if you make the time and have the energy.

Brighton's cemetery landscape at Woodvale has a colony of the peculiar **Collared Earthstar**, *Geastrum triplex*, on one of its woodland edges. These weird fungi have a soft bladder set within a fleshy white 'flower' of spreading petals. They look like flowers of the dead.

Summer Truffles, *tuber aestivum*, have been recorded from Brighton and Shoreham by Sea only 50 years ago. There's no particular reason why they shouldn't still occur, especially amongst any younger growth of Beech in our woods. And when you find one truffle species you tend to find several others. They attract a bizarre and very rare chafer beetle, *Odonteus armiger*, whose males have a honking great horn on their noses. You don't need a dog or a pig for truffling, just a good eye for habitat and for the little clouds of flies hovering over the site of subterranean truffles.

Morels occur in a number of species on our Downs. As a group they tend to like chalky woodland and scrub soils. I know of five *Morchella esculenta* sites on the Brighton Downs. Finding one of these weird golden honeycombs-on-sticks sitting in a May-time woodland full of songbird music and morning light takes a lot of beating. Don't pick them though. They are really scarce nowadays and are better enjoyed by all. They're very over-rated as an eating mushroom, too. Other wacky morel-like fungi come and go, like the **Ribbed Stalk-cup**, *Helvella acetabulum*, or the **Bleach Cup**, *Disciotis venosa*. You can find Bleach Cup as big as a frisbee sprawled across a bit of woodland floor. Spring's the time for Morels.

Scrub

Let's be Fair to Thorny Things!

FOR good reasons scrub has a bad image on our Downs. From the 1880s to the 1940s scrub crept across immense tracts of wonderful Down pasture as Europe dragged through a profound agricultural depression. And this process is still happening, particularly on the urban fringe and on many smaller derelict sites.

However, during the subsequent half century of rampant productivism, scrub was destroyed far more thoroughly even than the remaining species-rich Down pastures. So thoroughly, in fact, that very little *species-rich* scrub survives on the Downland plateau — for scrub isn't always made up of species-poor impenetrable stands of **Hawthorn**, *Crataegus monogyna*, or **Blackthorn**, *Sorbus spinosa*. Downland scrub *can* be a beautiful and diverse vegetation community, richly productive for birds and invertebrates. The Beeding Hill bostal descending north-east towards the old chalk pit is profoundly beautiful in its autumn colours, with the reds of hips and haws, the red-to-black umbels of **Wayfaring Tree**, *Viburnum lantana*, and **Elder**, *Sambucus nigra*, berries, the black grapelets of **Privet**, *Ligustrum vulgare*, and the clambering white webs of **Clematis**, *Clematis vitalba*, feathers.

Scrub needs to be valued in a more nuanced and rounded way than has been the case when both productivist farmers and despairing conservationists thought no further than just to hack and chop at its ranks.

Boring Scrub

T H E R E ' S still far too large a spread of species-poor scrubland sites, though, across our Downs, and their thorny uniformity means they are very little used or known.

Most of Newhaven's top-class coastal acid grassland and heath has been lost to dense Blackthorn and Hawthorn scrub. Beautiful old grassland sites like High Hill, and The Whiteway, Rottingdean, are disappearing under new scrub. Much of Waterhall's long grassy valleysides are sinking under a tangle of monotonous Hawthorn. The great majority of Moulsecoomb Wild Park's rich mosaic of old scrub and grassland has been lost to modern species-poor scrub. Other very large old grassland sites have been wholly lost to new scrub-cum-woodland, like Cuckoo Bottom, west of Lewes, and Ewe Bottom at the Devil's Dyke.

It's easy to recognize these new stands of species-poor scrub, at least in the spring. If you stand in May on the Ditchling Road, by High Park Corner, and look across to Dencher Bottom you will see that almost every bush on the hillside is white with May (Hawthorn) blossom. There's almost no other bushy species there. If you look across to Telscombe's 'E Piece' from Bullock Down, in April, whole thickets will be white with Blackthorn blossom. If you look up at some parts of the scarp slope from Underhill Lane in spring every bush is covered in the greeny-white new leaves of Whitebeam.

That's one central characteristic of boring scrub: it's just made up of one or two bushy species. Another is its tight density, allowing no glades or clearings.[4] Many invertebrates and birds and plants thrive best in the boundary area between scrub and grassland, using the scrub for some functions and the grassland for others. Scrub, too, which is structurally uniform in age, height, and spacing, like most of the Hawthorn thickets from Patcham's Sweet Hill to North Heath Barn, is much reduced in interest. It looks monotonous and attracts few special species.

Interesting Scrub

T H E scarp slope below Clayton's windmills, TQ 305 136, as far east as Clayton Holt, is one of nature's self-grown orchards. It's tussocky with Tor Grass, but if you are steady on your feet and can walk its neglected terracettes you will fall in love with the place. There's **Blackberries**, *Rubus fruticosa agg.*, and a **Crab Apple**, *Malus sylvestris*, tree, four species of Rose, including both the apple-scented **Sweet Briar** or **Eglantine**, *Rosa rubiginosa*, and **Small-flowered Sweet Briar**, *R. micrantha*, **Robin's Pin Cushion** (the gall wasp *Diplolepis rosae*), Sloe (Blackthorn) berries, pink and orange **Spindle**, *Euonymus europaeus*, berries, **Dogwood**, *Cornus sanguinea*, and **Buckthorn**, *Rhamnus catharticus*. If you count Bramble, **Dewberry**, *Rubus caesius*, and Clematis there's at least 25 scrub species there, 18 of which have fleshy and colourful fruits. 11 of its species are members of the Rose tribe — nature's special orchard family. There are a few oaks for acorns also and the nearby Holt is dense with nut-bearing Hazel coppice. So there's plenty to eat for beasts with fur and feathers in autumn, and oodles of spring and summer blossom for mini-beasts.

Few sites on these Downs will match the richness of Clayton Down.

Ashcombe Bottom, TQ 373 118, comes a close second. It has a few more bushy species, but, of course, it covers a far greater area. My sketchy list of bushy and climbing species there tots up to 28. Wayfaring Tree, which is especially emblematic of rich Downland scrub, seems to be uncommon, though Spindle and Dogwood are common enough.

Ashcombe Bottom has quite a different character to Clayton Down. It is mostly made up of dense scrub grading over into woodland, with hard, fenced boundaries. It is very Brackeny, *Pteridium aquilinum*, along its rides and in some of its glades, with **Silver Birch**, *Betula pendula*, and occasional Wood Sage. You can view Ashcombe in two ways. It is both old scrub on a transition to woodland, and recovering ancient woodland which has been through a very narrow 'bottleneck' in its recent history, in which almost all of it was lost, together with much of its ancient woodland character.

There are twenty or more bushy species on the scrublands of the Tertiary deposits west of Newhaven, but they, too, cover a much larger area than Clayton Down. They have areas dominated by **Gorse**, *Ulex europaeus*, and other areas, particularly near the cliffs, dominated by Blackthorn. Large stands of **Rosebay Willowherb**, *Chamaenerion angustifolium*, give colour, and **Honeysuckle**, *Lonicera periclymenum*, (which likes these less chalky soils) is common. As the scrub ages non-native species like **Horse Chestnut**, *Aesculus hippocastanum*, and Sycamore break into the canopy.

On the Downland plateau most scrubby sites have counts of around 10 or less bushy species. North of Waterhall, on Varncombe Hill's scrubby slope-top western fringe, I've counted eleven bushy and climber species, including Buckthorn, Wayfaring Tree, Oak, **Goat Willow**, *Salix caprea*, and a good fringe of Gorse. The Hill's scrubby top fringe actually extends around a lot of the long ridge from Varncombe Hill to Newtimber Hill, a bit like a monk's tonsure. This fringe

is distinguished by the presence of the pretty Broom called **Dyer's Greenweed**, *Genista tinctoria*, at most of its sites. It's very unusual to find this sub-shrub on the Downs, as it likes clay best and is most frequent on the Wealden Clay. Here, though, its presence faithfully marks the edge of this ridge's extensive topping of clay-with-flints. Heath Speedwell keeps it companion from the days when this clay-with-flints was covered with heather, commemorated by the nearby North *Heath* Barn.

Deep Bottom, south west of The Chattri, has a good stand of Hazel, with Oak, Holly, Goat Willow and others. Foxes Wood on the Brighton and Hove Golf Course south of Skeleton Hovel has at least 11 woody and climbing species. It's undoubtedly an old scrub site and used to have Whitebeam till recent decades. By contrast, Atlingworth Barn copse, just northeast of Mount Zion, has only five scrub species, but it has two epiphytic Door Snail species and several other shade loving snails. It must also be old.

Moulsecoomb Wild Park still has a rich old scrub community, and even its chalk grassland is distinguished by the sometimes-dominant presence of Rockrose, which, though it looks like an ordinary flower, is in fact a woody sub-shrub. There's 12 bushy and climber species at least, with Oak and Gorse upslope, Dogwood, **Yew**, *Taxus baccata*, and abundant Wayfaring Tree. The exquisite Green Hairsteak butterfly, an old scrub indicator species, is still present, and there's **Wasp Beetle**, *Clytus arietus*, and the primitive and scarce little **Masked Bee**, *Hylaeus signatus*, which likes scrub edge.

Gorse Scrub

Y O U wouldn't think Gorse is getting scarce on the Downs, would you?...It's so much a part of the old cultural stereotype of Downland — crowning every old pasture hilltop, flaming yellow in spring, and alive with the song of Linnets and Stonechat. How could it become scarce?

It is, though, for it has suffered not just from destruction by agribusiness, but from widespread lack of management, being gradually over-topped with high thorny scrub, and then eradicated by the onset of secondary woodland. Often you can find the skeletons of old Gorse bushes under the dark canopy of such new woodland.

Gorse tends to like the less chalky, richer soils of the plateau clay-with-flints, and the leached acidic soils where chalk heath previously existed. It grows most characteristically at the hill top break of slope, in much the same kind of places as ancient burial mounds are sited, though this association has mostly been sundered by the bulldozer in modern times, except on Kingston Hill, at Hollingbury Camp, and (just about) at Highdole Hill, north of Telscombe.

Gorse had many uses for humans, and still does to animals. It was extensively cut as fuel, particularly for bakers' ovens, as cattle and horse fodder, and for besom brushes. Special areas were harvested for it, and many 'fuel allotments' of Gorse and 'Furze Fields' ('Furze' is the old name for Gorse) were set aside both as residual commons after enclosure, or by private landowners. Locally, all of western Woodingdean Village, between Drove Road, Seaview and Warren Road was Furze Field 160 years ago, as was the ground around the southern edge of Woodingdean's Lawn Cemetery.

Many of the most characteristic birds of Downland, including **Dartford Warbler**, Stonechat, Linnet, **Whitethroat** and **Lesser Whitethroat**, have a strong association with Gorse. They nest in or under it, feed in it, and their males sing their songs from its tops. Indeed, Dartford Warbler — our only non-migratory Warbler — used to be called the Furze Wren. In winter **Goldcrest** and **Firecrest** can be found around its sheltered thickets.

In spring the smell of vanilla and coconut wafts from the golden bushes and in early summer the popping of the seed-pods cracks all around you in hot sunshine.

Those oily seeds are a favourite food of ants when they've fallen to the ground. Green Hairstreak butterflies use Gorse as one of their many larval food plants and can sometimes be found in Maytime in areas where Gorse is common. The caterpillars of the beautiful **Grass Emerald moth**, *Pseudoterpna pruinata atropunctaria*, depend entirely upon Gorse, **Broom**, *Sarothamnus scoparius*, and Whin. The little **Double-striped Pug moth**, *Gymnoscelis rufifasciata*, is also dependent on Gorse and other heathy plants. The **Gorse Shieldbug**, *Piezodorus lituratus*, can easily be found on Gorse from March right through until July (when the pods have all burst). It's a big beastie, green with a yellow stripe round its edge, and more than a cm long.

There are still big open thickets of Gorse surviving on both the top and the north side of Kingston Hill. Indeed — ridiculously — their presence was used to justify the exclusion of this north hillside from the right to roam provision. The hot, gorsey scrub on Kingston Hill makes it one of the places most evocative of the old landscape of our Downs. Waterhall has a large old Gorse thicket south of the golf clubhouse, but it is rapidly being over-topped by trees and taller Hawthorn. Freshcombe, north of Thundersbarrow, has an ancient Gorse thicket at its core, with Honeysuckle and a large swarm of heathy **Saw-wort**, *Serratula tinctoria*, at its only Downland site. The west slope of Rodmell's Mill Hill, also has a very old Gorse thicket, though this has been so dense with lack of management that access is nigh impossible. Hoathdown, by Peacehaven Golf Course, still has extensive thickets of very tall Gorse.

Gorse often marks the presence of now-gone chalk heath sites. At Whitehawk

Hill scrub management around the Gorse encouraged the flowering of Heath Groundsel after many years of dormancy.

Gorse seeds, too, can survive very long periods of dormancy. The National Trust's reversion of Fulking Tenantry Down to Down pasture after decades of corn growing, has allowed the miraculous re-appearance of the clumps of Gorse which had dominated it 50 years before

Juniper

O N the west flank of Newtimber Hill, above and below the Saddlescombe Road, lives a population of ancient **Juniper**, *Juniperus communis*, our most special and rarest native bushy species. It's been here a long time. It was in the advanced guard of woody species re-colonizing post-glacial Britain, and it is a classic species of the cold tundra grasslands. And just because it never grows taller than about 30 ft doesn't mean that it can't grow old. Indeed, the bushes, sometimes bent over in senescence, can grow to four hundred years. It would once have been widely found on the open Downs. In the chalk country of northern France it is still common and acts as a reliable indicator of old chalk pastures.

The Newtimber Junipers are the only native ones on the Brighton Downs, but it is only in the last 70 years that these old survivors, like Tolkien's Ents, have been reduced to such a desperate state. In 1937 Wolley-Dod[5] recorded it still as 'near Brighton, on the east, very rare', though 'abundant on the west';'a very few bushes above Keymer';'at Hogtrough Bottom' near Ditchling Beacon;'south of Streat'; and Newmarket Hill.

In the past Juniper was a big enough player to have attracted many other life forms into dependency and perhaps co-evolution with it. There's a whole gang of them. I know of one big Jewel Beetle, *Palmar festiva*, (not in Britain, though), one Gall Wasp, *Megastigmus bipunctatus*, (still at Levin Down, north of Goodwood),

six moths, a mite, *Trisetacus sp.,* (that destroys a large proportion of seeds), a Lacewing, *Aleuropteryx juniperi*, the **Juniper Shieldbug**, *Cyphostethus tristriatus*, and the **Juniper Waxcap** fungus, *Hygrocybe intermedia*, and I'm sure there must be more!

I'm not sure that our Newtimber survivors have any of the rarities, but they may well have some of the commoner things. Three of the moths are recent immigrants and do very well on cultivated Cypresses, because they are close relatives of Juniper. The Shieldbug has also got a new lease of life from all the new ornamental Cypresses.

I looked for the Juniper Waxcap at Newtimber before I read that it's only found in association with Juniper in Scotland! Here it doesn't seem to bother, and I've only found the Juniper Waxcap on Kingston Hill, where Juniper is not recorded.

Juniper is now planted on the A27 bypass at Stanmer, and the old Brighton Corporation planted it at the Devil's Dyke. Let's hope those young 'uns don't develop the same reproductive difficulties that seem to dog the old 'uns…

Hawthorn's Exotic Gang

H A W T H O R N can't claim scarcity value like Juniper or even Gorse, but it has many associates which are both secretive and beautiful. Thickets of young or coppiced Hawthorn have been much used by Nightingale. The thorn scrub at Waterhall and to its north, as well as the scrub thickets of Ashcombe Bottom, used to be well-known Nightingale haunts, though lack of management at Waterhall and the wider decline of the bird now makes its song a rare delight.

There's a little Jewel Beetle, *Agrilus sinuatus*, up to a cm long, whose larvae drill their burrows in Hawthorn's main boughs and trunks. They leave a characteristic D-shaped exit hole. There are dead Hawthorn bushes scattered over

Southwick Hill, which have been killed by this beetle. You're very unlikely ever to see it, but the stag-headed bushes give its presence away. I've found it at Dencher Bottom, High Hill and elsewhere.

There's one Morel, the supposedly-rare Thimblecap, *Verpa conica*, which is particularly associated with Hawthorn. Look for it in spring both underneath old Hawthorn and in the chalk grassland around it. It seems to have occasional years of especial abundance, followed by gaps when it is scarcely ever found. That would account for its description as a rarity, though its appearance so early in the season wouldn't help. We found it at five Brighton Downs sites in the spring of 2005, and none in 2006, to my knowledge.

Roses

T H E Brighton Downs are good rose country. You can have a lot of fun looking for the possible six native wild species we have and their many hybrids. I think of them as a 'midsummer flower', like Elder, but, though that's the time to enjoy their blossoms, it's not the time to identify them. That's best done in August and September, for it's the hips and prickles, leaves, sepals and glands that are the key to determining species.

Dog Rose, *Rosa canina*, turns up in every wild place, but the other species can be found with a tuned-in eye and nose.

The sweet apple-scent of Sweet Briar, *Rosa rubiginosa* — Shakespeare's Eglantine — can waft to you even some paces before the bush comes into view. It's got stalked, scented, viscid glands all over its underleaves and hip stems, which give off more fragrance when you rub them. It has a close relative, Small-flowered Sweet Briar, *R. micrantha*, which often occurs nearby, and is a fair bit commoner.

If you're very lucky you may come across the stumpy little **Burnet Rose**, *Rosa pimpinellifolia*, rarely more than knee-high, and often forming little mini-thickets. You can't mistake it. Its flowers are creamy white, its hips purplish-black, and its upright stems are hedgehog-covered in fierce straight prickles. It tends to be a coastal species, but it has just a few sites scattered across our local Downs. It occurs all over the 'Deer Park earthwork' by the Falmer Road, at the top of Loose Bottom. It's also hanging on at the Greenbank Quarry site, Saltdean, behind Greenbank Avenue. This is a sad and neglected site, which retains its old Down pasture interest against all the odds, in a mess of advancing Bramble, Bindweed and scrub. The owner doesn't use it, doesn't manage it, and doesn't turn it over for community use, either.

Butterflies of Scrub

T H E R E ' S a group of butterflies which are particularly constant to scrub. **Ringlet**, *Aphantopus hyperantus*, colonies tend to be associated with older scrub. For that reason we haven't found this butterfly at Whitehawk Hill, for though it is suffering from scrub incursion, this scrub is quite recent, except for the old Gorse thicket. **Hedge Brown** or **Gatekeeper**, *Pyronia tithonus*, has the same preference. **Brimstone**, *Gonepteryx rhamni*, needs the presence of Buckthorn on the Downs for it's caterpillars' food, and countryside rangers are adept at recognizing and leaving this species when they clear invading scrub.

Surprisingly, **White Admiral**, *Ladoga Camilla*, can be seen on Mount Harry and at Ashcombe Bottom, for there's plenty of Honeysuckle for its caterpillars in the scrub thickets of those heathy highlands. This butterfly is usually confined to Wealden woods.

Special Things

T H E R E ' S one very special scrub species which we can claim for our Downs, particularly after its discovery in 2005 on the edge of Coombe Plantation, under Mount Harry. This is **Fly Honeysuckle**, *Lonicera xylosteum*, our second

Honeysuckle species, and it is as rare as its sister species is common. It was recorded for the first time in 1801 by Borrer (our famous Sussex botanist) in the scrubby rew below Amberley Mount. It's since been recorded at Wilmington Holt in a similar scarp-foot situation, and a couple of bird-sown bushes occur at Balsdean and Burpham, and that constitutes its entire native population in Britain. I discovered the Coombe Plantation bush when it was in full flower in May, with the Warblers in full song and **St George's Mushrooms**, *Calocybe gambosa*, Early Purple Orchids and unseasonal **Wood Mushrooms**, *Agaricus silvicola*, scattered across the woodland floor.

If you travel to the Pyrenees or the Alps you will come across Fly Honeysuckle and two, three — up to five — other Honeysuckle species around their rich, humid mountain thickets. Our own solitary bush must be one of the furthest outliers of those far off vegetation communities.

When I was 12 I saw my first Fly Orchis below the Devil's Dyke's scarp bottom woodland fringe, in scrubby chalk grassland above Poynings Pond, and its velvety body and realistic antennae made it a winner. Later, I read that orchids got their name from the Greek word for testicle and that the Fly Orchis roots looked just like them. So my brother and I dug one up to see (and replanted it after). They do…(But don't do this. It will damage the plant).

Fly Orchis, is one of those orchids (with Twayblade, Butterfly Orchid and Broad-leaved Helleborine) which can be happy in scrub, or even in shady chalk grassland, as well as woodland. My findings of it seem mostly to have been around scrub and glades.

Two springs ago I bought a new toy. I've always been intrigued by Clearwing moths. Most of them use tree and scrub species for their caterpillar food plants. You hardly ever see Clearwings, and before last year I can recall every one of the few occasions I've come across them. They're really dainty. They mostly mimic little solitary wasps and have narrow largely transparent wings and mostly-black bodies with stripes and patterns of yellow and red. Now it's become dead easy to see them. You can buy — as I did — pheromone lures that work by attracting the males to a synthetic replica of the female sex pheromone. The moths come very quickly to the lures — within minutes — so you can walk round several potential sites within less than an hour.

So I spent lots of bits of time in June and July hurrying round scrubby sites on the Brighton Downs looking for clusters of Wayfaring Tree, which is host to the scarce **Orange-tailed Clearwing**, *Synanthedon andreaneiformis*. It's caterpillars burrow into the branches.

I soon found a strong distribution pattern for this moth. I found it all along the scarp slope, but at only one site on the dip slope plateau.

I saw it in a necklace of six scarp slope sites from Beeding Hill via the Devil's Dyke, Newtimber Hill, Streat Hill, and Mount Harry to Offham Down. At all these sites there were significant swarms of Wayfaring Tree across the steep slopes. Only on the scarp slope facing the Ouse valley did I draw a blank, but this was no surprise because these slopes above Iford and Northease have little old scrub and there is no old slope bottom rew.

Out of 17 plateau and urban fringe sites looked at I found Orange-tailed Clearwing only at Moulsecoomb Pit in the Wild Park. Dip slope sites with large cover of scrub, like Mill Hill Shoreham, Southwick Hill, Waterhall. Ladies Mile, Bevendean Down and Halcombe valley Piddinghoe, all bore little or no Wayfaring Tree and no accompanying Clearwings.

Wayfaring Tree had been planted abundantly along parts of the A27 bypass, but what pheromoning I did there proved negative.

Wayfaring Tree is a good indicator of species-rich Downland scrub.[6] The scarcity of Wayfaring Tree on the Downland plateau points up that its large cover of surviving scrub is mostly recent. The scattered Wayfaring Trees there are not frequent enough to have Orange-tailed Clearwing and the Bypass plantings have not attracted them, at least yet.

Orange-tailed Clearwing seems likely locally, then, to be a refined indicator for old, rich Downland scrub communities — even better than its Wayfaring Tree host.

Footnotes

1 'Large-leaved Limes on the South Downs' — Frances Abrahams and Francis Rose, *British Wildlife*, Dec. 2000, Vol 12, No 2, pages 86-90.

2 Veteran trees have been increasingly recognized for their importance to wildlife and their aesthetic contribution in the last decade or so. Paradoxically, Britain has more veteran trees than the rest of Europe put together, despite our small cover of woodland, because of the tradition of pollarding, which greatly extends the life of many species.

3 *The Sussex Tree Book* — Owen Johnson, (Pomegranate Press, 1998), page 83.

4 'Scrub Ecology and Conservation', in *British Wildlife*, Oct. 1996, Vol. 8, No. 1, pages 28-36.

5 *Flora of Sussex* — Edited by Lieut.-Colonel A.H. Wolley-Dod. First published in 1937. (The Chatford House Press, 1970), page 534.

6 *British Plant Communities, Vol. 1, Woodlands and Scrub* — J. Rodwell, (Cambridge University Press, 1991).

THE GEOLOGY AND LAND
FORMS OF THE DOWNS

— THE PATTERNS OF DEEP TIME

And then we'd scramble up and chase
  cloud-shadows on the Downs;
  Or hunt for chalk-pit fishes; or
  for stones called "*Shepherds' Crowns*"[1]

NOWADAYS I love picking along
the chalk cliffs and quarries and
walking the winter ploughlands
for fossils as much as I love hunting
for insects and flowers or listening to
birdsong. And the questions about how
our Downland was formed arise with
every flint we pick up and every combe
we descend.

So here's an attempt to answer some of
those questions.

The Downs are all made of chalk, aren't they?

THEY are indeed — the vast bulk of them,
anyway. Most of the chalk was laid down
in a huge sea that stretched across Europe
as far as Kazakhstan[2] and the Crimea. The
nearest land would have been islands
formed by the present Scottish mountains
and southern Ireland, or, to the south east,
the Belgian Ardennes.

It formed at depths between 100m and
500m across the UK, mostly below the
level of wave-action. There's an awful lot
of it. Under the North Sea today the chalk
rock layers are up to 1300m thick — more

than five times the height of Ditchling
Beacon!

When was the chalk formed?

IN the end period of the Age of Dinosaurs,
which was called the 'Cretaceous' — a
word that actually means 'made of chalk'.
Major chalk formation started about 100
million years ago and ended around 65
million years ago — so that's a period of 35
million years.

It was a time of great global warming,
so the polar ice caps melted away, which
caused the seas to expand greatly across
the continental shelves.

We don't have the youngest, uppermost
chalk layers on the Brighton Downs
because they were eroded away very early
on across Southern England.

What is chalk made of?

IT's made of calcium carbonate. It's
basically a soft, white friable limestone.

On the Brighton and Eastbourne Downs
we are used to thinking of chalk as a
dazzlingly white rock, for our cliffs are that
colour. That is because they are made of
what used to be called the Upper Chalk
(now called the White Chalk), which is
very pure — over 98% calcium carbonate.
It is pure because it was laid down at a
great distance from land at a time when

the expansion of the seas was at its greatest. If it had been laid down nearer the land it would have been mixed with sediments transported by rivers, which would have discoloured it. By contrast, the Lower and Middle Chalks (now called the Grey Chalk) contain up to 40% clay minerals, together with a little sand, quartz and glauconite. They were laid down in shallower seas, nearer to the land.

When you travel eastwards along the Lewes southern bypass look out at the chalk pits which come into view as you approach the Southerham roundabout (only if you are a passenger). You'll notice that the tall Southerham Cliffe chalk pit on the left towards Lewes is a shining white. That's because it is made of these pure Upper Chalks. The two chalk pits — one in front and one to your right — which come into view next, close to the roundabout, are a much creamier, greyer colour. These two Southerham Grey Pits don't dazzle in the sun like the Cliffe chalk pit. They are made up of the less pure Lower and Middle Chalk.

The marly Grey (Lower) Chalk is excellent for crop growing, and where it surfaces in a wide band along the base of the north scarp slope, the Saxons focused their chief plough lands and built a string of villages. Underhill Lane passes right through these Grey Chalk cornlands.

But *how* was the chalk formed?

I T was formed by a continuous rain of the skeletons of plankton falling from the surface layers of the warm sea down to the sea floor. It was formed, that is, entirely from the dead bodies of living things. Our chalk Downs are a giant bone-yard of multi-millions of years of life. We live on a pile of the heaped skeletons of aeons of oceanic life forms.

In that sense, the *whole* of the Brighton Downs are one gigantic pile of fossils. Don't get too excited, though, because you won't be able to see these tiny skeletons

except with a powerful microscope. You could get 30,000 of them[3] on a pinhead!

The skeletons of microscopic animals, called foraminifera, together with shell fragments, make up a coarse fraction[4] of about 5-10% of chalk, which is embedded in a fine matrix of the skeletons of planktonic algae. Their little algal bones are called 'coccoliths'. They form the major part of chalk. Algae are a sort of plant and photo-synthesise, like green plants on land. Seaweeds are giant forms of algae. The planktonic algae would only have lived in the surface layers of the sea because only there did the sunlight penetrate.

Ok. But why don't you see many obvious fossils in the chalk?

W E L L , actually you do. It depends where you look. In some fields under the escarpment big fossils are as common as those you can find on the beach of Dorset's Jurassic Coast. All those wiggly flints, too, which look like branches and tubes and Henry Moore sculptures, are the fossils of the burrows of sea floor creatures, often animals in the crab and prawn family. They are like plaster casts of their burrows.

It's true, though, that some parts of the chalk are relatively poor in large fossils, whilst others are much richer. The Grey Chalk has much better preserved assemblages of Ammonites and fossil fishes, and some sea shells, because a lot of these creatures had shells made of aragonite, which is a type of crystal of calcium carbonate that preserves in clay, which the Grey Chalk contain, though it doesn't in chalk. However, some layers of the White (Upper) Chalk have spectacular fossil Ammonites, like those you can see on the beach at Peacehaven.

The echinoderms, some sponges, brachiopods and other sea shells, belemnites (octopoid creatures) and sea mats all had shells made of calcite, which is a type of calcium carbonate crystal that does preserve in pure chalk. That's

One of the giant Ammonites, *Parapuzozia*, on Peacehaven's undercliff beach.

Experts use their many evolutionary forms, together with other sea urchins, as indicators of level in the chalk strata. I find them on dip slope hilltops. Nearer the scarp top I have found the **'Fairy Loaf'**, *Micraster*, sea urchin. The *Micraster* species are found in older, lower chalks than *Echinocorys*, even though I found them in higher ground. That's because — though the scarp top is higher than the dip slope hills — the chalk is older at the scarp top because of the way the chalk strata tip upwards towards the north.

why you find fossil echinoderms, like sea urchins and bits of sea lilies and starfish, commonly in the White Chalk.

Some of these sea urchins were fossilized as flints, and these tend to survive much better on exposure to the open air. It's the flint sponges and sea urchins that turn up most obviously on ploughed fields high on the Downs.

So where can you find these fossils?

Y o u can find them amongst the flint pebbles on the beach. You can find them in the chalk reef and on the cliff face (careful though, because the rock is unstable and may fall). You can find them on the ploughed Downland fields and the fields just north of the northern escarpment, as well as in the old quarries that pit the northern face of the Downs and slopes along the river valleys.

Each layer of the chalk has its own fossil assemblage. The **'Shepherd's Crown'** *Echinocorys scutata* sea urchins are common on the Downs as well as in the cliff face and on the chalk reef platform.

The oldest, Grey Chalks, which are rich in ammonites, outcrop along Underhill Lane at the base of the scarp and around the edges of the Vale of Brooks, especially at Iford and on the two brookland Rises. They used always to be corn growing land, but now many of the fields are used for horse grazing. In autumn the plough annually turns up new rocks, which often contain the Ammonite, *Schloenbachia varians*, and Inoceramid bivalves, but also occasional Nautiloids.

On the cliff face you can find fossil worm tubes, looking like tiny versions of those worm casts on a garden lawn. You can find fossil corals and tiny sea mats, *bryozoa*, and many bits of sponge. The Brighton Downs has one characteristic large fossil sponge, called *Siphonia koenigi*, which turns up very commonly on winter fields and is sometimes spectacularly preserved. You can often

Schematic Downland Section Between The Devil's Dyke and Hove Beach

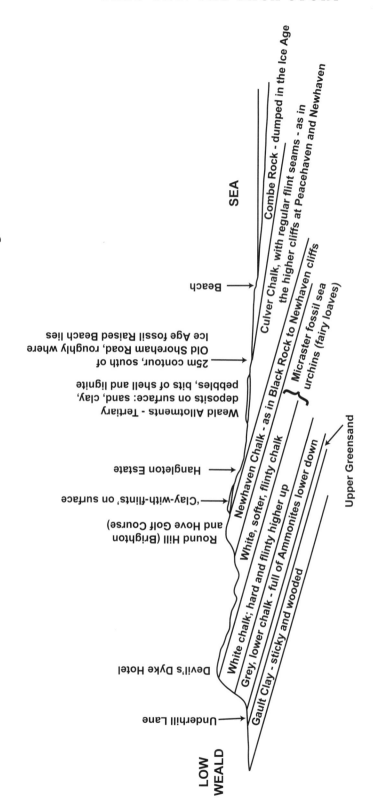

Combe Rock - dumped in the Ice Age

Culver Chalk, with regular flint seams - as in the higher cliffs at Peacehaven and Newhaven

SEA

Micraster fossil sea urchins (fairy loaves)

Chalk - as in Black Rock to Newhaven cliffs

Beach

Ice Age fossil Raised Beach lies

Old Shoreham Road, roughly where

25m contour, south of

Weald Allotments - Tertiary deposits on surface: sand, clay, pebbles, bits of shell and lignite

Hangleton Estate

Upper Greensand

'Clay-with-flints' on surface

Newhaven Chalk

White, softer, flinty chalk

Ammonites lower down

Round Hill (Brighton and Hove Golf Course)

White chalk; hard and flinty higher up

Devil's Dyke Hotel

Grey, lower chalk - full of Ammonites lower down

Underhill Lane

Gault Clay - sticky and wooded

LOW WEALD

Based on cross sections from BGS 1:50,000 Geology Series Sheet 318/333 and Sheet 319/334, with the permission of the British Geological Survey, under permit IPR/103-17CX.

find bits of the broken tentacles of Sea
Lily Crinoids. And you can find all sorts
of shells and bits of shell, some very like
modern species, and some belonging to
the now-near-extinct order of brachiopods,
which look like bivalve molluscs, but are
actually more closely related to worms.

One winter recently we found a total of
22 Ammonite and four Nautiloid species
on and just under the Downs between
Wilmington and Washington. Very often
you just find fragments, but those small
bits can still be enough to identify them.
Sitting amongst the Bluebells in a tiny
edge-of-Downland shaw this spring I
casually picked up a frost-cracked lump of
Grey Chalk. It was jam-packed with fossil
Ammonite bits.

The more you look the more you find.

What is flint?

FLINT is formed of silica, a substance
similar to glass, which is very common in
nature. Indeed, perhaps 50% of the earth's
crust is made up of it. Chalk deposits on
the sea floor contained the remains of
many silica-rich simple animals, such as
Glass Sponges. Over time, this silica was
redistributed after dissolving in the sea
water, solidifying in places often associated
with decaying animals, especially old
burrows and shells.

There are regular bands of flint all
through the White Chalk. In fact, in the old
days, the White Chalk used to be called
'Chalk with Flints', to separate it from the
Grey Chalk, which is largely free of these
bands. Experts reckon that the regularity of
the banding of flint and marl in the chalk is
somehow related to long climatic cycles[5]
— called 'Milankovitch cycles' — caused
by variations in the shape of the earth's
orbit altering the amount of solar radiation
reaching us. Very eerie and sci-fi!

The flint in our Downs is mostly black
with a white skin, or cortex. Up in Yorkshire
their flint is grey and more tabular.
Sometimes the flint comes in different
colours, such as dark red, like jasper. You

My Fossil Chalk Pit Lobster

Lorries and cars, trains and vans
Roar past, or chunder, halted for a jiffy.

Lights at night. Noise always.

Funny place to find a Lobster.

Six miles southwards the real sea lies,
With clanking dredgers and the
Haul of fishing's meagre pickings
— A haul to scarcely fill a few
Cold marble market slabs
Nowadays.

My Lobster's a survivor.

She's survived
NINETY FIVE MILLION YEARS
She has!

I see her in the cracked grey rock,
Her near-eternal hidey-hole.
I peer with eyeglass. Squint up close.

I see her spines and pincers black
Glossy and black as plain to see
As though she'd died but yesterday,

Not long before whole mountains reared —

Whole mountain chains from plain and
                                    undersea
That reared and groaned and raised their
                                    bulk
In time i n f i n i t e s i m a l l y long,
While she lay still within her chalky tomb.

And now she lies within her broken home
Cupped in my hand.

I'm like a god, I think, to span such
God-like numbing tracts of time
In my mind-speeding wonder.

NINETY FIVE MILLION YEARS!!

Some gods we are!

Who make our own sea empty
And empty all the land
Of life except our own.

My Lobster's owned more of eternity
Than we will ever know.

Part of my collection of over 20 Ammonite species found on the Brighton Downs.

seem to find those bits around 'Clay with Flints' deposits. They can also come in various shades of grey, azure (often very beautiful) and pearly white, and sometimes they are beautifully translucent. There used to be a little Brighton industry in polishing and cutting these stones for sale.

Sometimes on the Downs you can find small boulders of **crystallized chalk — calcite** — of great hardness. Often they have beautiful elongated translucent crystals. It's easy to overlook them, especially when they're muddy or have bits of vegetation on them, but once you 'get your eye in' you start spotting them. They used to occur on Brighton beach under the soft cliffs where Marine Parade is now. Were they the rocks that Lower and Upper Rock Gardens were named after?

You can find blobs of **iron pyrites** on Downland fields or on bare ground under bushes and trees. Often the blobs have a most beautiful cubic crystal structure. Sometimes these lumps are broken, and when you take them home to display them they crumble into dust over time. Other lumps are more stable. Iron pyrites can be quite attractive and is sometimes called 'fool's gold'.

On the top of the Newhaven chalk cliffs there's a big cap of other rocks — pebble and sandstone. What's that all about?

T H O S E rocks were laid down much later than the chalk. There's probably around a 25 million years gap in age between the top of the Newhaven chalk and the bottom of the pebble bed that sits immediately above the chalk. That's a big gap!

At the end of the period of chalk deposition the tremendous accumulated weight of ocean bottom chalk was pushed up into a huge dome of low mountains — which geologists call the Wealden Dome — under the influence of gigantic flexings and grindings of the earth's crust. To the far south the African continent crashed into Europe causing the great process of Alpine mountain building. About 15 million years worth of chalk that used to sit on top of the existing Newhaven chalk was eroded away, before the pebbles and sands were laid down on top.

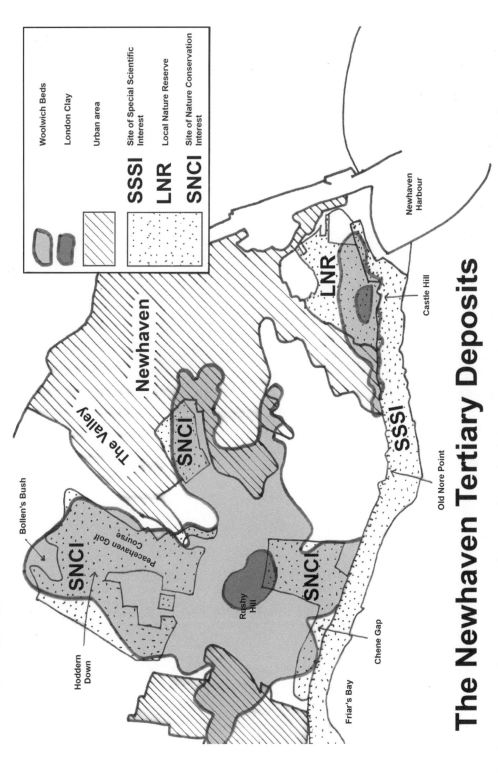

The Newhaven Tertiary Deposits

Based on map extracts from BGS 1:50,000 Geology Series Sheet 334, with the permission of the British Geological Survey, under permit IPR/103-49CX

Section of the Strata at Castle Hill, Near Newhaven Harbour

From *Geology of the South East of England*, pages 54-56, by Gideon Mantell. (1833).

Though some of Mantell's names have changed the same clear stratigraphy can still clearly be seen in the perched soft cliffs above the chalk at Newhaven's Burrow Head, behind the harbour breakwater.

1. *Sand and pebbles* — from 10 to 15 feet.

2. *Coarse argillaceous rock*, chiefly composed of oyster shells, with a few tower shells (Cerithia), etc — 5 feet.

3. *Foliated blue clay*, with an immense quantity of shells; the upper part contains shells of the bivalve genus Cytherea and Cyclas; the lowest divison Cerithia, shark's teeth, and a few Cyrena genus shells — 10 feet.

4. *Reddish brown marl*, more or less slaty, bearing impressions of leaves, wood, cones of a plant of the palm tribe? and casts of Potamides and Cyclades — from 4 to 5 inches.

5. *Lignite or surturbrand* - from 4 to 6 inches.

6. *Blue clay*, with marl of a sulphur colour, including gypsum, both crystallized and fibrous — 20 feet.

7. *Sand*, of various shades of yellow, green, ash colour, etc, without fossils — 20 feet.

8. *Breccia* of pebbles, broken flints, and green sand, strongly impregnated with iron, forming a hard conglomerate — 1 foot.

9. *Ochraceous clay*, containing *hydrate* and *sub-sulphate of alumine*, with gypsum, etc — 1.5 feet.

10. *Chalk*

The age in which these Newhaven sands, pebbles and clays were laid down was a very different one from the Cretaceous age of chalk. The Dinosaurs went extinct at the end of the Cretaceous, and with them went the Ammonites and many other ancient life forms. In the new age mammals rapidly expanded to dominate the world. It was named the Tertiary (that means third) period.

Those pebbles and sands were themselves erosion products that had been washed into a new, but shallow, warm sea that had formed over the eroded chalk. Later there are charcoal-like lignites and plant fossils that must have been laid down in swampy lakes and cut-off rivers. Later still the sea deepened and London Clay was laid down. It survives on the top of Rushy Hill and Castle Hill.

These Newhaven Tertiary deposits can be very fossiliferous and the bare exposed ground is sometimes powdered white with shell fragments. Sharks' teeth are frequently found, as well as big crystals of selenite gypsum. There are rare minerals, too, like jarosite and aluminite.

All of the Downland would have been covered in these Tertiary deposits, but locally they only survive in their original layerings at Newhaven and Peacehaven, and around Falmer and Shoreham Harbour. The deposits under Peacehaven were quarried for brick making when the town was built in the 'twenties and 'thirties.

Brighton parks, like Stanmer Park and the Old Steine, have lots of 'sarsen stones'. What are they?

THE Downs north and north east of Brighton are a sarsen locality. Sarsens are a hard sandstone. Sometimes they contain bits of pebbles, like currants in a pudding. The Goldstone, in Hove Park, is like that. Sometimes they are just pure sandstone. They come in all shapes and sizes, though they are mostly rounded.

Sarsen stones — sometimes known as 'greywethers', or 'druid's stones' — were

made in the Tertiary period, though they were not laid down under water, like the Newhaven deposits, but were made when the Downs had a hot, desert environment. They are a product of occasional rains pooling, and, flushed with silica, cementing the softer sandstones they soaked into. Stones very like sarsen are still being made in places like the Kalahari Desert and Australia.

When the Tertiary 'pie-crust' on top of the chalk eroded away, all the sarsens were scattered. However, they remained common enough on parts of the local land surface to influence Saxon place naming. Hence, *Stan*mer (stony pond), *Stan*dean (stony valley), and Old *Steine* (staene = stony place). On other Downland ranges, like the Wiltshire Downs, sarsen stones were use to build stone age monuments, like Stonehenge and Avebury, and even on the Kentish Downs you can find 'megalithic' (= large stone) tombs. The sarsen on the Brighton Downs wasn't big enough for monument building, although it is possible there were prehistoric stone circles where Hove Park now is, and north of St Nicholas Church — Brighton's old parish church.

Sarsen stones occasionally survive as boundary stones, for instance on Whitehawk and Kingston Hills and around the Hangleton Parish boundary. They also get incorporated in old flint walls, for instance of medieval churches.

...and Clay-with-Flints... What's that?

IT's a mixture of often-reddish earths and flints found on the tops of Downland hills. The flints within it are often stained yellowish. Clay with Flints can be found near to surviving Tertiary deposits and is probably a combination of jumbled-up Tertiary sediments and wind-blown earth (loess) brought here in the Ice Age (Quaternary) period.

Clay with Flints has a much less alkaline chemistry than the chalk. Indeed, leaching over the centuries often made it very

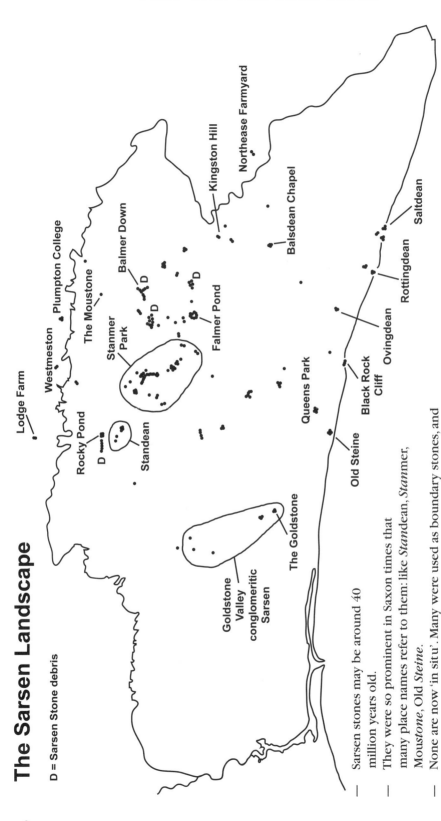

The Sarsen Landscape

D = Sarsen Stone debris

Lodge Farm

Westmeston

Plumpton College

The Moustone

Balmer Down

Kingston Hill

Northease Farmyard

Balsdean Chapel

Saltdean

Rottingdean

Ovingdean

Stanmer Park

Falmer Pond

Queens Park

Black Rock Cliff

Old Steine

Rocky Pond

Standean

Goldstone Valley conglomeritic Sarsen

The Goldstone

- Sarsen stones may be around 40 million years old.
- They were so prominent in Saxon times that many place names refer to them: like *Standean, Stanmer, Moustone,* Old *Steine.*
- None are now 'in situ'. Many were used as boundary stones, and they can be seen in some old flint walls. Brighton Parks Department have placed many decoratively on roadsides and in parks.
- Sarsen debris can be seen on bare fields in some places.

Reproduced from 1940 Ordnance Survey map bases with the kind permission of the Ordnance Survey.

acidic. For those reasons, Clay with Flints areas often developed into large heaths, and can sometimes be identified by their surviving heathy place names (like North Heath Barn, for instance).

Clay with Flints is found on the flatter Downland areas, and, with care, can grow good crops. For that reason those Downland heaths are now almost extinct on our local Downs, though on the North Downs and Chilterns they survive more widely.

The prehistoric people often homed-in on Clay with Flint areas for their flint tool-making workshops and encampments.

Tell me why the Downs are so high, since chalk is so soft?

THEY are high because they don't erode very easily, despite their softness. They don't erode because they soak up water like a giant sponge, rather than repelling it and forcing it to form fast streams that would cut down and erode the rock. Paradoxically, it's the softness and permeability of the chalk Downs that enables them to survive at such heights, rather than eroding away like the Wealden Clay, to their north.[6]

This exceptional permeability means that the chalk sponge soaks up enough water to provide 98% of Brighton's water supply.

OK, but the Downs are still broken up and small, compared to the giant chalk sea they were formed from. That's erosion, big-time!

VERY true. Indeed, when you stand on the scarp at the Devil's Dyke and look across to the North Downs on the horizon it's gob-smacking to know that our South Downs originally joined up with them.

Remember that the flat chalk sea-bed was forced up into the Wealden Dome in the Tertiary period. That dome would have been heavily cracked and strained. It eroded easily. The edges of the dome did not suffer nearly so much distortion, and

have survived as the North and South and Hampshire Downs.

Most of that erosion took place way back, not geologically long after the Dome was raised. What survived of the Dome, around its edges, has actually been remarkably stable. So stable, in fact, that parts of the land surface of the Downs go back more-or-less to those early Tertiary times.

It's obvious that the land surface of the chalk under the Newhaven Tertiary deposits has been preserved ' in aspic' at least since those deposits piled up on them. But the land surface of the top of parts of the chalk scarp, and at the top of the sub-scarp where there is one, may also be that ancient, partly preserved under layers of Tertiary material.

Well, I mustn't exaggerate…It would have shrunk greatly because of chemical weathering. Like a jelly cube or some aspirins the chalk of the Downs dissolves in water — just a lot slower. So the crest of the Downs was much higher and further north back in the time when palaeo-horses were only as big as dogs. It's flatness, though, is a relic of its ancient form. It's not cut greatly by valleys. It's a pretty steady line, like the original flat chalk beds. That's what makes the South Downs Way such nice easy walking. You don't have to switch-back up and down too many valleys to walk along it.

So how did those dip slope valleys form?

IF the escarpment crest were only one mile further south, you'd be up and down like a yo-yo as you walked the South Downs Way.[7] The number of valleys or 'wind-gaps' cutting the crest would more than treble, reducing their average spacing from about one valley every three km to less than one km between valleys, for the dip slope dry valleys all start just south of the crest.

The obvious explanation for this is that those long dry valleys are actually not

Downland Landforms

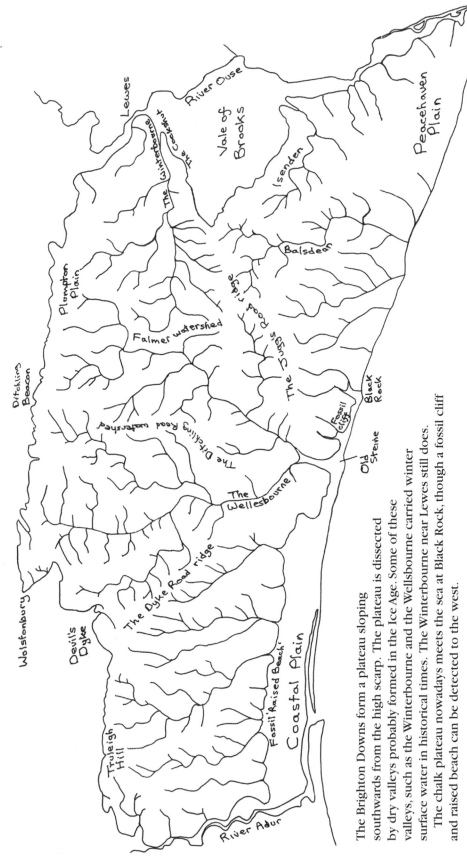

The Brighton Downs form a plateau sloping southwards from the high scarp. The plateau is dissected by dry valleys probably formed in the Ice Age. Some of these valleys, such as the Winterbourne and the Wellsbourne carried winter surface water in historical times. The Winterbourne near Lewes still does.

The chalk plateau nowadays meets the sea at Black Rock, though a fossil cliff and raised beach can be detected to the west.

Modern soil

Ice Age Involutions

Chalk strata

The Ice Age land surface of the Downs is preserved only a few inches under our thin soils. These are corrugated 'involutions' created by freeze-thawing.

very old, going back only to geologically recent glacial times — a matter of tens of thousands, not multi-million years. The retreating escarpment has not had time to behead more than a small number of dip slope valleys.

It's likely they formed as a result of periglacial processes, such as melt-water torrents and frost action, rather than continuously flowing streams. The combination of 'sheetwash' (wide films of water washing down slopes), 'solifluction' (the movement of saturated soil over permafrost sub-soil), and 'rill action' (where mini-streams join to cut deeply into the land surface) carved out our combes and deans.

They also dumped huge quantities of soil and rubble into the valley bottoms and out onto the coastal plain and the Weald in great fans of debris. That dumped material is called 'Coombe Rock' and 'Chalk Head', and often makes good corn growing land.

You're telling me that those Downland valleys never had continuously running streams?

CORRECT, mostly. Of course, the water table used to be higher, so springs would have occurred further up the valleys. There are also winter streams, like the Winterbourne flowing into Lewes, and the Wellesbourne, which used to flow down Brighton's Level and across the Old Steine.

If all that erosion was going on how come the Downs are so rounded?

ALSO because of periglacial erosion. Water (from sheetwash and solifluction) would have increased in volume and speed with distance down-slope, thus scouring the middle slopes more than the tops. Hence the gently convex hill brows and steep slopes.[8]

**But why is the scarp slope so steep
— almost like a cliff?**

AGAIN, maybe because of periglacial
action. The Downs are very high there,
over the Lower Chalk, Greensand and
Clays, so the erosive power of sheetwash,
rills, solifluction and avalanching on the
frost-eroded chalk falling from that height
must have been very great.

**How come the Rivers Ouse and Adur
cut through the chalk and are not
deflected round it? They can't be
periglacial!**

NO, they are much older, and probably
go back to early Tertiary times. They were
cutting down into the chalk before the
Wealden Dome crumbled away, and have
kept their courses since. In fact their beds
cut very much deeper than they do now,
for their valleys have been 'infilled' since
the end of the Ice Age. The River Ouse
used to cut 30m deeper in glacial times
than it presently does at Newhaven, and
sea levels then were up to 130m lower
than they are now. In those days the rivers
were also faster flowing and with much
steeper gradients.

Footnotes

1   From 'A Letter to an Old Sweetheart', by
    Charles Dalmon, page 50 of *The Sussex
    Bedside Anthology*, collected and arranged
    by Margaret Goldsworthy (The Arundel
    Press, 1950).

2   *British Upper Cretaceous Stratigraphy*
    — R.N. Mortimore, C.J. Wood and R.W.
    Gallois. Geological Conservation Review
    Series. (JNCC, 2001), page 3 onwards.

3   *Ibid.* page 29.

4   *The Wealden District* — R.W. Gallois.
    British Regional Geology series, British
    Geological Survey. (London HMSO, 1965),
    page 39.

5   *Fossils of the Chalk*. Palaeontological
    Association Field Guides to Fossils: No. 2,
    edited by Andrew B. Smith and David J.
    Batten (The Palaeontologial Association,
    London, 2002), page 4.

6   'The Landforms of Sussex' — R.B.G.
    Williams and D.A. Robinson, in *Sussex,
    Environment Landscape, and Society*
    (University of Sussex, 1983), page 40.

7   *Ibid.* page 44.

8   'Periglacial Phenomena in the South
    Downs' — R.B.G. Williams, in *The Scientific
    Study of Flint and Chert* edited by G.
    de Sieveking and M.B. Hort (Cambridge
    University Press, 1984), page 164.

PATTERNS MADE BY PEOPLE

The Ancient Peoples

I T ' S both fascinating and depressing to walk the Brighton Downs looking for signs of the ancient peoples. You can see most of the big prehistoric camps, of course. You can see some barrows and field systems and cross dykes and even Bronze Age house sites. But the ancient landscape has faded to a pale shadow over the past 60 years. The bold traces of Roman peasant farms north of Cockroost Hill, Portslade, have been bulldozed to oblivion, as has the Eastwick Barn field system at Patcham (though lots was also destroyed by the Brighton Bypass). Whole surviving prehistoric landscapes have disappeared.

Keep searching, though. The burial mound you are looking for may now be only a faint rising of the surface, compared to the big tump it was 100 years ago, but it may still be visible. Don't let the farmers and landowners persuade you to write-off this landscape.

Recently I found what may turn out to be a Bronze Age platform barrow or round house site, with a dense scatter of worked flint flakes strewn around. It was hidden in woodland with no right of access, so no-one had previously made this discovery. There's **loads** still to find.

Barrows: The Landscapes of the Dead

W H E N my mum was in the Land Army in the last World War she used to work with a lugubrious old bloke. Up and down the furrows they'd shuffle, backs aching and gloves wet, cutting cabbages or dibbing in potatoes. Each time he'd pass her he'd say *"every step forward is a step nearer the grave"*.

He was right, of course, but do we want to be reminded of it every day?

Well, the folks in the Bronze Age did. They turned the highest parts of the Brighton Downs — the long ridges, the landmark hills and the long scarp ridge — into a landscape of the dead. All along the ancient track marked now by the South Downs Way, a necklace of burial mounds was strung out, big and small, clustered or in isolation, looking down on the field workers southwards on the plateau. Many of these mounds are situated not on the highest points, where they'd be invisible to people below because of the rounded upward curve of the slope, but on the false crest of the ridge (which you always hope is the top as you struggle up the slope, only to have the real top revealed as you approach) where they'd have the maximum impact.

We Stand on the Shoulders of all Past Humanity

WHEN I was a teenager, and strongly influenced by all the pervasive nonsense of racism, I used to think **The Chattri** — the oriental-style monument to the Indian dead of the First World War, high on the Downs north of Patcham — was an alien intrusion on the good Saxon landscape of old England.

I don't anymore. I can hardly think of a more appropriate and timeless tribute to our dead. For all around are scattered the funerary monuments of the ancient peoples who shared these Downs with us. Just half a mile southwards from The Chattri on the spine of **Ewebottom Hill**, by the dewpond, is another cemetery of at least six 'bowl barrows', now sadly flattened by modern ploughing. And three quarters of a mile southeast of The Chattri, on the top of **Tegdown Hill**, is another cemetery of at least five barrows, including a famous 'ring barrow'. Only two miles southwards along the **Ditchling Road** ridge and its side spurs to **Ladies Mile** and **Stanmer Woods** lie scattered barrow sites and the high barrows within **Hollingbury's Iron Age Camp**. Indeed, the name by which this whole ridge was called till modern times — 'The Patchway' — commemorates a pagan Romano-British temple and burial site, behind nearby Upper Lodge Wood. 'Patchway' is a mutation of *'Peccel's weoh'* and *'weoh'* is the old Saxon word for a pagan temple or sacred site. Four miles southwards on the horizon you can see **Whitehawk Hill**, where the Neolithic people made the sacred landscape of its causewayed camp long before Stonehenge was dreamed up — and where the modern landscape of the dead at Woodvale now continues that ancient tradition.

The South Downs Way

SCATTERED along the thirteen miles of the South Downs Way that lie between Beeding Hill and Offham Down there are at least 183 ancient prehistoric 'barrows'. (They are called 'tumuli' on the map and 'barrows' by archaeologists. The archaeologists' name is nearer to their old folk name of 'burghs', which comes from the Saxon *'beorgh'*, meaning rounded hill or mound). They are all circular in plan, like the houses of the Bronze Age peoples who made them, though they have at their hearts the bodies of the dead, not the hearths of the roundhouses. They are the homes of the departed loved ones of those peoples.

Sometimes these barrows form dense clusters, like the 25 or more on **Western Brow**, east of Ditchling Beacon, or the circa 22 just **west of Blackcap**. Sometimes these clusters are of quite small barrows, without ditches. Often these 'barrow fields' were of pagan Saxon origin, though perhaps mixed in with earlier Bronze Age barrows. You can still see such a pagan cemetery above Woodingdean at **The Bostal**, or between Newmarket Hill and Kingston Hill, **south of the Jugg's Road**, or up on **Offham Down**, just south of Coombe Plantation.

Don't expect to be able to see the sights our grandparents saw, though, for farmers have trashed the great majority of the barrows which survived into modern times. The important cluster of nine barrows on **Beeding Hill** has long been destroyed. You won't see anything now if you go up onto **Falmer Hill**, or **Pickers Hill** above Saltdean, or **Mill Hill** Rodmell, or **Houndean Farm** above Ashcombe House — all of which had large barrow cemeteries into modern times.

Famous Barrows

WHENEVER I've gone to visit the **Money Burgh** at Dean's Farm, north of Piddinghoe, I've had to pick my way over a couple of barbed wire fences. It's always worth it, though, to get to stand on this so-ancient Neolithic long barrow and

Known Barrows (Prehistoric Burial Mounds)

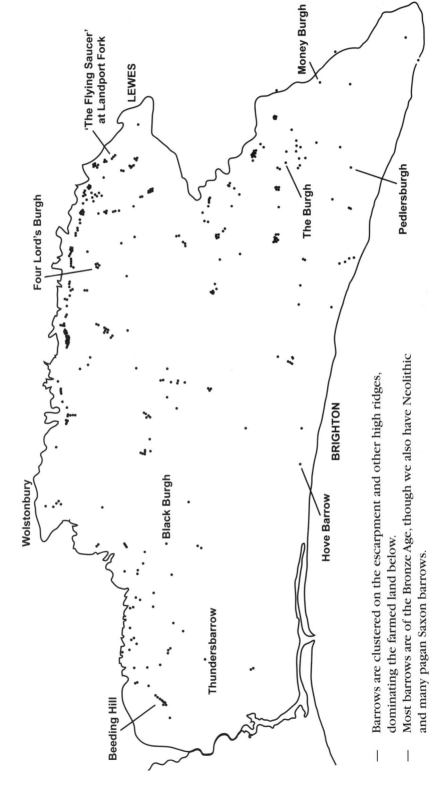

Four Lord's Burgh

'The Flying Saucer' at Landport Fork

LEWES

Money Burgh

Pedlersburgh

The Burgh

Wolstonbury

Black Burgh

BRIGHTON

Hove Barrow

Thundersbarrow

Beeding Hill

— Barrows are clustered on the escarpment and other high ridges, dominating the farmed land below.

— Most barrows are of the Bronze Age, though we also have Neolithic and many pagan Saxon barrows.

Reproduced from 1940 Ordnance Survey map bases with the kind permission of the Ordnance Survey.

look across the narrowing valley of the River Ouse, which the barrow commands, and to enjoy the tiny Downland flowers — Pride of Sussex Rampion amongst them — which still mantle this old mound. In recent years we've also had to avoid a high-fenced game release pen on the steep slope that drops away north of the long barrow. Who knows what the money was that someone once found whilst plundering this grave? Was it some votive offering buried here later in Iron Age or Roman times?

Visiting **Thunders Barrow** north of Southwick Hill is also an evocative experience. Go there especially in the dusk or dawn. It's a big barrow even now, though it was half dug away on its south side in the nineteenth century to make way for a dew pond. The name could not be more apt, for it is the sky that dominates this place and a clap of Thor's thunder would be no surprise here. The name cannot be traced earlier than 1801, though. Was it an old folk name surviving outside written culture, like the old custom of dancing kiss-in-the-ring round the Hove barrow?

Last year I walked the site of the **Black Burgh**, just south of the Devil's Dyke Road and right at the head of the long valley which drops down to Toad's Hole and The Goldstone in Hove Park.

All you can see when the field is fresh ploughed is a scarcely-raised scatter of white flints contrasting with the earth of its surroundings. I paced backwards and forwards and found a fragment of old pottery right on the burgh site. It would have been lovely if it had been a piece of Bronze Age earthenware, but of course it wasn't. Maybe, though, it was part of a broken jug used by the Victorian excavators of the burgh, led by the famous General Pitt Rivers. That'd be something.

The Black Burgh revealed to its excavators a rich early Bronze Age internment. Accompanying the skeleton

of a woman were at least 65 shale beads, a bronze pin, a bronze dagger, and — most interestingly — a little earthenware cup. Curwen tells[1] us *"the cup is decorated with what looks like a pair of eyebrows — a conventional representation of the human face which, though not uncommon on pottery in the Aegean area, as at Troy, and also in Denmark and Spain, is possibly unique in Britain"*. Well, well!

The Danish connection was even stronger at the famous **Hove Barrow**. It was dismantled so that its earth could be used for the new Palmeira Square Gardens in 1856-7. Think of the origins of that brown earth next time you pass those flower-beds. The barrow was one of the most prominent landmarks on the whole of our end of the coastal plain. It could be seen from the whole cirque of the surrounding Downs and — perhaps as importantly — from a great stretch of the open sea. For the big chief whose grave the barrow contained obviously traded, or perhaps had family links, all along the seaway to Denmark. The 12 ft high by 200 ft diameter mound contained the famous amber cup (which is one of the City museums' most precious possessions), and a stone-axe hammer both of probable Danish provenance, as well as a dagger and whetstone.

The South Downs Way will take you past the site of the **Four Lords' Burgh**, south of Blackcap. There's not much to see now except fences, but the cluster of barrows here was obviously once prominent enough to make it the convergence point of four separate manors: Westmeston/ Novington, Chailey/Warningore, St John's sub Castro, and Balmer. Barrows were often used as boundary marks of manors and parishes and many local examples still remain.

Does **Skeleton Hovel**, near the clubhouse of West Hove Golf Course, mark an opened and cleared barrow, now long forgotten? It is likely that at least some of the isolated inhumations found on the Downs were once marked by barrows cleared for their flints or to make an even plough surface.

Most of the barrows in this list of the more famous have gone. That's the reality of our Downs nowadays. But some have been handsomely commemorated even in their destruction. **Southease and Piddinghoe churches** are built on the probable sites of large pagan barrows. **Brighton's old parish church of St Nicholas**, up on Church Hill, may also have been located there to challenge its status as a pagan sacred site. There may have been a sarsen stone circle, and an urn and two Bronze Age grave beakers were found there.

Camps and Enclosures

PREHISTORIC hillforts and enclosures have survived fairly well compared to other parts of the ancient landscape. **The Devil's Dyke** is still marked by the 'poor man's wall' round its whole circumference, though the Iron Age hillfort has never been excavated, so little can be said about its date or usage. The hillforts at **Thundersbarrow, Wolstonbury, Hollingbury** and **Newhaven's Castle Hill** all have their origin in the Late Bronze Age, not the Iron Age, though their usage continued into that time. Half of Castle Hill has been lost to the sea or damaged in modern times, but it's still a wonderful place. **Offham's Neolithic causewayed camp** has been half lost, too, but this time to the deep chalk pit adjacent. It's sister camp at **Whitehawk** has survived better, though roads and the racecourse have damaged big chunks. Till recently, the plough crossed and re-crossed most of **Ditchling Beacon's Iron Age enclosure** so that little of it is now visible. The part that is visible contains a small fragment of derelict chalk heath, complete with ageing Ling Heather bushes.

It gets more rank and brambley every year. Brighton Council owns that part. They don't care.

There are also several medieval enclosures and fortifications surviving, like the small Norman motte on the top of **Edburton Hill**, west of the Dyke (though this probably incorporates prehistoric earthworks). **Old Erringham Farm** is embraced by a 10th century defensive ring bank, contemporary with the invasions of the Vikings. You can just about make parts of it out on the ground. There's another **Castle Hill** at **Balsdean**, behind Woodingdean, with an ancient rectangular banked enclosure on it. Our forebears were free-er with the term 'castle' than we are!

Ancient Farming Landscapes

EIGHTY years ago G. Holleyman[2] started systematically walking the Brighton Downs to finds traces of the prehistoric peoples' farming landscapes. He worked out that 18% of our Downs were *still* covered by the lynchets of the 'Celtic' field system! They stuck out like the ribs of some giant sleeping animal, highlighted by the strong shadows of early morning and dusk. By the 'Celtic' field system he meant that of the peoples of the Iron Age, from around 2800 BP to around the end of Romano-British culture at say 1500 BP.

His was not an estimate of the *total* footprint of land on the Downs which was cultivated in pre-modern times. He was only able to estimate what he could see. We now know that prehistoric fields also filled in large areas between his lynchetted areas, for instance between Round Hill, Hangleton and Foredown, Portslade. They were a busy lot those early farmers.

The quiet haven of **Buckland Hole**, on **Balmer Down**, opens up before you as you walk the farm track skirting south of the round top of Balmer Huff. Under grass again now, after post-war decades of damaging modern ploughing, it is still crossed and recrossed by the bony banks

Hillforts, Castles, Rings and Enclosures

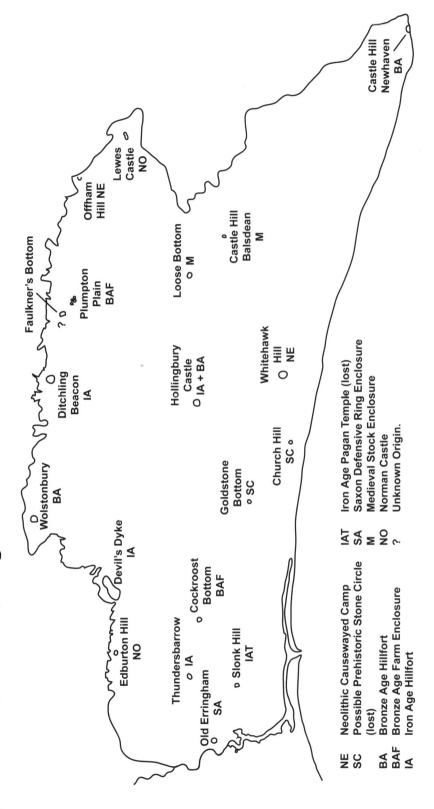

Castle Hill
Newhaven
BA

Lewes
Castle
NO

Offham
Hill NE

Loose Bottom
○ M

Castle Hill
Balsdean
M

Faulkner's Bottom

? ○

Plumpton
Plain
BAF

Ditchling
Beacon
IA

Hollingbury
Castle
○ IA + BA

Whitehawk
○ Hill
NE

Wolstonbury
BA

Goldstone
Bottom
○ SC

Church Hill
SC ○

Devil's Dyke
IA

Edburton Hill
NO

Thundersbarrow
○ IA

Cockroost
○ Bottom
BAF

Old Erringham
○ SA

○ Slonk Hill
IAT

NE   Neolithic Causewayed Camp
SC   Possible Prehistoric Stone Circle
     (lost)
BA   Bronze Age Hillfort
BAF Bronze Age Farm Enclosure
IA   Iron Age Hillfort

IAT Iron Age Pagan Temple (lost)
SA   Saxon Defensive Ring Enclosure
M   Medieval Stock Enclosure
NO   Norman Castle
?   Unknown Origin.

Reproduced from 1940 Ordnance Survey map bases with the kind permission of the Ordnance Survey.

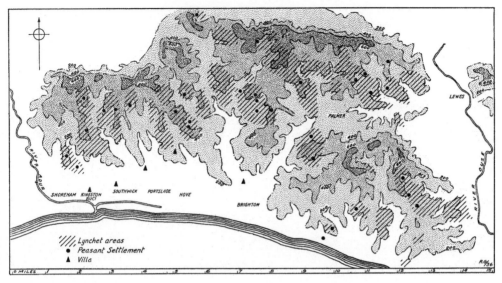

FIG. 84.—DISTRIBUTION OF PEASANT SETTLEMENTS, VILLAS AND LYNCHETS IN THE BRIGHTON DISTRICT
After G. A. Holleyman
The hatched areas were under cultivation in the Roman period

> **We now know that prehistoric cultivation covered many other areas (in addition to those shown) at different times.**

of a Romano-British pattern of fields. They have lain there under the turf since the abandonment of this farming settlement sometime around the end of the Roman occupation. These surviving banks are high — too high even to be easily destroyed by modern farm machinery. There's just a flavour of an Irish landscape here. The fields were small and square and each of these banks are topped with a thin line of flaming gorse and thorn. It must have been a large community, with at least two hamlets, roads, ponds, and a large urn cemetery, uncovered in 1849. It is a remarkable survival — probably **the best surviving 'Celtic field' system on the South Downs.**

Walk north from this tranquil place to Four Lords Burgh. To the north-west, north of Moustone, lies a lovely high dry valley, flowery, and dotted with gorse and sheltering trees. At the very head of this valley, below **Plumpton Plain**, there is a most remarkable survival — the

intact remains of a **Bronze Age peasant farming settlement**, traceable in its entirety beneath the protective turf. With a good map you can trace each household's enclosure, the sunken circle of each round house, their ponds, fencelines, little platforms, plough-banks and trackways.

Why has it survived so perfectly when so many of the visible signs of this period have disappeared? Perhaps because the land to the east — Ashcombe and Boxholt — was always filled with old woodland, which expanded to embrace the Plumpton Plain site after its abandonment. Beneath the wood the traces of the hamlet survived all subsequent local ploughing right up until modern times.

To the west and the east of **Thundersbarrow** the Iron Age/Romano-British field system is also still very visible. The big lynchets to the west were known as **'Thunders' Steps'**. The lynchets to the east are mingled with medieval lynchets and a wartime firing range bunker!

High Dole, above Telscombe, also still shows its lynchet system in the evening light.

The Neolithic peoples who first started serious clearance of the Downs have not left much visible evidence of their farming activity. They were doing a sort of scratch agriculture with hand tools, and their plots would have been obliterated by later cultivation or have left few signs. Under the turf, though, there are many signs both of their activity and of the Mesolithic (Middle Stone Age) gatherer-hunters who preceded them. They would probably have cleared some ground to facilitate their hunting activities and domestic activities. **Red Hill, Patcham** — now just a spaghetti junction of roads at the crossing of the Dyke Road and the Brighton Bypass — was an important Mesolithic flint knapping site, taking advantage of the clay-with-flints deposits. They left a generous litter of scrapers, flakes, axes, knives, burins, arrowheads, piercers, picks and blades. Later the Bronze Age people farmed the land. **West Hill**, above Saddlescombe on the same ridge, was also a busy place for those gatherer-hunter flint knappers.

Field Walking

O N E early spring day I walked a freshly ploughed hilltop field where a clay-with-flints cap was marked by dark earth and large flint nodules. It seemed a good

place to look for the debris of prehistoric flint working. After only a few minutes I spotted out of the corner of my eye a little white flint whose edge had been carefully chipped (or 'retouched' as the archaeologists say). The edging looked a bit like a tiny version of the thumbprints pressed into the edge of a pie crust. The flint was a rounded oval biscuit shape about 1.5 inches by 2 inches. No doubt about it: this was a prehistoric scraper tool — probably Neolithic. Perhaps some hunter or early herder had knelt right here to scrape clean the skin of a Roe Deer brought back from the surrounding woods, or maybe one of their own oxen. I walked on. After just an hour and a half I had found three more scrapers, a tiny flint 'saw' — only 1.5 inches long with teeth all down one edge — a blade, and a scatter of flakes left from the worked flint nodules. The hands that had last touched those tools were the hands of our ancestors working perhaps five thousand years before our time.

It is not hard to find prehistoric worked pieces of flint on our winter ploughlands, though you have to be lucky to find those sort of concentrations. You just need to familiarize yourself with the shapes and subtleties that identify them, the same way as bird watchers learn to interpret the 'giz' of birds they fleetingly see.

An unfinished neolithic axe recently found by David McOmish on Plumpton Plain.

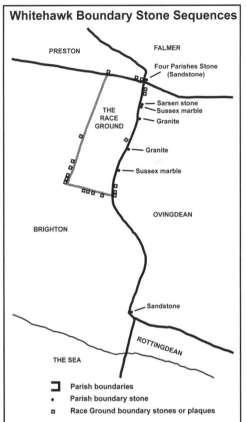

Whitehawk Boundary Stone Sequences

PRESTON

FALMER

Four Parishes Stone
(Sandstone)

THE
RACE
GROUND

Sarsen stone
Sussex marble
Granite

Granite

Sussex marble

OVINGDEAN

BRIGHTON

Sandstone

ROTTINGDEAN

THE SEA

Parish boundaries
Parish boundary stone
Race Ground boundary stones or plaques

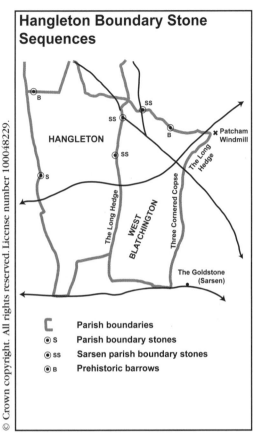

Hangleton Boundary Stone Sequences

B

SS

SS

HANGLETON

B

x Patcham Windmill

SS

S

The Long Hedge

WEST BLATCHINGTON

Three Cornered Copse

The Long Hedge

The Goldstone
(Sarsen)

Parish boundaries
S   Parish boundary stones
SS   Sarsen parish boundary stones
B   Prehistoric barrows

In some areas farmers' flint picking machines have removed much of the surface evidence, and the repeated passing of farmers' giant machinery has crushed and splintered much that survived. The repeated ploughing, too, levels out the post holes, the banks and ditches and the buried remains.

With a watchful eye and a bit of knowledge gleaned from books and experienced field walkers, though, you can still add to what we know of where our ancestors lived and worked.

So...if you look westwards towards **Benfield Hill** from its immediate east in certain afternoon lights you can see what looks like slight east-west corrugations across the top of the Hill. Are these the traces of ancient 'ridge and furrow' ploughing? If you walk the grass alongside the **Brighton Racecourse** north of the

garden centre you can see slight humps. Are these the attenuated remains of prehistoric barrows? If you look across from Whitehawk Hill to the **east flank of Sheepcote Valley** you can see a faint circle of greener turf. Is there a Bronze Age enclosure there?

Keep looking.

Medieval Marks: Downland Boundaries

W H E N I walk the Downs with visitors to the area they'll often say "they've uprooted all the hedges!" They're wrong, for this has certainly been a largely hedgeless landscape at least since medieval times. Pre-modern farms, manors and parishes marked their boundaries by noting isolated thorn bushes, banks, stones, barrows,

Medieval Parish Boundaries

Meeching

(Newhaven)

Southease

Piddinghoe

St John
Sub Castro

Rodmell

Telscombe

Chailey
detached
(Warningore)

Hamsey

St Anne
Without

Iford

Kingston
near
Lewes

Rottingdean
(Balsdean
chapelry)

Rottingdean

Westmeston
detached
(East Chittington
and Novington)

St John
Sub Castro
detached
(Ashcombe
Bottom)

Falmer

Ovingdean

Plumpton

Street

Westmeston

Stanmer

Brighton

Keymer

Ditchling

Falmer
detached
(Patchway)

Clayton

Preston

Pyecombe

Patcham

Hove

West
Blatchington

Aldrington

Newtimber

Hangleton

Poynings

Portslade

Edburton

Southwick

detached

Beeding

Old
Shoreham

Kingston
Buci

New Shoreham

Reproduced from 1940 and 1873 Ordnance Survey maps with the kind permission of the Ordnance Survey.

lynchets and furrow edges. Except around farmsteads and some parish boundaries they didn't use hedges.

Mostly these old boundary features have been eliminated or replaced by wire fences, but some relics survive. West Blatchington parish boundary is still marked by long sequences of the Long Hedge surviving inside and outside the built up area. Its northern boundary is still marked by two sarsen stones and a Bronze Age barrow. Benfield Hill still has a Hangleton-Portslade boundary stone and, of course, the Brighton-Ovingdean parish boundary is still marked by a long necklace of boundary stones across and below Whitehawk Hill. Part of the boundaries of Telscombe Tye's 'D' and 'E' pieces are still marked by these simple banks and furrows

The patterns that the boundaries make tell significant stories, too. The Newtimber parish boundary follows

the course of an ancient (probably Roman or older) trackway for two miles northwards from near the Brighton and Hove Golf Course clubhouse all the way to Beggar's Lane, Newtimber. The eastern boundary of Newtimber also follows the probable Roman road route from West Hill to Varncombe. It seems that the Saxon officials who negotiated the boundaries of Newtimber with its neighbouring parishes chose to fix them on ancient trackways for almost the whole of its Downland area. They were, maybe, basing their decisions on far older estate boundaries.

Seven parish boundaries (Preston, Patcham, Falmer, Kingston, Rottingdean/Balsdean, Ovingdean, Brighton) come together in a star shape on the **Warren Road/Jugg's Road ridge** from Race Hill to Kingston Hill. All seven needed access to its huge heathy pastures.

Stanmer parish sat oddly on the Downs surrounded by the fragments of Falmer parish from which it was carved. Patchway (around the Ditchling Road) was still a detached part of Falmer till modern times, and its ancient boundary banks are still obvious in the landscape west of Stanmer Park.

Nearly all the **scarp foot and river valley villages** have a characteristic linear shape, tracing long narrow fingers from the Weald up over the Downs, to divide up all the available soil types and resources.

Roads and Tracks

ROADS of both inter-parish and wider importance mostly followed the higher ground on the ridge tops and the plateau lands towards the high scarp top.

The **South Downs Way** along the scarp top takes a route that must have been travelled since deep in prehistoric times. It is one of several such long distance routes on the chalklands, like the Ridge Way and the Icknield Way along the Wiltshire and Berkshire Downs and the Chilterns. Like the Icknield Way, though, the South

Medieval Parish Boundaries

- Patcham and Falmer had the biggest Downland footprints.
- Stanmer, though, was carved out of Falmer in 765 AD, leaving a detached fragment of Falmer at Patchway.
- Parish boundaries often converged on wild, remote Downland. At Hazelholt, where ancient woodland maybe survived, the parishes of Shoreham, Edburton, Portslade and Southwick may have converged to share the common wood.
- Seven parishes converged on the Jugg's Road ridge between Brighton's Race Hill and Newmarket Hill. Four of them converge at the 'Four Parishes Stone'.
- Four parish territories converged at 'Four Lord's Burgh'; four more on High Hill, Rottingdean; and four more near Golf Farm, Devil's Dyke Road.

Downs Way had a scarp foot alternative route, which followed the lower chalk and greensand 'bench' and passed through the spring-line villages. East of Clayton it is officially called the Underhill Lane (though I use that name for the whole length of the Sussex Downs scarp foot lane). Which route a long-distance traveller would take must have depended upon the season, their purpose, and the weather.

There was no road up the estuarine and marshy Adur Valley (where the present A273 lies). The highway inland from Shoreham and Brighton mounted Mill Hill northwards to Beeding Hill before descending into the Weald. A second, parallel highway from Brighton in Shoreham parish went inland over Slonk Hill, past Buckingham Barn, above Mossy Bottom and over Summer Brow to meet the first route on Beeding Hill. This route is now no longer even a right of way and has disappeared completely at its northern end. The valley road to Beeding and Steyning up the riverside was not constructed till the nineteenth century!

The **Jugg's Road** connecting Brighton with Lewes also took the high ground via Race Hill, Newmarket and Kingston Hills. It was a continuation of the old coastal highway along the line of the **Old Shoreham Road**, which must have been at least Roman (and probably much earlier) in origin. It would have serviced the Roman villas at Southwick, West Blatchington and Preston, as well as the port on the Adur estuary. It runs roughly along the southern edge of the chalk outcrop, where it meets the alluvial coastal plain. For some of its length, west of Fishersgate, it tracks roughly along the 15m contour, which, as far west as Chichester, has been associated with the fossil Ice Age feature known as the 'Brighton-Norton Raised Beach'. It must have taken this inland route partly to avoid crossing the lower Wellesbourne river after it had been doubled in size at the confluence of its two main streams (from the London Road and Lewes Road valleys) at Viaduct/ Union Roads. After risking wet feet there, travellers would mount the steep chalk white road now marked by Elm Grove, and go on across the Downs to Lewes.

It seems unlikely that either the present London Road or the clifftop route of the A259 were main roads before the modern growth of Brighton. The London Road valley would have been soggy in winter. (See how Patcham and Preston old churches are raised up on their hillsides from the valley bottom). The run of cliffs to Newhaven held no villages except Rottingdean. The route from Brighton to Rottingdean was a bit inland over Red Hill, through Ovingdean, and over Beacon Hill. Beyond Rottingdean there was a very bleak and lonely five miles till you got to Meeching (Newhaven).

There were a number of medieval (and prehistoric, no doubt) **fords and ferries** across the Rivers Ouse and Adur, and these would have carried the important ridgeway and coastal routes onwards. The lowest medieval bridges across the Adur and the Ouse would have been at Beeding and Lewes, and these were not built until comparatively late. The first record of a bridge at Beeding was not until 1086, though the main Adur channel (by St Mary's Bramber) is first recorded as bridged as late as c.1230. The first record of a Lewes bridge was not until 1150. And if you wanted to cross below these bridges you forded (or ferried) across the Adur at Old Shoreham, or at Botolphs, where the river is at its narrowest and the ridgeway comes down on both sides. For the Ouse you crossed at Meeching/ Newhaven (not bridged till 1784), Stock Ferry (commemorated in Stock Cottages), Southease-It*ford* (bridged in 1810) or Southeram.

The **Roman engineers** who built their straight road south from London Bridge to the Clayton wind gap would probably not

Some Ancient Roads

(Not including swine pasture droves)

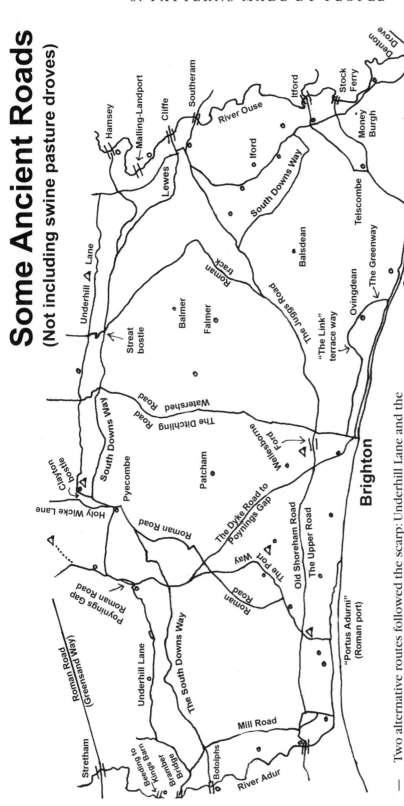

— Two alternative routes followed the scarp: Underhill Lane and the South Downs Way along the ridge.

— Most Downland routes followed the ridges, not the valleys.

— The rivers were crossed by a number of ancient fords and ferries.

— The Old Shoreham Road roughly followed the line of the fossil Ice Age seashore: the 'Brighton-Norton Raised Beach'.

Reproduced from 1940 Ordnance Survey map bases with the kind permission of the Ordnance Survey.

have been aiming directly southwards to Brighton as their final destination. Instead, it's more likely they had Portslade harbour in mind. Their road passed up over the eastern flank of Wolstonbury and down Pyecombe village street. After that it probably climbed West Hill along the South Downs Way, then tracked down the ridge of Varncombe Hill (roughly where the medieval parish boundary was fixed), and in a straight line (along the Monarch's Way route) up onto Foredown and down into Portslade and the Copperas Gap.

They may, however, have taken the well-established prehistoric route over Summer Down (also the later parish boundary) and around Round Hill down through later Hangleton. That route is known as the **Port's Way** and its strong bank can still be followed for a mile as a terrace way around Round Hill. It is said that coaches still travelled it as late as the 17th century.

From that time **Turnpike Trusts** began to create new roads with tolls chargeable at entry tollgates. They survived until the railways and improved local government killed them. A turnpike to Brighton was created in 1770, which devised a new route through Clayton Gap and on down past Withdean and Preston. Another turnpike was created along the present route of the A259 from Newhaven towards Brighton, skirting round the northern flank of Rushey Hill. It replaced the ancient highway up past Meeching's medieval church and over the top of the Hill. That route still survives as a pot-holed and windy track.

This is, though, a blessedly roadless countryside. Surveyors have had very little to do with the great majority of the tracks across our open Downs, which were created by users along lines of convenience. The straight, right angled paths at the northern end of Cockroost Hill are **surveyors' alignments**, laid out upon the 1860 enclosure of the Portslade Tenantry Down.

Most paths across the high pastures were 'braided', that is, they took whatever line the traveller (or herd or flock) felt was most convenient and avoided mud and ruts. This pattern of **braided paths** was *still* evident as late as 1946, when the superb RAF aerial photo series reveals them. Now the vast majority of such old 'desire-line' braids are gone — fenced in and ploughed out — and only a few relics survive.

Such braided paths can be very rich in wildlife. The deep gullied tracks offer a whole series of micro-habitats, from close-cropped Sheep's Fescue turf on the bank tops, to scree-like banks, bare chalk and mud, and areas of tall herb growth in the abandoned gullies. There are a whole series of aspects, too, from sun-drenched to deep shade.

The line of the South Downs Way has several of these braids. There is a section of braid between Newmarket and Newmarket Plantation, halfway between Falmer and Lewes. On West Hill, west of Pyecombe, a derelict braided section survives. Summerdown, near the Devil's Dyke, has a section south of the road. Perching Hill has a tiny section. Mill Hill, Shoreham has a section just west of the road. The west side of Newtimber Hill has a superb section, both upslope and downslope of the road, which the National Trust are gradually clearing of scrub. Here juniper survives in its only native East Sussex locality. And the wind gap at Clayton Hill has an exceptional braid (though with none of the lovely atmosphere of the braids out on the old Down pastures) with a bit of prehistoric track, the line of the Roman road, two abandoned Turnpike alignments and the modern A273!

Drove roads, made to facilitate repeated and regular stock movements, can make distinctive patterns on the Downs, though most of them are now lost to modern agriculture and built development.

Patcham's Drove Roads

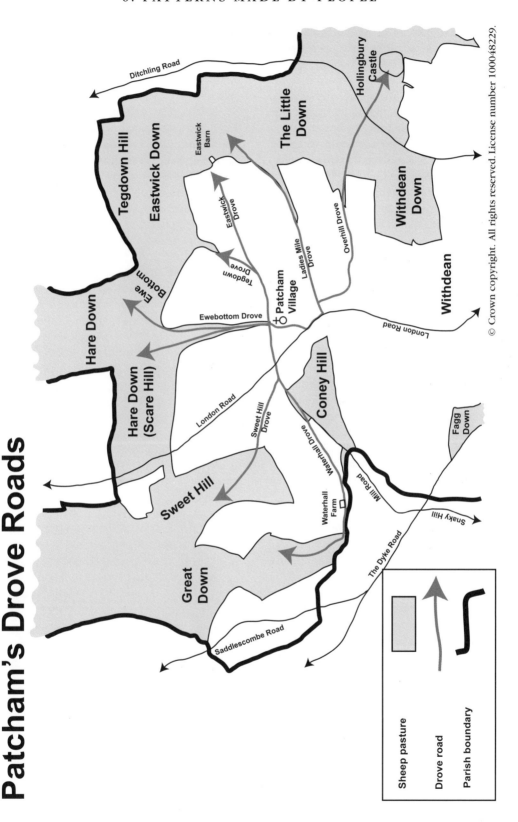

Legend:

- Sheep pasture
- Drove road
- Parish boundary

Map labels:

Ditchling Road

Tegdown Hill

Eastwick Down

Eastwick Barn

The Little Down

Hollingbury Castle

Withdean Down

Eastwick Drove

Tegdown Drove

Ladies Mile Drove

Overhill Drove

Withdean

Hare Down

Ewe Bottom

Ewebottom Drove

Patcham Village

Hare Down (Scare Hill)

London Road

London Road

Sweet Hill Drove

Coney Hill

Fagg Down

Sweet Hill

Waterhall Drove

Waterhall Farm

Mill Road

Snaky Hill

The Dyke Road

Great Down

Saddlescombe Road

Patcham parish's drove roads out to its huge and distant sheep pastures made a clear fan of radial spokes out from the village centre. Ladies Mile served the Park Bottom pastures (where ASDA is now). A drove to Eastwick Barn and another branch drove to Tegdown Hill served those pastures in the northeast of the parish. Another drove going northwards served Ewe Bottom and Deep Bottom, with a branch drove to Scare Hill. And two further droves tracked north-west and west to Sweet Hill, North Heath, Varncombe, and Waterhall.

Preston parish, now almost entirely built up, still has its two long western and eastern droves, from Hove Park to Race Hill. The first section, west of the old village ('The Drove'), is so steep that no-one could be under any illusion that it was made for wheeled traffic.

Long distance drove routes took stock (sheep, pigs, cattle) far into the Weald and onto the river brooklands, and the next chapter will describe those connections. Suffice it to say, here, that many of these routes imprinted themselves very deeply on the soft chalk landscape. As they tracked diagonally down steep places they cut deeper and deeper into the chalk. Animals and their herders would not spread out in braids across the pastures, as they did on the more level ground. To the contrary, they would pick a safe path and then walk it repeatedly until it had cut so deep as to make them invisible in its gully from the surrounding landscape. The drovers and shepherds **'bostal'** paths in these steep places, like the braided paths, are exceptionally rich in micro-habitats for wildlife. On the scarp they are hung with crinkly mats of the mosses *Neckera crispa* and *Ctenidium molluscum*. They hold colonies of the rare scree-loving **Many-toothed Snail**, *Abida secale*, and the only home on our Downs for Spiny Restharrow. Their short, open swards hold Chalkhill

Blue and Glow-worm in summer and are dotted with Waxcaps in autumn.

Most of our deepest bostals are on the steep scarp, but some occur on the plateau, where the paths descend steep places. Slonk Hill, near Holmbush, has a stretch a third of a mile north west of Slonk Hill Farm. Southwick Hill has a very deep one descending above the eastern portal of the A27 Bypass. Waterpit Hill has a long one on Falmer's old swine pasture route to the Weald. Bullock Hill and High Hill, east of Woodingdean, both have bostals descending to old Balsdean, and Stanmer Down (a mile north of Sussex University) and Halcombe's south slope (south of Dean's Farm, Piddinghoe) have tracks which are more like terrace ways than bostals.

Water

EVERYONE who knows our Downs knows that they are now waterless. Once, great Ice Age torrents rushed down our valleys and frost and sheetwash ate away at our valleysides. Sometimes in more recent prehistory the water table within the chalk has been much higher. That meant that some of the ancient peoples were able to take advantage of streams flowing much higher up our dry valleys. And even in medieval times the seasonal rivers of the London Road and Lewes Road valleys still ran in winter, giving their name to the medieval Brighton Hundred of Wellesbourne. 'Bourne' was an early Saxon word for a clear stream or river. Nowadays pumping stations bring water up from deep in the chalk aquifer.

Ponds

IN modern history, though, animals on the Downs have had to rely on ponds for water. Luckily, sheep's need for water is much less than cattle. The **dew ponds** which are so famous on the Downs are of uncertain provenance, though evidence of pond construction can be found right back to the Bronze Age. In the last century and more there was a surge of pond construction. Dew ponds were made using layers of puddled clay, straw and burnt lime — and a protective layer of flints, too, if cattle were to use the pond.

There are still some lovely dew ponds surviving on the high Downs, though many have gone. The pair on Kingston Hill are amongst the most evocative. Ditchling Beacon has a good example opposite the car park, and there are two more nice ones either side of the Ditchling Road at Piddingworth.

I have three personal favourites, though. What makes them so is the thought that I could easily spend a sunny day beside them quietly, with a picnic and something to read. Two of them are twins, sitting next to each other on Pond Brow, just over half a mile due south of Saddlescombe. Once they watered the great flocks on Ewe Bottom, but now all that is thickets and golf course. They still water the flock on the valleyside below, though. The other is the beautifully restored dewpond east of Hollingbury Castle, on the brow above Moulsecoomb Pit. It no longer waters stock, but, in this case, who cares? No misguided attempt has been made to plant it up, and dogs splash about in it, whilst their owners stand and chat. All around is yellow gorse, and linnets and pigeons nest in the mature scrub. It's a lovely airy spot, and you have shelter from the breeze, too.

Some ponds, however, definitely should *not* be restored. The dried out pond on Red Hill, above Sheepcote, whose soft turf now displays good Waxcaps and Fairy Clubs in autumn, is one of those, as is the dried Middle Brow dew pond on Pyecombe Golf Course, with its Downland turf and Fragrant Orchis. Tegdown's dry pond (north of Patcham) looks far better than any fenced and over-vegetated restoration would do — for that is the problem with dewpond restoration. The character of an old dewpond was of a

bleak and open watery lens reflecting the sky. Only **Flote Grass** and (rarely) **Water Crowfoot** decorated the open water, and sheep and little Downland birds drank from the bare earth rims. Restored ponds, by contrast, are often fenced *against* livestock. They are often planted with an exotic range of emergent water plants, more often seen in garden ponds or shady Wealden lakes, and their untrampled rims quickly succeed to rank bramble, tall herbs and bushes. Rocky Pond above Standean, with its rim of huge Sarsen stones, has lost all its old Downland character now it is fenced. It looks just like a tiny developing thicket.

Though the old dew ponds were functional and their aesthetic unadorned they had their own complement of very special wildlife. We spent half a delightful afternoon, some years ago, hauling Screech Beetles, Newts, Daphnia, Cyclops, and snails out of one Downland pond. Some dew ponds have all three species of British Newt in them. The dried pond on Newtimber Hill is dappled with orange and yellow Waxcaps round its rim in autumn.

Some ponds do not hold water all the year round. They are seasonal, and that can mean very special creatures and plants are able to find a living. For much of the year one such pond on the Brighton Downs — I shall not say where — is a mere muddy hollow, with, at best, a mat of soft Silverweed. Yet in the weeks after heavy rain it gradually comes to life with a quivering, darting spawn of **Fairy Shrimps**, *Chirocephalus diaphanous*, (or Sea Monkeys, to many folk). These strange crustaceans can only grow in seasonal ponds where they do not face the competition of fish or other big predators. Once, many ruts on farm tracks and similar small puddles held them, but this is now their only local site. They can survive for years of drought encased in the dry mud, but when the rains come they magically spring to life.

In modern times farmers made or restored their dew ponds with concrete linings, but these ponds can still have important wildlife. The examples on Newmarket Hill, just east of the Falmer Road, and on Balmer Down, by the South Downs Way, still hold water.

The iron pan under the Tertiary sands and clays west of Newhaven, and across the footprint of Peacehaven, led to wholly untypical areas of impacted drainage across these Downs. As a result, there were several marshy areas, natural ponds, and at least one large mere. Most of this mere has been filled in for housing development, but a rather sad fragment of it survives off Sutton Avenue, near the Peacehaven Meridian Centre.

On Newhaven's cliffs, however, one tiny spring-fed pool — heavily invaded by scrub — survives at Burrough Head, with its little outflow trickling down the cliff face. Here two species of nationally scarce water beetle have been found. Could this have been the site, too[3], of the rare flightless water beetle *Noterus crassicornis*, for which we have an historical record from a pond "on Newhaven cliff"?

On the cliffs, just east of Chene Gap, Peacehaven Heights, there is a tiny overgrown pond with a most peculiar mixed flora of native and introduced species. Spotted Orchis blooms near to **Galingale**, *Cyperus longus*, **Sea Club-rush**, *Scirpus maritimus*, **Greater Pond Sedge**, *Carex riparia*, **Greater Spearwort**, *Ranunculus lingua*, and **Yellow Flag**, *Iris pseudacorus*, whilst *Crassula helmsii* mats the open water. Odd.

Every farmstead and village had its pond. Most of them are now gone. Hangleton's famous pond on the green below lonely St Helen's church was drained in the 1950s, after housing had crept up around the green. It could easily be restored. Patcham's pond outside its ancient church is now also just a depression in the turf.

Saddlescombe pond is about the best surviving example, and Falmer's is still attractive, though far too wildfowl-infested and becoming a bit 'municipal'. The very rare **Pennyroyal**, *Mentha pulegium*, a herb of grazed pond edges, still clings on there. Both Fal*mer* and Stan*mer* were named by Saxon folk after their meres, and they may well be natural in origin. Falmer Pond is much bigger than all other Downland ponds and of an irregular shape. It sits right on the watershed between the old Wellesbourne draining down through Brighton, and the Winterbourne draining through Lewes into the Ouse.

Springs and Winterbournes

THE line of villages and manors along Underhill Lane, under the scarp slope, were each located where cold sparkling spring water gushed out of the bare chalk rock. Most of those springs still flow, despite the lowered water table of modern times. It is only those streams of the Ouse and the Adur that arise from that chalk springline that have the same character of crystal clear cold water as the more famous chalk rivers like the Hampshire Test, Itchen and Avon. Our two local rivers are muddied in their final slow glide through the Downs to the sea by their higher sources on the clays, alluvium and loams of the Weald.

The Winterbourne as it flows into Lewes, then across the Railway Lands Nature Reserve to the Ouse, reminds one of those clear Hampshire trout streams. So does the stream below the spring at Poynings, as it arises in the deep gill between Newtimber Hill and the Devil's Dyke. Willow, Ash, Maple and Hazel bow down towards it from the gill sides above a spring-time cover of Bluebells, **Sanicle**, *Sanicula europaea*, **Dutchman's Clock**, *Adoxa moschatellina*, and Celandine. **Blackcap, Chiffchaff** and **Willow Warbler** make their music at dawn and dusk, and big plates of **Dryad's Saddle Bracket**, *Polyporus squamosus* — creamy white in the green shade — decorate old Hazel stools.

At Edburton and Fulking, too, clear chalk springs arise amongst green shade at the scarp foot. At both those springs a most exciting find was made recently. Larvae of the very rare and beautiful **Hill Soldier Fly**, *Oxycera pardalina*, were discovered living there. This little beast has not before been found in Sussex, and is usually found in the milder and wetter west and the north. It is one of those 'Atlantic' species, which cling on as relics of that time (5-7000 years ago) when such a climate was dominant across the whole of Britain. Those streams were once sheep washes, and were often ponded for watermills. Such mills existed till modern times at Poynings (where the pond — a Victorian attraction — has been restored in recent decades) Clayton, Keymer and Plumpton.

The spring water which flows into the deep Pellbrook Cut, below Offham Chalkpit, is cold and clear, though floating vegetation can camouflage it in summer. I tried to wade the stream one summer, thinking to take a short cut back to the upper road, after dipping the Brooks for beetles and leeches. I made the rest of the hike back dripping and draped from shirt downwards in bits of duckweed and starwort. Much of the Lewes Brooks, especially in their upper reaches near to Lewes, have that clear, calcareous character, at its best on Spring Barn Farm towards the Celery Stream.

The Bevern Stream, whose multiple fingered streams arise in the chalk between Westmeston and Plumpton still has both **Brown Trout** and migratory **Sea Trout**.

Where the chalk meets the coastal plain and the two river valleys, small winterbournes would once have run. A chalk stream ran through Southwick Green till just in living memory. It was made into a covered drain, as was the big Brighton Wellesbourne, by the Council.

A small winterbourne may once have influenced the siting of Benfield Manor, Hangleton. The site of the Saxon manor and the present Benfield Barn are up on the shallow valley side, above what would once have been the wet dean bottom. Neighbouring Greenleas Park, just south of Hangleton Manor was the old Great Meadow of the parish, and meadows were features of streams and riversides. We can speculate that by the 1540s, when Hangleton Manor was built, the winterbourne had stopped flowing, for Bellingham built his manor house right on its old course.

Some small wet inlets into the chalk hills do survive, like Old Erringham Combe, just north of the Farm, or those at Halcombe, south of Dean's Farm Piddinghoe, or The Wish, south of Piddinghoe.

Pumping Stations and Reservoirs

F R O M Victorian times water pumping stations have dotted the urban fringe and the open Downs. Their bylaws have affected patterns of built development (forbidding development over the heading tunnels drawing in deep water) and the water companies' vigorous land purchases have formed the core of the Brighton Council Downland estate. Now all the ornamented old pumping houses have gone except for the Goldstone works, now the Engineerium, though the rather grim superintendents' houses often survive, as at Waterhall, Mile Oak and, picturesquely, deep in Coombe Bottom, below Keymer Post.

The reservoirs dotted over the hilltops have a more lasting value for wildlife. Often important chalk grassland has developed on their turfed sides and tops, and, on the Brighton Downs, they hold superb Early Spider Orchis and Green Winged Orchis swarms, important lichen heath and good Waxcap and Pink Gill assemblages. They might be small, but they're still important.

Chalk Pits

WE'VE always dug pits in the chalk.
Ancient people mined for flint, mostly
to the west of the Adur, and many of
our hilltop clay-with-flints deposits have
shallow pits dotting them where folk have
dug, right through into Victorian times.
Wolstonbury Camp is pocked with the
pits of (probably Victorian) flint diggers,
as is Southwick Hill at its southern end.
On the spur north of Keymer Post there
are extensive surface diggings, too, and
Red Hill, above Sheepcote, and High Hill
also have such flint pits. At Bollens Bush,
near Newhaven, the diggers would have
been interested in the sandy gravel of the
Tertiary Deposits.

Though every Downland common and
manor would have had a small chalk pit, it
was only from Tudor times onwards that
large-scale chalk extraction really took
off, with the increasing use of masonry in
building and therefore the need for lime
putty mortar.[4]

There are only two working chalk pits
left on the Brighton Downs now, one on
the slopes of Wolstonbury overlooking
the London Road, and one at Golding
Barn, below Beeding Hill.[5] They're largely
working around and below the join
between the Upper, or White Chalk and
Lower, or Grey Chalk. Till recently, the
huge Blue Circle Pit on the River Adur at
Beeding was worked, but that awesome
moonscape is, at present, magnificently
derelict. The Offham Chalk Pit also worked
on a modern scale, lowering chalk down
a still-existing twin tunnel ramp under the
road to barges below. Its infrastructure was
constructed two centuries ago, around
1805-9. The Meeching Quarry, which
was worked to make Artex, like the still-
working Tarring Neville Pit on the other
side of the Ouse, now houses the company
headquarters.

It's along the escarpments facing the
Weald and the river valleys that the
majority of our chalk pits are situated.

Most of them are small, and sometimes it's
difficult to tell them from very steep bits
of natural slope. They are always delightful
places to go, and the grassed-up ones
are great places to take the kids, because
there's loads of fun to be had scrambling
about and making camps and feeling just
a tiny bit unsafe (but not really). Often the
level turf on top of the spoil heaps has old
fire sites left on it, so clearly many people
already love them.

The importance of these old quarries
for Downland wildlife is immense. Because
of their steepness and skeletal soils they
often retain a fine short Sheep's-fescue
turf, with much bare soil and rock. The
rare Grayling butterfly needs exactly this
habitat, and survived till very recently in
Offham and Saddlescombe chalkpits. The
tiny rare Musk Orchis and Frog Orchis also
both like such short quarry swards. Old
grassland fungi like Persistent, Blackening
and Chalkland Waxcaps, and Earthtongues,
enjoy grassy quarrysides, and when the
spoil heaps have become bushy and
nettley, they become good places to search
for spring Morel fungi.

The main conservation importance of
such old quarries may well be for their tiny
chalkland mosses, lichens and liverworts,
however, which are wholly dependent
on such early successional stages, and
love these damper, shadier locations on
the north facing scarp. Five of the seven

Quarries and Pits

— The scarp slope is dotted with small common and farm pits.

— Pits reached an industrial scale in Victorian times, as at Offham, and Beeding Cement Works.

— Only two commercial pits are still being worked: at Golding Barn and Wolstonbury, though the Penfold Pit at Mile Oak was recently worked, and small pits are occasionally used for local needs.

Quarries and Pits

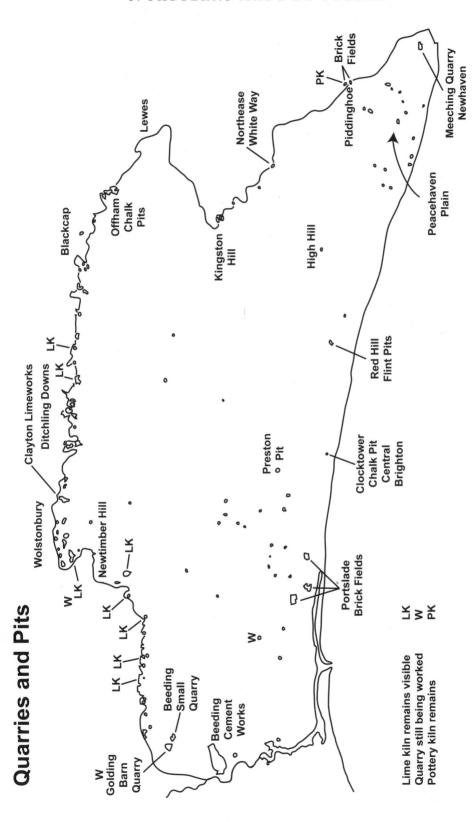

Brick Fields

PK

Piddinghoe

Meeching Quarry
Newhaven

Peacehaven Plain

Northease
White Way

Lewes

High Hill

Kingston Hill

Offham
Chalk Pits

Red Hill
Flint Pits

Blackcap

LK
LK

Ditchling Downs

Clayton Limeworks

Clocktower
Chalk Pit
Central
Brighton

Preston
o Pit

Wolstonbury

Newtimber Hill

LK

W
LK

LK LK

LK LK

W

Portslade
Brick Fields

W

Beeding
Small
Quarry

Beeding
Cement
Works

W
Golding
Barn
Quarry

LK   Lime kiln remains visible
W   Quarry still being worked
PK   Pottery kiln remains

Reproduced from 1873 and 1940 Ordnance Survey maps bases with the kind permission of the Ordnance Survey.

The restored Victorian lime kiln at the base of Perching bostal.

Chalk pits are also great places for fossilling. Though our pits on the White Chalk of the Brighton Downs are not as easy to work as the Grey Chalk it is easy to find Inoceramid seashells, and persistence will bring you many other finds, too, such as tiny, perfectly preserved brachiopod shells. The Offham Pits were known as good hunting ground for the teeth and palates of fossil fish and for the free-swimming *Marsupites* Sea Lily (of Black Rock and Friars Bay fame). Clayton Limeworks at the base of Clayton Hill turned up excellent fossils. Many of the Booth Museum's Willett Collection fossils came from there. The extensive pits are now draped in woodland and exposures of bare chalk are rare, but on a recent visit I found a cluster of good Inoceramid shells.

best chalk grassland sites Francis Rose[6] surveyed on the Brighton Downs in the early '90s for mosses and lichen contained core chalk pit habitats. They are difficult plants for people to scale down enough to appreciate, but they are truly beautiful. Lichen are often bizarre in form and colour, like aliens from outer space.

The huge Blue Circle Beeding Quarry often has **Raven** and **Peregrine**, and a local traveller who was acting as an unofficial security guard there told me that he had had excellent views of a 'big cat' at the far end of the quarry; a sighting which has been confirmed by other observers.

Old limekilns, into which the quarried chalk was tipped for burning, can still be found at the base of these old deserted scarp foot quarries. Saddlescombe, the Devil's Dyke, and one of the Fulking chalk pits still have such kilns, and they are marked on the 1873 first edition O/S maps as occurring at many of the escarpment chalk quarries between Wolstonbury and Plumpton.

The dip slope of the Downs had no big pits, but the plateau is dotted with small pits, which would have been dug for agricultural and building lime, often for just the local farm. Many of these have now been lost within Brighton's built-up area, but with the help of old maps and a good eye many of them can still be detected. The old Knoll chalk pit, in the angle between Hangleton Road and Old Shoreham Road, was still in existence till recent decades, and now has sheltered housing built within it. During the 1960s an oil well worked by a donkey pump was located there. There was another long-used chalk pit on the Dyke Road between the Clock Tower and upper North Street on the west side. Despite the modern buildings the indentation in the hillside can still be made out. The Preston Pit, just under the railway bridge west of Preston Manor, has now been lost to the widened Millers Road, but a small exposure of white chalk still peeks out from the draping ivy and other undergrowth near the junction with The Drove. The pit was well known in Mantell's time for its fossil fish remains.

Footnotes

1 *The Archaeology of Sussex* — E. Cecil Curwen (Methuen & Co. 1937), page 161.
2 *Antiquity* ix — G.A. Holleyman (1935), pp. 443-54. Quoted in *Ibid.*, page 299.
3 *Castle Hill, Newhaven Entomological Survey Report No. I* — Peter Hodge (2000), page 4.
4 Article by Don Cox, page 110 in *An Historical Atlas of Sussex,* edited by Kim Leslie and Brian Short (Phillimore, 1999)
5 Plus a very small one on the Mile Oak Road run by Penfolds.
6 *Report on the Bryophytes and Lichens in Chalk Grassland in West Sussex* — Dr Francis Rose (1993) for West Sussex County Council and the Sussex Downs Conservation Board.

BUILDINGS ON THE
DOWNS

THE places where we can feel deep time, and sense our direct connection with nature and with other peoples now long-gone, are profoundly attractive. Several sorts of places give me those strong feelings. Veteran trees, rejuvenated by centuries of pollarding, always bring that sense of wonder and kinship. So, too, do prehistoric barrows, and doubly so, for they are mostly to be found on hilltops and ridges where the vastness of sky, vale and sea draw especially close.

And ancient buildings do that too, and particularly our oldest, simplest medieval churches. I have tested the patience of many friends over the decades, when, walking or cycling from village to village, I have insisted on turning the great black church door rings and pushing open the ancient doors to walk into musty, dark interiors. For all my adult life I have felt the paradox in this, because for all that time I have been an atheist. In fact, it was whilst visiting a village church that I first gained the confidence to call myself one. Whilst others must have come to believe in their religion in such places, I paced the nave and looked up at the cool stone, and surprised myself with the thought that... "yes, there is no god, but the world is just as full of wonder — and so is this

lovely place". So don't walk past our 'little lost Down churches'. Their lichen-covered stones, their rafters, worn pews and hummocked grave-yards are full of truths to be seen and stories to be told.

Though the surviving buildings of the old Downs only very rarely approach a millennium in age, the settlement patterns within which they lie are consistently older. The necklace of spring-line villages along the base of the northern escarpment go back at least to early Saxon times and probably much further. The same is probably true for most of the coastal villages. Many of them will have been enlivened by the migration of homesteads from off the high Downs in the 'mid-Saxon shift', when the Downs were left largely bare of farmers for the first time in several thousand years. Thus, the people of early Kingston Buci may have descended from those who deserted the Romano-British village on the hill by Thundersbarrow.

The legacy of old buildings that the farming communities have left are built mainly in the materials that were at hand: flint, chalk rock, and a lime-sand-and-gravel mortar, which together were used for 'bungaroosh' walling, timber and wood and plaster. Most roofing would have been of thatch, using furze and turf for poorer buildings, as well as reed and straw.

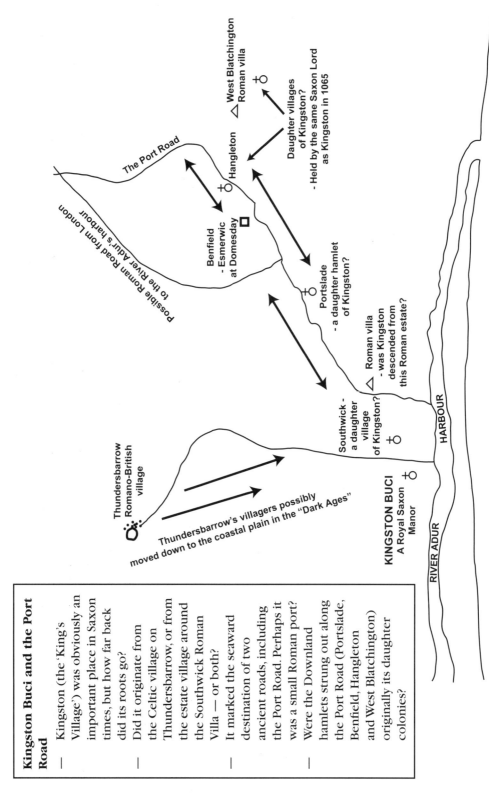

Kingston Buci and the Port Road

- Kingston (the 'King's Village') was obviously an important place in Saxon times, but how far back did its roots go? Did it originate from the Celtic village on Thundersbarrow, or from the estate village around the Southwick Roman Villa — or both?

- It marked the seaward destination of two ancient roads, including the Port Road. Perhaps it was a small Roman port? Were the Downland hamlets strung out along the Port Road (Portslade, Benfield, Hangleton and West Blatchington) originally its daughter colonies?

West Blatchington Roman villa

Hangleton

Daughter villages of Kingston?
- Held by the same Saxon Lord as Kingston in 1065

The Port Road

Benfield
- Esmerwic at Domesday

Portslade
- a daughter hamlet of Kingston?

Possible Roman Road from London to the River Adur's harbour

Thundersbarrow Romano-British village

Roman villa
- was Kingston descended from this Roman estate?

Southwick -
a daughter village of Kingston?

Thundersbarrow's villagers possibly moved down to the coastal plain in the "Dark Ages"

KINGSTON BUCI
A Royal Saxon Manor

RIVER ADUR

HARBOUR

Court Farm Falmer's magnificent thatched barn under snow. April '08.

From medieval times onwards, thatch would have gradually been replaced by tile, and Horsham slabs on the better buildings. Only with the coming of trains, then motors, did more distantly sourced building materials — slate and brick and a far greater range of stone — come to be used.

Those buildings that survive best are the buildings of the ruling class or the well-off intermediate classes. Only very occasionally do the small homes of the poor survive. The deserted village of Hangleton was excavated in the 1950s and the discoveries made were used to reconstruct a medieval single storey cottage at the Weald and Downland Museum at Singleton. It's worth a visit.

Many old villages of the Brighton Downs are still dominated by **flint building** — like Stanmer, old Patcham, Saddlescombe, old Ovingdean and Rottingdean, Iford, Rodmell and Piddinghoe. And many, like New Shoreham, Lewes, and Brighton up to early Victorian times, have far more flint buildings than seems at first sight, for modern aspirations to status dictated

the covering of flint walls with stucco, and wooden walls with brick. Sometimes, though, flint was used as a material of high prestige right into modern times, with regular knapped flint working almost to a mosaicist's standard, as in the Old House, 199 Preston Road, opposite Preston Manor, or parts of the re-built Falmer church, or at the superb Newtimber Place.

The Brighton Downs are not an area where **thatch** has survived more than very occasionally, but where it does it can be spectacular. Undoubtedly the finest thatched building is the great barn at Court Farm, Falmer, a gigantic building, and one of the best surviving vernacular buildings around Brighton. Old Shoreham's little group of old thatched cottages is memorable, too.

Timber domestic building, also survives only rarely, though not as rarely as the outward appearance of buildings display. The old cottage at the rear of Moulsecoomb Place may be the oldest secular building within Brighton's boundaries, dating probably from Chaucer's time. There are fine examples in

Fulking and Clayton, Pyecombe Street, and other villages, and Lewes.

Grand timber roofs, though, are very common, and the most magnificent of them are in our old barns. Many of them plainly out-class the roofs of our medieval churches.

Here is my personal list of the finest buildings of the Brighton Downs, restricted to no more than six in each category.

Prehistory

- **The Devil's Dyke.** TQ 260 110. A fine Iron Age hillfort.
- **Whitehawk Hill's Neolithic Causewayed Camp,** TQ 330 048, whose upstanding banks have survived for 5000 years and are one of only ten well-preserved examples of that class of monument in Britain.
- **Hollingbury Castle,** TQ 321 079. A hillfort, barrows and house sites of Bronze and Iron Age date.
- **Plumpton Plain Bronze Age village.** TQ 358 121. Site preserved in aspic over several millennia.
- **The 'flying saucer' barrow at Landport Fork, Lewes,** TQ 403 110. A fine Bronze Age barrow. One of a cluster of three.
- **The Money Burgh.** TQ 424 036. Neolithic long barrow guarding a fording place of the Ouse.

Castles

- **Lewes Castle.** Need I say?
- **Edburton motte and bailey.** TQ 238 110. Norman. Humps under the turf. In origin probably a prehistoric hillfort and barrows.

Medieval Churches

- **Old Shoreham.** Saxon and Norman. Baronial and fine.
- **Kingston Buci.** Humble and grand, cluttered and yet clear. Full of the accretions of the centuries.
- **Hangleton.** A Saxo-Norman church of shepherds and peasants. Lovely herring-bone flintwork.

- **Poynings.** Baronial, but the feeling is of a mosque: a space of peace — not feudal wars.
- **Clayton.** Saxo-Norman. The finest of the medieval frescoed churches of the Brighton Downs.
- **Southease.** Pure loveliness. In its time a church of the sea, of the brooklands and of the Downs.

Barns

- **Kingston Buci Manor Farm.** A great russet expanse of roof.
- **Patcham Court Farm.** Huge and bendy, like a whale's back
- **Falmer, Court Farm.** A thatched masterpiece. Fourteen embayments!
- **Stanmer Home Farm.** Warm sun on wooden walls.
- **Northease Farm.** TQ 411 065. A giant of russet tiles and flint.
- **Old Hoddern Farm, Piddinghoe.** TQ 422 022. Another russet roofed whale of a building.

Cottages

- **Fulking.** The posher end of the cottage spectrum.
- **Old Portslade village.** Flint, flint, flint.
- **Old Patcham village.** Ditto. One cottage 15th century.
- **Iford.** Nice scatter of old places.
- **Rodmell.** Flint, brick and timber.
- **Piddinghoe.** More flint.

Manor Houses

- **Old Erringham Farm.** TQ 205 077. Lovely old flint hilltop house, with a medieval chapel outside.
- **Hangleton Manor.** TQ 261 069. Tudor and older. Warm mullions and old flint. Best pre-modern house in Brighton.
- **Newtimber Place.** TQ 268 137. Truly superb Queen Anne moated masterpiece of flint.

Old Erringham Manor House — Flint, dressed stone, Horsham slabs, tile and brick.

- **Danny.** TQ 284 149. First class Elizabethan E-shaped warm brick mansion.
- **Plumpton Place.** TQ 360 134. Moated bourgeois Shangri-la. Tudor, Stuart and Lutyens.
- **Swanborough Grange.** TQ 400 078. An outstanding medieval survival.

Windmills

- **West Blatchington Mill.** TQ 278 068. Painted by Constable.
- **Patcham Mill.** TQ 291 084. Landmark.
- **Jack and Jill, Clayton.** TQ 303 134. First sight of home for weary commuters.
- **Rottingdean, Beacon Hill.** TQ 365 024. Landmark.

Modern Buildings

- **Brighton and Hove Golf Course Clubhouse.** TQ 269 091. 120 years old and still temporary.

- **Devil's Dyke Farm.** TQ 260 102. Built circa 1950. The last generation of traditional farm buildings.
- **The Chattri.** TQ 304 110. Monument to Indian soldiers who had died at the Brighton Pavilion military hospital in World War One. It is at the end of a 5000 year funerary tradition.

Best Assemblages

- **Saddlescombe.** Lovely in every way. Preserved in aspic.
- **Stanmer.** Barns, houses, church and teas!
- **Ashcombe.** TQ 386 085. Lovely setting.
- **Rodmell.** Large variety of cottages.
- **Southease.** Village green, church, brooks and hills.
- **Telscombe.** Nestling in the crook of the Downs.

DOWNLAND
CONNECTIONS

I F you stand on Ditchling Beacon or Streat Hill and look north across the vastness of Wealden woods and fields you will be looking at country which the medieval peasants of Stanmer and Falmer knew almost as well as they knew the fields around their villages. It was not a wilderness to them. Some of them trudged backwards and forwards up the Wealden roads right as far as the Surrey border several times a year.

If you walk the South Downs Way along Iford Hill and down through Southease, you will look across the fertile cornfields and pastures of the Brooks and the tiny scarp foot villages. The villages below you, though, were once fishing ports, landing herring by the boat load. When the sea retreated their lush brookland meadows provided hay for all the dry settlements of the higher Downs.

The medieval farming economy of the Downland villages could be self-sufficient for some of its needs. It could not meet all them. The Brighton Downs had long been largely stripped of its timber. The Downland commons could not give best nourishment to fatten up spring lambs, pigs and cattle, or to feed them through the winter. Salt and fish had to be found elsewhere, as did iron, glass and many other items. Even honey — that valuable forest product — was thought important enough to figure in the Domesday taxation assessment, where Beeding was obliged to yield up two 'sesters' of honey from its distant Wealden forest of St Leonards.

The resources of the wooded Weald, the lush meadows of the Ouse and Adur and their tributary streams, and the sea, were intimately connected to the Downland communities from the very earliest times. At first the linked communities of the Downs and the Weald would have 'inter-commoned' the woods, heaths and grasslands. No one settlement would have had exclusive rights to the uninhabited tracts between them and their neighbours. But as South Saxon society stabilized the wood pastures and meadows would have been parcelled out to individual communities under the new manorial lords.

Swine Pastures and Drovers Roads

S T A N M E R parish was carved out of the pre-existing community of Falmer at some time between 760 and 771 AD by the King of Sussex and given to the church for the building and upkeep of a minster church. This was less than a century after the return of Christianity to Sussex. Great swathes of Wealden lands were granted to Stanmer in a line due north, all the way to

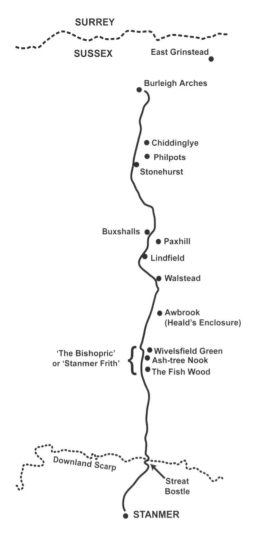

Stanmer's Swine Pastures

— Stanmer commanded a huge territory in medieval times.

— In 765 AD the King of Sussex, Aldwulf, carved out a great chunk of Down and Weald to fund a minster, or monastery.

— Probably the peasants were already working this land unit.

— Later the land passed to the College of South Malling, Lewes, which was held by the Archbishop of Canterbury.

— Hence the names 'Burleigh Arches' and 'The Bishopric'.

— Over the centuries the Wealden peasants wrested power from the Stanmer peasants to leave Stanmer a much-reduced place.

Ardingly village and past Wakehurst Place, Philpots and Chiddinglye. Don't stop. Keep walking north again up the high ridge to Turner's Hill and down into the wooded Burleigh valley beyond, under the Crawley Down ridge. That's a 16.5 mile stretch as the crow flies. Much longer the way those herder's walked, with all the chivvying and chasing they'd have had to do to keep the pigs on course. You have been walking on, or close to, medieval Stanmer village land the whole way.

How many of us modern softies could do that walk even once nowadays? We'd have sore feet and aching bones enough to need a weekend's rest! Yet imagine doing that walk on a muddy, stony track, a quagmire if the rain caught you, guiding a grumpy herd of pigs, all with tuskers that would make a nasty mess of you if they lost their temper. All you've got is your fellow swineherds, young and old, and your dogs to keep your precious porkers 'on track'. Only mud-floored huts for shelter on the way, and carrying all the supplies you need for the weeks of woodland herding ahead.

the wilds of Worth Forest on the Surrey border.

Take a trip northwards from Stanmer village, up the track along the side of Bow Hill and to the crest of Streat Hill. Much of what you see due north to the far distance was Stanmer ground. The zig-zagging bostal track down Streat Hill makes deep, steep sided cuttings. Herds of swine, cattle and sheep would have cut down through this chalk for centuries.

Take the straight lane north to Wivelsfield Green, then north again to Walstead, Lindfield, Paxhill and Buxshalls, keeping on the east side of Haywards Heath. Keep walking northwards through

Most paths on the Brighton Downs track northwards from the coastal plain, except to the east of Brighton, behind the cliffs. Relatively few paths cross from east to west. Beyond the Downs these paths continue northwards and can be traced right up to the edge of the old Saxon Sussex kings' royal forests of St Leonards and Worth. They have at least 1500 years of use, back to early Saxon times, and probably much more — way back to Iron Age times, before the Romans, and beyond.

Tracking northwards up Kingston Lane from the twin manors of Kingston Buci and Southwick the swineherds would have crossed Thundersbarrow, up over the hump of Tottington Mount, down the bostal, through Tottington Woods, across Oreham Common, past the east side of Henfield and across the infant River Adur to Shermanbury. If they were headed for their other outlier at Woodmancote they'd have gone slightly to the east, cutting down the deep bostal on the side of Southwick Tenantry Down (just west of Mile Oak Farm), up Summersdean, over Edburton Hill and down the winding bostal to Truleigh Manor Farm. Then they'd have tracked north past over Truleigh Sands, across Horn Lane (the old Roman road) to Woodmancote.

All along the scarp you can be sure that the bostals that are carved the deepest into the chalk — as deep as railway cuttings sometimes — are partly the work of those early trudging herds on their seasonal drives to and from the Wealden woods, for autumn acorns, beech mast and fungi, or for spring sweet browse of lime, elm and other young shoots, or meadow pastures.

The steep bostal cuttings on Fulking Hill mark the paths of the Portslade and Southwick herders, going northwards towards Bolney. The long cleft down the spine of the spur north of Keymer Post, and the Burnhouse Bostal to the east, mark the route of the herders and cultivators from Withdean manor as they made their way east of Keymer, via the present Oldlands Mill, up to their outlying meadows and woods at Ote Hall, Lunces, and Hurst, just south of the old Lunatic Asylum at Haywards Heath. The peasants of Bevendean, Falmer and Balmer would have carved the deep bostal cuttings down Plumpton Hill and Blackcap on route to their wood pastures way north at East Grinstead, Standen, (by the Weir Wood reservoir) and Horsted Keynes.

Meadows

ONLY to the east of Brighton is the pattern of north/south Downland pathways altered. Here the pattern of pathways tracks *north-easterly*, from the scattered farms and villages, like Rottingdean and Telscombe, across the scarp and down to the scarp foot villages of the River Ouse brooklands.

One reason for this altered trackway pattern was the presence of the extensive meadowlands down on the watery eastern flood plain.

Meadow was generally found only in small quantities in medieval England and it was the most valuable kind of agricultural real estate there was. Meadow was lush grassland, often near waterside, which was enclosed for a late spring or summer hay crop, and then opened for grazing.

Meadow hay was vital for feeding oxen, and the Downs, like the rest of the medieval countryside, were heavily dependant upon oxen for ploughing and hauling. Spring lambs, too, could get an early bite on those brook pastures, before the Downland grass recovered from winter.

Only two thirds of the manors on the dry Brighton Downs recorded meadow present in the Domesday Survey of 1086 (against about 80% of English settlements overall). Many Downland manors, too, had meadow only in very small quantities. Brighton had only seven acres, probably down on the damp grassland of The Level. Pangdean (which included Pyecombe) had

Saxon Swine Pasture Drove Roads

Hailsham

Piddinghoe

Waldron

Rodmell

Northease

Iford

St John sub Castro
Lewes

Hamsey

Barcombe

Ashdown Forest

Balneath

Horstead Keynes

East Grinstead

Balmer

Falmer

West Hoathly

Wivelsfield

Bevendean

East Grinstead

Wivelsfield

Stanmer

Patcham

Clayton

Withdean

Preston (with Hove)

Pangdean

Wivelsfield

Hangleton

Cuckfield

Portslade

Cuckfield

Southwick

Woodmancote

Kingston Buci

Shermanbury

St Leonards Forest

Beeding

- 'Swine pastures' were woodland where the pigs were herded to eat the 'mast': acorns, beech nuts, wild service berries, crab apples, fungi, and so on.
- Downland manors held swine pastures across the Wealden forests as far as the Surrey border.
- The drove roads crossed the plateau, down the scarp bostals, and then struck out across the Weald.

Reproduced from 1940 Ordnance Survey map bases with the kind permission of the Ordnance Survey.

only one acre. Kingston Buci, despite being on the coastal plain, only recorded four acres.

The scarp foot villages of the River Ouse brooklands, in contrast, record very large acreages. Iford had 208 acres, Hamsey 200 acres, Rodmell 140 acres and Southease 130 acres in Domesday. For many centuries these brooklands were managed in common, like the Tenantry Downs, only being broken up into private holdings from the 17th century onwards.

Right down to enclosure in 1845 the tenants of the dry village of Telscombe had the right of 'cut-and-away' — taking a hay crop — on the commonable brooklands of their twin parish of Southease. The big farm of Challoners, in Rottingdean, too, had cut-and-away rights over part of Southease's meadow.

To this day, there is a lonely meadow out on the brooklands south of Lewes called 'Bormer Brook'. It's a lovely place, haunted by Snipe and Reed Bunting, and with brooks full of Frogbit, Sticklebacks, Eels and water beetles. This must have been the detached meadow of the manor of Balmer, three and a quarter miles to the west, though it has long lost that usage.

The other group of manors that had a large Domesday meadow resource were those of the Saxon royal town of Ditchling, with the villages of Clayton, Keymer and Withdean, which shared access to its huge resource of Wealden territory. (Stanmer and Falmer would have shared in that wealth in earlier Saxon times, but by Domesday their Wealden 'empires' had largely collapsed).

Salt Houses

O u r Downs have the sea to the south and rivers to the east and west. In early medieval times these rivers were salty estuaries, with ocean going trading vessels and fishing craft plying up them to St Cuthman's harbour by Steyning church, and to Lewes.

The medieval Adur was far narrower than the Ouse's wide valley and mostly given over to salt marshes. It never became as important for brookland pasturage. Its 'saltings' though, had there own economic importance for Downland. All the way up the River Adur from Kingston Buci to Wappingthorn (half way between Bramber and Henfield) the saltings bore crowded clusters of 'salterns', great mounds of sandy waste from the salt extraction industry, which belonged to each riverside community. This was a great wealth producer. Monastic houses like Boxgrove, Sele Priory at Beeding, or Cokeham Hospital at Sompting held 'salt houses', as did Wealden manors like Wiston and Washington.

The scale of the industry is shown by the fact that in the decades around 1300 AD, seventy 'saltcotes' were destroyed by the sea in late medieval floodings. It was an old industry, too, for archaeologists have found 'briquetage' — the broken up remains of baked salt cooking clay ovens and containers — up on Mill Hill, Shoreham, with associated pottery of middle Iron Age date. At its height it must have presented a semi-industrial scene, with smoke rising from the numerous salt houses where the briny liquor was boiled down. The saltings would have been busy with workers raking and scraping up the tidal sand, dragging it on sledges across to the filter troughs and stoking the fires of the boiling houses.

Kingston Buci was assessed for 9 salt houses and had to find 10 'ambers' of salt for tax in the time of Domesday. Erringham had one or two salt cotes, too, and Beeding had many, but the majority were on the other side of the river at Lancing, Applesham, Coombes and Annington.

The River Ouse, by contrast, had only two clusters of salt houses, at Rodmell and Beddingham, both very prosperous manors, though further up, on the Glynde Reach levels, there were lots. It is possible that Northease and Southease take their names from the Rodmell salt industry,

A World Away — The Domesday Book villages, 1086 AD.

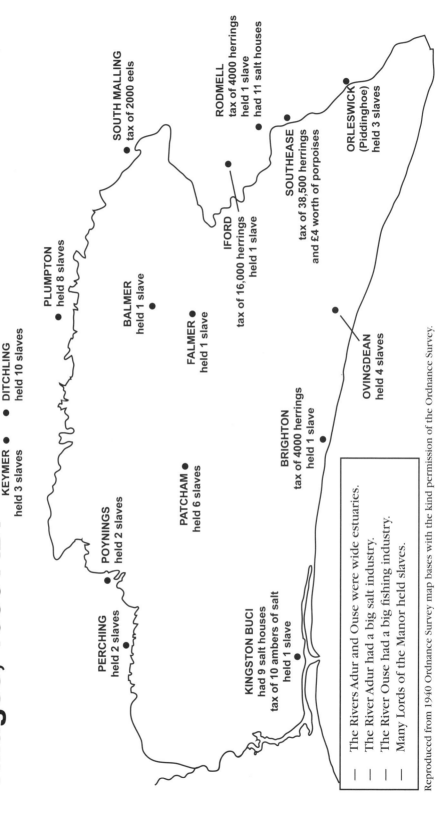

KEYMER ●
held 3 slaves

● DITCHLING
held 10 slaves

SOUTH MALLING ●
tax of 2000 eels

RODMELL ●
tax of 4000 herrings
held 1 slave ● had 11 salt houses

ORLESWICK ●
(Piddinghoe)
held 3 slaves

SOUTHEASE ●
tax of 38,500 herrings
and £4 worth of porpoises

IFORD ●
tax of 16,000 herrings
held 1 slave

PLUMPTON ●
held 8 slaves

BALMER ●
held 1 slave

FALMER ●
held 1 slave

OVINGDEAN ●
held 4 slaves

BRIGHTON ●
tax of 4000 herrings
held 1 slave

PATCHAM ●
held 6 slaves

POYNINGS ●
held 2 slaves

PERCHING ●
held 2 slaves

KINGSTON BUCI ●
had 9 salt houses
tax of 10 ambers of salt
held 1 slave

— The Rivers Adur and Ouse were wide estuaries.
— The River Adur had a big salt industry.
— The River Ouse had a big fishing industry.
— Many Lords of the Manor held slaves.

Reproduced from 1940 Ordnance Survey map bases with the kind permission of the Ordnance Survey.

for the 'ease' bit of their names means brushwood or underwood, and could have indicated a small coppice industry provisioning the salt rendering ovens.

Now little remains of the saltern mounds, for the big farmers ploughed them out in the 1960s and only the clusters north and south of Bramber are still there to see. They are there, too, at New Monks Farm, Lancing, though those salterns have been buried under builders' rubble for the new golf course development there.

Herring and Porpoise

THE wide estuary of the Ouse gave the under-Down settlements there a dual character in medieval times as fishing villages as much as farming communities. Indeed, two of these villages still have this maritime character, for the tidal river still laps below Piddinghoe's church, and old Meeching's Norman church still sits up above the busy riverside, though now long surrounded by the modern riverside town of Newhaven.

Iford, Rodmell, and Southease had major taxation assessments in fish in the Domesday survey. South Malling, too, was assessed for 2000 eels. Iford was assessed for 16,000 herring, Rodmell for 4000, and Southease for a massive 38,500 herring

and four pounds worth of porpoise — a fortune in modern money! Clearly, Southease was a very important fishing port and the first to be reached as you sailed inland from the sea. Newhaven didn't exist. Neither did Seaford, yet, and even Meeching and Piddinghoe may not yet have existed, though they may have been present under different names. By comparison the only other local community assessed for its fishing fleet was Brighton, which paid tax of a mere 4000 herrings.

Though the fishing industry waned with the silting up of the river and the draining of the marshes to form brookland meadow, the memory of this maritime past lingered. Periodic flooding of the Brooks still occurs, and it is little over a century since winter flooding meant that a boatman could scull up to the ancient hard of Rodmell, just as his forebears had done a thousand years before. Right up till 1623 the steward of Southease manor recorded that the tenants were customarily given six good herrings at Lent (four if they came across the river from the manorial outlier of Heighton), as if herrings were still easily obtained in a village now stranded four miles from the sea!

BRIGHTON — A DOWNLAND CITY

BRIGHTON doesn't just sit on the coastal plain at the edge of the Downs, like Eastbourne or most of Worthing. Its suburbs, roads and industrial estates actually sit upon the Downland hills. There is huge interpenetration of views between town and Downs.

In that respect Brighton is more like Lewes or Arundel. It is a *Downland City*.

Many views from the City encompass the Downs. The view from Race Hill across Brighton and the Bay of Sussex is as spectacular as Amalfi or some other Italian hill town.

Many views from Downland encompass the City. The views from the high Downland at the Devils Dyke are painfully interrupted by the distant high rise blocks of Brighton's sea side and the sprawl of Patcham's suburbs.

Every big thing that's built in Brighton affects remote Downland.

And the development of Brighton has sprung from the most peculiar mix of business selfishness and far-sighted social planning. Brighton both painfully intrudes upon Downland and — sometimes — happily integrates with it.

'The Deans' and 'The Octopus'

BRIGHTON'S 19th century expansion served the rich and the pleasure seekers.

Whilst big property speculators laid out the Regency squares and terraces of the seaside, smaller operators built the densely packed working class houses and lodgings across the open fields of Brighton and the coastal plain of Hove. Those slums of Carlton Hill and Conway Street housed the service workers needed by the seafront's rich visitors and retirees.

Early Council Housing: Sensitive Social Planning in 'The Deans'

WHEN the labour movement finally gained the strength to contest for government after the First World War, one of the first major reform successes was the unleashing of a giant programme of council house construction. This movement burst the bounds of the old medieval parishes of Brighton and Hove in a dramatic way. The Council's Moulsecoomb estate and Bevendean were built in the 1920s and '30s on old Patcham parish land and completed from the 1930s to the '50s on old Falmer parish land. The Queen's Park estate up on the slopes of Whitehawk Hill around Pankhurst Avenue was built in the 1920s, and the Whitehawk estate, on old Ovingdean parish land, was built from 1930, to be joined by the Manor Farm estate from 1935 onwards. In Hove the Knoll estate was built on the Downs lower slope down to Old Shoreham Road.

The early phases of construction were strongly influenced by the idealism of the Garden City movement, and The Avenue in Bevendean looks like nothing so much as the eighteenth century Dorset model village of Milton Abbas, tucked, as Milton is, into a fold of the chalk Downs. The only substantial difference is that Milton's model semi-detached cottages are thatched! Most of these early Downland estates of the council housing movement have substantial gardens, generous public greens, and proximity to large Downland allotment sites.

Much of this phase of council house building was carefully adapted to fit within the valley bottom contours of Brighton's Downs and thus to minimise the landscape damage to wider Downland. The deepest part of these **'deans'** became housing and the hilltops remained green. Remarkably, too, the boundaries between the new valley bottom housing land and the higher, open slopes were often roughly the same as the medieval boundaries between the valley bottom arable lands and the high sheep walks.

Thus, even now, despite the additional construction of Coldean on ex-Stanmer estate land from 1950 onwards, the high dome of Hollingbury Hill still stands completely above the council estates filling the valleys on its eastern and north eastern sides, when viewed from the remote Downs of Balmer and beyond, or even closer by on Falmer Hill. The Hill still feels as much part of the wild open Downs as it has for aeons of time. That was good planning!

'The Octopus': The Housing Market Goes Haywire

As cheap motorized transport and rail electrification took off in the 1920s and as land prices bottomed in the deep farming depression, house building exploded across the countryside. London doubled its immense size in twenty years.

Working families desperately wanted to make their home amongst green fields. Speculators' 'ribbon development' stretched out along every arterial road, as along great stretches of the Old Shoreham Road from Sackville Road to Shoreham. Large housing projects were proposed in all sorts of crazy locations to suit the whims of speculator landowners.

Sometimes their locations were semi-rational, as with the Ladies Mile/Mackie Avenue estate in Patcham built by George Ferguson in the 1930s. Though it was built in remote Downland it did, at least, hug the valley bottom and was accompanied by large commitments of public open space, the largest of which now forms the Ladies Mile Local Nature Reserve.

Many of the schemes, however, showed an utter disregard of landscape or of the proximity of services and employment. If angry opposition and incompetence had not stalled many of them our Brighton Downs would now be as wholly destroyed as are the North Downs, where housing swims right to the crest of the escarpment. The Devil's Dyke was bought for a major housing development. Remote Standean, south west of Ditchling Beacon, teetered on the edge of division into 40 development plots, and Sweet Hill, north of Waterhall was parcelled up into 'plotlands'. All those sites were saved by Brighton Council's purchase. Woodingdean was first developed as a 'plotlands' self-

Milton Abbas: An 18th Century aristocratic model village sunk in the Dorset Downs.

build speculation, and both Peacehaven, Saltdean, and bits of Rottingdean were developed by the appalling fraudulent speculator, Charles Neville, in the inter-war period. Lovely Hoddern Down, between Peacehaven and Newhaven, north of the A259, was 'fingered' by Neville and his fellow speculators, as was most of the wild cliffland between the two towns around Chene Gap and Rushy Hill. Only the speculators incompetence and gross under-investment saved (some of) this cliff landscape from painful development.

None of these developments took any account of land form or amenity. Woodingdean was first constructed on land between 400 and 500ft high and Saltdean and Peacehaven were constructed on tall cliffs above sharp chalk reefs with an almost total absence of beach.

200 and 300ft Contours

THE extreme public anxiety about the loss of open Downland in these inter-war years did bring a strong response from the local councils, though weakened by lack of planning powers. In West Sussex, which included Southwick and Shoreham Councils, a contour boundary of 200ft, above which development would not be tolerated, was fixed in the 1930s, with the cooperation of most landowners. In East Sussex a boundary contour of 300ft was chosen, with the higher contour as a concession to the need to avoid making

expensive compensation to landowners whose schemes were thus thwarted.

This crude 'rule of thumb' planning could not work in the long term, for adherence to it would have meant tolerating building stretching along the whole of the valley between Brighton and Lewes; right up the London Road valley as far as Pyecombe; and all over the eastern Brighton and Newhaven Downs including Balsdean, Breaky Bottom and Telscombe. It would, however, if implemented earlier, rigorously, and permanently, have prevented painful landscape damage at Mile Oak, north Hangleton, along the slopes on either side of Dyke Road Avenue, at Patcham, on the west slopes of Hollingbury Hill, and Woodingdean. So it goes.

Later Council Housing: Driven onto the Hilltops

IF early council housing was excellently located, in landscape terms, the later phases suffered from the competition of the private sector which gobbled up all the best sheltered valley land. At Withdean, Westdean, and all along the Goldstone Valley around Hove Park it was the private sector which monopolized the development opportunities, taking advantage of pre-existing landscaping, which had already matured over as much as one or even two centuries.

The Hangleton council estate, built in the late 1940s, was thus forced up onto high Downland — around 250-350ft — north of West Blatchington's little church, windmill and manor house. The 1950s Woodingdean council estate was built largely on the highest land in the suburb. Much of Bexhill Road, at 550ft, was as high as the landmark Cissbury Ring! Though the council was successful in confining much of the Hollingbury estate, built in the late 1940s and '50s, below the 300ft contour, the Stanmer Heights flats and the roads

Bevendean: A 20th Century model council estate sunk in the Brighton Downs.

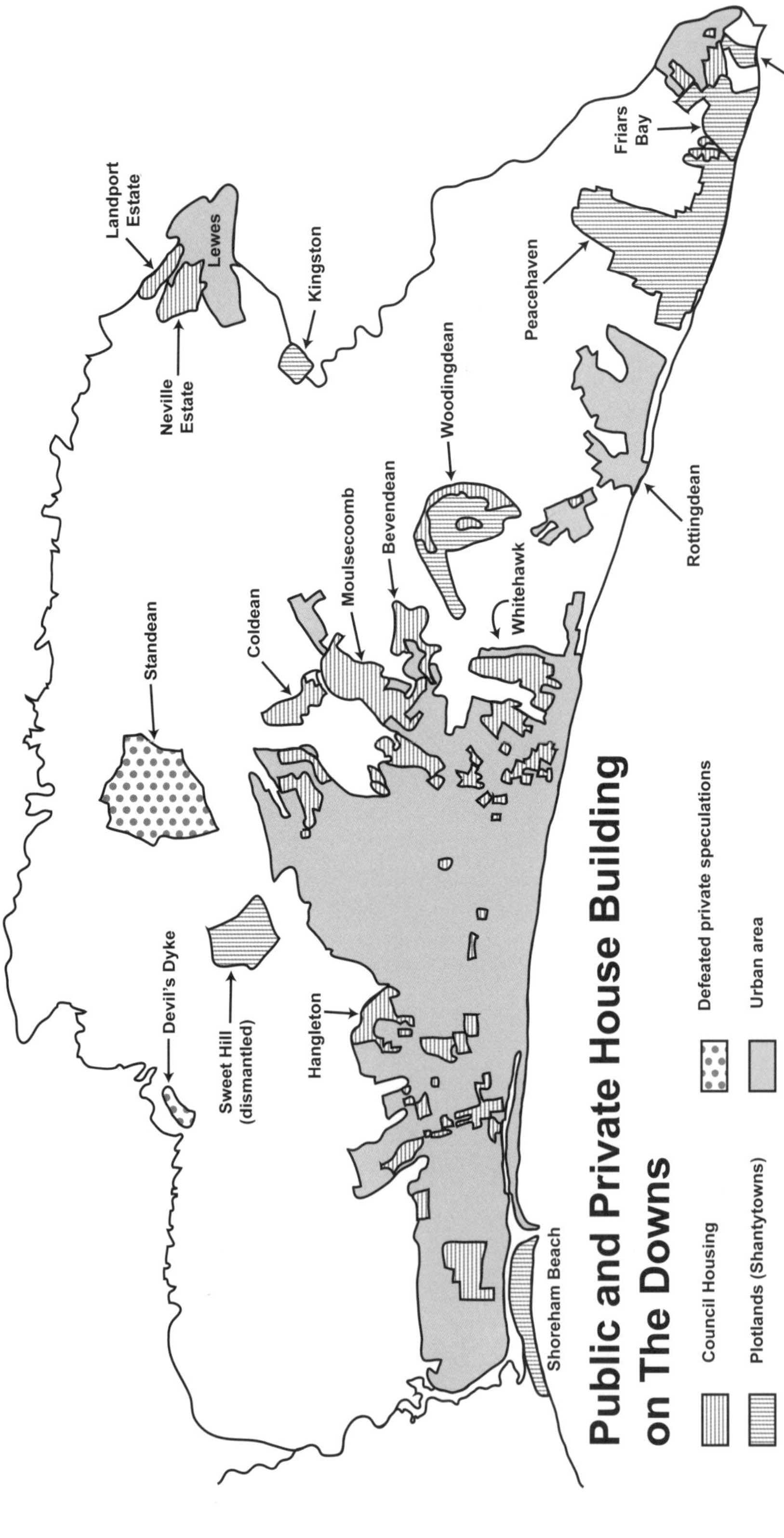

Public and Private House Building on The Downs

Newhaven

Friars Bay

Peacehaven

Rottingdean

Landport Estate

Lewes

Kingston

Neville Estate

Woodingdean

Whitehawk

Standean

Moulsecoomb

Bevendean

Coldean

Devil's Dyke

Sweet Hill (dismantled)

Hangleton

Shoreham Beach

Legend:
- Council Housing
- Plotlands (Shantytowns)
- Defeated private speculations
- Urban area

around Rotherfield Crescent are painfully prominent across huge swathes of the Brighton Downs.

The wave of council high-rise development in the 1960s even brought giant tower blocks to the head of Whitehawk Valley, at Swanborough Place, almost obscuring race-goers views of the far reaches of the race course. Only on the cheap ex-Stanmer estate land at Coldean and at unfashionable North Portslade were the councils able to built substantial council estates without major damage to wider landscape assets.

After the Thatcher/Blair halt to council house building only small amounts of social housing have been built, all by housing associations, and projects have very often had the character of urban 'infilling'. However, housing associations, like later council housing, have been forced by private sector competition onto open, often high and exposed Downland sites. Thus, the appalling Causeway and Monument Way developments on the top of Whitehawk Hill actually bit into the edge of the Neolithic Whitehawk Hill enclosure (which should, in justice, have incurred a £20,000 fine on the council for damaging a Scheduled Ancient Monument). Further housing association developments encroached on the Hill's southern and south eastern slopes, and on the edge of the Local Nature Reserve at Sea Saw Way. Again, at Hollingdean (Brentwood Road) and Portslade (Fox Way/Foredown) housing association estates were forced onto the highest open Downland.

We Preserve for Them to Destroy.

CAPITALIST development does not take place at an even rate. No calm process of collective decision making governs building activity, despite the apparatus of Planning Acts and council planning departments. Rather, it takes place in a series of pulses and contractions, as the cycles of boom and bust unfurl. And economic activity and technical innovation always slide to areas of lowest costs and richest resources. Public planning processes merely serve or ameliorate the dominant economic force of private capital.

In this context, paradoxically, the qualities that lead to the protection of special areas and sites can, in the long term, also be the qualities that attract major new development. It is for that reason that the stories of Benfield Valley, Stanmer Park and Black Rock, need telling.

Benfield Valley: Saxon Estate to Sainsburys Superstore.

TILL the Brighton bypass and the Hangleton link road were built around

---

Public and Private House Building on the Downs

The first (inter-war) generation of council housing was rationally planned. It was mostly placed in 'the deans' — the dry valleys of the Downs at the urban edge.

By contrast, private speculative developments, both of shanty 'plotlands' and more wealthy housing, reached a lunatic irrationality. The entire wild white cliffland between Rottingdean and Peacehaven was ruined, and the tops of the Downs at Woodingdean, the Devil's Dyke, Standean, and Sweet Hill, Patcham, were threatened. Sadly, Woodingdean was lost.

After World War Two council housing was sometimes forced up onto the high ground, too, by competition from the private sector.

Crazy speculative developments on untouched landscapes were stopped, though, by the Labour government's new 'Town and Country Planning Act' of 1947.

1990, a green corridor of Downland extended south from Benfield Hill right down into urban Hove as far as the Old Shoreham Road. The Benfield Valley was a remarkable survival. It retained landscape features going back a thousand years to late Saxon and early Norman times. Its ancient hedged boundary banks originally marked out the estate of a Norman knight given part of a giant Saxon estate carved up into three bits by the Norman overlord. (The other two bits were Hangleton and West Blatchington.)

In 1908 the West Hove Golf Club took over Benfield Valley and Hill, still within the property boundaries it had occupied for about 900 years, except for the open Downland north of Benfield Hill which was severed from the holding. For the next 80 years the golf course preserved Benfield Valley, the Hill and the farmstead in aspic, complete with its old hedged closes, huge old barn, farm cottages and white farm tracks. At night a ghostly barn owl glided across the paddocks and pipistrelle bats played above the golf greens. Hangleton Lane's quiet hedgerows remained as they always had been: a lovely place to take the family blackberrying on hot summer afternoons.

Though development crept up and surrounded the Valley on both long sides, the golfers and the planners of Hove Council stood fast to preserve this quiet valley and hill.

Yet when the Brighton bypass project first seriously arose in the 1980s, the very qualities which Benfield had preserved became the qualities which made it perfect as a route for the new Dover to Honiton superhighways' only new link into the town centre. The valley was sheltered, bordered by screening trees, penetrated right into the town centre, and was without obstructing buildings or competing economic interests.

Despite a long campaign the bypass was built. Now, where children blackberried and golfers, walkers and allotmentees

enjoyed the summer evenings, huge Sainsburys lorries trundle to the superstore. Hangleton Lane is now a dangerous slip road to the bypass. Benfield farm cottages are now in ruins, burnt out after Sainsburys, having evicted the last tenant, left the cottages and their lovingly tended gardens empty and vulnerable. The beautiful cluster of Victorian farm buildings has fallen further into ruin. The two medieval farm closes are destroyed. One is the scrappy new golf club car park and the other is built on. The lower valley is lost to the Sainsburys superstore, car park and link road.

Stanmer Park: Bosky Playground or Developer's Landscaping?

STANMER Park's eighteenth century aristocratic owners didn't like the beauty of the bare open Downland sheep walks and huge, hedgeless corn fields. Their idea of a model landscape was based on the medieval deer park, with its bosky woods, lawns and bushy slopes. So that's what they planted up and nurtured to maturity over two hundred years. The park that they made and that Brighton Council bought in 1947 had very different qualities from the Downs around it. It was enclosed by shelter belts and the Great Wood. Its long views were broken up by clumps of trees and woods covering the ridge tops and infilling the combes.

Such enclosed, sheltered parkland makes a lovely playground, and Brighton's purchase was an act of great foresight.

Enclosed countryside has other advantages, too. It shelters and hides built development far more effectively than could be done otherwise on Brighton's bare and inter-visible Downs. And that's been Stanmer Park's most important function. It has served as visual screening not just for one, but for TWO universities! One of these universities is the size of a small new town. It has acted as shelter for the development of the large Coldean Council estate, remote from the city centre

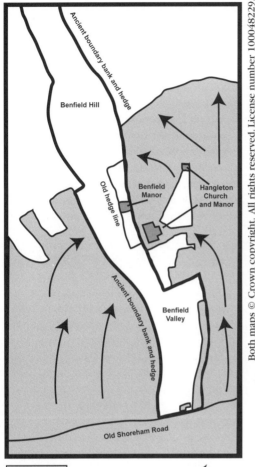

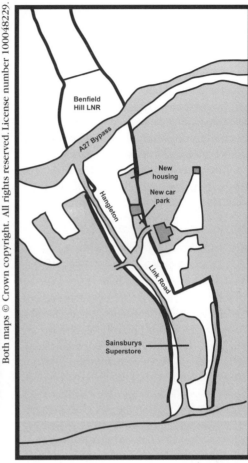

 Built-up area ← **Direction of urban development**

A. Benfield Valley in the 20th Century

— Housing crept up around the Valley.
— The valley, though, was preserved as a golf course within its medieval manorial boundaries.

B. Benfield Valley and the Bypass

— The preserved Valley proved to be a perfect site for the new Hangleton link Road and a giant superstore.
— Its preservation had merely facilitated a new round of mega-developments.

but beautifully laid out. It gives some acoustic and visual screening for two miles of the Brighton A27 bypass. And, now, it provides a new expressway out-of-town site for the Albion Football Stadium — as good a location as any "big box on the bypass" superstore or warehousing utility could ever dream of.

This woody screening has also provided a home to other folk, too. All the different communities of travellers — English traditional gipsy travellers, Irish travellers, new travellers and van dwellers have encamped in the Duke's Car Park, up at Chalk Hill and along the main drive to the big house, as well as in the sheltered hollow below Marquee Brow. This is one of the main areas around Brighton where travellers can easily park up for short periods with relatively little conflict or difficulty. Yet whereas the universities and the football club relentlessly press their proposals for expansion, travellers come under more and more pressure — from new park-wide parking restrictions and from the football club's plan to route an access road through part of the Duke's Car Park, as well as from the everyday pressure to move on from the Council and some settled local residents. Freedom to roam has never been a right the settled community has easily allowed our real nomads.

The Marina: Dubai Kitsch Meets Crabs, Anemones and Chalk Cliffs

B L A C K Rock was a great place for kids free play. It isn't any more.

It was a bit of a hike from central Brighton (though Volk's Railway will still get you there nicely) but at least you knew you had definitely reached the edge of town. After more than a mile of the boring concrete cased-in cliffs of Madeira Drive, you came at last to the Real McCoy: dazzling white cliffs, stretching away to Rottingdean, with squabbling **Jackdaws, Fulmars** and **Rock Pipits**. Admittedly, the Undercliff Walk — built in 1930-33 — had made the cliffs a lot more bland. Cliff hanging workmen had chamfered the cliff face to an even backwards angle, knocking off all the irregularities, the crags, ledges, and over-hangs. That meant no big beach tumbles of chalk rock, brought down by winter storms, to pick over, and no cliff bottom nooks and crannies to explore. It was still a children's paradise, though, and the Undercliff Walk meant that nanny and grandad could enjoy the walk out towards Rottingdean, too. You could take the kids rock pooling for crabs and anemones. The open air swimming pool was a great place to go on hot days, and the Peter Pan Playground was just a short walk away. You could watch the fishing dingies being winched up the beach and sneak a glance at the nudist sun worshippers.

And for some local kids, like ex-milkman Rob White, the Black Rock cliffs revealed other wonders to their patient observation. For the cliffs could be read like a story book of the history of the land right back through the Ice Age to the Age of Dinosaurs. Picking over the basal layers of cliff rock Rob came across the remains of an ancient fossil Sea Lily in a semi-complete form. This peculiar creature looked like a little upside down geodesic dome with a Medusa's hair of wavy tentacles. It free swam the hot, tropical seas about 84 million years ago. Long, long extinct, the familiar modern relatives of this beastie are the starfish and sea urchins. Rob's fossil hunting at Black Rock started him on a lifetime of local exploration, which now makes him one of the top local experts on chalk fossils.

Black Rock had marked the end of Brighton and the beginning of the Downs for 180 years, since the building of the Gas Works in 1818-19 and the construction of Sussex Square in the 1820s. Despite

---

A. Stanmer Park circa 1870

| Stanmer's aristocratic landowners didn't like the open fields and prairie pastures of the old Downland 'champion' landscape.

| Instead, they created a copy of an enclosed medieval deer park, with its woods and surrounding hedges and copses.

B. Stanmer Park 2008

| In our time this enclosed landscape has proved perfect for landscaping and hiding two universities, a planned football stadium, a trunk road bypass, and parts of two council estates within its sheltering woods.

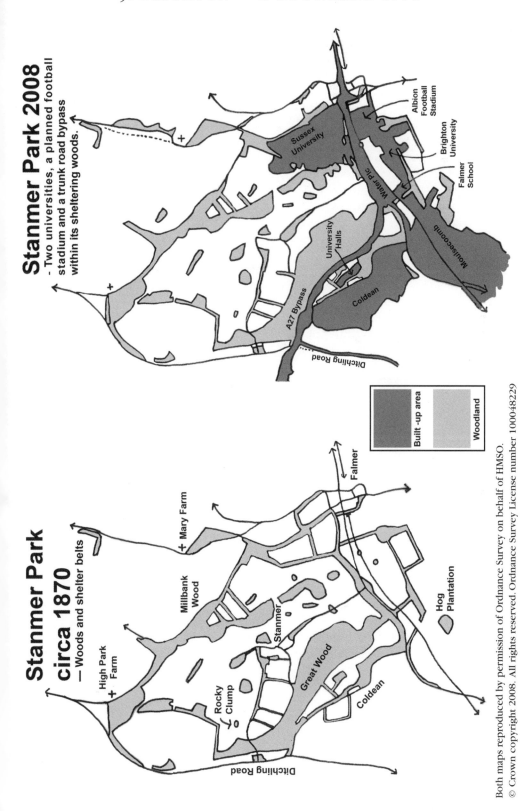

Stanmer Park 2008
- Two universities, a planned football stadium and a trunk road bypass within its sheltering woods.

Sussex University

Water pic

Mouisecoomb

Albion Football Stadium

Brighton University

Falmer School

University Halls

Coldean

A27 Bypass

Ditchling Road

Stanmer Park circa 1870
— Woods and shelter belts

High Park Farm

Mary Farm

Millbank Wood

Rocky Clump

Stanmer

Great Wood

Coldean

Hog Plantation

Falmer

Ditchling Road

Built -up area

Woodland

Both maps reproduced by permission of Ordnance Survey on behalf of HMSO.
© Crown copyright 2008. All rights reserved. Ordnance Survey License number 100048229

piecemeal encroachments, like Roedean School or St Dunstan's, or the new housing at Ovingdean and Saltdean, the chalk cliffs marked the beginning of the wilder sort of open landscape of the Downs.

The coming of the Marina from 1971 changed all that. Driven away from Kemp Town beach by local protest, the Marina developers switched their plans to the unspoilt cliffscape to the east. Now the Black Rock cliffs are a backdrop to the business of weekend shopping at Asda, and the Marina houses a several thousand strong community in its pastiche Georgian apartment blocks.

But the future plans for the Marina make the present place look like Toy Town. The Emir of Dubai would be proud of them. The owners and their developer cooked up a scheme for eleven huge tower blocks up to 16 stories high, dominated by one 40 story skyscraper which tops out at 420 feet (120m) tall. This monster will be taller than ancient Whitehawk Hill, to its north, taller than Red Hill above Sheepcote Valley, taller than Mount Pleasant at Woodingdean and almost twice the height of Beacon Hill, Rottingdean. It will be taller than High Hill above Rottingdean, Rushy Hill at Newhaven and as much as 40m taller than the high white cliffs of Seaford Head, which mark the eastern end of the monster's viewshed.

All around the cirque of the Downs from Worthing's Highdown Hill, Cissbury, Chanctonbury and Lancing Ring; all along the South Downs Way past Truleigh Hill, the Devils Dyke and Wolstonbury to Ditchling Beacon and Firle Beacon; and all along the chain of chalk cliffs at Roedean, Ovingdean, Telscombe Tye to Seaford Head the tower will be visible in a viewshed which is 25 miles by 6.5 miles across.

Brighton's planners have abandoned all pretence of defending Downland's wider integrity. The towers will be a "book-end" to the conurbation, they say, "providing a visually stimulating marker for the city's edge" and "providing confidence to the national and international investor and development market".

And now a second phase of Marina high rises is proposed, which will wall off the Black Rock Ice Age cliffs behind an avenue of tall blocks, obliterating any possibility of us seeing many long views of this feature.

Who cares, though? Who needs nature when you've got a tower block to admire?

One That Failed: Motor Racing on the Portslade Downs

THE former are three stories of disaster for Downland conservation. Sometimes, though, conservationists have won. The story of the attempt to build a huge motor racing circuit on the open Downs between Portslade and the Devil's Dyke is a story of a disaster that was avoided by a hair's breadth.

At the very same time (1928) as Brighton Council were being praised by the Duke of York (later George V1) for preserving the Devil's Dyke and other recently bought Downland as "not merely a local, but a national possession" they were agreeing in principle to lease 1,100 acres of its Downland estate just west of the Devil's Dyke for a gigantic motor-racing track. The proposals were originally cooked-up by the off-road trail bikers of the Brighton and Hove Motorcycle Club and by 1928 the proposals also included an aerodrome. All the land between New Barn Farm (north of Foredown Tower) and Fulking Hill was to be taken by this giant serpentine course. Brighton's councillors eyed the profits that Brooklands and the Isle of Man races garnered and concluded that "looking at it from a business point of view there must be money in it."

All the usual flannel was added in. The track would conform with the natural contours (in fact, it travelled right along the crest of the Mount Zion ridge for a mile and right along the Benfield Hill ridge for another mile), and would be disguised by a six foot fence painted tastefully in a neutral tone. The grandstand would be collapsible and race meeting timings limited. In any case, the scheme's promoters said, there were no rights of way (the core of the site has now been opened up as statutory access land) most of the valley was cultivated (now all of it is managed as permanent ESA grassland) and amenity was already impaired by derelict farm buildings (the lovely old Atlingworth Barn — later bulldozed in the 1960s — and New Barn Farm) and a water tower (now the Foredown Tower Countryside Centre) and isolation hospital. It would only occupy a small portion of the Downs (in fact it occupied almost the whole width of the open Downs at that point and a further connecting road to the Devil's Dyke was proposed).

Till the motor racing track was proposed Brighton Council had been working with its neighbours to create the Brighton, Hove and District Joint Town Planning Committee, but the vigorous opposition of its neighbours, including Portslade where the project was to be located, put Brighton's leaders' noses out of joint and Brighton resigned from the Joint Committee, which, within a month, had collapsed.

A greater disaster then ensued, for Brighton's intransigent support for the motor racing track destroyed the chances for the passing of the South Downs Preservation Bill which both East and West Sussex County Councils were promoting in Parliament. The 1934 bill would have given the Councils much stronger planning powers, in the absence of a comprehensive national town and country planning regime. Brighton saw the bill merely as a "dead set at Brighton over the motor racing track" and not only refused to join with it but gave angry evidence against. They used a populist rhetoric against their snobbish opponents in the House of Lords whose opposition to the despoliation of the Downs was mixed with a strong dose of exclusivist opposition to mass public access.

In the event, only lack of finance and the coming of the Second World War scuppered the plans for the Portslade motor racing track.

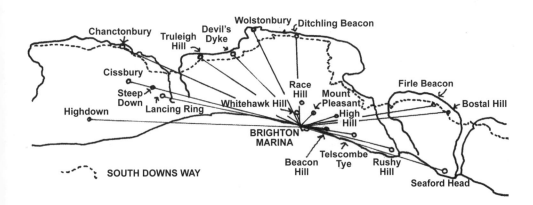

Who's Looking at Who?
— The visual impact of the Brighton high rise developments will be immense.
— Many Downland high points will be intruded upon by the giant Brighton Marina towers and other high-rise developments.

Reproduced from 1911 Ordnance Survey map bases with the kind permission of the Ordnance Survey.

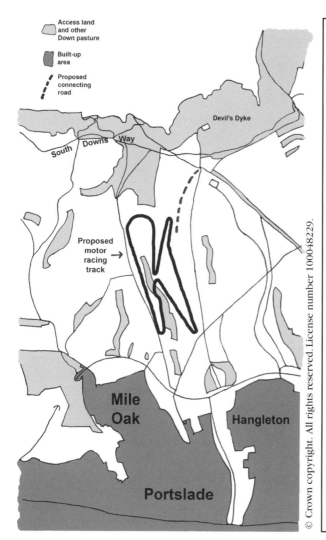

The Portslade Motor Racing Track Proposal circa 1935

— Brighton Council vigorously pushed the proposal, arguing that this stretch of Downs was unsightly, that the track would not damage the landscape in any case, and that it represented people's democratic aspirations. The modern Council's case for the Falmer football stadium closely paralleled the way the pre-war Council argued for the racing track.

— If the track had been created the highest Downs would have been breached by built development, just as the North Downs have been.

— The plans were halted by the outbreak of the Second World War in 1939.

The Continuity of Brighton's Political Culture

WHAT is remarkable about the 1930s debate over the Portslade motor-racing track is how close it parallels the debates over the Falmer football stadium and the Marina Towers and other sky-scraper proposals. Brighton's pre-war vision for economic development was entirely conventional in its view that prosperity must mean major expansion of the conurbation at the expense of open Downland. Community prosperity would come from the 'trickling down' of wealth created by ordinary capitalist activity.

Even the vision of Sir Herbert Carden, whose energy lay behind the acquisition of Brighton's Downland estate, was wholly developmentalist, despite his 'municipal socialism'. The creation of 'Greater Brighton' — watering place of the Empire — was the key to *greater* prosperity. Any sense that *the real key to prosperity lies in an alternative project,* (based on re-distribution and planned, socialised production for use rather than the market) has so far formed only a minority current in Brighton politics.

Just like the pre-war dispute, the fight over the location of the Brighton and

Hove Albion's new football ground took place in the context of a fierce debate over strategy for the wider protection of the South Downs. After 70 years the proposal for a National Park was at last becoming a real political possibility. Though the idea was opposed by most of the local authorities on the South Downs, as well as Brighton's Council Leader Steve Bassam, it was embraced by the new Labour Government's left-leaning Minister of the Environment, Michael Meacher. In this national context, and as leader of the only Labour Council on the South Downs, Bassam did an about-face and expressed his support for the National Park proposal. This support for the principle of the National Park, however, was not allowed to damage the possibility of further expansionist built development on Brighton's Downland edges.

Thus was born the proposal for the new Falmer football stadium. It was vigorously argued that no alternative urban sites were available (in fact there were lots, including a string of sites which were never seriously investigated). It was argued that the Falmer site was already damaged by proximity to the University (an argument which could be used to justify built encroachment at any urban fringe location); that the stadium would be a positive beautification of the Downs (an argument that would justify any built encroachment if a sufficiently posh design could be commissioned); and that there would be significant job creation for this disadvantaged area of east Brighton (though the vast majority of the jobs may be part time, unskilled, ancillary roles). A populist argument was used that minority conservationists were attempting to frustrate a mass campaign, (whereas the truth was that Councillors were too broken-backed after years of political retreat to do the campaigning necessary to secure an urban site which would benefit urban regeneration *and* conserve the environment).

The same contradictory 'unmaking with the one hand what the other hand was doing' characterizes the Council's attitude to the Marina skyscraper proposals. Despite the Council's continued expressions of support for the National Park project, the implications for the Downland setting of Brighton of the new pro-skyscraper policy of the Council were never seriously discussed. The 'Special Planning Guidance' passed by the Council avoided facing the implications for Downland of city centre skyscrapers, assuming that the landscape damage would only occur with towers on high ground or the urban fringe. Yet the damage already done by such giant seaside monoliths as Sussex Heights (at 330ft, higher than Benfield Hill and Foredown and almost as tall as Southwick Hill) and the County Hospital tower was plain to see. They clearly disrupt the remoteness and visual integrity of the Downs right up to the South Downs Way and all along the coast.

The Guidance talks of the function of the chalk cliffs as no more than a useful visual screen, "mitigating" the effects of tall towers, not a valuable natural landform in their own right, despite the designation of the whole of the cliffscape from Black Rock to Newhaven as a geological SSSI (Site of Special Scientific Interest).

The Council's Special Planning Guidance for the Brighton Marina went even further in ignoring the Downs and cliffs. At no point does the two volume Guidance ever mention the proposed National Park or Area of Outstanding Natural Beauty, yet the Council's own proposed boundary for the National Park comes to within half a mile of the Marina skyscrapers and proposes the inclusion of the cliffs and the chalk reefs in the new Park.

The political culture of market developmentalism means that the Council can state with frank innocence that the present Marina has "no landmark features, no statement of identity or destination", despite marking the beginning of a backdrop of seven and a half miles of shining white, 100 ft high, 85 million year old chalk cliffs!

This culture means that the Council can propose motor racing tracks up to the top of the Downs, skyscrapers interrupting their views, and football stadiums in their midst, whilst still proclaiming their passionate commitment to preserving this precious landscape!!

THE URBAN FRINGE

THE open Brighton Downs are made up of three layers. There are the urban fringe Downs, lying just within and without the urban edge. There are the Downs of the high plateau beyond, dissected by long dry valleys, mostly running southwards. And there is the high scarp.

Received wisdom may make us think that the Downs are richer in wildlife and historic interest the further we travel from the busy modern urban edge.

It is not so.

The 'Sandwich'

OUR Downs are, in fact, layered like a sandwich. The high scarp is *outer layer one* of the sandwich, with its ribbon of steep chalk grassland and necklace of ancient burial mounds and fortifications. The *filling layer* in the middle of the Downs is the wide, corrugated plateau. It is a relatively meagre feast, poor in surviving Down pasture and surviving cultural monuments. It is also relatively inaccessible beyond the rights of way system, which largely serves to bring urban visitors across it, between the high scarp and the urban edge. *Outer layer two* is the Downs near to the urban edge. They are rich in wildlife and cultural heritage, varied in aspect and vegetation, and relatively open to public access.

Paradox

THEREIN lies the paradox. The urban fringe Downs, close to the muddle of housing estates, roads, industrial estates and retail parks have — proportionately — a greater resource of wildlife and historic landscape, and more access land than the more distant Downs of the plateau. They do not, of course, have the qualities of tranquility and remoteness that the farther Downs still hold. The damage that the A27 bypass has done has been profound. Even so, deep tranquility can still be found in some places right up close to the urban edge. Falmer and Balsdean Bottoms, below Castle Hill, are a world away from busy Woodingdean, only a few hundred yards away. Only the occasional rusting, burnt-out car testifies to the closeness of Brighton.

A combination of factors has allowed us to retain this urban edge richness. Often this Downland is steeply contoured, with many south-facing sites (as at Mill Hill, Moulsecoomb Wild Park, Bevendean valleysides and Whitehawk). Often it has had long management as open space, (as at Ladies Mile, Whitehawk Hill and Beacon Hill). And often farmers have retreated from managing the land there in the face of the necessity of assuming a public role (as they did at Hog Plantation

The 'Access Sandwich' has No Filling!

Lewes

Newhaven

Kingston Hill

Peacehaven

Blackcap

Telscombe Tye

Ditchling Beacon

Brighton

Kemp Town

Devil's Dyke

Portslade

Truleigh Hill

Shoreham

Town

Statutory Access Land and other Downland with public access

Edges of access zones

- There's plenty of 'bread' — the top slice of accessible Downland along the scarp, and the bottom slice along the urban edge.

- However, most of the 'filling' of the Downs — the remote, tranquil plateau landscape — has little Downland with extensive and statutory rights of access.

Moulsecoomb, Bevendean Down and Sheepcote Valley).

Urban fringe Downland open spaces often go way back. The oldest of them all is Whitehawk Hill, officially open to Brighton pleasure seekers from 1822. Moulsecoomb Wild Park and East Brighton Park were formally opened in 1925, Beacon Hill became a Corporation open space from its purchase in 1929, and, similarly, Ladies Mile Down from 1937.

The Good

THERE are some places on the urban fringe where farmers have *not* given up in the face of the need to manage public access. The best-managed site is Southwick Hill, where the tenant farmer has continuously grazed the Hill, despite the death and injury of stock, for both the National Trust and Brighton Council. The result is that the Hill retains much of the wildlife lost elsewhere, and is a delight of soft old Downland turf to walk upon. Happy Valley, next to Woodingdean, is still grazed, as access land, from Ovingdean Farm, and Falmer and Standean Bottoms, also close to Woodingdean, are still grazed by Balsdean Farm.

There are many places, too, where local activists have brought about the return of grazing and other farming techniques to derelict and un-grazed sites. The friends of Telscombe Tye, lovely Bevendean Down, Benfield Hill, Mill Hill Shoreham, and now both Sheepcote valleyside and Beacon Hill Rottingdean, have all defied the cynics who say that farming and the urban public do not mix.

The Bad

THERE are too many depressing stories, however. Toad's Hole Valleyside, next to the Hangleton Estate, was brought back into management by a partnership of local residents, progressive Hove Council officials and the landowner. For a year or two in the early '90s this previously-derelict site looked better and better. The scrub was pushed back, the grass was mown, a dew pond was built, a management plan was drawn up, and the rubbish was cleared. Then the landowners had their application to develop the valley bottom for the new Albion Stadium rejected by the Council. In response they ended the agreement, stopped the management work, and banned the public from the site. The valleyside has deteriorated ever since, and is now plagued by trail bike riders and disappearing under bramble, litter and scrub.

The wildlife-rich ancient Down pasture sites of Waterhall and Moulsecoomb Wild Park have suffered many decades of neglect. Their ancient grasslands and gorse brakes have been left to succeed to a tedious and inaccessible blanket of thorn scrub and incipient secondary woodland. The result is they have become largely inaccessible to the public. Largely cut off, now, by the busy A27 and A270 from the neighbouring housing estates, they are no longer safe to many local children. Grand in scale though they are, their potential is largely ignored by the Council, who own them.

Whitehawk Hill and (till recently) Hog Plantation, Moulsecoomb, too, are disappearing under a sea of encroaching rank vegetation. At Whitehawk, cumulative encroaching developments additionally threaten its core qualities.

To the east, most of Newhaven's magnificent cliff landscape has disappeared under impenetrable thorn scrub and cumulative development. This sub-landscape is unique on the Brighton Downs and is — still — a lovely wild place, and one of the best sites in Sussex for invertebrates. These qualities have not saved it so far, though, and the town and cliffs await another onslaught of gentrifying development. At Lewes, the old Racecourse Down, uphill from the Prison, is disappearing under a sea of thorn and rank grass, despite its rich chalk grassland wildlife and archaeology.

And The Ugly

URBAN fringe farmsteads have suffered badly from a kind of ramshackle modernization, which has turned some of them into places more like mini-industrial estates. Several of them are significant eyesores.

In 1980 Brighton Council sold off the old Ovingdean Grange farmhouse, cottages, timbered barn and old farm buildings and built a new farmhouse and yard on the adjacent open ground. It now sprawls painfully up the valley, adding a further urban note to the encroaching townscape. Patcham Court Farm had earlier suffered the same fate. Mile Oak, New Barn and Upper Bevendean Farms have now become significant clusters of industrially produced buildings, only exceeded by the sprawling mess of Coombe Farm, Saltdean. Home Farm, Stanmer and Court Farm, Falmer are still dominated by their beautiful and grand vernacular wooden barns, but neither farm has found a solution to the problem of how to preserve their old structures and incorporate new public uses. The Falmer thatched barn has now been covertly sold by Brighton Council.

Suburban Farmyards

FOR those farms separated by development from open Downland, the story is even more depressing. Old Shoreham Farm, by the ancient church, has long gone, as has nearby Buckingham Farm. Its lonely flint dovecot sits isolated on an empty green, surrounded by suburban houses, like some piece of tokenistic sculpture in a shopping mall. The nearby Regency manor house is an empty shell, part in-filled with new houses. Kingston Buci's huge ancient barn survived better as a community resource, but new developer-owners threaten it. Benfield Farm has suffered painfully from developer greed and Council under-funding. Its cottages have been burnt down and demolished and only its wagon barn survives intact. Hangleton Manor, close by, lost its beautiful

woodland surroundings in 1970 to a Hove councillor-developer who'd bought the empty manor house, and got the permission of his fellow councillors to surround it with a cramped housing estate. The Rottingdean farms — Challoners, Court Farm, West Side and the rest — have all been long separated from their farmed land and turned into suburban villas, but Lewes's lovely Landport Farm survives a little better, on the edge of the Landport Council estate, its farmhouse turned into council flats.

For the rest, most remain only in memory. West Blatchington Manor House, dating right back to Chaucer's time, was bulldozed in 1955; Hodshrove Farm, dating back to the 13th century at least, was demolished in 1936/7; and Moulsecoomb Home Farm in the 1960s. Lower Bevendean Manor was lost in the late 1940s. Spital Farm in Lewes survives only as a barn conversion, and Meeching Court Farm, in the centre of Newhaven, has long gone, though one of its flint barns survives as a community hall.

New Cultural Landscapes

THE huge growth of Brighton was accompanied by the growth of new kinds of cultural landscapes on the Downs. From the late 1880s Brighton saw the birth of the **golf landscape**, utilizing the same ancient sheep pastures beloved of walkers, picnickers, naturalists and antiquarians. From the last quarter of the nineteenth century there was a dramatic expansion of municipally-provided **allotments**, to address the needs of the urban poor of the Brighton slums. This, together with a new increase in smallholdings catering to the huge new food market created by the expansion of Brighton, changed whole tracts of Downland. Then, from the beginning of the twentieth century, there was a whole new settlement movement of urban people seeking cheap and independent housing by the seaside or in open country. This **'plotlands'** movement had its first major local impact in the Edwardian shanty settlement of Shoreham Beach, but after the First World War the movement took off on a grand scale in tandem with the land speculations of Charles Neville on the cliffs east of Brighton. From the 1950s there was a steepening rise in the amount of urban fringe — and remote — Downland which was devoted to horse keeping — **'horseyculture'** — as prosperity gave more and more folk the chance of horse ownership.

All these new landscapes have represented attempts by urban people to return in some way to a greater closeness to nature and the countryside. But such brave attempts are always mediated by class and opportunity. Whilst the middle and upper class golfers changed the Downscape least — in the short term anyway — they achieved a real privatization of previously open Down pastures. The working class allotmentees and small holders changed the physical appearance of large areas with their huts and fences, but they re-created a pattern of food growing — the old strip cultivated peasant open fields — going back well over a millennia. Though the democratic aspirations of the plotlanders were worthy to their core, they were in the hands of antisocial land speculators who did not recognize the difference between a shanty town and a garden city, and cared even less about preserving historic landscapes.

The Land of the Golf Course

The Brighton Downs are the land of the golf course. Between Brighton and Newhaven there are an astonishing nine golf courses, as well as two miniature golf courses, not to mention a further two courses and two half courses now long gone. In Hangleton parish alone there are three courses. If you drive up the Dyke Road to the Devil's Dyke you pass three courses on your way.

The contrast with the rest of the South Downs is startling. The whole of the 46 km of Downland between the River Adur at Shoreham and the Hampshire border has only four golf courses (two at Goodwood and two north of Worthing). The open Downs between Lewes and Eastbourne have six courses, but two of these are at the foot of the Downs at Eastbourne.

Golf was originally a game of coastal dunes, with its headquarters on the sandy coast between Edinburgh and St Andrews. It was a game that required open landscapes, a well-drained soil, preferably sandy, and a springy turf. In England this largely meant utilizing the tiny numbers of surviving commons, as well as other heathlands and old Down pastures. The concentration of golf courses on the Brighton Downs is a marker both of the past character of its breezy, close-shorn Downland turf, and of the up-market national status of the resort.

On all except the new West Hove Golf Course the courses were laid out to take advantage of the existing sheep pastures. Indeed, the Brighton and Hove course, off the Dyke Road, continued to be grazed by the Church Farm sheep flock for at least the first 40 years of its existence — till the 1920s — as it had been for long centuries before. The municipal Hollingbury Golf Course was grazed right up till 1962[1].

Despite many decades of neglect or damage to the ancient grasslands of their roughs and fairways, the Brighton Down's golf courses still retain many important ancient chalk grassland sites. At Benfield the importance of the chalk grassland is recognized by Local Nature Reserve status, and the roughs on the hillside have been regularly winter-grazed by sheep and cattle over the last 10 years. This is the only Brighton Downs course which has achieved the re-introduction of grazing, although it was considered at the Brighton and Hove Golf Course a decade ago. This latter course has one of the best chalk

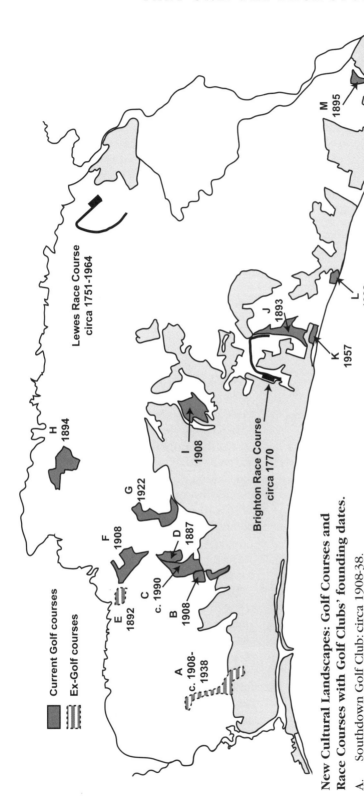

Lewes Race Course
circa 1751-1964

Brighton Race Course
circa 1770

M
1895

L
1938

J
1893

K
1957

I
1908

H
1894

G
1922

F
1908

E
1892

D
1887

C
c. 1990

B
1908

A
c. 1908-
1938

Current Golf courses

Ex-Golf courses

New Cultural Landscapes: Golf Courses and Race Courses with Golf Clubs' founding dates.

A. Southdown Golf Club: circa 1908-38.

B. Benfield Valley Golf Course: started 1908 as West Hove Golf Club.

C. West Hove Golf Club: circa 1990, when moved from Benfield Valley.

D. Brighton and Hove Golf Club: 1887.

E. Brighton and Hove Ladies Club: 1892.

F. Dyke Golf Club: 1908.

G. Waterhall Golf Course: built privately 1922. Taken over by Brighton Council 1936.

H. Pyecombe Golf Club: 1894.

I. Hollingbury Golf Course: 1908.

J. East Brighton Golf Club: 1893.

K. Roedean Miniature Golf Course: 1957.

L. Rottingdean Miniature Golf Course: 1938.

M. Peacehaven Golf Club: 1895. The Course used to run down to the cliff top.

grassland sites on the Hove Downs and the Club has worked with the Hove Ranger to clear large amounts of scrub.

Both of Brighton's two municipal golf courses at Waterhall and Hollingbury have important ancient grassland sites, though the grassland at Waterhall is in a wretched state and receives no significant management. The great majority of it has grown rank and poor in species, or disappeared under dense scrub, and only rabbit grazing keeps small biodiverse islands open. The Dyke Golf Course was municipally controlled till 1966 when it was leased to the Club.

Nowadays when one plays the Dyke course or Waterhall, with their impenetrable Hawthorn thickets on all sides, it is difficult to imagine their previous open character. Whether by default or design, the course managers have obliterated the very qualities which made this a landscape of golf courses in the first place.

The Pyecombe and Peacehaven Golf Courses are especially important, for they hold the only significant extant 'chalk heath' sites surviving on the Brighton Downs, incidentally saved by the sympathetic mowing regimes of the grounds staff, but largely unrecognized for their importance. At present, though, the chalk heath at Pyecombe continues to be slowly strangled, despite the input of the Countryside Rangers and the sympathy of the Club. A much more vigorous management intervention is needed if this important site is to be saved.

Brighton's golf courses still hold all the special wildlife of the ancient sheep pastures. Stonechat and Linnet still nest in the thick Gorse of the Hollingbury Camp, where, too, Early Purple Orchids make a delightful spring display. Adder may still be present on Benfield Hill and is present at Waterhall and maybe other courses, too. Chalkhill, Adonis Blue and Brown Argus butterflies occur at Brighton and Hove

Golf Course and Little Blue can be found at Benfield and Waterhall. Glow Worms form a magical midsummer display at Benfield, and occur on old lynchets within the new West Hove course, as well as at Waterhall. Brighton and Hove has the primitive Purse-web Spider and still has the ancient medicinal herb Field Fleawort, which often marks the presence of prehistoric sites.

Recently we have discovered a whole, previously unsuspected, layer of interest in these golf courses during our surveying of the Brighton Downs for colourful Waxcaps and other fungi which characterize ancient unimproved grassland. Benfield, the Dyke, Hollingbury, East Brighton, Pyecombe and Peacehaven golf courses have all proved to have special assemblages of these fungi, and there is much still to discover.

The best sites were on chalk heath or acidic grassland relics, and Peacehaven Golf Course, lying on the mossy, sandy soils of the Newhaven Tertiary Deposits, stands out as exceptionally good. Here we found 28 old grassland fungi species, including swarms of colourful Waxcaps like Scarlet Hood, and many others. Pyecombe Golf Course's chalk heath, too, had big displays, including the ancient grassland indicator Crimson Waxcap.

As well as being a sport of the middle and ruling classes, golf was a game dominated by men. If women played at all they largely just putted. Women fought to change this, and in 1892 the women golfers of the Brighton and Hove Club decamped to found the Brighton and Hove Ladies Club at the Devil's Dyke, when the established male club refused to admit women members. Difficulties with finance obliged them to partner with a new Men's Club course laid out at the Dyke around 1908, however. The old women's course was to the west of the Dyke, where cows now graze, not to its south, where the present course lies. Later the continuing marginalisation of women players led them to cut loose again, this time to the newly formed municipal Waterhall Golf Course, in 1936, where they formed a Women's Section.

All bar one (West Hove's new course) of the Brighton Downs golf courses are more than 70 years old. The Brighton and Hove Course is the oldest. It was founded on the high sheep pastures of Round Hill, Hangleton in October 1887 — a month after the opening of the Dyke Railway. Indeed, much of the platform of the Golf Club Halt still exists. In the 1890s four new courses were built. The Ladies Course at the Dyke (now gone) started in 1892, East Brighton in 1893, Pyecombe in 1894 and Peacehaven in 1895. At some early stage there was a golf course up on Slonk Hill, by Holmbush Farm near Shoreham, and later this was replaced by the Southdown Golf Club, north of Buckingham Barn, with a club house at New Erringham Farm, but this had all gone probably by the late 1930s.

In 1908 the West Hove Golf Course was started at Benfield, and in the same year the present Dyke Golf Club and the Hollingbury Golf Club were founded. In 1922 a private golf course was started at Waterhall, which became a municipal course when Brighton Council bought the West Blatchington Estate in 1936.

Golf play has proved a more benign usage of the Downscape than commercial agriculture. Even so, the wildlife and landscape assets of our Downland golf courses are not fully appreciated, or managed for, by most clubs, who still plant trees and bushes on fragments of ancient grassland and do not see the importance of rolling back scrub invasion, or regularly mowing the roughs. There is much work still to do.

Allotment and Smallholding Landscapes

IN the last quarter of the nineteenth century there was a dramatic expansion of municipally provided allotments, to alleviate the appalling poverty and over-crowding of urban areas, such as the Brighton slums of Carlton Hill, Hanover and Kemp Town. In this provision Councils were also responding to a broader agitation for land rights, which saw the re-birth of agricultural trade unionism and land resettlement schemes in England, and major land rights movements in Ireland and Wales. A wave of new Allotments Acts were passed between 1887 and 1925 which made the provision of allotments a statutory duty.

Early allotment and smallholdings were centred on three sub-landscapes. One was on the wide slopes of Whitehawk Hill, on the site of Brighton's old open fields and Tenantry Sheep Down. Another, smaller one was around the busy semi-industrial villages of Portslade and Portslade by Sea. Later on, after the First World War, the County Council laid out extensive smallholdings and allotments on the flat brickearth fields south of West Blatchington Court Farm and windmill. They were to cater partly for returning ex-soldiers.

Even now, a century and a quarter later, allotments are still clustered primarily around the broad arc of east Brighton and around Portslade and Fishersgate, as well as around Nevill Avenue, West Blatchington.

At their height, in the early 1920s, an allotments and smallholdings landscape stretched over 2.5 miles of high Downland top and valley on the Whitehawk/Jugg's Road ridge as far as the Falmer Road at Woodingdean. Another landscape stretched up from Hollingdean Lane over the Hollingdean ridge for nearly a mile by one third of a mile wide. These were wonderful places, with a complex interaction of detailed plantings and long, uninterrupted high views, and a rich culture and wildlife.

These landscapes were also messy and higgledy-piggledy, with shacks and hutments everywhere (and after the

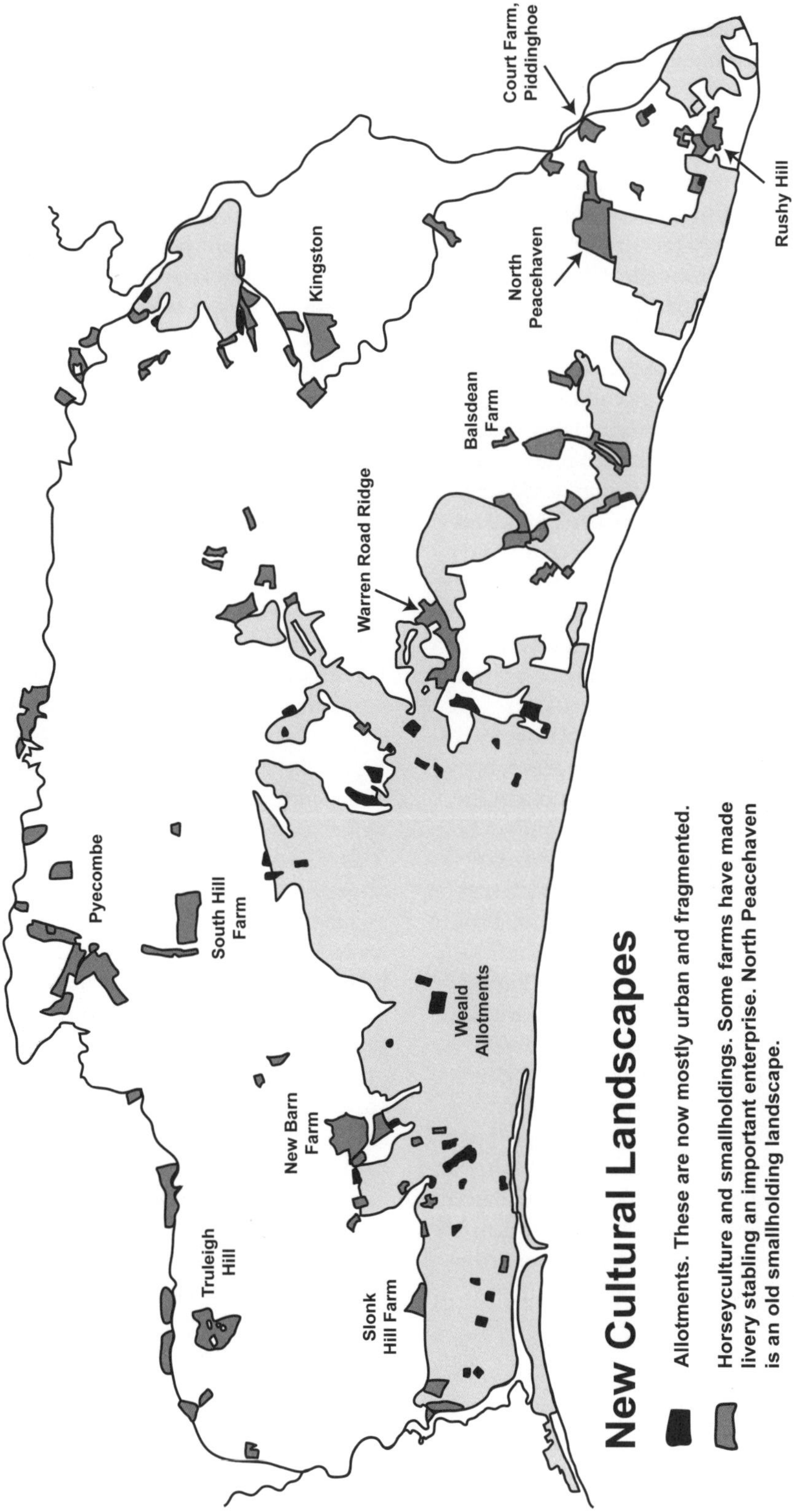
Truleigh Hill
Slonk Hill Farm
New Barn Farm
Weald Allotments
Pyecombe
South Hill Farm
Warren Road Ridge
Balsdean Farm
Kingston
North Peacehaven
Court Farm, Piddinghoe
Rushy Hill
New Cultural Landscapes
Allotments. These are now mostly urban and fragmented.
Horseyculture and smallholdings. Some farms have made livery stabling an important enterprise. North Peacehaven is an old smallholding landscape.

Second World War many ex-servicemen re-started their home lives camping out in the allotment huts of Natal Road and elsewhere). They were, though, immensely productive, generating — nationally — an estimated 10% of all British food production in 1944, at the close of the World War. They were, too, a great place for children to play, learn and work. Growing up near the Hollingdean allotments one lady born in 1939 says[2], **"I feel sorry for kids, nowadays. They think they're street wise, but they're not. The things that I learnt about nature was from just going up the allotment and playing at the golf course. I take my grandchildren in the country and they're bored to tears, and yet that was our playground. Vandalism was unheard of in those days. When we got hungry we scrumped an apple or some blackberries or strawberries to keep us going for the afternoon. But we never damaged anything — it was harmless fun."** And another allotmentee[3] reminisces of those earlier days: **"under the door of our hut we had a wild bees nest there which we left alone. And we had mice in the hut. My father used to put a few seeds and potatoes out for them rather than poison. He said they wouldn't get into his sacks of saved vegetables if he put a bit of food out for them. But in those days you didn't feel you needed to protect wildlife because there was so much of it."**

Indeed, these allotment landscapes are extraordinarily rich places for wildlife. Whilst surveying part of the Race Hill Farm derelict allotment site for wildlife an expert collected a peculiar little beetle, which proved to be completely unknown from this country. This tiny (less than 2mm long) flightless Soldier Beetle was christened by him the **"Whitehawk Soldier Beetle"**, though the experts know it better as *Malthodes lobatus*. The survey work prior to the public inquiry into a

proposed housing development (which we won) identified 22 rare insect species, as well as the scarce Yellow Vetchling, on and around this threatened and neglected ex-allotment site. Then there were all the special birds, like Whitethroat and Stonechat, the big Lizard colony and the huge and noisy population of Great Green Bush-crickets.

Glow-Worm used to occur on the grassy paths of the Tenantry Down allotments right up until the late 1940s, having probably survived on this hillside for many millennia (till rendered extinct, probably by modern horticultural chemicals).

In addition, the disturbed habitats of Whitehawk Hill's allotments have other layers of new interest, which are of great value in their own right. There are the drifts of blue Asters on the hilltop, and the tall Japanese Spindle and Cherry Plum hedges on the Race Hill Farm allotments which have gained this area the nickname 'Little Ireland'. (The hedgerow Spindle, or the Cherry Plum, may be hosting the larval stages of the Whitehawk Soldier Beetle). Or there are the flaming sheets of Rosebay Willowherb, which host the caterpillars of the huge **Elephant Hawk-moth**, *Deilephila elpenor*, which crash into our moth-trap lights in summer and delight the kids.

Grass Snakes love compost heaps, as on the now-gone allotments of Benfield Valley. Slow Worms and Lizards love bits of tin and wood and rubbish piles, which can also provide homes for Carder Bumble-bees, Field Mice, Shrews, Field and Bank Voles. Scarce species such as the Dartford Warbler and **Woodcock** — notable even in the wildest countryside — can be seen on Whitehawk Hill's allotments.

Moulsecoomb Place Allotments, better known as the Moulscoomb Forest Garden, play host to **Badger, Fox**, Blue Tit and Wrens nests, Morel fungi, *Morchella elata*, on the wood chip mulch, and Smooth Newts by the net-full in the pond.

The allotments in the little valley of Roedale, Hollingbury, embraced by Down Plantation's trees.

A short spring stroll in Cross Road Allotments in Southwick showed **Tawny Mining-bees**, *Andrena fulva*, lovely golden Flower-bees, *Anthophora plumipes*, and Early and Buff-tailed Bumble-bees, *Bombus lucorum* and *B. terrestris*, nectaring on the flowers of Primulas and Lungwort and early blossom.

The high point of the allotment movement is now long gone, though it is undergoing a smaller revival. The great allotment and smallholding landscape of the Warren Road ridge was lost to the building of Woodingdean village, the conversion of the smallholdings to horseyculture, and the post-war abandonment of most of the allotments. The whole of Craven Vale and Freshfield Road became Council housing, as did the Hollingdean allotment landscape. The allotments of the steep south west slope of Whitehawk Hill, and the south slope of Lower Bevendean have now grown up to tall, shady woodlands in the space of just half a century!

The large area of allotments and smallholdings south of West Blatchington Court Farm and windmill has mostly gone, too. Corn, though, was still grown behind the houses of Nevill Avenue right up to the construction of the Polyclinic there, and The Weald and North Nevill Allotment sites still have an astonishing 529 busy plots, with waiting lists.

The decline of the allotments movement has lain these cultural landscapes open to the threat of development on a large scale, and often allotments are treated as a mere piggy bank of future development land. The large Eastbrook Farm allotment site, owned by Brighton but located just over the border with Adur District in Fishersgate, is presently the subject of such predatory proposals.

Allotments sites are often the only repository of disappearing landscape character. Only in the extraordinary Tolkienesque Roedale Valley, or in the Moulsecoomb Forest Garden, can the sheltered, sun-drenched warmth of these lost wooded Brighton combes still be appreciated fully. Only on the broad slope of Natal Road Allotments can you appreciate the wide openness of the Moulsecoomb Valley. Only on the flat expanse of the Wealden Allotments, or the Eastern Avenue Allotments in Shoreham, can you still get any sense of the lost old fertile landscape of the coastal plain, punctuated only by lines of hedgerow elms, the distant church tower of New Shoreham and Southwick church's spire, and the tall windmill of West Blatchington.

The 'Plotlands'

THE cheapness of land, transport and new prefabricated materials powered a huge energy amongst poorer folk desperate to leave the over-crowded 'wen' of London and the other industrial cities and make a new life with clean air and access to space and nature.

Even before the First World War there was a "rash of temporary dwellings and shacks" next to Brighton racecourse on the smallholdings and allotments between Warren Road and The Drove. After the war this was consolidated as the Brighton Heights Estate. At Telscombe cliffs, too, the Cavendish Estate Company made a feeble pre-1914 effort to lay out a clifftop settlement, but it went no further than a few houses and a lot of derelict-looking land.

After the First World War, however, this homesteading movement really took off with the vigorous intervention of the morally dubious Charles Neville, who, with his allies acquired much of the four miles of open cliffland between Rottingdean and Newhaven. This speculator had already been involved in buying mineral rights in New Guinea by selling trinkets to the local tribes, and in land development in Canada and Australia.

Neville's method was to stage a competition in which thousands of entrants were told that they had won a free plot[4], but were asked to pay three guineas for legal fees for the transfer of the land. Neville stood to gain a profit of 30 pounds for every acre of land. When he was inevitably taken to court (in an action in which the Daily Express paid the legal fees of the would-be plotlanders) Neville was found guilty and the judge concluded that the plots were absolutely worthless

and that the scheme was no more than a clever fraud[5].

In return for their money the homesteaders had no sewage system (relying at best on leaky septic tanks), which quickly made the land "sewage sick", no made-up roads and no street lighting. The cliffs were in retreat, of course, from coastal erosion at an average rate of 18 inches per year. Only in 1949 was the clifftop fenced, after a young child tragically fell from it, and only in the 1970s was the undercliff protected by a new sea wall.

Neville was also the developer of Saltdean, and when his Saltdean Estate Company got going in the later 1920s he must have felt that housing to a higher standard for a middle class clientele, rather than the make-shift plotlanders, would answer some of his critics. He was right, and Saltdean is now often praised as the attractive face of Downland property speculation, in contrast to down-market Peacehaven, whose plotland pioneers have now been replaced by the tenants of new housing association developments, particularly in the north of the town. Yet this must be largely a *social* judgement, not an *aesthetic* one, for the effect of 'tasteful' Saltdean upon the wider Downland landscape is plainly far larger than the effect of Peacehaven. Built in a landscape of Downland hills, Saltdean's housing rises up those slopes, and is painfully visible from all the surrounding ridges. In contrast, Peacehaven lies on the wide, flat plain between Telscombe Tye and Hoathdown/ Rushey Hill and is relatively unobtrusive from the surrounding Downland.

The plotlands have largely gone the same way as the allotments and smallholdings landscapes and have been consolidated into serviced townships, with their derelict spaces infilled, their roads made-up, and schools and modern shopping centres built.

Only in two areas do the original plotlands landscapes survive. One is in the gap between Newhaven and Peacehaven, with the failed townships of Friars Bay, Peacehaven Heights and Harbour Heights, and the other is at the northern end of Peacehaven on the slopes around Valley Road, where the town's old smallholdings district survives to this day. Caravan and mobile homes parks, pony paddocks, dense thickets of thorn and gorse, rutted and pot-holed roads, and an assortment of bungalows and houses dot these plotland fragments.

Peacehaven's Valley Road used to be a place of vegetable plots, chicken and rabbit farms. It is no longer busy with these small enterprises, and is now largely a leisure landscape, but the tall hedges, occasional tilled plots, sheds and outbuildings give it a real character. Local people have fended off major housing developments here, but it is remarkable that no attempt was made to include the area within the proposed National Park, for it richly deserves that status.

The Peacehaven — Newhaven gap is a remarkable sub-landscape. Huge swathes of thorn scrub advance and retreat before bursts of clearance and dereliction. The rutted plotland roads, deep puddled in winter, still display their street name signs — Charleston Avenue, Cuckmere Road, Links Avenue — as though they were ordinary suburban streets, though rank grass and gorse surrounds them, and half buried builders rubble and debris lies scattered along their kerbs. Despite strict planning protection the social character of the place is changing, as plot owners go up-market, with smart villas, dressage paddocks and high walls where there used to be cottages, small bungalows and shacks.

Elsewhere, only the smallest resonance of these plotlands survives. Sweet Hill's short-lived colony north of Waterhall has only one or two smallholding buildings to remind you of that episode. The small modern self-build developments of Sea Saw Way off Wilson's Avenue, Golf Drive

in the Roedale Valley, and Hog's Edge in Bevendean, with their wooden walls and verandas, like log cabins in the woods, or Heidi's house in the Alps, come nearest to the lost homesteaders spirit which once touched so many peoples' lives.

Horseyculture

FROM the eighteenth century horse racing and leisure riding on the Downs had been a core reason for Brighton's popularity. The Brighton Race Course embraced a whole square mile of the east Brighton Downs. There was a training gallops running high up from Thundersbarrow Barn to Truleigh Hill. The Lewes Race Course encompassed another three quarters of a square mile. Lewes continued to host a clutch of racing stables for years after the closure of the Race Course in 1964, and the course still has a busy training stables. Working with and getting to know horses and ponies has long been the aspiration of many thousands of children of all classes. It has, however, taken the combination of rising local prosperity and the recent farming depression to provide the basis for the substantial conversion of land to horse pasturage.

The world of the stables is made up mostly of women — and children — in refreshing contrast to the more masculinised world of farming, and they constitute busy communities on the larger yards.

This new land usage creates a distinctive sub-landscape. Fields tend to be sub-divided by a variety of fencing types, and field sheds appear, which vary from the ramshackle to the very smart. The pasturage tends to be over-grazed, sometimes to a point when the grassland type is difficult to recognize at first. The paraphernalia of artificially surfaced dressage paddocks, floodlighting, security lighting, new stabling and mobile homes appears around farmyards. Byways and bridleways near to livery stables tend to be heavily poached by horse traffic, and regular encroachment of horse riders onto Down pastures can have serious effects upon the sward and its specialist wildlife.

Horseycultural landscapes are increasing across the whole Down landscape, but they are particularly common on the urban fringe and around the scarp foot villages. The pattern of their occurrence is distinctive, with little on the northern edge of Brighton and Hove, but distinct clusters between east Brighton and Newhaven, and around Portslade, Southwick and Shoreham.

The old plotlands landscapes of north Peacehaven and Rushey Hill/Hoathdown have big concentrations of horse and pony keeping, as one would expect. The old smallholdings landscape around the Warren Road ridge, next to Brighton Race Course has been run as horse pasturage for over 40 years now, since Brighton Council bought out the famously smelly and fly-ridden piggeries there and let most of the land for grazing paddocks and stabling. The prosperous area around Ovingdean, south Woodingdean and Rottingdean has a substantial fraction of its farmland turned over to horseyculture. The pony paddocks down in Portslade's old village, hard by Easthill Park and the old flint walls of the medieval church and manor house, bring a little bit of the country into the town many decades after housing development has surrounded them.

Two major new livery establishments, at New Barn Farm, Portslade, and New Barn Farm, Ovingdean, hide painful stories of past farming errors. Both farms were the locations for disasters back at the end of the 1980s when autumn ploughed corn lands in the dry valleys were soaked by heavy rain, and brought flooding and mud slides crashing down on the residential areas below them. Following this trauma the farmer at New Barn Portslade converted all the farm to permanent grassland, and the livery grazing around the farmstead now comprises about 20% of the holding. At Ovingdean the livery grazing is less, but the valley above the stables is now barraged by three earth dams.

The new horseyculture can bring many possibilities for wildlife, from tiny insects to bats and birds.

Many pony paddocks now have a red, very spiny, knapweed-like plant called **Red Star Thistle**, *Centaurea calcitrapa*. It used to be very rare, and Sussex is still its British HQ, but you can now expect it to turn up anywhere on the Brighton Downs where horses are exercised. It occurs on the paddocks at Mile Oak, as well as on Southwick Hill, and over on the Downs east of Brighton.

Horse pastures can be great places for mushrooms, and some species clearly target the mounds of stable litter, too. Horse Mushrooms, *Agaricus arvensis*, appropriately enough, love those dung heap piles. Walking on the line of the old Lewes Race Course I have found four eating mushroom, *Agaricus*, species on the stable litter banked up against the hedge.

If the pastures are unfertilized and the horses not treated with strong vermicides, then they can set up a food chain of marvellous richness. The cornerstone of this diversity is horse dung! On the Race Hill paddocks forty years of grazing without pesticides and fertilizers have made an island for wildlife. Flocks of Rooks, Crows and Jackdaws, with Green Woodpecker, pick apart the dropped dung for beetle and fly grubs. Overhead Swallows and House Martins sweep by, trawling for the flying insects of the fresh dung. At night a party of Serotine Bats fly all the way — two miles — from Coldean to hunt for flying chafers and other beetles. And, round the perimeter of the paddocks, you can find Badger latrines full of the shiny, iridescent wing cases of Dor Beetles snatched as they wander from the dung heaps under which they make their nest burrows.

And other, rarer and more spectacular insects are found there, too. Race Hill's horse paddocks are the 'mother ship' for a colony of one of Britain's biggest — and most handsome — flies: the **Hornet Robber-fly**, *Asilus crabroniformis*. You will find them in late summer, like funny inch-long, ochre-and-gold-coloured trolls, perched on cow pats waiting to leap out and capture passing flies or grasshoppers.

Horseyculture can be very bad news for wildlife and the open Down landscape, too.

It can enclose and privatize previously open grasslands. Thankfully the pony paddocks dividing up part of the ancient grassland above the Balsdean Pumping Station have now been removed (June '08). They threatened an important site for Early Spider Orchis, Frog and Bee Orchids. The wayward troops of exercising horses on Sheepcote Valley and Race Hill's slopes cause disturbance to locally important ground nesting Skylarks and Meadow Pipits. The National Trust has had to fence open Down to prevent persistent damage to rare Man Orchids from wandering horse riders.

There is much to be negotiated to make for harmony for all Downland users.

Footnotes

1   Of course, many rural courses on common land are still grazed. The New Forest golf courses are simply specialist managed parts of the common grazing pastures.

2   Judith Spence in *Seedy Business — Tales from an Allotment Shed* by Warren Carter (Moulsecoomb Forest Garden and Wildlife Project, 2001): www.seedybusiness.org

3   Sheila Groom in *Seedy Business* by Warren Carter: www.seedybusiness.org

4   I remember my granny telling me she'd won a plot at Peacehaven in the newspaper competition (she lived in Luton then) but later had to give it away for lack of money to develop the plot!

5   See *Cotters and Squatters: Housing's Hidden History* — Colin Ward (Five Leaves Publications, 2002). Also *Peacehaven: A Pictorial History* — Bob Poplett (Phillimore, 1993) and *The South Downs* — Peter Brandon (Phillimore, 1998)

THREATS TO OUR
DOWNLAND

T HOUGH conservationists have won some big victories in recent decades the old threats remain and have been added to by new ones.

Neglect

MANY important wildlife-rich Down pasture sites are suffering from both lack of grazing and scrub management. They may be in public or private control. If they are in public control the problem may be local government funding constraints, ignorance and indifference, or inability to properly challenge protected farm tenants. It may also be because of a lack of available local grazing stock. If they are in private control the problems are usually commercial, coupled with indifference and ignorance, if not hostility, and game shooting demands.

Threatened public sector sites include the nationally famous scarp sections at Ditchling Beacon (Sussex Wildlife Trust) and Blackcap and Mount Harry (National Trust), the Newhaven cliffs (Lewes District Council), Hoddern Down (Lewes DC and private owners), as well as outstanding places like Whitehawk Hill and Moulsecoomb Wild Park (Brighton Council).

Threatened privately owned sites include areas round the South Downs Way like Streat Bostal scarp, Offham Chalk Pits, Spital Down by Lewes Prison, Cold Coombes by Kingston Hill, High Hill north of Rottingdean, The Beeches and Pyecombe Golf Course, and Freshcombe, north of Portslade.

Few acts of neglect are challenged, because the deterioration of these sites

Rank grass and spreading thorn thickets creep across the south slope of Freshcombe, north west of Mile Oak.

Protected Downland Sites

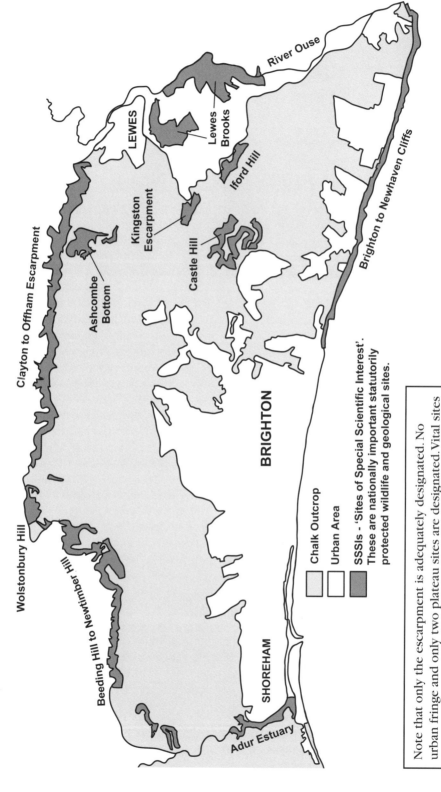

Legend:

Chalk Outcrop

Urban Area

SSSIs - 'Sites of Special Scientific Interest'. These are nationally important statutorily protected wildlife and geological sites.

Note that only the escarpment is adequately designated. No urban fringe and only two plateau sites are designated. Vital sites like Dencher Bottom, Waterpit Hill and High Hill are excluded.

Labels on map: River Ouse, LEWES, Lewes Brooks, Iford Hill, Kingston Escarpment, Castle Hill, Brighton to Newhaven Cliffs, Clayton to Offham Escarpment, Ashcombe Bottom, BRIGHTON, Wolstonbury Hill, Beeding Hill to Newtimber Hill, SHOREHAM, Adur Estuary

A lonely fragment of ancient Down pasture in a sea of cultivation. Balsdean, north of Rottingdean.

is slow and therefore less noticed, and most of the sites are poorly known or understood by the public.

Intensification

GROSS damage to ancient chalk grassland and archaeology still goes on, often at sites away from areas of public usage, or on small sites, though large-scale damage is now largely halted in the face of overwhelming public pressure. In any case, most easily cultivable ancient Down pasture sites have long been destroyed by farmers, so some of the drop in the level of attrition of such sites is simply due to their extreme scarcity and low utility to farmers.

However, the situation may take a turn for the worse as farmers respond to raised food prices with a new cycle of intensification. Already huge areas are being put back into cultivation after years of reversion to pasture.

The recent destruction by agro chemicals of part of the mile long pastures east of Mount Zion, on New Barn Farm, was a scandal that went unmarked, despite their being in Brighton City Council ownership. The destruction of the Scabby Brow scrubs and glades was challenged locally, but the institutional response was pathetic. Similarly, at Halcombe slope, Piddinghoe, where the landowner erected a pheasant pen on prime chalk grassland for which he was receiving environmental payments, the state showed a shyness in enforcement that they would certainly not show towards dodgy benefits recipients. There was enforcement action at Casterbridge, Pangdean, when the tenant bulldozed an area where there had already been a trail bike circuit, but the site remains at risk. At Coombe Farm, Saltdean, small areas of an old Down pasture site were sold off for incorporation in neighbouring gardens. The City Council intervened and hopefully this practice will not be repeated.

Traffic Increases and Road Building.

SINCE the 1990s the new Brighton A27 bypass has destroyed the tranquility of most of the near-urban Downland plateau, and increased traffic has done the same for all of the rest of the A27 and A23 corridors. Now traffic pours in a continuous roar past Waterhall and Patcham windmill, and the bypass junctions at Shoreham and Falmer sprawl as wastefully as any American beltway. And after the Albion Football stadium is built it is a safe bet that a Woodingdean bypass across the Downs will be proposed at some point.

The old villages road from Lewes to Newhaven is now jammed with traffic at peak times and sees tailbacks to Rodmell from the coast. Peacehaven-bound traffic spills onto the little Downland road through Telscombe, even though its final section is a deeply rutted dirt track

The destroyed site of Scabby Brow, Ashcombe (seen here from Kingston Hill) showing as crop marks in a huge arable field. Scabby Brow's bushes and flowery glades were ploughed out only recently.

with only bridleway status. The quiet hilltop roads to the Devil's Dyke and Saddlescombe and across Ditchling Beacon are no longer safe for cyclists and walkers as motorists roar up there at crazy speeds.

Air and Aquifer Pollution

DIFFUSE atmospheric pollution is one of the worst enemies of surviving wildlife-rich old Down pastures.

Nitrogen-based pollution from motor vehicle emissions, intensive farming, and so on, reduces species diversity at current rates of deposition on our Downland, and more strongly close to road corridors, like the A27 and A23. It particularly hits the sensitive moss, lichen and fungal communities, as well as wild flowers and less aggressive grass species. It is noteworthy, for instance, that the rich Waxcap fungal community on the top of Whitehawk Hill fruits very thinly. That may be due to the taller grass on that site, which is known to inhibit fruiting, but it may also be due to the nitrogen oxide and other pollutants from the

busy surrounding roads. It also does so indirectly, by stimulating the spread of coarse and blanketting Tor Grass.

Though gross forms of pollution, like sulphur dioxide, have come under some control in recent years and enabled the recovery of some lower plant populations, other pollutants, even at far lower concentrations, continue to erode the most sensitive plant communities, and prevent their recovery.

Pollution of the chalk aquifer by farm fertilisers and other agro chemicals now has a significant effect on our drinking water and obliges Southern Water to install expensive purification equipment at the more damaged pumping locations. Those big metal tanks that have appeared at Waterhall and Newmarket pumping stations do a job that should not need to be done.

Climate Change

THE direct effects of climate change may include the creation of extra stresses on vulnerable communities of shade and

Tranquil Areas Map: South Downs Area of Outstanding Natural Beauty.

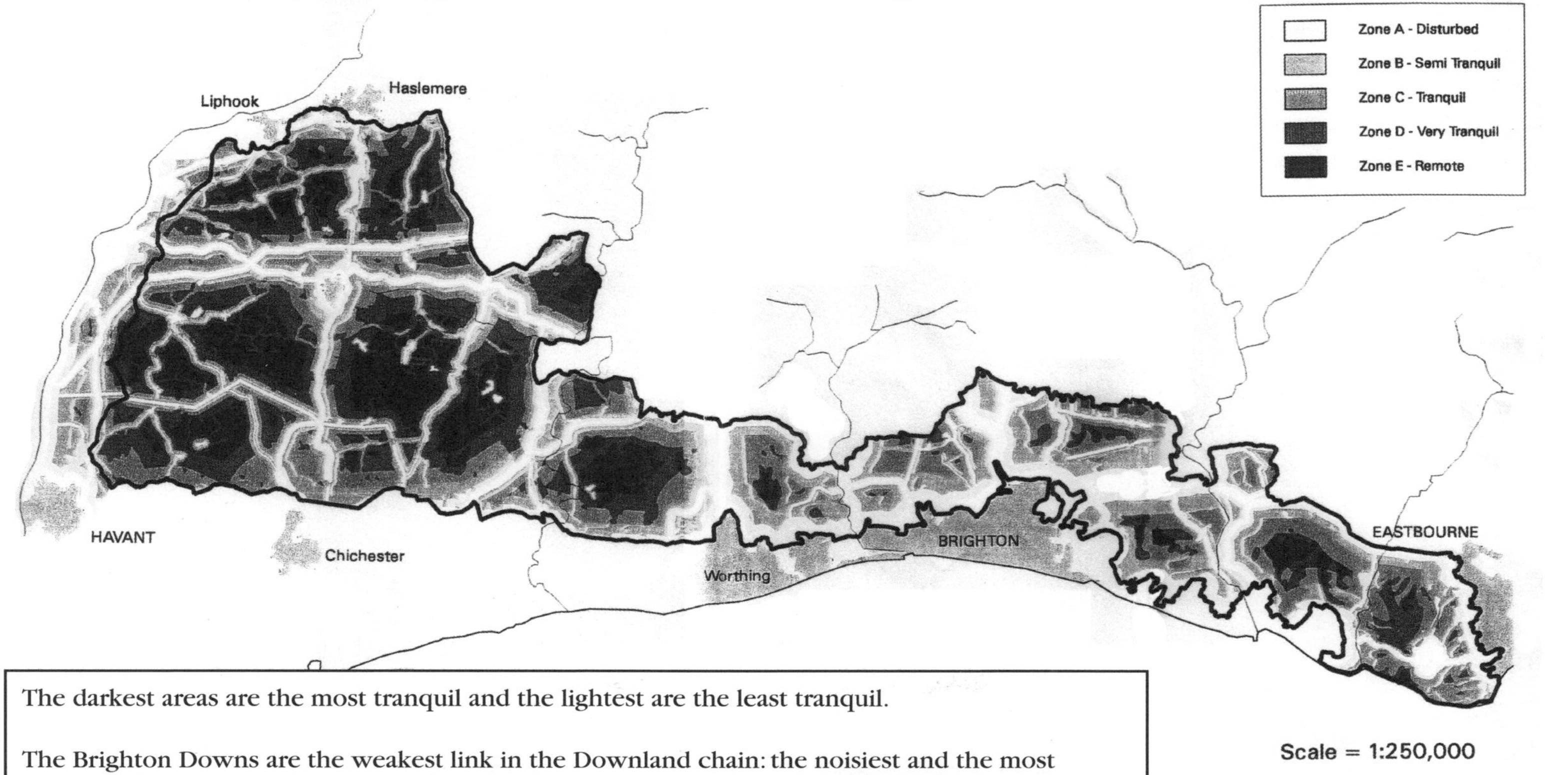

TRANQUIL AREAS

Zone A - Disturbed
Zone B - Semi Tranquil
Zone C - Tranquil
Zone D - Very Tranquil
Zone E - Remote

Scale = 1:250,000

EASTBOURNE

BRIGHTON

Worthing

Haslemere

Liphook

Chichester

HAVANT

The darkest areas are the most tranquil and the lightest are the least tranquil.

The Brighton Downs are the weakest link in the Downland chain: the noisiest and the most visually damaged. The A23 and A27 corridors do the most damage. To find real tranquility we have to hunker down in the remotest valleys.

Brighton seen from the South Downs Way at Truleigh Hill. There's no escaping the egotism of high-rise development. From whole stretches of the South Downs Way Brighton's high-rises are visible. No proper assessment of the visual impact of these schemes has ever been done.

moisture loving Down pasture plants, especially mosses and liverworts. Plants and animals which are on the edge of their range this far north, like Horseshoe Vetch and the Adonis and Chalkhill Blue butterflies, may benefit from warming, though other changes, for instance in rainfall patterns and quantities, could cancel these benefits out for some species. Groups like old grassland fungi are very dependent for fruiting on rainfall and we already see dramatic differences in abundance from year to year. It is difficult to predict how this will pan out in the long term. Wildlife which is already stressed and declining from other human causes may not be able to tolerate further pressures. Rainfall patterns just in the last two summers have caused steep declines in the populations of our local bumble-bees, butterflies and moths.

Climate change will certainly encourage the more mobile species to colonize from the continent. Already we are seeing many new insects arriving. We will lose others, though.

Sea level rise will bring new erosive pressures to those portions of the chalk cliffs which have so far escaped coastal engineering, and in the long term may threaten part of the existing pattern of settlement on the coast. Settlements in vulnerable areas, for instance on the flood plains of the Ouse and Adur, or in some areas facing the sea, may ultimately require relocation.

The indirect effects of climate change may mean that the planning constraints on the development of wind farms and other intrusive renewable energy developments are weakened. Capital will always seek ways of exploiting new opportunities at the expense of nature — even when the rationale is the mitigation of the effects of damage to the natural climatic system.

High Rise and Built Development

WITH the A27 bypass has come the Holmbush mall, the wrecking of the Benfield Valley, and now the Albion football stadium. Developments on the Downs, when they come, tend to be large and very damaging.

Other developments off the Downs can still affect them. The growth in air traffic from Shoreham Airport has badly dented the tranquility of the Adur Downs, and will do so more if the Airport expands.

The pushing through of a new permissive policy towards high rise development by Brighton Council had backing from some Greens, who argued that it's better to stack people high than spread them low. That thinking ignored the real motors of high rise development (in the push by capital to service the consumerism of the rich, and in the over-heating of the regional economy). It also ignored the effects of high rise development on the wider landscape of the Downs. Now we are faced with a 450 ft Marina tower block next to Sussex's white cliffs and only a third of a mile from the National Park boundary, as well as other blocks which will be visible within a radius of twenty miles of National Park Downland.

Other disasters are waiting to happen. The derelict Beeding Chalk Pit is eyed up by all sorts of predators anxious to build things they would never otherwise get permission for on open Downland. The last sections of Sussex chalk cliff still free of coastal engineering — at Telcombe Tye and Newhaven — may be threatened with such works as their erosion takes them back towards the coast road and residential property.

Landfill

LANDFILL may mean the loss of the geological and fossil resources of the working pits at Wolstonbury and Horton Farm. Both pits have received waste already, in some measure. The worst threat is likely to be to the two adjacent Southeram Grey Pits and the Balcombe Pit at Glynde, with their superb fossil-rich Grey Chalk sections. The southern Southeram Grey Pit is a geological SSSI.

Already there has been talk of them being used for London's rubbish.

Game Shooting.

IN the last generation there has been a massive expansion of intensive game bird shooting on the Brighton Downs. Some areas (like Balsdean Bottom and the Downs between Southease and Piddinghoe) now have the character of intensive poultry rearing enterprises, with the period from July to January full of the noise of whirring wings and the echoes of shotguns, the calling of pheasant and partridge, and the sight of scuttling poults and rotting carcases.

Game shooting is anathema to any project for a public, democratic Downland, and for the restoration of an open Down pasture landscape. Gamekeepers challenge innocent usage of the countryside — walking, nature study and play — and attempt to remove the public from their ground. They challenge members of the public even on Access Land and Rights of Way. They encourage the destruction and fragmentation of chalk grassland by scrub encroachment because such scrub provides cover for the semi-wild pheasants. They have built large rearing pens on old chalk grassland and within scrub and woodland, and planted cover crops on old chalk grassland.

About 75,000[1] metric tonnes of toxic lead shot are discharged annually on a national scale — with unquantified effects on the soil fauna and flora and on birds of prey and other predators that take game birds.

The huge biomass of pheasant and partridge radically alters the balance of wild species.[2] Stoat, Weasel, and Fox, for instance, are encouraged by the huge numbers of naïve birds released and are then trapped and shot mercilessly. And the effects of game birds intensive foraging on old Down pasture herbs and insects has not been assessed. In ancient woodland such foraging replaces the ancient

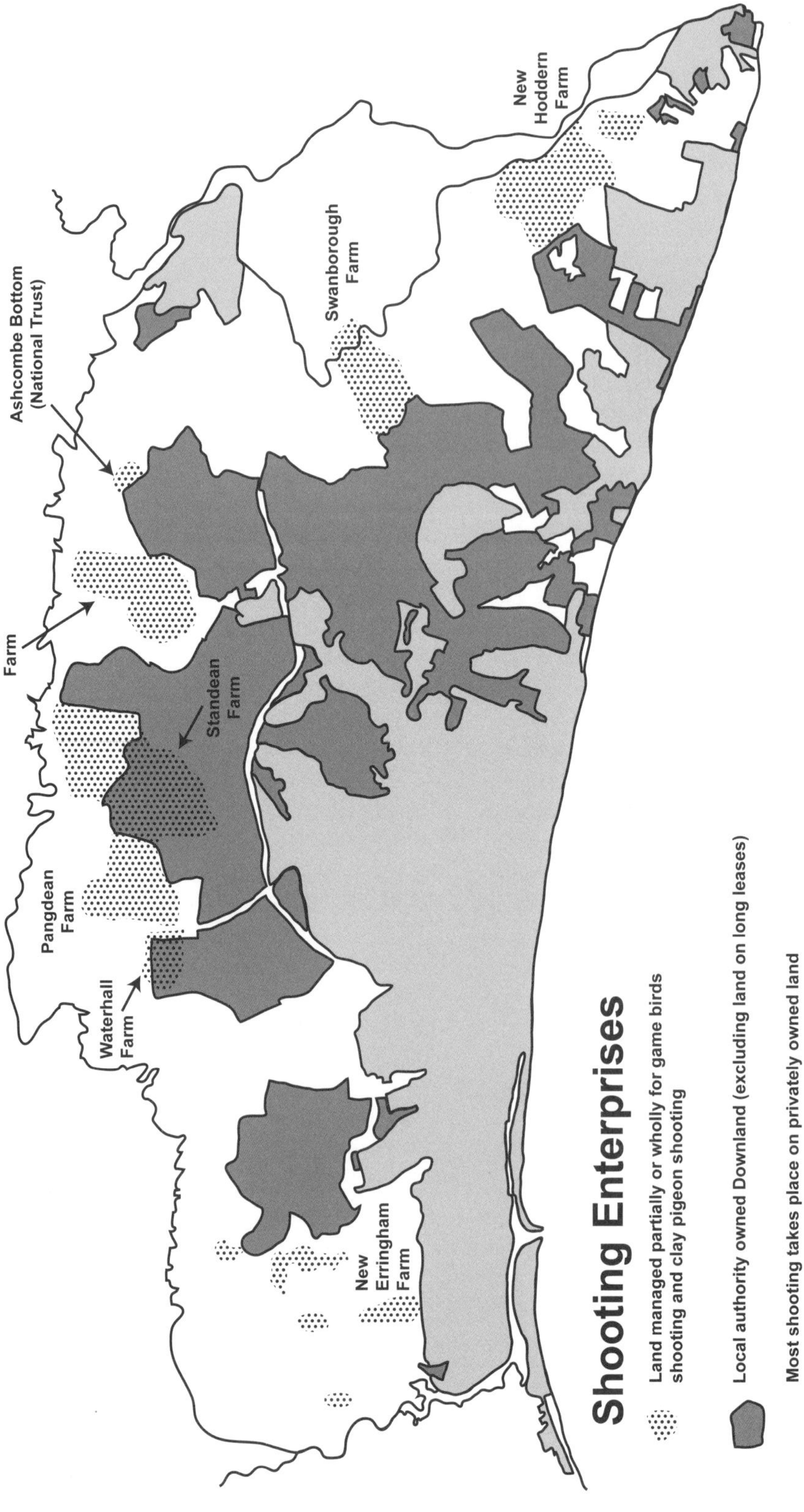

Shooting Enterprises

New Hoddern Farm

Swanborough Farm

Ashcombe Bottom (National Trust)

Mary Farm

Standean Farm

Pangdean Farm

Waterhall Farm

New Erringham Farm

Land managed partially or wholly for game birds shooting and clay pigeon shooting

Local authority owned Downland (excluding land on long leases)

Most shooting takes place on privately owned land

woodland herbs with weedy species and bare ground.[3]

In centuries past farmers would have ridiculed the idea that the Downs would become pheasant country, for pheasants are a woodland bird. Pheasant rearing was done locally only in Stanmer Woods and some rew woods of the scarp. Now, the spread of scrub and woodland has brought them all over our Downs. And where there are no pheasant there are reared Partridge.

Luckily, Brighton Council ownership has kept intensive game shooting off large swathes of Downland. Even there, though, two Brighton tenant farms — Standean and Waterhall — continue to host such shoots and at least two other tenant farmers host shoots on land they manage nearby.

New agro-environmental measures have obliged farmers to cease using some vulnerable sites for game rearing, but often pens remain even after they are no longer used, such as at Freshcombe and Dencher Bottom, or Pangdean Holt.

We have had some success in campaigning against abuse, such as at Halcombe Farm, Piddinghoe, where the farmer was obliged to remove his pen from the majority of an ancient Down pasture site. It is not enough, though. The trend is for further acquisition of land for shooting and more farmers are making deals with syndicates. The end result is that wonderful sites such as The Beeches at Pyecombe and Nore Down at Piddinghoe are lost to nettles, scrub, rank vegetation, and mindless slaughter.

The Invasion of Problem Species

OLD Down pasture is threatened by the spread of a number of species, some native, like Tor Grass and Hawthorn, and some escaped alien species, often of garden origin.

Tor Grass is spreading at a dangerous rate. Large under-grazed sites like Cold Coombes and Kingston Hill, and large parts of the northern escarpment, are turning from a springy short turf to a mat of tussocky Tor Grass, unpalatable to commercial sheep and cattle except for a short time in spring. A combination of under-grazing and the effects of nitrogen-based air pollution encourage its spread. The grass was always present, but only as a small component of a diverse sward. Now some sites are moving close to becoming Tor Grass monocultures.

The Brighton Downs are a redoubt of the traditional Sheep's Fescue turf, though the neighbouring Firle Beacon Downs and the Surrey and Kentish Downland, have long suffered from heavy Tor Grass infestation. Now the problem has hit our Downs, too.

The spread of several garden **Cotoneasters**, *Cotoneaster spp.*, is also becoming very serious. Only occasionally seen a few decades ago, Cotoneasters can now be seen even on the remotest, most intact sites. Chalk pits and steep slopes with thin open turf are especially vulnerable. The Cotoneaster species with low growth and a wide horizontal spread are the worst because they quickly shade out the short turf underneath. At Moulsecoomb Pit the most valuable slope is at risk of total loss to Cotoneaster invasion. The north side banks of the A27 Bypass cutting through Slonk Hill and Mill Hill, Shoreham, are succumbing to a mass of Cotoneaster, through lack of management by the Department of Transport. This ground-level thicket acts as a seedbed for the expansion of the shrubs onto vulnerable sites.

Buddleia, *Buddleja davidii*, is at present only a minor threat, particularly to sites with much bare ground, like bostal sides, quarries, and tracks. It does expand rapidly, though. The huge Beeding Chalk Pit is gradually becoming carpetted with Buddleia, and Offham Chalk Pits are vulnerable, too.

Other species pose local threats. The **hybrid Bluebell**, which lacks the elegance and deep colour of the native species, is spreading next to the urban fringe and in some woods. Folk also deliberately plant it even in remote areas, such as near Thundersbarrow, or accidentally introduce it by dumping garden waste.

Such species are a serious problem when they challenge native species or threaten biodiversity. Most alien species easily become ordinary parts of the native plant and animal communities, but a minority 'take off' when conditions are right. The **Harlequin Ladybird**, *Harmonia axyridis*, brought into Europe as a biological control, has come to threaten many native Ladybird species in just a few years.

Horseyculture

T H E growth of horse and pony keeping can be a very positive thing. It is not always well managed, though, and when it is not

damage can be done. Over-grazing is the most frequent problem, but others include the unsightly spread of field shelters, the fragmentation of big sites into fenced paddocks, the dumping of stable muck, and the poaching of tracks and pastures by frequent usage. Disturbance to ground nesting birds and trampling of rare orchids are two problems that have caused local grief.

Footnotes

1 'Pheasant shooting in Britain — the sport and industry in the 21st century' — Peter Robinson, Consultant Ornithologist, page 2.
2 *Ibid.*
3 'The ground flora of ancient semi-natural woodlands in pheasant release pens in England' — Rufus Sage, Clare Ludolf and Petere Robertson. *Biological Conservation* 122 (2005), pp. 243-252.

FIGHTBACK

WITHOUT the past campaigning by the Society of Sussex Downsmen (now the South Downs Society) and many local and national activists, the Brighton Downs would have been largely lost by now, just as the Surrey Downs due north of us are gone, except for 'precious fragments'.

In recent decades, though, conservationists have won a wave of crucial new victories.

The South Downs 'Environmentally Sensitive Area'

IN the mid 1980s the Conservatives under Selwyn Gummer adopted the idea of agri-environmental support for countryside restoration on a landscape-wide scale. It was a fine idea. Instead of a scatter of funding of individual farmers wherever they may show interest, a series of endangered landscapes of national value would be targetted for a coordinated programme of landscape restoration. Farmers would get subsidy for using traditional methods of extensive grazing and would be paid for the restoration of pastures, scrub clearance, fencing and other capital works.

Many areas were suggested for possible inclusion. Led by Paul Millmore and Phil Belden, a small team of activists launched a major lobbying campaign to make sure that the South Downs were chosen. Massive mailings winged out to all those with influence. They were successful, and the South Downs was included within the very first tranche of chosen landscapes, alongside areas like the Norfolk Broads, the Pennine Dales and Loch Lomond.

The scheme has made a profound difference. Some farmers included most of their farms in the scheme, and many sites that had been neglected for decades were brought back into management. Sheep and cattle began to reappear in substantial numbers in a landscape dominated by cereals production for half as century. The scheme provoked emulation from Brighton Council's new Labour administration (untarnished yet by years of retreat) who developed their own mini-scheme for those areas left outside it, until the ESA's success enabled it to extend its boundaries and embrace some of those excluded areas.

There were many limitations to the scheme. It was seriously under-staffed and monitored, and the detection of abuse was often left up to members of the public. Because it was driven by the priority of supporting existing farm businesses many imbalances were created. Areas of productive newly created pasture were enthusiastically grazed, whilst neighbouring old Down pasture fragments often received only enough grazing to fulfill the minimum requirements of the scheme — if that — and not enough to bring them back into pristine condition. Sometimes, too, areas were over-grazed. The payment levels were not enough to bring many businesses into the scheme. Yet, for all that, the ESA scheme has made a bigger difference to the survival chances of old Down pasture on our Downs than any other single act of policy since the Second World War.

Paul Millmore, Phil Belden and their band of campaigners have much to be proud of.

The future may unravel these gains, though. ESA payments are being replaced by new subsidies (such as Higher Level Stewardship), and the pressure for new cultivation from rising grain prices and bio fuels is intense.

Stopping the Sale of the Downs

I N late 1994 activists in Brighton got wind of a proposal by Brighton Council's Blairite leadership to sell-off the 11,000 acres of Downland farms the Council had so laboriously acquired over the past century. The money was to be used to help finance capital works such as re-wiring the Brighton Centre and re-doing the Marine Parade balustrades.

A coalition of community activists and wildlifers hastily got together and — under the name 'Keep Our Downs Public' — swung into action. The economics of the privatisation were nonsense, of course. The let farms were likely to attract only half the price they would get with vacant possession, and with the government taking half the capital generated, and other shortfalls, it was likely the council would be able to utilize only *one fifth* of the sale price!

KODP took the argument into the Labour Party, addressing almost all their ward parties and taking motions to their ruling bodies. They exposed the Council's poor past management of the farms and the fantastic potential they had missed. They exposed the wretched record of the tenant farmers who the Council was proposing to sell the land to. They demonstrated the likely future of the Council farms, if sold, by comparison with neighbouring private sector farms, and they argued, picketed and lobbied the media.

They were pretty much on their own. None of the other well-funded conservation bodies — the Downsmen, the Ramblers, the Wildlife Trust and so on — supported their stand. They all believed that struggles against privatisation could not be won. All were prepared to settle for the most flimsy of reassurances from the Council.

It did not matter in the end, for our message was heard. Labour Party members, as well as the Tory and Lib Dem opposition, did not want the sell-off. Decades of agri-business destruction told its own plain story of what happens to the countryside under commercial private ownership.

The privatization proposals were quietly dropped, though desultory talks continued with the National Trust, who had earlier bought the Devil's Dyke and Saddlescombe Farm from the Council. Even within the Trust, though, we had friends and the case was strongly made that the Trust should not 'cherry pick' already publicly owned conservation land and provide political cover for a squalid municipal sell-out.

It has taken a decade since then for the longer term proposals of the campaigners to be heard, but, at last they bear some fruit, with the opening up of Stanmer Park and parts of the Ditchling Beacon Downs to public access and the spread of council in-hand conservation management.

And KODP's stand may have had even greater effects, for since those days, trade unionists and community campaigners have halted or reversed no less than three other major City Council privatisations. The ripples from one dropped pebble can spread very wide.

Like our successes with the ESA scheme, though, these gains are coming under new threats. Labour made several piecemeal sales on Downland, and new national and local policy shifts may encourage new asset sales. New campaigns will be necessary.

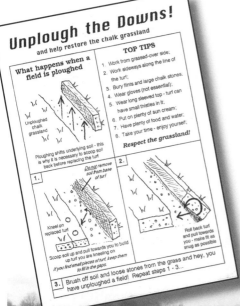

The 'Un-Ploughing' of the Downs

As the General Election of 1997 approached another major crisis developed. Conservationists heard that a farmer was threatening to plough up large chunks of the lovely Offham Down, which is in the SSSI (Site of Special Scientific Interest) that stretches along the escarpment from Clayton to the River Ouse at Offham. SSSI's are the 'crown jewels' of nature in the UK, but had only limited legal protection.

Negotiations had been going on for months between the farmer, who wished to grow flax on parts of the SSSI, and English Nature, who were responsible for safeguarding SSSI's.

The talks broke down because EN were not able to offer sufficient compensation money to the farmer for the profit he would forgoe by not planting the flax, which was being promoted under the

Campaigners heaving back the turves of Offham Down in 1997. And here's their little instruction sheet!

EU's Common Agricultural Policy as a new industrial crop at an astonishing subsidy of £591 per ha. English Nature — always feeble in standing up to landowners and business — refused to place a 'Nature Conservation Order' on the site, arguing that they couldn't justify it because parts of the SSSI were not of sufficient value.

The farmer started to plough the SSSI, mostly at night. Early in April a party of conservationists went up there and confronted the farmer just as he was about to start ploughing the most sensitive part of the Down. Their action forced him to leave the site. He came back, though, and continued ploughing in darkness.

That was enough. Activists from Earth First! and the local Friends of the Earth occupied the partly ploughed Down. FOE and the Wildlife Trust organized a large demonstration on the site. The issue hit the national news in a big way. The local Labour Party candidate came out strongly against the ploughing. Both Conservative and Labour vied to denounce the madness that allowed a farmer to be paid to destroy a nationally important nature conservation site. The future of Offham Down became an election issue

Public support for the site occupiers escalated. One Sunday afternoon 250 people turned up on the Down to 'unplough' the damaged sward. Everyone who was fit enough joined in to heave over and replace the ploughed turfs. Even the farmer, Justin Harmer, came up to the site and joined in.

English Nature had egg on its face. Selwyn Gummer, the outgoing Tory minister, ordered his officials to find him good reasons for preserving the site whatever English Nature might say. The reasons were obvious, with Sussex Rampion, Bastard Toadflax and many other old Downland herbs a-plenty on the site.

As one of his last acts in office Gummer slapped on a Nature Conservation Order, and the site was saved. The farmer did

well, too, gaining a very generous level of compensation. The law had encouraged vandalism.

The Offham Down victory provided all the arguments for much stronger legislative protection of nature conservation sites, which was one of the early achievements of the new Labour government.

But the victory had broader repercussions. It showed that the public would demonstrate, occupy, and take direct action against the destruction of nature even on remote sites where they had no right of access.

The Right to Roam

ONE part of Labour's past radicalism that survived the coming of New Labour was a commitment by the new government to the 'right to roam'. Ramblers and labour movement activists had campaigned for this for well over a century, and it was well past time that this simple reform should have its day. Michael Meacher, the Labour Minister of the Environment, was personally committed to it.

A public debate kicked off about what form this new freedom should take. Two forms of access were debated. On the one hand, many activists wanted an inclusive right. They argued that we should adopt the long-standing Swedish model of comprehensive open access, subject to the obvious conditions that no damage should be done and that the privacy of people's homes should be respected. The Swedish call this 'Allemansratt', or Everyman's Right.

The large access organizations argued, however, for a more limited right of access to 'open country', which had come to be defined in law as: mountain, moor, heath, down, common, woodland, coast and waterside. Their view was shared by Meacher.

Landowners and their allies launched a strident campaign against any kind of freedom to roam, be it inclusive or limited. They filled many pages of the conservative

'Right to Roam' Trespassers walking a forbidden footpath at Falmer from Ridge Farm to Balmer Farm. 1998.

papers and much air-time in denouncing the outrageous consequences of letting folk walk freely in the countryside.

Access campaigners on the Brighton Downs wasted no time either, and under the banner of 'The Land Is Ours', the land rights organization founded by George Monbiot, they organised a campaign of mass trespasses on the eastern Downs to highlight the nonsense of public exclusion.

The local situation was very stark. Not more than 20% of the old Down pasture and scrub had public access, though such habitat itself comprised a mere 9% of the open Brighton Downs. The public had an existing right of access to perhaps 4% of the Brighton Downs in total, despite the fact that about two thirds of these Downs were in some form of public ownership, and despite the forthcoming National Park project.

We walked. Our first walk attracted about 60 folk on a trespass ramble around the Ditchling Beacon Downs. It was a success, despite the police attempting to persuade our hire bus driver to abandon us on the Downs and despite the squally weather.

Our second walk attracted 120 on an exhilarating route from Falmer across Balmer Down to Offham Down.

The press publicity began to roll in, with us providing a double act with the 'legal' wing of the movement: the Ramblers Association and the Open Spaces Society. Mark Thomas did a special TV programme on the Brighton Downs, and came on our first trespass.

Over the summer of '98 we organized five big trespasses, culminating in a glorious ramble on all the forbidden Downland around the Long Man of Wilmington, which attracted at least 170 folk, including contingents from London, Kent and all over Sussex. Des Turner, the Brighton Labour MP, addressed our rally under The Long Man.

We gained good coverage on all the main national TV and radio news bulletins

Not-So-Free-To-Roam

Unimproved Down pasture which has been open to the public from 2004 under the Countryside and Rights of Way (CROW) Act, 2000.

Other old Down pasture and scrub excluded from the statutory freedom to roam.

Tottington Mount

Devil's Dyke

Clayton Down

Offham

Southease

Sheepcote Valley

Brighton

and did interviews on everything from Farming Today to You and Yours.

We continued the trespass walks all through the following winter of '98-'99, culminating in a 60 strong trespass into Arundel Park, where the Earl of Arundel had bricked up the northern entrance to the Park, near to his pheasant rearing pens.

The right to roam passed into law. There is no doubt that the combination of legal lobbying and organized trespassing highlighted the access campaigners side of the debate as nothing else could have done.

That was not the end, however, for we were then faced with a three year campaign to gain the optimum amount of Access Land from a designation procedure which was heavily biased against public intervention. Despite providing complete maps and site details for every acre of eligible access land on the Brighton Downs (and the whole of the rest of the 80 mile South Downs chain) no DEFRA official ever approached us for a face to face meeting, or sought to test our proposals in discussion. Landowners were allowed to appeal against site designation, but the public were not allowed to appeal against site exclusion. Some sites which appeared on the first draft maps disappeared from the later drafts, presumably after their owners had objected. They never reached the appeals procedure because they were dropped from the candidate site list before designation.

Many small sites were excluded, which, given that the Down pasture on the Brighton Downs was shattered into around 180 fragments — many of only a few acres — was a major loss. Golf courses were excluded, despite the fact that all bar two of them on the Brighton Downs was constructed on ancient Down pasture. And sites which were at all anomalous or unusual clearly 'threw' the DEFRA officials so that they simple excluded them. Thus, the gorsey slopes north of Kingston Hill

were excluded, though they have probably had Down pasture cover for several thousand years. Old Down pasture that lay in larger land units was excluded, though these land units were often of recent origin and bore no relation to traditional patterns of land use or land ownership. Woodland had been dropped from the categories of eligible land during the consultation, so places like Coombe Plantation, Clayton Holt and Newer Copse continue as close-kept secrets, despite their loveliness.

Even now, some Access Land on our Downs has no stiles or gates or notices of entitlement because of continuing farmers opposition, and timid Council enforcement.

In the first year after designation I was challenged several times for walking on designated Access Land sites. Those challenges have lessened, though they still occur. As recently as May 2008, I was challenged aggressively on a Brighton Council owned farm by the tenant farmer, who denied that the site was Access Land.

For all that, the Right to Roam provisions of the CROW Act (Countryside and Rights of Way Act, 2000) has shifted public consciousness gradually and brought many places to public attention.

The assemblage of Access Land sites will be reviewed after 10 years have passed. We must expect challenges, then, to the continuance of some sites as Access Land, as well as having to fight for the inclusion of all those previously excluded sites.

The National Park

S i x t y years ago, when the idea of British National Parks first passed into law, they were not considered to be areas where the landscape should be publicly owned — as they are in the United States. Landowner and farmer interests were too strong. The Parks were merely areas that received a higher level of planning control and funding. Only in Scotland was the public ownership of National Park landscapes seriously proposed — and

The Downs are Ours at Night, Too.

(I wrote this poem in June 2000 as part of the lobby to prevent Parliament restricting the right to roam to day time. I got bored with ordinary letters of objection and thought a poem would be more effective.)

At night you can hear the vixen scream.
At night you can see the white owl
    sliding past your sideways vision.
At night you can see the dark owl calling
    from the tall tree
At night the glow-worms of midsummer
    shine like the firmament.
Their magic is worth the lights of any city.
At night the bats hunt, the chafers buzz,
    the moths take their wonky flight.

Night is the republic of silence. The place
    where all hiding creatures reign. The
    place where people reign who wish
    for quiet peace — from cities, from
    noise, from other parts of their own
    lives, from too much work, from
    sadnesses, from thought, from light.
Night is a bath. It soothes. It envelops. It
    renews. It re-kindles.
Night is where companiable walking
    needs no talking.
Night is where you go with your lover to
    celebrate your love.
Night is where you can hear the cows
    comfortable chewing. Smell their
    breath. Hear their shuffling.

The stars still shine in country skies.
    The light which has travelled for
    millions of years reaches our eyes
    where house lights, street lights,
    entertainment lights, son et lumiere
    lights, security lights, car lights,
    industrial lights drown it.

At night you can smell the scent of wild
    roses and white butterfly orchids,
    the scent of grass, hear the waving
    and swooshing of trees, the way-off
    voices of bed time.

Night is the republic of bats, moths,
    cats, badgers, nightingales, foxes,
    glow-worms, owls, nightjars,
    dumble beetles, mice, voles, shrews,
    luminous millipedes, hedgehogs,
    night scented flowers and blossoms.

Are we all to continue banned from
    this whole half of life, so that the
    antiques, white goods, and jewellery
    of a selfish few should remain
    double and triple protected?

Country night is not just for patrolling
    gamekeepers, security guards, and
    paranoid second homers.

Country stars, the scudding moon, and
    silk black night belong to us all!

The Proposed National Park Boundaries

— East Brighton does very badly, with the exclusion of most of the Racecourse landscape, including Whitehawk's Neolithic camp and ancient Down pastures.
— The exclusion of Newhaven's cliffs and Downs is potentially disastrous.
— The exclusion of the iconic white cliffs and seashore between Rottingdean and Newhaven is inexplicable. They should be CENTRAL to the National Park's identity.
— By contrast, the posh, enclosed countryside of the Weald, to the north, has been generously included.
— Let us see what the boundaries are when the Park is finally designated.

Proposed National Park Boundary in the First Public Enquiry Inspector's Report

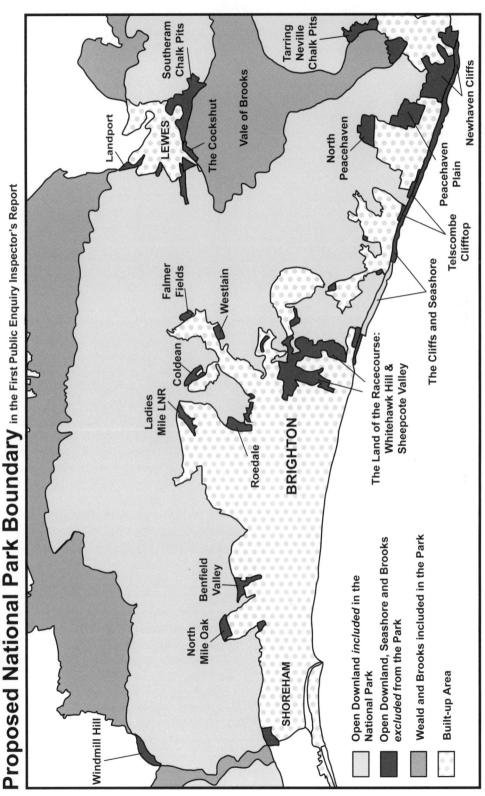

Southeram Chalk Pits

Tarring Neville Chalk Pits

Landport

LEWES

The Cockshut

Vale of Brooks

Newhaven Cliffs

North Peacehaven

Peacehaven Plain

Telscombe Clifftop

Falmer Fields

Westlain

Coldean

Ladies Mile LNR

Roedale

BRIGHTON

The Land of the Racecourse: Whitehawk Hill & Sheepcote Valley

The Cliffs and Seashore

Benfield Valley

North Mile Oak

SHOREHAM

Windmill Hill

Open Downland *included* in the National Park

Open Downland, Seashore and Brooks *excluded* from the Park

Weald and Brooks included in the Park

Built-up Area

rejected by Westminster politicians, who then stalled the designation of Scottish Parks till political devolution made them inevitable.

The National Park system in Britain had other biases built into it. Thus, upland landscapes in the west and the north (like Dartmoor and the Lake District) were favoured for designation, because they were of marginal economic value and fitted the fell walking taste of the key civil servants and politicians who drove through the National Parks and Access to the Countryside Act in 1949. The softer chalk landscapes of lowland England — like the Cotswolds, the Chilterns and the various Downlands — though they were as greatly loved and used by urban dwellers, were never seriously considered for designation, for their productivity and land values were far higher.

Only the South Downs escaped that bias and was listed for designation. The widespread love that was felt for them could not be ignored. However, by the time the question was seriously considered the plough had trashed most of the extensive and easily walked old Down pastures. In 1956 our Downs were rejected for designation.

That was not the end. Determined campaigners kept up a heroic fight over the next forty years, at last gaining a manifesto promise from the Labour Party to designate the South Downs a National Park. When they acceded to government in 1997 Michael Meacher, the new Environment Minister, was as good as his word. He announced a project to create a National Park of a new type — committed to the *restoration* of the old Down pasture landscape.

Since then there has been a lengthy public enquiry, resulting in an Inspector's Report accepting the principle of designation, followed by a second public enquiry to re-address the disputed matter of the boundary.

Campaigners in Brighton worked hard to gain a boundary that included the vital urban fringe. They fostered an unlikely alliance of Conservatives, Greens and dissident Labour councillors to win Council endorsement for a proposed National Park boundary that included Toad's Hole Valley, Whitehawk Hill, Sheepcote Valley and the white cliffs and shore. Though this was partially undermined in a City Council committee and by council officers, it gave local activists a clear field to argue at the public inquiry for an inclusive cling-film boundary round the built-up area.

We argued that the Countryside Agency's draft boundary was biased against working class communities. We pointed out that they had held consultation events in Rottingdean's prosperous community but done nothing in Whitehawk. We showed how they had been generous with their own criteria to include damaged Downland next to well-off communities, like Saltdean, but had ignored spectacular landscape at Newhaven Cliffs and Whitehawk Hill. We demonstrated how working class communities' failure to participate in the formal consultation process did not reflect their heavy usage of their much-loved Downland.

We occupied Toad's Hole Valleyside to undertake neglected conservation work and gained good and sympathetic press coverage.

When the Inspector's Report came out we had made some important gains. Toad's Hole Valley, part of Sheepcote Valley and the Brighton chalk cliffs were included in his proposed boundary.

We await the final results of the latest public inquiry.

Despite its limitations there is no doubt that the final success of this eighty-year struggle will qualitatively increase the survival chances of our Downland.

WHAT SHOULD THE FUTURE LOOK LIKE?

Two things stand out when the fate of our Downs is considered. One is **the ravages of the market economy on the Downs,** making them the butt of movements in the profitability of food commodities and the imperialist politics that bolster the British food industry. The other is **the democratic deficit,** which means that decisions are made without reference to Downland users and workers, and mostly in the interests of landowners, managers and farm tenants. The large measure of public ownership on the Brighton Downs mitigates this, but the public sector's methods of management remain bureaucratic and covert and mostly serve the corporate interest of the local Councils (chiefly Brighton) rather than the public.

This needs to change.

Much more land needs to come into public ownership. At the moment conservation bodies tend only to purchase land which is of the highest conservation status: SSSIs and the like. Their budgets are too constrained to do otherwise. Yet the critical problem for old Down pasture is its fragmentation. *Public expenditure needs to be increased* so that councils and other conservation bodies are able to acquire connecting land and degraded land, which can be restored to publicly accessible species-rich Down pasture. The shattered fabric needs to be stitched back together under public control.

The land which is publicly owned needs to be managed democratically by the collective body of its workers and users. Firstly, *councils need to work to end the letting of their farmed land, and its replacement by direct in-hand council management*. At present, *most* of this land is let on long agricultural tenancies, which give the business farmers a huge measure of management control. Conservation and access initiatives are stymied and alternative farming systems remain unconsidered. Instead, our farmers and farm workers should become ordinary salaried council employees, with all the security, protection and accountability which public sector employment can give. Such direct council control is a pre-condition for enabling all aspects of the Downs' usage — protection of the chalk aquifer, food production, public recreation, and the conservation of historic features and biodiversity — to be treated as equal objectives.

Secondly, *local authority Downland estates need to be managed by executive bodies made up of representatives chosen by all the involved interests*: local site protection groups, the staff trade unions, specialist conservation, heritage and access groups, farming experts, and so on. There are a number of partial models for this, but nothing that can be copied satisfactorily. It must be worked out anew.

At the moment, public sector landowners' management structures lack accountability and are fragmented and contradictory in their purposes. Thus, the day to day farming oversight of the Brighton City Council farmed estate is contracted out to distant managing agents who also manage many private aristocratic and business estates. Their culture reflects that portfolio of clients. Senior Council managers are mostly unfamiliar with, and do not prioritise, the detailed conservation problems of the Downland estate, and lower management layers are constrained by that lack of political will.

Thirdly, *we need to be sure that the income generated from the local authority Downland is ring-fenced, so that it is primarily ploughed back into the management of the Downs* and not creamed off to cross-subsidise other council services which the ruling parties neglect, as has always been the case.

Fourthly, *we need to empower less privileged folk to enjoy using the Downs, and to take over the work there,* so that farming is not just confined to the hereditary control of a few farming families, as happens at present even with the farm tenants of the Brighton Council-owned estate. At the moment, middle class people make up a large proportion of Downland users. We need to encourage working class people, women, ethnic minority folk and children to enjoy the Downs and take on new roles in more sustainable alternative farming systems.

These changes can only take place with a powerful public movement behind them, but, though the times are bad, we can start that process. People's usage of the countryside is deeply inhibited. Most of us scarcely go there, and when we do

we stick to footpaths, and scarcely roam more widely even when larger stretches of landscape are open to our use.

These changes are doubly important now the imperatives of restraining fossil fuel usage dictate that we should focus on better access to our local landscapes, rather than damaging travel to more distant places.

The emerging new threats to the wider integrity of the Down landscape from built development must also be addressed. The threat from high-rise development wrong-footed the conservation movement and has still not penetrated the consciousness of many 'greens'. *Downland conservationists need a broader vigilance. They need to make wider alliances with groups concerned with the built fabric: progressive campaigners for social housing, townscape conservationists, and opponents of gentrification and property speculation.*

What You Can Do (Apart From Just Enjoying The Downs)

EVEN **the smallest things you do are valuable.** Reporting site abuse or damage to wildlife can be crucial. Carry a spare plastic bag to pick up unsightly rubbish. Just the act of walking the remoter sites lets landowners know you care about them. Let the Booth Museum of Natural History or the Biological Records Centre at Woods Mill know of any interesting wildlife sightings.

— **Join your local site-based Downland protection group** (like the Benfield Wildlife Group, the Friends of Sheepcote Valley, or the Castle Hill Group in Newhaven). There are lots of them, particularly around the edge of the Brighton conurbation.
— **If there isn't a group then set one up yourself.** Don't be tempted to

lean too heavily on Council support. Remember, they will often be your opponents. Rely instead on the advice of other neighbouring groups and campaigners. Too-close Council involvement comes with a cost to your independence and a limitation to your view of what is possible. Don't invite your local councillors along. They often exploit people's deference to argue for their own agenda. You wouldn't invite the boss to your trade union branch meeting, so no need to invite them to our 'trade unions of the Downs'.

— **Join wider environmental campaigning organizations.** Here's a rough rule-of-thumb to go by...if the organisation has titled people on its headed notepaper (*Sir* Something or *Lord* Somebody or Fred Oojamaflick *CBE*) then don't bother joining. Anyone who thinks that the prestige of ruling class big wigs does their long-term interests anything but harm needs to think again...

— The problems of nature and the countryside will only be addressed by wider societal changes, so look for organisations that anticipate that by calling for much greater public expenditure, an end to inequality, and much greater public ownership. Use those criteria whether the organization you are interested in is a single-issue campaign or a political party.

— **Come in and help revive the weakened movement for land reform.** Till only a few years ago the movement was still 'on the up' with organisations like 'The Land Is Ours', The Labour Land Campaign, and the Scottish Parliamentary land reform proposals. We live in very reactionary times, but the movement will wake up. It's our job to help it...

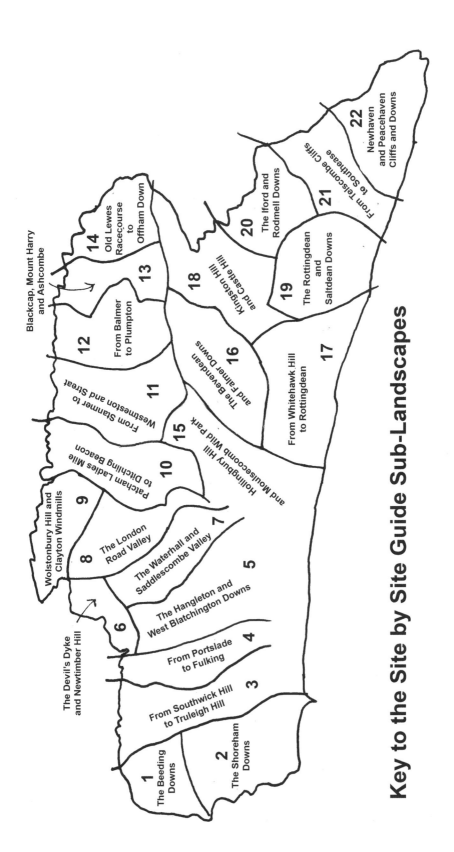

Key to the Site by Site Guide Sub-Landscapes

1 The Beeding Downs

2 The Shoreham Downs

3 From Southwick Hill to Truleigh Hill

4 From Portslade to Fulking

5 The Hangleton and West Blatchington Downs

6 The Devil's Dyke and Newtimber Hill

7 The Waterhall and Saddlescombe Valley

8 The London Road Valley

9 Wolstonbury Hill and Clayton Windmills

10 Patcham Ladies Mile to Ditchling Beacon

11 From Stanmer to Westmeston and Streat

12 From Balmer to Plumpton

13 Blackcap, Mount Harry and Ashcombe

14 Old Lewes Racecourse to Offham Down

15 Hollingbury Hill and Moulsecoomb Wild Park

16 The Bevendean and Falmer Downs

17 From Whitehawk Hill to Rottingdean

18 Kingston Hill and Castle Hill

19 The Rottingdean and Saltdean Downs

20 The Iford and Rodmell Downs

21 From Telscombe Cliffs to Southease

22 Newhaven and Peacehaven Cliffs and Downs

Reproduced from 1940 Ordnance Survey map bases with the kind permission of the Ordnance Survey.

PART TWO
SITE BY SITE GUIDE

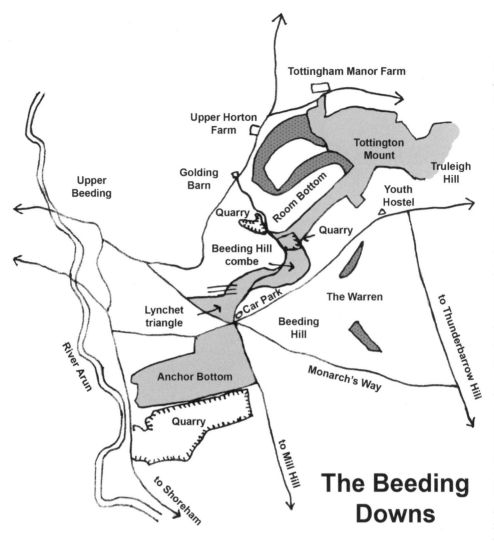

Tottingham Manor Farm

Upper Horton Farm

Golding Barn

Upper Beeding

Quarry

Room Bottom

Tottington Mount

Truleigh Hill

Youth Hostel

Beeding Hill combe

Quarry

Lynchet triangle

Car Park

The Warren

Beeding Hill

River Arun

Anchor Bottom

Monarch's Way

to Thunderbarrow Hill

Quarry

to Shoreham

to Mill Hill

The Beeding Downs

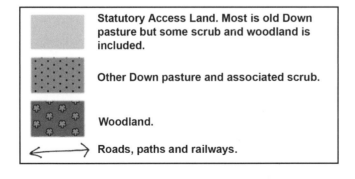

	Statutory Access Land. Most is old Down pasture but some scrub and woodland is included.
	Other Down pasture and associated scrub.
	Woodland.
⟷	Roads, paths and railways.

1: THE BEEDING DOWNS

GORGEOUS, dramatic Downland with many top-quality sites. This sub-landscape has drifts of Blue butterflies (Adonis, Chalkhill, Small, Common), Green Hairsteak, Small Copper, *Lycaena phlaeas*, Brown Argus butterflies, Short-eared Owl (sometimes), Adder, abundant Waxcap fungi, Dark Green Fritillary butterfly, *Mesoacidalia aglaja*, Green-winged Orchis, Dodder, *Cuscuta epithymum*, Heath Snail, *Helicella itala*, Stripe-winged Grasshopper, Stonechat and abundant Glow-worms. It has magic remnants of the ancient Downscape.

If you stand on the South Downs Way and scan the scene to the west you will see: Chanctonbury, Cissbury Ring, Steep Down, Lancing Ring and Lancing College Chapel, and down to the ancient hamlet of Coombes on the far side of the River Adur. You will see the blue sea at the mouth of the estuary and the deeper blue Western Weald through to Blackdown.

Anchor Bottom. TQ 205 092.

THIS is one of the best sites on the whole of the Brighton Downs. It is part of an SSSI (Site of Special Scientific Interest) and is well farmed from Old Erringham Farm. Here you can capture the feel of the Downs two centuries ago (but for the distant traffic noise, the pylons and the chimney of the redundant Beeding Cement Works). The soft valley sides are contoured, as of old, with the terracettes made by the regular meanderings of the resident herd of cattle. It is called Anchor Bottom because the riverside at its base provided an anchorage in the past.

When I visited soon after dawn in late July the slopes were colourful with Scabious, Knapweed, Red Clover, *Trifolium pratense*, Betony, Sussex Rampion, Restharrow, *Ononis repens*, Ragwort, *Senecio jacobaea*, Pyramidal Orchis, Eggs and Bacon, Viper's Bugloss, *Echium vulgare*, and Ox-eye Daisy, *Leucanthemum vulgare*. Several Yellowhammers were already singing. (The 'hammer' bit of the name comes from the German for 'Bunting'. People call them the 'Scribble Bunting', too, because their eggs look as though some child has drawn all over them with wandering brown lines). A very sleepy Dark Green Fritillary sat on my hand and let me admire her. She looked like something out of a Tropical Butterfly House. I looked in all the 'bells' of the Harebell, *Campanula rotundifolia*, and the very first one had a Bellflower Bee asleep in it. Others, more prosaically, had sleeping Earwigs and Flea Beetles! All over the wet grass flat, whitish snails were out. They mostly have light brownish stripes and big 'belly buttons' at the centre of the shell whorls. These are the rare Heath

Anchor Bottom, looking a bit bleak in early spring.

Snails. This is one of the only sites on the whole of the South Downs with a vigorous, healthy population, thanks to the cattle grazing. In olden times this snail would have been one of the commonest on Downland.

The steepest, shortest turf near the valley bottom is best for Adonis Blue butterflies.

Beeding Quarry. TQ 205 089.

THIS derelict quarry is a surreal, lunar landscape. Everywhere we are surrounded by tall white walls, scree slopes of graying flint and chalk, and banks of Buddleia. The

Heath Snail

resident Peregrine Falcon does not like our presence and circles restlessly, her harsh alarm call grating on our ears and our conscience for intruding on her peace. There are well-attested stories of a Big Cat living in this white desert, though she must be strong-minded to hide up alongside all the trail bike riders who periodically hold events here.

The quarry is of importance to geologists for its chalk exposures. We were tipped off about the presence of beautiful calcite crystals at the base of one cliff, and, indeed, they were there. One crystal we found was as good as anything in a Crystal Shop.

This is a dangerous as well as interesting place. I go there with caution.

Reservoir Corner, or Lynchet Triangle, north of Beeding Hill car park. TQ 207 098.

THE 'cultivation terraces' marked on the OS Landranger map mark attempts by land hungry medieval peasants to win further arable strips from increasingly unsuited ground, The whole of the valley floor between here and Castle Town, as well as Windmill Hill, was organized in the medieval strip cultivated open fields right through till the middle of the nineteenth century.

This slope is winter grazed, so the grass is tall in summer. It has rank Hogweed around the entrance by Beeding Hill car park, but don't be deceived, it's a lovely site and is part of the SSSI.

There's lots of Yellow Rattle, *Rhinanthus minor*, and I've counted three orchid species. I've seen Common Heath and Latticed Heath, *Chiasmia clathrata clathrata*, moths here (they're both day flying) and Grizzled Skipper butterfly has been recorded in the past. There are Glow-worms here.

The area downslope and to the west end of the site is poorer.

Bostal from Beeding Hill car park to Golding Barn.

THIS is a lovely sunken trackway, with overhanging Wayfaring Tree and Old Man's Beard (Wild Clematis). The bostal sides retain a good chalk grassland flora, with Horseshoe Vetch, Orchids and Harebell, but are becoming overgrown because of lack of grazing. This bostal should be fenced in to Reservoir Corner or the up slope

combe and grazed. Otherwise the ancient grassland will be lost.

Glow-worms are present.

Beeding Hill Combe and disused quarry. TQ 212 100.

A beautiful mosaic of species-rich scrub, short and long grass and bare ground (at the quarry). All part of the old Beeding Hill Tenantry Down. Part of the larger SSSI. The 'hills and holes' of the grassed over quarry spoil tips are rich in flowers and insects, though trail bike riders have damaged the sward.

Great place for a picnic and for blackberrying. DON'T light fires, though.

The slopes have abundant yellow Cowslips in spring, and in autumn you may be lucky to find the yellow blobs of Persistent Waxcap. Wild Clary, *Salvia horminoides*, was present a few years ago, and probably still is. Lots of Devil's-bit Scabious and much Tor Grass. Corn Bunting seen.

Beeding Hill: Summer sunset and distant Chanctonbury.

The abundant Wayfaring Tree has the scarce Orange-tailed Clearwing moth. Ringlet and Green Hairstreak butterflies — which both like scrub edges — are present, as well as Adonis Blue and Chalkhill Blue.

The short turf around the quarry is my favourite place, with lots of little old Down pasture species: mosses and lichen, tiny Moss Snail and Scree Snail, and Chalk Carpet moth.

Room Bottom. TQ 213 107.

THIS used to be *Broom* Bottom, but some map-maker in Victorian times left out the 'B' by mistake. 'Broom' makes much more sense because parts of the hilltops had heathy vegetation till the last century.

It's a tranquil and remote valley normally, but when the trail bike riders rev up it can be very noisy. They used to use the steep slope at the head of the combe, too, but that's been banned.

The **south side of the valley** has a tussocky sward, with scattered scrub. It's not very interesting up-slope, but there was a thriving colony of our local speciality, the Cistus Forester moth, some years ago. Is it still there? There's Dingy Skipper and some Chalkhill Blue, too.

The steep **east end of the valley** is derelict chalk grassland heavily invaded by Tor Grass and still scarred by the trail bike riders' tracks. It does, however, retain much interest, with lots of Rockrose and an associated Web-cap fungus, and the little black Earth Tongue, *Geoglossum umbratile*. There's Brown Argus, Adonis and Chalkhill, Sussex Rampion and Ploughman's Spikenard, *Inula conyza*.

The **north side of the valley** has a very dry, almost continental feel. It's also very steep, though the terracettes allow one to walk it. There's lots of rabbit activity, so we find Field Pepperwort, *Lepidium campestre*, Field Forget-me-not, *Myosotis arvense*, and Hound's Tongue. It's got three Blue butterfly species, plus Small Heath butterfly, *Coenonympha pamphilus*, and Yellow Belle moth, *Semiaspilates ochrearia*. The Heath Snail hung on here till about 1992.

West and north west slopes of Tottington Mount. TQ 210 110.

THESE slopes were very heavily horse-grazed in the 1990s and it took some close looking to realize that the bowling green sward still had its suite of old Down pasture herbs. Now the slopes are lightly grazed by Sussex cattle and the Down pasture wildlife is returning, although there's much Tor Grass. There's lots of 6-spot Burnet moth and Marbled White,

Beeding Quarry: A weird white moonscape — watch out for Daleks!

with Harebell and Sussex Rampion. At the bottom of the north slope, opposite Tottington Manor Farm, is a nice old rew woodland with a very old rookery. It used to have Fly Orchids in the 1960s and probably still does. There are large old Beeches, Wych Elm, Nettle-leaved Bellflower, Primrose and Bluebell.

Tottington Mount. TQ 218 110.

I T ' s lovely to sit near the bridlepath that crosses the top of Tottington Mount and look west towards Chanctonbury. You can see the three medieval churches of Botolphs, Bramber and Steyning, and you would be able to see Beeding church, too, but for its surrounding trees. All four of these churches marked early river landing points. Botolphs and Beeding marked Saxon fords or early bridges. Bramber marked the Norman baronial causeway and bridge, and Steyning marked the busy Saxon *Portus cuthmanni.*

Around 1960, not long after our family moved back to Hove, we had a picnic sitting on the top of Tottington Mount. Munching our sandwiches we watched the white steam from the tank engine of the Horsham Flyer as it pulled its two red coaches across the brooks towards Bramber station. Now that peaceful railway line marks the route of the Bramber bypass and its low roar disturbs the peace every hour of the day.

Most of Tottington Mount lost its ancient pastures, but the steep slope above the head of Room Bottom didn't, and it's pretty with a carpet of flowers. I found an excellent bivalve fossil there last summer and saw a colourful Ichneumon Wasp, *Protichneumon pisorus*, nectaring on the umbels of Hogweed. This orange-and-black beauty is an endoparasite of Hawkmoths. Maybe it blew in from the Sallows of the Adur brooks below, for some of its Hawkmoth victims use them as larval food plants.

The Warren, Beeding Hill. TQ 218 094.

T H E Warren was given its name just over a century ago when the squire of Buckingham Place, Shoreham, attempted to turn the old Beeding Tenantry Down sheep common into a commercial rabbit warren. The attempt failed, but the place grew even more bramble, thorn and gorse thickets than it had before.

It must have been a wonderfully remote place. Nightingales sung there.

All along the crest of Beeding Hill, just south of the road up to the Youth Hostel, was an important cluster of Bronze Age burial mounds — nine or more of them. No above-ground sign of them remains. Decades or relentless ploughing have eliminated this important cluster.

In 1945, after the Second World War, the West Sussex County Council gave this plateau landscape — 352 acres — to the National Trust. Before they did so, however, they leased the land out to farmers on 999 year leases. What a mixture of generosity and foolishness! Over the next few years these farmers bulldozed and ploughed all of these ancient pastures and their archaeology and wildlife. Now nothing remains to tell you of the National Trust's token ownership except their signboard next to the fly-tipped and scruffy Beeding Hill car park.

After decades of farmer's vandalism the land was returned to permanent pasture in the 1990s. There was new environmental money to be had there. The barbed wire remains, though, and no freedom to roam exists on these wide acres.

Tiny fragments of Down pasture exist on the eastern slope of Beeding Hill — Harebells and Common Blue Butterflies and some bits of Gorse.

There was a cricket ground in the Prince Regent's time on the southern side of the Monarch's Way, TQ 210 095, as it tracks east from the Beeding Hill car park. Must have been windy.

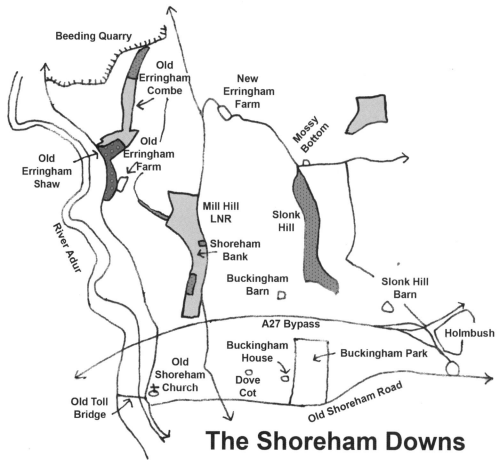

The Shoreham Downs

Beeding Quarry

Old Erringham Combe

New Erringham Farm

Mossy Bottom

Old Erringham Farm

Old Erringham Shaw

River Adur

Mill Hill LNR

Slonk Hill

Shoreham Bank

Buckingham Barn

Slonk Hill Barn

Holmbush

A27 Bypass

Buckingham House

Buckingham Park

Old Shoreham Church

Dove Cot

Old Toll Bridge

Old Shoreham Road

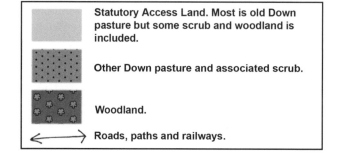

Statutory Access Land. Most is old Down pasture but some scrub and woodland is included.

Other Down pasture and associated scrub.

Woodland.

Roads, paths and railways.

2 : THE SHOREHAM DOWNS

Shoreham Bank, Mill Hill.
TQ 212 071.

STANDING at the slope top on Mill Hill is almost like standing on a cliff, for the bank is very steep and offers panoramic views out across the silvery meanders of the Adur Estuary to the sea. In fact, Shoreham probably takes its name from this bank or 'scora', as the Saxons would have called it.

This place is a most peculiar hybrid of the ancient and the modern. The new stuff hits you in the face and roars in your ears. There's the continuous din of the A27 bypass and the penetrating noise of planes circling overhead from Shoreham Airport, and there's the big-ego architecture of Lancing College's pseudo-French chapel, though at least that makes a conscious connection with our past. Yet, also opposite you on the Lancing Downs is the quietness of Applesham Farm, which was a prosperous village way back at the time of the Domesday Book in 1086; and at the north end of Shoreham Bank is another Saxon farm, Old Erringham, which King Alfred's successors fortified to defend the estuary. To the south, too, you can see the Norman church of Old Shoreham almost on the banks of the Adur, and next to it the wooden piers of the 1781 Toll Bridge,

which still collected traffic tolls right up to the 1960s.

Forty two years ago I came to the lane under Shoreham Bank to photograph a gypsy encampment that I had spotted from the road. The family had some black lurchers, and a black cart horse grazing in the meadow. They had a beautifully painted wooden waggon with smoke drifting from its chimney. They were friendly, though they must have got fed up with the curiosity of people like me. That place now lies directly under the A27 spaghetti junction, which cuts Shoreham Bank in two.

Shoreham Bank was famous from the 1820s to butterfly lovers for its many rare varieties of the Chalkhill Blue butterfly, which, with the Adonis Blue, are still the 'flagship' species of this Hill. In May the hillside is dusted yellow with Horseshoe Vetch — the butterflies food plant — and in August the butterflies can still be found in large numbers, dancing above the turf in the hot sunshine.

They had a narrow escape, though. Back in the 'fifties and 'sixties myxomatosis hit the Rabbit population severely and the bank became covered with tall grass and

Shoreham Bank, alias Mill Hill Local Nature Reserve, or 'Coney Hanger' (to give it its extremely old name).

scrub. The new owners, Adur District Council, even banned grazing from the bank, though it had been grazing which created its butterfly interest. By the seventies only a few Chalkhills and Adonis survived in a tiny area of an acre or so which was kept mown. These mistakes were rectified as a result of strong action from the community of wildlifers, and a combination of vigorous scrub bashing, the recovery of the Rabbit population, and the return of sheep and cattle grazing.

Not all species were able to survive this bottleneck, though. The special mosses and lichens went, and in the 1990s you often found empty shells of the extinct Heath and Carthusian Snails. Most, if not all, of the other special chalk grassland molluscs were eliminated, too.

In August the hillside is colourful with pink Centaury, *Centaurium erythraea*, the tiny white pinpoints of Eyebright, and the white umbels of Wild Carrot, *Daucus carota*, Wild Parsnip, *Pastinaca sativa*, St John's Wort, *Hypericum perforatum*, and Basil, *Clinopodium vulgare*.

Alongside and next to the hill top road you can see the long grassy grooves made by the braided paths of the old highway by which all traffic passed from Shoreham to Beeding before the building of the valley road in modern times.

Shoreham Bank is a Local Nature Reserve, but that status doesn't automatically bring management resources to it. The northern and the southern end of the bank are both scrubbed up and the scrub at the base of slope is encroaching, too. Even formally protected sites are not necessarily that safe in practice, and Shoreham Bank's two centuries of fame didn't stop the bypass smashing it in two.

Old Erringham Farmstead.
TQ 205 076.

THIS farmstead is one of the nicest on the whole of the Brighton Downs. It has a lovely old flint farmhouse with great chimneys and part-Horsham slab roofing, and ramshackle old flint barns. It has one of only two remaining medieval manorial chapels on the Brighton Downs (the other is at Swanborough Manor), which now functions as a front garden shed for one of the modern farm workers cottages just to the south of the old farmhouse. It has a tiny ecclesiastical window on its south face. The farm has a tenth century 'ring work', presumably built as a defence against the Vikings, though it's difficult to pick it out amongst the grassy plats now. It's a mixed farm with corn crops, beef cattle, a bit of livery stabling, and hay meadows — one for Boot Fairs — and management of the gorgeous sites of Old Erringham Combe and Anchor Bottom to its credit.

Around the farmstead I counted bits of Red Star Thistle, *Centaurea calciptrapa*, (the Brighton Downs speciality), Musk Thistle, *Carduus nutans*, Spear Thistle, *Cirsium vulgare*, Welted Thistle, *C. acanthoides*, Creeping Thistle, *C. arvense*, Teasel, *Dipsacus fullonum*, and Viper's Bugloss all adding summer colour, as well as prickles, though none in the sort of numbers that would lead anyone to curse them.

Old Erringham Combe and Shaw. TQ 205 081.

As you walk down into this secret valley the road noise stops as though you've pressed a switch. Only the Yellowhammers lazy song can be heard. What blessed peace!

The Combe's old-fashioned mosaic of habitats and aspects make it a great refuge for Downland wildlife. The south-facing bank is the hottest place, but below it there are willows and a tiny tongue of wet grassland where I noted Lesser Marsh Grasshopper, *Chorthippus albomarginatus*, some years ago. Autumn Ladies Tresses orchis occurs on the banksides with Bastard Toadflax, Rockrose, Betony, Thyme and so many other herbs. Wall Brown, *Lasiommata megera*, and Clouded Yellow, *Colias crocea*, butterflies, and day flying moths like Yellow Belle, Dusky Sallow, *Eremobia ochroleuca*, Common Carpet, *Epirrhoe alternata alternata*, and Grass Moths enjoy the drying grassland.

This site used to be part of a 'cow down', and it is maybe because of those centuries of cattle grazing that the rare Carthusian Snail, *Monacha cartusiana*, clings on in this combe.

The upper valley has clay pigeon shooting apparatus hidden in a thicket and the pasture is crunchy underfoot with shattered clays. Clearly those shooting folk don't believe in picking up their own mess.

Old Erringham Shaw is a tangled wood of Sycamore, Ash, Elm and thorn. It's more open at the northern end facing the combe, where the remains of four big old

Lancing College chapel

Old Erringham Combe and Shaw. Remote and delightful.

broken beeches and lots of may blossom make it a good place for insects.

Slonk Hill. TQ 222 070.

S L O N K Hill's steep eastern slope has an island of old Down pasture in a plateau landscape damaged by decades of agribusiness. I have tended to visit on summer evenings when long shadows frame the hills and the warmth of the evening sun is more forgiving. The best places on this hillside are the old bostal, which tracks down this slope at its southern end, and a patch of hillside a few hundred yards north, surrounded by Iron Age field lynchets. These places escaped when the farmer sprayed this hillside perhaps twenty years ago. For a while it was a sad place, for the sprayed areas simply developed coarse grassland and a huge mess of Creeping Thistle. But now, with time and the recovery of Rabbit populations, the hillside is again colourful with herbs. The intact areas have Pyramidal and Spotted Orchid, Meadow Oat-grass, *Avenula pratensis*, and Crested Hair-grass, *Koeleria cristata*, and Sussex Rampion is common. There used to be a lot of Chalkhill Blues around the bostal slopes. Perhaps they're still there.

Slonk Hill takes its name from the Saxon word 'slog' — part of the verb 'slean', as in 'slay' — so there may have been some memorable bloodshed in the distant past. There were at least two Bronze Age barrows and a little Iron Age settlement on the Hill, and the barrows continued to be a sacred place right through until the end of Roman times. In Iron Age times they were surrounded by a rectangular ditched enclosure and perhaps made into a 'temenos' or temple[1]. Ritual deposits of animals and coins were buried at the site. The evening shadows still show many intriguing dips and hummocks at the Hill's southern end, though the trench digging of the large army camp that came here during the First World War must be the explanation for most of them.

Mossy Bottom east slope, TQ 226 082, and New Erringham Farm.

S I X T E E N years ago I was surveying the wildflowers on this steep eastern slope of Mossy Bottom, and watching the distant fleet of combine harvesters away over by the barn. As I watched I saw a combine — it must have been a third of a mile away — peel away from the others and trundle across the field towards me. At the bottom of the slope it stopped. The cab door opened and the farmer called out to ask me what I was doing. I told him. He demanded that I go. I asked him why? He hesitated, and said I was damaging the wildlife. I asked him how? Just at that moment a Partridge exploded from cover between us and winged away. "You're scaring off that old Partridge for a start," he said. I said "you've done a mighty sight more damage by spraying that lovely slope of Slonk Hill over there!" He said, "If you don't go I'll call the police!" I said "call them then!" He thought for a sec, then shouted "well, make sure you don't do any damage" and drove off again to join the others.

I've had many exchanges like that on our Downs.

That slope is now open to the public under the new right to roam 'CROW' Act.

It's got lovely boney Iron Age lynchets across it made by the peasant farmers who lived in Thundersbarrow village. They used to be called "Thunder's Steps." There are big old anthills, Large Thyme, Dropwort, Cowslip, Basil, Harebell and Rampion. It's a bit of a mess from past attempts to clear and cultivate it, but it's still a nice spot.

Large herds of beef cattle wander this landscape now, lowing for their offspring or just for the sheer pleasure. The place is a bit like the Wild West, only a lot tamer and with a lot more wire fences. Only fifteen years ago New Erringham Farm and almost all this landscape was covered with grain crops, except for the little patch I was sitting on. Then one of the farmers decided to enter his land into the 'Environmentally Sensitive Area' (ESA) scheme to attract subsidy by reverting it to permanent pasture. Over five years an estimated 25,000 pounds of our money was spent sowing wildflowery pastures. Then, in 1997 another local landowner bought that land. Taking advantage of the five year break clause in the ESA Agreement he re-converted the farm to arable production. Our taxes had been wasted. Now the landscape is back under permanent pasture and we're still paying the farmer in subsidy.

Mossy Bottom derives its name from 'Muster' Bottom — where the shepherd mustered his sheep. The spine of the Slonk Hill ridge had another coaching road along it from Brighton to Beeding, way back in Stuart times. It's gone and there isn't even a footpath there now — just game cover crops.

Old Shoreham village, TQ 208 059, Buckingham Park and Little Buckingham Farm. TQ 222 062.

THE Norman church of Old Shoreham is timeless and beautiful. It's all that is left of the port which so soon moved down to New Shoreham. It sits close to the river, together with some good surviving old flint, timber and thatch cottages and the toll bridge.

This Downland used to be part of the estate owned by the Bridger family who were based at Buckingham Park, now separated from the hills by the bypass and two streets of housing.

Buckingham Park still has a few surviving veteran Sweet Chestnut trees. They are huge. Hidden away behind the western boundary of the Park is the neo-classical ruin of the two hundred year old Buckingham House, where the Bridger's lived. And if you walk up Downsway, just a couple of streets westwards from the House ruins, you will come across an old flint dovecot sitting stranded on a bit of suburban amenity grassland. It's all that's left of Little Buckingham Farm apart from the modern Buckingham Barn, to the north of the bypass.

Footnotes

1   *The Archaeology of Sussex to AD 2000*, edited by David Rudling (Heritage Marketing and Publications Ltd and University of Sussex CCE, 2003), page 122.
     Also *Prehistoric Sussex* — Miles Russell. (Tempus, 2002), page 137.

Old Shoreham's Norman church and wooden toll bridge by the River Adur.

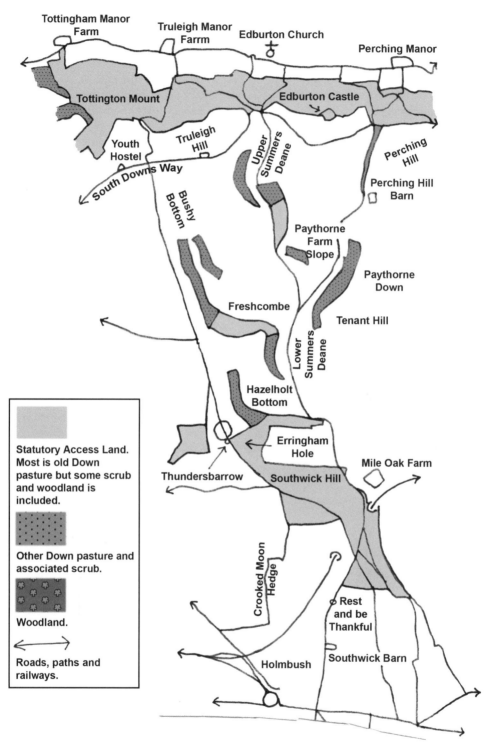

From Southwick Hill to Truleigh Hill

3: FROM SOUTHWICK HILL TO TRULEIGH HILL

PORTSLADE and Southwick folk are so lucky to have these Downs on their doorstep! Southwick Hill and the smaller sites connected to it are the second biggest surviving complex of ancient Down pasture on the entire plateau of the Brighton Downs. (The biggest is around Castle Hill, near Woodingdean). And, to the north, we have the wonderful high scarp and its intact grasslands and deep carved bostal paths.

The Thundersbarrow ridge takes us away from noise and urban clutter, to the south, to the peace and stillness of the high Downs, where Buzzards mew, lambs bleet, Meadow Pipits sing, and the wind rustles the tall grass.

Kingston Buci old village, TQ 235 052, and Southwick old village, TQ 239 053.
THUNDERSBARROW may have been the centre of a large estate in the post-Roman dark ages. In early or mid-Saxon times the people may have re-located down off the hill to Kingston, where the medieval church, rectory, manor house and huge old barn still make a lovely cluster — now stranded three quarters of a mile from the Downs. It's the same thing that may have happened at Cissbury, where the people came off the hill to form Findon, and at Mount Caburn, where people

re-located down at Beddingham. The church was extensively re-modelled in the thirteenth century when the ever-shifting river estuary temporarily made Kingston a port town. The 'king' of the name 'Kingston' may have been a Saxon King of Sussex. The 'Buci' bit of the name comes from the Anglo-Norman owners' home town of Bouce in Normandy.

Southwick was a dependent settlement of Kingston in origin, but had its own church by the time of Domesday in 1086. The medieval church with its spire, the Green, old farm houses, barns and cottages still have a strong feeling of countryside-in-the-town.

**The Crooked Moon Hedge.
TQ 233 070.**
I FIRST explored the Crooked Moon Hedge and its valley whilst trudging north from the Holmbush shopping mall up to Southwick Hill on a very hot summer day, already feeling dusty and sweaty.

Hedges are very rare on these Downs, except around farmsteads, so this one is worth a special look. It lies on the top of a prehistoric field lynchet, for these southern slopes of Southwick Hill were covered with an Iron Age field system whose banks lay regularly on east-west and south-north axes. Most of them have long been ploughed out but this one survived, probably because it was too tall. At its northern end it became the boundary between Kingston Buci and Southwick parishes and at its southern end it bounded Kingston Buci sheep Down to the west, and one of the parish open fields to the east.

The hedge may have been bird-sown, as, I suspect, these few Downland hedges mostly were. Yet it contains a lot of Maple and Ash and it is difficult to see how their 'keys' (winged seeds) could travel long distances. On the coastal plain a lot of the medieval open fields were hedged, so it may be that the southern part of the hedge was planted to shelter the open field.

I paced the hedge in 30 m sections, counting its tree and shrub species as 'Hooper's Rule' for assessing hedge ages tells you to do. The number of species per section is meant to roughly equal the age of the hedge in centuries. By this rule the hedge is three to four centuries old.

It peters out to the north, but just before its end, as my attention was wandering, I noticed the huge, rugged bole of an old ash pollard between its veil of leaves. This is a whopping great tree by ash standards, and it has a smaller companion next to it. As I gazed I noticed a fresh Woodpecker nest hole high on one limb. Then I heard a soft humming drone from the rear of the bole. Braving the nettles I crept round it. Just above my head was a mass of honeybees emerging from their nest hole, obviously on the point of swarming…a tiny fragment

of the wildwood right out on these bare Downs!

The 'Rest and be Thankful' stone. TQ 238 069.

T H E large flat block of lichen-covered stone by the path to Southwick Hill from Southwickhill Barn marks a corner on the old parish boundary between Kingston Buci and Southwick. It isn't sarsen stone. It's a bit far west to be of that provenance, for the nearest sarsen locality is around Goldstone and Hangleton. With all that shipping activity at the harbour, though, getting a big lump of hard stone for this spot was hardly a problem.

Still, I wonder when it was put there. It was famous enough to show on the Victorian Ordnance Survey maps.

Southwick Hill. TQ 237 077.

T H E dark smudges of Southwick Hill's thorn thickets mark it out in many a long view from other parts of the Brighton Downs. It is a time capsule from a particular period of Downland history, that of the long agricultural depression from 1876 to 1940, when scrub took over many old pastures and cattle replaced many sheep flocks.

Southwick Hill is now the best-managed site on the entire urban fringe of the Brighton conurbation. That's not because its managers are super-competent (though they may be!). It's much simpler than that. It's because the Hill has long had a

View of Southwick Hill from Erringham Hole.

continuity of grazing by cattle from Mile Oak Farm, whilst the scrub has been controlled and monitored by the Hill's owners, the National Trust.

Walking anywhere over the Hill you may come across its contented herd with their calves playing round about and maybe a huge and mellow old bull. And the Hill's many dog walkers simply walk past them all, admiring and accepting their presence.

It must be very difficult at times for the farmer to continue this practice, for cows have been killed by vandalism in the recent past. He deserves our thanks, for the grazing is the key to the survival of so much of interest here.

In autumn parts of the short turf may be as colourful as a garden with splashes of yellow, red, orange, white, and even purple, black and blue, from the many waxcap and other old meadow fungi. There are puffballs everywhere, and fairy rings, and you may find a troop of Blue Legs, *Lepista saeva*, or the flaming orange of Velvet Shank, *Flammulina velutipes*, on some rotten old stump.

In high summer you may see Chalkhill Blue occasionally on the bostal path, as well as Rampion, blue Scabious and Autumn Gentian, *Gentianella amarella*. The turf is too tightly grazed for a big display of colour, but at the hill's northern end, on the south side of the bridlepath, there is an un-grazed triangle with a taller sward. Here, Rabbity lawns with Purging Flax, Eggs and Bacon, Squinancywort, Eyebright and Basil, mingle with tall herb patches of Parsnip, Greater Knapweed, Ragwort, Hogweed, St John's Wort and Basil. You'll find Raspberry bushes, *Rubus idaeus*, and Rose-bay Willowherb. You may see Common Blue, Clouded Yellow, Small Heath, Comma, *Polygonia c-album*, Red Admiral, *Vanessa atalanta*, Painted Lady, *Cynthia cardui*, or day-flying moths like Treble-bar, *Aplocera plagiata plagiata*, and Dusky Sallow.

In spring on the Hill the Gorse is yellow and coconut-fragrant and the May blossom is white and narcotic-sweet on the air. Bird song fills the scrub thickets. At midsummer the northern Down and the bostal path have glow-worms a-plenty.

In 1985 local residents were presented with the plan for an A27 bypass smashing through the Hill. Through the vigorous campaigning of activists from ABBA (the Anti-Brighton Bypass Association) the road was re-routed through a tunnel under the Hill rather than a cutting through it. It was the only big victory in this battle against the road. This was, however, the last major roads scheme to go through before the onset nationally of mass direct action campaigning against the roads programme — at Twyford Down in 1992. Indeed, many of the activists of South Downs Earth First!, based in Brighton, who co-ordinated the direct action campaigning, agonized over whether they should focus on Twyford Down, or on building a direct action campaign against the Brighton bypass. Whether they made the correct tactical decision or not, the result of those years of direct action resistance is that major roads schemes everywhere received a massive blow. Progressive residents of Worthing can thank those campaigners for the present shelving of the Downland bypass scheme there.

Thundersbarrow, TQ 229 083.
S T A N D I N G on Thundersbarrow in August I heard a commotion in the sky to the west. Looking across I saw a Buzzard being mobbed by a Crow. After a while the Crow got bored and left and the Buzzard was joined by first one, then two more of its kin. The four magnificent birds wheeled and soared above the valley, whilst nearer to me a pair of Swallows shot by, a Kestrel hovered and a Meadow Pipit parachuted down into the long grass.

It is only at this distance from the bypass that the silence of the Downs and the sound of the birds are bigger than the noise of the road. This point marks the beginning of Downland tranquility.

The ramparts of Thundersbarrow's late Bronze Age and Iron Age camp are still tall enough for us to walk them all around, though they get a bit vague on the eastern side because of plough damage, and because the Romano-British villagers built their houses just outside the rampart — and right up against it — on that side. When the village was excavated in 1932 two corn-drying ovens were found, still with soot in the flues and bits of charred grain.

Erringham Hole, TQ 231 082.

THIS is the bushy combe just down to the east of Thundersbarrow, whose celtic villagers built the huge field lynchets, parts of which are up to 12 feet in height. It was called 'Erringham Hole' because it was part of Old Erringham Farm. It's

not to be confused with Whitelot Bottom which is the ploughed land further east down the combe. Old Erringham Hole has flowery chalk grassland, scrub, rank grassland and lots of Rabbits. The bunnies encourage, perversely, lots of Rabbit-resistant plants like the tall woolly Mullein, *Verbascum thapsus*, (complete with Mullein Moth, *Shargacucullia verbasci*, caterpillars) and Hound's-tongue, Vervain, *Verbena officinalis*, Ground Ivy, *Glechoma hederacea*, and Eyebright. In the spring there are plenty of Cowslips and birdsong.

Hazelholt Bottom. TQ 235 084.

A LOVELY tranquil slope with large flowery glades. There are often Roe Deer in the wide corn field below the slope. The National Trust own the south slope and Whitelot Bottom further south, but Whitelot was ploughed up after 1945 and has never been returned to public use. Hazelholt has rich old chalk grassland with Adonis and Chalkhill and lots of other butterflies.

At the head of the combe there's more old grassland and great blackberry thickets... big juicy blackberries! Hazelholt is a nice place to see Brimstone butterflies because there is Buckthorn in the thickets

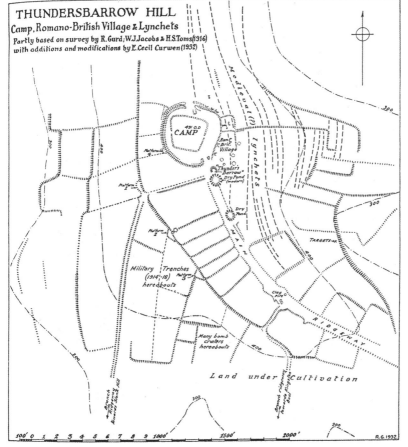

(which their caterpillars munch). There's Devil's-bit Scabious in September and Cowslips in spring.

Lower Summers Deane's west slope. TQ 233 090.

THIS rather scruffy, gorsey slope has lots of red-purple Betony, Yellow Rattle, Rampion, Ragwort and Red Clover. There's Hairy Violet, *Viola hirta*, in spring and Whitethroat song from the Gorse. Cattle do a good job grazing it. I'm not sure whether Chalkhill Blues are still there.

Freshcombe. TQ 230 092.

THIS is a very special place. It's north facing and very feels very remote. Its slopes have very old Gorse thickets on them which are shown as well established on the 1873 O/S map, and may be centuries older than that.

It has one very special plant, Saw-wort, which looks like a slimmer version of Knapweed, and still blooms profusely in a little glade amongst the Gorse. This is its only site on the whole of the South Downs. It's a survivor from the days of the Downland heaths. It survives here because the soil must have a strong clay-with-flints influence. The glade where it blooms is colourful with its flowers and Betony, Red Clover, Hawkbit and St John's Wort. Gorse pods pop all around in summer and Linnets twitter. Large flocks of young Starlings use the scrub thickets, and Wood Pigeons coo.

It's another site owned by the National Trust, but sadly leased away from their management. It is lovely but declining and very threatened by scrub expansion and insufficient grazing. Chalkhills may have gone from there. They used to be frequent, but I have seen none for the last year or so.

Bushy Bottom. TQ 226 093.

THIS is a landscape in recovery. It was bulldozed and cultivated for decades, though the east and west slopes of Bushy Bottom retained threadbare relics of their old heathy pastures. Now it's been back down as permanent pasture for nearly twenty years and gets better every year.

The big herds of cattle attract the rare Hornet Robber-fly, *Asilus crabroniformis*, our largest and handsomest fly.

All the landscape is silence and rustling breeze and the soft horizontals of the hilltops. There's Small Heath and Common Blue butterflies and Harebell, Dropwort, and Field Woodrush, *Luzula campestris*, and you could see a Hare, if you're lucky.

Upper Summers Deane's west slope. TQ 231 105.

THIS site lies just south east of Truleigh Hill Barn. It, too, is in recovery after being surrounded for decades by arable cultivation. It has a slightly less chalky soil chemistry, and has Lesser Stitchwort, *Stellaria graminea*, Sorrel, and Gorse as well as more chalk-loving Restharrow, Quaking Grass, Bladder Campion, *Silene vulgaris*, and Thyme.

Upper Summers Deane's east slope. TQ 233 101.

SMALL but perfectly formed, this slope has five orchid species, lots of colourful wild flowers and butterflies, interesting fungi and bushy bits for the birds. When we last went there on 1st August a big flock of mostly adolescent Whitethroat were restlessly feeding through the bushes — darting out from perches to swipe flying insects and twittering to each other.

This site lies just north of the spot where Summersdeane farmstead stood till the Canadian artillery flattened it during the Second World War. It was an old farmstead, going right back to the 13th century at least. In 1840 it was a daughter farm of Horton Farm to the north west, over the far side of Tottington Mount. The farmstead's grove of Beech trees survives, though.

Just a hundred yards or so further south from the grove on the fence line is a shapely Wych Elm (TQ 233 097). I hope it's not lonely out here all on its own! · That same fence line is an old manorial boundary, and further southwards, just over the hill crest, it crosses over two prehistoric round barrows. Boundaries were often marked by barrows on the Downs, and the same boundary is marked by a further (largely ploughed out) barrow (TQ 239 090) when it swings across to the top of Tenant Hill on the other side of Summers Deane.

This slope has the rare Bastard Toadflax, Carline Thistle, *Carlina vulgaris*, and Horseshoe Vetch, with a few Chalkhill Blues.

Lurid Bolete is present, attracted by the Rockrose which it mutually depends upon, and there is Mosaic Puffball, Persistent Waxcap and lovely little bluey-black Pink-gills, *Leptonia*.

Paythorne Farmstead slope. TQ 235 098.

PAYTHORNE Farm, like Summersdeane Farm next to it, was demolished by the Canadian artillery in the last World War. This Paythorne Farm was originally built as an outlier of the main Paythorne Farm to the north, under the Downs at Edburton, though it has long been owned by Brighton Corporation. Farmworker Ron Russell knows this Corporation land as the Rat's Ramble, no doubt because of its poor fertility. Children who played around the two lost farms called it Dead City, and all knew the story of the woman on the farm who fell down the well. Ron, who has worked for Paythorne Farm (the main one) for the last 45 years, continues to live in the 'new' Paythorne Cottage that the Corporation built just south of Mile Oak Farm to replace the war-ruined one. He has a nearly three mile cycle to work over the Downs — uphill in the morning and downhill when he's homeward in the evening.

The little surviving chalk grassland site next to the vanished farm can be picked out from a distance by the bushes upon it, but it's mostly ancient pasture. It's extra-special because it's only one of six south facing sites on the whole of the Shoreham to Patcham Downs. The rare Heath Snail and Carthusian Snail only recently became extinct here, but Adonis Blue and Chalkhill Blue may both still be clinging on. It has Autumn Ladies Tresses, Rockrose, Bastard Toadflax, and Chalkland Waxcap. All small fragmented sites are vulnerable to the extinction of their special species, unless the process of Down pasture re-creation saves them in time.

It is sheep grazed through the seasons now, so you are unlikely to see much of the flowers.

Paythorne Down, on the west side of Tenant Hill. TQ 239 095.

THIS site is over a third of a mile long, but you'll have to look carefully to pick it out from the surrounding recent pastures. It has very little scrub except some Gorse and thorn at the northern end, and there is strong lynchetting at the southern end, where there was a Roman peasant farm. At the northern end, at the base of the Gorsey slope, there was a medieval peasant farm.

The site has the rare Field Fleawort, which flowers in late spring and early summer and is often associated with prehistoric sites. In spring, too, it has Cowslip, Hairy Violet, Skylark and Meadow Pipit, and you may find Lizards.

You won't see great displays of flowers here, especially because of the year long grazing, but many Downland sites keep their treasures unseen. This site has three minute snails: the Blind Snail, *Cecilioides acicula*, the Scree Snail, and the Moss Snail – all three indicative of the antiquity of this pasture. The Blind Snail is weird. You can find it in anthills, where it lives underground, and it is eyeless and colourless, like many creatures of darkness. Its tiny pointed shell (only half a centimeter long) is transparent, too, when it's fresh, but when you usually find the old shells it has gone opaque and white.

Perching Hill's west slope.
TQ 241 105.

THIS is a very remote place. Just sheep, pylons, a rusting barn, huge modern pastures, and a slim fragment of the old Down pastures — where the steepness of slope halted the plough. When we visited the site, in high summer, an adolescent Cuckoo was sitting on a post by Perchinghill Barn. It looked very queasy and ruffled, but I think they always do at that age. Apparently this slope used to be a fine place to see Cuckoos gathering before their late summer retreat south to Africa. Along the slope we spotted a party of three Wheatears: an adult and two juniors, also readying themselves for departure. At that same moment a Brown Hare sat up, then loped up the slope and over the brow.

The site has many good old Down pasture species, including Spring Sedge, *Carex caryophyllea*, two orchis species and Devil's-bit. It used to have Heath Snail, but it's gone now.

Tottington Mount scarp. TQ 218 112.

AN ethical crime took place here about a quarter century ago. No law was broken, so this crime went unpunished. But a crime it was nonetheless. An agrochemical-bearing light aircraft systematically sprayed the whole of the north-facing slope of Tottington Mount, and in a few passes utterly ruined its millennia-old flowery pastures.

We had thought that these steep, unploughable slopes were safe from farmers' greed, but they were not.

Great patches of Nettle and Creeping Thistle sprawl over the slope and coarse grasses, White Clover and weedy species have replaced the dainty Downland herbs. Only Cowslip managed to survive, scattered here and there.

Truleigh Hill. TQ 224 110.

I CAME up here one morning in early summer, sweating up the narrow footpath from Truleigh Manor Farm. I stopped for a rest. Up behind me came a couple — a younger woman and an elderly man. They stopped, too. Any excuse to catch your breath! The man told me why he had come. He had been stationed on Truleigh Hill for part of the last World War and was bringing his daughter up to show her where he had spent his army years. He told me that under the hill top great caverns had been excavated, full of equiptment, work spaces and facilities. There he had helped staff a radar station monitoring the skies and intercepting enemy movements. It was a vital part of the war effort.

It's been a radio relay station ever since. There are four masts on the Hill and their red lights can be seen across this Downscape for many miles. All around them is much clutter. There are bungalows and derelict sheds, scruffy tree plantings (which do not thrive in these skeletal soils), barns, a big modern house — Freshcombe Lodge — and the Youth Hostel. For decades the Society of Sussex Downsmen fought to prevent new radio masts being erected here. It was a dogged and necessary battle, but there is little to show for it now.

The views across the Downs to the west and south are spectacular. It is best to enjoy the southerly views in a hazy light, however, for when the sun shines on the buildings of the Brighton conurbation there is a painful sense of intrusion. The white towers of Sussex Heights and its sister sky-risers punctuate the serene horizontals of the Downscape and seascape in a way that the eye cannot avoid.

All the distant intrusion and nearby mess destroys the sense of remoteness this place once had. There is more sense of the integrity of the landscape and more unimpaired connection with nature down in some of the nearby valleys.

Edburton Hill. TQ 237 110.

A MAGNIFICENT place. The banks of the Motte and Bailey castle, built by the

Truleigh Hill scarp with Newtimber Hill in the distance

Norman overlord soon after the Conquest, probably on the site of much older earthworks, are a great place for a picnic, though anywhere on these slopes is lovely. The castle cannot have been occupied for long and was of timber construction only. It's scarcely bigger than a farmyard. Later, in 1260, the Lord of Perching got a licence to build a fortified manor house down under the Hill, and you can still see crop marks where it used to stand.

There were four manors in the parish of Fulking-Edburton: Truleigh, Aburton (spelt the way old Sussex folk pronounced Edburton), Paythorne and Perching, and each had its chunk of Down pasture, its rich malm and greensand arable under the Downs, its sticky wooded patch of gault clay beyond, and fertile lower greensand at the northern end. Each of these four farmsteads still exist below you, though only Truleigh Manor still has its old working farmyard. Each of the farmsteads had a daughter farm to the north on the lower greensand — Truleigh

Sands, Edburton Sands, Nettledown and Perching Sands. The woods of Tottington-Longlands and Perching Hovel mark the poorly-drained gault clay. And the spire of Hurstpierpoint church and the glaring white cottages of Nep Town, Henfield, mark the extension of the lower greensand ridge to the north.

There was a scatter of Bronze Age round barrows along this scarp top, but only one is now in good condition — on the South Downs Way just east of the cross roads in the dip between Truleigh and Edburton Hills. There was thought to be another at the base of slope above Edburton church, but it is unlikely to be of that provenance. Sitting on that tump a year or so ago I watched a Turtle Dove for half an hour on the trees and bushes at the slope bottom.

Edburton church is a lovely place, full of the peace of the centuries. It's named after a Saxon woman, Eadburh. She founded this church and was a nun and a granddaughter of King Alfred (so it is said).

The grassland of these slopes varies in its 'walkability'. You will find traditional Sheep's Fescue turf and other mossy close-grazed areas, but there are also more tiresome areas of tall grass and tussocky Tor Grass, which is expanding. Often the slope top can have longer grass, but sometimes this is not so.

In spring the slopes are whitey-green with the new leaves of Whitebeam, and there are many Cowslips. You may find Green Hairsteak and Brimstone butterflies. The banks of the Motte and Bailey have Field Fleawort, and you may find some patches of Chalk Milkwort — much more sky-blue than common Milkwort, and almost unknown to the west of Brighton.

At one point you may come across a miniature bush of Spiny Restharrow, *Ononis spinosa*, which is extremely rare on these Downs, preferring the Wealden clays.

These slope have two deep-cut bostals, one coming up from Truleigh Manor and one from Perching Manor.

The Perching bostal. TQ 241 111.

THE Perching bostal is superb. It is so deep in parts that it looks like a quarry, with bare blocks of chalk forming its walls. Water gushing down it during storms forms a bare runnel down its floor. In one place Tufted Hair-grass, *Deschampsia cespitosa*, and Hard Rush, *Juncus inflexus*, can be found, as though this was a Wealden meadow, not dry chalk country. In hot weather the glaring white chalk roasts you with the reflected sun. Mats of moss cling on precariously. In high summer Carline Thistle and cushions of Thyme thrive, whilst other plants would wilt, and Wall

Brown butterfly, Chalk Carpet and Black Pyrausta, *Pyrausta nigrata*, moths enjoy the aridity.

One June I walked at late dusk from the Truleigh Youth Hostel to look for Glow Worms in the bostal. The wind was zinging through the pylons and night clouds scudded overhead. It was a bit eerie. But when I scrambled down deep into the bostal the wind stopped, and there around me I could pick out the tiny greenish lights of the Glow Worms. That was enough to cheer anyone up.

At the base of the bostal is the grassed over remains of a chalk pit with its Victorian lime kiln beautifully restored. There's another one south of Edburton church, too.

Edburton springhead and the scarp foot rew woods. TQ 231 112.

THE spring at Edburton is buried deep in the scarp bottom woodland and feels like a very secret place. Damp loving Yellow Archangel, Moschatel, Hard Fern, *Blechnum spicant*, and Male Fern, *Dryopteris filix-mas*, thrive there. The crystal clear water gushes from the hill at several points and deep green liverworts and mosses clothe the clefts. In the stream the stones are speckled white with little clinging Caddis Fly cases. There's a rookery overhead and a big Badgers' sett nearby. The early farmers settled here for good reasons.

It's fun to walk along the scarp bottom rew, especially in spring. There are Bluebells and Ramsons, Three-veined Sandwort, *Moehringia trinervia*, occasional Primrose and the odd patch of Gooseberries, *Ribes uva-crispa*.

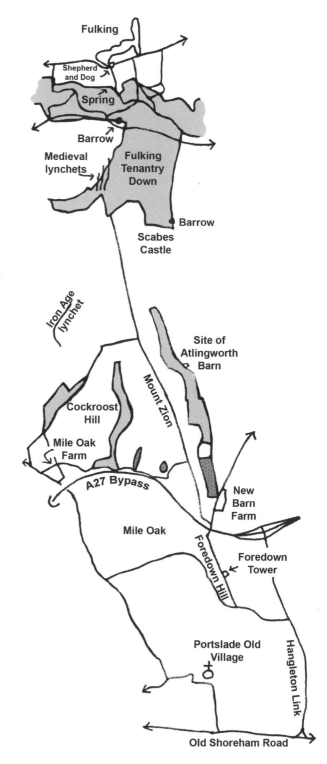

Legend

Statutory Access Land. Most is old Down pasture but some scrub and woodland is included.

Other Down pasture and associated scrub.

Woodland.

Roads, paths and railways.

Fulking

Shepherd and Dog

Spring

Barrow

Medieval lynchets

Fulking Tenantry Down

Barrow

Scabes Castle

Iron Age lynchet

Site of Atlingworth Barn

Mount Zion

Cockroost Hill

Mile Oak Farm

A27 Bypass

New Barn Farm

Mile Oak

Foredown Hill

Foredown Tower

Portslade Old Village

Hangleton Link

Old Shoreham Road

From Portslade to Fulking

4: FROM PORTSLADE TO FULKING

Here, the open South Downs are only two miles across. It is their narrowest point in the whole chain. And they only survive at all by perverse fortune, for if it had not been for the outbreak of the Second World War the entire landscape between Foredown Hill and the Devils Dyke would have been filled with a roaring, sprawling motor racing circuit, complete with grandstands and new roads. If that had happened then the battle for the integrity of the Downs would have truly been lost, as it has on the North Downs.

The dip slope landscape retains a scatter of small but high quality ancient Down pasture sites. It's owned by Brighton Council and let to two tenant farmers, whilst the Fulking scarp is in the safe hands of the National Trust.

Portslade old village. TQ 255 063.

If you explore this landscape make sure you enjoy the old village as well. Till the 1850s you could walk from Portslade old village to the Shepherd and Dog at Fulking without ever leaving common land. The warm flint tower of medieval St Nicholas church and the eye-stopping Victorian brewery and its chimney dominate the village centre, but there is a maze of old flint walls, cottages and twittens. Next to the church are the ruins of the 12th century Norman manor house within the grounds of its 19th century replacement, now an Emmaeus Community with an excellent second hand furniture store. The old village still has pony (and llama) paddocks, old allotments and secret manor house gardens (only approached by a tunnel under the road!) and a series of nice 19th century villas still in their grounds, including Easthill Park.

The **Foredown Tower Countryside Centre, TQ 256 071**, has been created in a Victorian water tower that is the only building remaining from the grim Foredown Isolation Hospital. It has a large camera obscura at its top and is a grand place for kids to have the night sky explained. It's future is threatened by Conservative Council cuts. In the medium term the coming National Park Authority might find a role for it, but will it survive long enough to utilize their help?…That's up to us…

It lies only two thirds of a mile south of the gorgeous east slope of Mount Zion on New Barn Farm (see below). Yet, to my knowledge, no partnership has ever been made with the farm to encourage public enjoyment of that site by Tower visitors.

Cockroost Hill, Mile Oak. TQ 24 08.

Cockroost Hill was part of the last redoubt of the Great Bustard two centuries

Portslade old village, with medieval church and Victorian manor house on the hill behind.

Looking northwards, the corn fields before you cover the remains of much Iron Age and Romano-British farming activity. At one time the quantity of finds led archaeologists to suppose there was a Roman encampment there. Little visible survives, except crop marks to be seen after ploughing, though one tall, bushey lynchet remains in the valley bottom between Cockroost and Tenant Hill.

The **east slope of Cockroost Hill, TQ 248 084**, has a half mile long Down pasture site which is noisy at its southern end but tranquil to the north. Right on the line of the bypass, in Cockroost Bottom, a large 4000 year old Bronze Age settlement was found during the bypass rescue excavations. There were two bowl furnaces for metal working (very rare) and the charred remains of a burnt out round house with all the domestic clutter right where it was when the peasant family ran from the flames. Under these remains was a much larger circular ditch and bank that Miles Russell, the excavator, thought to be a 'henge' (as in Stone*henge*) though that is disputed. Deer bones were found — and Deer still use this valley. There are many Rabbits here, too. In autumn you may find yellow Fairy Clubs and black Earthtongue meadow fungi.

Just east of the Bronze Age site there is a **grassy hillock, TQ 251 080**, with some trees. It's a piece of modern archaeology, for in the Second World War this tump was built as a gun emplacement to guard the valley. Its slopes have acquired lots of the Downland herbs which ploughing later eliminated from the fields surrounding it.

Mount Zion's east slope. TQ 254 085.

THIS is a delightful mile-long site, with a little copse two thirds of the way up. Its

ago and maybe takes it's name from those birds, who always roosted on high ground to give themselves long views of any approaching danger. These prairie grasslands were broken up following the enclosure of Portslade's commons in 1861, but two fragments remain.

The **west slope of Cockroost Hill, TQ 242 085**, has a restored dew pond and a beautiful old Down pasture fragment. If your children are old enough to walk properly and you want to try somewhere a bit further than the delights of the ducks and rabbits round Mile Oak Farm shop, then bring them up here. It's an easy walk. Bring a picnic. The children will have lots of fun and you'll love the views and the peace. The site has some remarkable wildlife survivals. Walking there recently I saw a pure white moth that was not at all familiar. It turned out to be the rare Pyralid *Sitochroa palealis*, which occasionally breeds on seaward sites along the south coast. This is a very colourful wild flowery place, and the scarce ones include Field Fleawort and Yellow Vetchling, *Lathyrus aphaca*. For such a small site there's an impressive number of butterflies and moths, including Chalkhills, Brown Argus, Small Heath and Mother Shipton moth.

turf has never suffered from lack of grazing (as so many surviving old Down pasture sites have) and it is springy under the feet and dotted with old anthills. North of New Barn Farm it has three gentle combes, and the northern two feel quite remote. The most northerly combe has the little copse, with Hazel and Dogwood. Goldfinches and Linnets enjoy its peace.

You may be lucky enough to find Bee or Fragrant Orchis, and in high summer the pasture has a tinge of light blue across it from Scabious flowers. The Creeping Thistle at the slope bottoms is a good place to find nectaring butterflies, which include Green-veined White, Chalkhill, and Common Blue. The northern end of the site has a slightly more acidic soil chemistry and Small Copper enjoys the Sorrel found there on bits of bare ground. In the ant hills the tiny subterranean white woodlouse lives. It has the lovely name of *Platyarthrus hoffmanseggii*.

There used to be an old flint hovel and yard called Atlingworth Barn next to the copse. It's name had a thousand years of history behind it, for 'Atlingworth' was the paramount manor of Brighton and this remote place must once have been part of that manor. The old Brighton parish church of St Nicholas was probably built as the church for Atlingworth manor and there's still an Atlingworth Terrace off Marine Parade. Back in the 'sixties the keen new tenant of New Barn Farm bulldozed the Barn. Only scattered bits of stone remain.

There were Adder and Early Purple Orchis in the bushey places nearby, but the tenant bulldozed all the ground — many acres — that he could drive his machinery over. Cropping for corn was big money. If the Adders survived that they wouldn't have survived the 1970s, for in those years the over-grazing of the old slope turned it yellow and parched and all cover for Adders was eliminated. He started scrambler bike racing across the slope, too, and the track scored great loops and gouges out of the ancient turf and even through the little copse. It was a kind of 'racers revenge', really, because it was in this valley that a major motor racing track had been planned between the two World Wars. The bike racing was too much for Hove Council, though, and they used a special planning procedure (an 'Article Four Direction') to ban it.

Mount Zion's east slope: Kipling's *Bare slopes where chasing shadows skim.*

After all this damage there seemed no point in visiting this farm. There'd be nothing to see.

Then came the crunch. The heavy rains of October 1987 went on for two days and more, and suddenly the householders of Hangleton Valley found their houses and gardens awash with a brown flood of earth and rainwater torrenting down from the farm's exposed autumn ploughlands.

That was enough for the tenant. He was one of the first to enter the new Sussex Downs Environmentally Sensitive Area support scheme set up that year. Now none of New Barn Farm grows arable crops and great flocks of sheep and herds of cattle dot the newly-greened slopes.

Too late for the Adder and the Early Purples, though, and too late for the marks that the ancient peoples made. Too late for Atlingworth Barn, where we searched for Horse Mushrooms.

And still the damage had not ended, for some years ago the southern combe of this slope, TQ 255 081, was treated with chemicals and most of the ancient herbs disappeared under a nitrogen-green improved sward. The City Council, as landowners, took no enforcement action following this disaster.

Yet this farm has been owned by the people of Brighton for more than a century!

Fulking Tenantry Down. TQ 250 105.

THIS is one of the three surviving Down pasture commons on the Brighton Downs.

On the western side of its **dip slope** there was a working medieval strip-cultivated open field until early Victorian times. It had 23 strips in an area that can't have been much bigger than that number in acreage. The very tall old lynchets of these strips, TQ 246 103, are where the old Down pasture wildlife survives on the dip slope. There are bits of Betony, Rockrose and Rampion, and in autumn there's Scarlet Hood, Golden, and Chalkland Waxcaps, making splashes of colour.

Almost as interesting, though, is the way the rest of the common's dip slope has recovered under the National Trust's management since it was put back down to grass after half a century of tillage. Before its bulldozing there had been big Gorse thickets on the common. As soon as the pasture returned the Gorse reappeared miraculously from the long-dormant seed bank. After a few years Snowy Waxcap, *H. virginea*, and Blackening Waxcap, *H. conica*, also reappeared.

The Tenantry Dwn had at least four prehistoric barrows, but only two are now visible above ground. One of them marks the southern end of the eastern boundary of the common and the other sits by the South Downs Way above the Fulking Hill western bostal. That is a fine example, still with its flowery turf. Just to its west on Perching Hill the South Downs Way proceeds through a deep hilltop cutting which shelters you from the wind and brings all the little herbs and mosses up to your eye level.

The **scarp slope** grasslands and bostal have their aboriginal turf intact and full of interest. I have found Fly Orchis there with Spotted and Twayblade orchids. The short turf where the two bostals cross near the bottom of the slope is very rich with herbs and chalk loving butterflies. There are lots of cowslips.

Hidden up the combe above the Shepherd and Dog is the **Fulking springhead, TQ 247 111.** It's a lovely cool spot with pretty Monkeyflower, *Mimulus guttatus*, matting the gill floor. There's Fool's Water Cress, *Apium nodiflorum*, and the stream bed has hundreds of tiny Caddis cases, just like the Edburton springhead. The rew woodland is pretty with flowers in spring, too.

Fulking village, TQ 247 115, is very pretty and has smelt strongly of serious money since before I first knew it nearly fifty years ago. No farm worker (if their jobs still existed) could afford those cottages.

5: THE HANGLETON AND WEST BLATCHINGTON DOWNS

THIS is part of 'the land of the golf course', with three courses. There is much history here, with two Roman roads, a superb Tudor manor house, a well-preserved Norman church, a windmill painted by Constable, and the remains of a lost railway.

The landscape has benefitted from environmental campaigning. Much arable land is returning to grass, the Benfield Hill Local Nature Reserve has been created, and two new Access Land sites designated. However, the A27 Bypass and Hangleton Link Road have been disastrous and the peaceful Benfield Valley has been fragmented and partially developed.

There are two long ridges — the Benfield ridge and the Round Hill ridge — and two valleys — the Benfield Valley and Toad's Hole Valley.

There is only one sizeable ancient Down pasture site — the golf course slope east of Round Hill — but a whole series of excellent 'secondary' Down pasture sites.

Old Hangleton.

HANGLETON village was deserted about 600 years ago, apart from the manor farm. The deserted village was excavated in the early 1950s and a reconstruction of one of the peasant dwellings can be seen at the Weald and Downland Museum, Singleton.

Hangleton Manor, TQ 264 069, is a large and rambling flint-built Tudor manor house with a fifteenth century wing. There are some decorated stones taken from the old St Pancras Priory at Lewes built into the main doorway, and the main room has beautiful Elizabethan panelling and an embossed plaster ceiling. In the gardens is a seventeenth century flint dovecot, lovingly restored.

In the early 1960s the manor lay empty, and myself and other local kids used to roam its ghostly rooms smashing the still-remaining fittings and stomping through crumbling floorboards. Several local folk — including my mum — mounted a vigorous campaign to save it. In the end Hove Council agreed a shameful compromise, whereby the councillor-developer who had bought it was allowed to built on half the grounds — bulldozing the wood and its rookery that protected the character of the place — in return for conserving the buildings. The manor's salvation still had to wait till its sale to conservationists, who carefully restored it as a pub.

The church of St Helen's, TQ 264 072, at the top of the Green is over 900

The Norman shepherd's church, St. Helen's, Hangleton.

years old and retains parts of its medieval wall paintings. We found 54 species of lichen on its walls and gravestones. At **Benfield Farm, TQ 263 071**, a two century old flint and timber barn with a huge roof and wagon entrance survives, but the Victorian cottages and other farm buildings are crumbling into ruin as developer-leaseholders of Benfield Golf Course manoeuvre for advantage with the City Planning Department. The farm is a sad place. After the building of the Bypass one of the cottage tenants unsuccessfully resisted rehousing, for he had lived all his life there. Soon after Sainsburys (the then leaseholders) had got rid of him the empty cottages were burned down.

Benfield Ridge.

B E N F I E L D **Hill, TQ 261 078**, is becoming famous for its magnificent Glow-worm displays on midsummer evenings. The Hill slopes are mostly good 'secondary' chalk grassland, for all but the steepest part on the east side and a lynchet on the west side were used for crop growing, probably until late Victorian times. These grasslands have matured into diverse and beautiful places. On the steep east side of the Hill there is much Large Thyme, *Thymus pulegioides*, and Autumn Gentian, and Bee Orchids can be found. You can see Brimstone butterfly in spring, and Small Heath, Marbled White and Common Blue in summer. Green Hairstreak and Ringlet have been seen in the past. On the western side of the Hill the gentle slope has long-standing populations of Small Blue and

Brown Argus. The tall grass encourages magnificent displays of Burnet moths.

Nearly a mile northwards, on the **east side of the Benfield Ridge, TQ 260 093**, there is another interesting 'secondary' Down pasture site. The flattish top of the ridge was where the ancient chalk grassland used to be, but many species 'hopped' off it onto the derelict arable land on the steep slope. Then the ridge top land was ploughed out in the 'sixties and this secondary chalk grassland was all that survived. It is steadily improving and now has Autumn Ladies Tresses, Violets, Thyme, Milkwort, *Polygala vulgaris*, and Carline Thistle.

To the north of the Parish/City boundary this good secondary chalk grassland continues on **Devil's Dyke Farm land, TQ 260 095**. A **prehistoric barrow, TQ 258 094**, marked that boundary, but is now only detectable by a slight rise in the fence line as it crosses the ploughed-out mound. In a good evening light you can see the lynchet lines of an Iron Age field system in **Adder Bottom, TQ 253 101**, just west of the Devil's Dyke Farm. The Devil's Dyke Farm's barns and cottages were built around 1950 and are the very last generation of farm buildings to be built with relatively traditional uses and proportions.

The boundary bank and bushy fence, that marches north up Benfield Valley from Hangleton Manor as far as the old Dyke Railway goes back to just after 1066 when the Norman lords divided up the old united manor of Benfield, Hangleton, and West Blatchington.

Old West Blatchington. TQ 278 068.
T H E **Norman church of West Blatchington** fell into ruin probably after the manorial tenants became Quakers in the 17th century. It was only restored in 1890. Only the south and west walls are (mostly) original. Look at the two tiny Norman windows in the west wall.

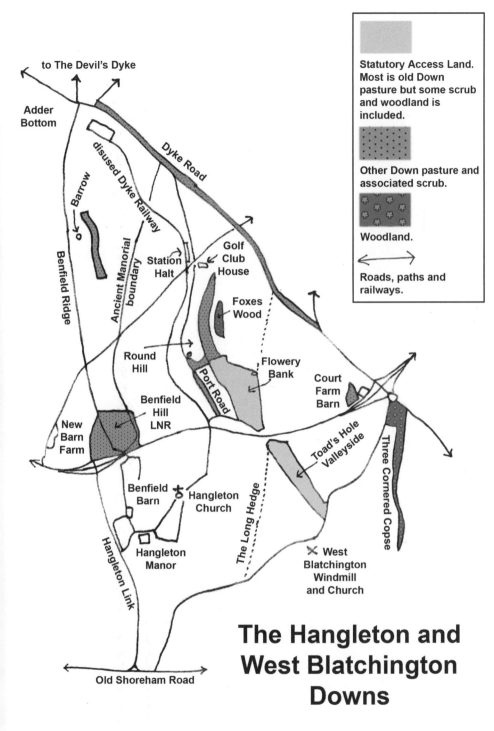

The Hangleton and West Blatchington Downs

Benfield Wildlife Group members enjoying a summer evening on the Hill after their founding meeting. The white scar of the new A27 bypass lies behind.

The **windmill** was built about 200 years ago and Constable, the landscape painter (who spent loads of time in Brighton), did a sketch of it a few years afterwards. The **manor house** was a lovely building, of the 14th, 15th and 16th centuries, with a Victorian addition. It stood just east of the church, where The Mount flats now stand. It was stupidly demolished in 1955. One of the founders of the Friends of Toad's Hole Valleyside spent his honeymoon in the deserted building shortly before its demolition. It's nice that the old building was shown some love just before its demise.

Toad's Hole Valleyside. TQ 277 075.

THIS site is a scandalous mess. The landowners should hang their heads in shame. If we lived in a just society this land — adjacent to a large council estate with many children — would be confiscated from them. Though the slope is designated as Access Land it is rapidly degenerating into an impenetrable mess of Bramble and Bindweed with spreading thorn scrub

and Sycamore and Ash woodland. The slope top has a broad band of Nettles hiding decades of fly-tipped rubbish. The remaining grassland is mostly rank, though Scabious and Vetches and other flowers survive in places. The old Hove Council managed the site beautifully for a year or so in cooperation with the landowners, and the site began to look good, but the landowners then withdrew their consent.

At the base of this slope, next to the bypass, the woodland has grown out from an old hedge line that has several woodland snail species. Perhaps the hedge was a relic of the old hanging woodland commemorated in the name *'Hangratun'*, or Hangleton?

'The Flowery Bank': Round Hill's south eastern slope. TQ 273 080.

I am told that the farmer calls this slope 'the flowery bank'. It is a good name. All of the bushy slope is colourful, but it gets progressively more diverse in wild flowers as you walk from the south to the north end. This is because the whole slope, like Toad's Hole Valleyside, is 'secondary' chalk grassland which was ploughed up till the last century. After it reverted to pasture it was gradually re-colonised from its northern end by the wild flowers of the ancient chalk grassland over the fence on the golf course. Thus, you can find Sussex Rampion, and wonderful displays of Cowslip and Fragrant Orchis at the northern end, but have to make do with Knapweed and Scabious at the southern end. The north end has Forester moths.

The Norman Parish boundary.

A T the north east corner of the Access Land described above is a **sarsen stone, TQ 273 082**, of the same type as the Goldstone further down the valley in Hove Park. There is another **sarsen stone, TQ 275 089,** on the west bank of the Dyke Road a short walk south of the gateway to Golf Farm. Both these stones are Norman boundary stones between Hangleton and West Blatchington parishes. Much of West Blatchington's 900 year old parish boundary can still be traced. To the south of the Bypass it becomes the **Long Hedge**, now trapped between Amberley Drive and

Applesham Avenue. On its eastern side the boundary between West Blatchington and Patcham survives as **Three Cornered Copse**, between Woodland Avenue and Woodland Drive.

Round Hill, TQ 268 085, and around.

T H E R E are so many signs of the past around this Hill. The name **Skeleton Hovel** (for an old flint barn, **TQ 269 090**) probably commemorates a prehistoric burial unwittingly discovered during farming work. On the crown of Round Hill is a Romano-British round barrow, TQ 268 084, and the site of a second, and the famous Bronze Age **Black Burgh** barrow, TQ 268 097, stood by the Devil's Dyke Road. There are the remains of prehistoric field systems on Round Hill and right across the Benfield Valley and ridge. Just north of the Golf Clubhouse two minor Roman roads intersect: **The Port Way**, running north on a double lynchet along the western side of Round Hill's crown, and the road to Clayton Hill that comes from the west across the Benfield Valley and Hill.

The platform of Golf Club Halt, still visible 70 years after the Dyke Railway's closure.

The **Golf Clubhouse, TQ 269 091**, itself is a great piece of Victoriana and still has its iron stove in the middle of the lounge, with a stovepipe rising from it through the roof.

Both the **Dyke Railway** and Golf Club were opened in 1887, and in 1891 the Club acquired its own **Golf Club Halt, TQ 267 093**. The northern part of the Halt platform, complete with its line of Japanese Euonymus bushes at the back of the platform, survives, though the railway was closed in 1938. Several of the Dyke Railway's embankments still retain bits of old open grassland and the Dyke Rail Trail embankment due east of Northlane Barn, TQ 266 085, still has Glow-worms present. North of Skeleton Hovel the Dyke Rail Trail is forced back onto the nearby bridlepath and road because of the farmers opposition to the use of the old rail track.

The Rail Trail is scrubbing up with thorn and Ash, Parsnip and even Japanese Knotweed. Like so many old railway cycle trails it could become a tunnel of vegetation through which you get occasional glimpses of the surrounding landscape. At its southern and northern end this process has advanced a good way.

There is a bit of living railway archaeology on the nearby steep **eastern slope of Round Hill, TQ 269 087**, for one evening a summer or so ago I found a dainty tuffet of Pale Toadflax, Linaria repens, flowering there. This little plant is pretty rare, all in all, and often occurs on railways, banks and roadsides, usually on chalk. Maude Robinson (of Saddlescombe fame) recorded it in 1930 as having been "for many years" about the Dyke Railway.[1] It may well have come with the railway, then jumped off the scrubbing-up disused track and made a new home on this adjacent site.

The Round Hill eastern slope is the best of Hove and Portslade's Down pasture sites. Not the best managed (for it strongly needs grazing and more scrub control) or with the longest management continuity (that accolade goes to Mount Zion's east slope), but the richest for old Downland wildlife. It has Field Fleawort (as you would guess from so much archaeology), Chalk Milkwort, Orchids, Cowslips, Hairy Violet, Rockrose, Crested Hair-grass and Devil's-bit. There are Adonis and Chalkhill Blue butterflies. There's Fox Moth, *Macrothylacia rubi*, and Common Heath Moth, Purse-web Spider, Moss and Pygmy Snails. The crown of the Hill still has a tiny patch of chalk heath, with Ling heather and Heath Speedwell amongst the Gorse.

The old scrub thicket below the slope is known to all local people as Foxes Wood.

It is sad that this, the senior of all Hove sites, is not designated as Access Land, like the two 'secondary' sites south of it. Being part of a Golf Course excluded it.

Footnotes

1   *The Flora of Sussex*, edited by Lt.-Col A. H. Wolley-Dod (The Chatford House Press, 1937, reprinted 1970), page 319.

***Is this a face I see before me?* The cup found when the Black Burgh barrow was excavated.**

6: THE DEVIL'S DYKE AND NEWTIMBER HILL

SHEER magnificence!! Two whale-back mountains pointing into the blue Weald.

Together they constitute one of the most intact survivors of the ancient Down pasture landscape on the whole 80 mile South Downs chain.

Stand on Summer Down and look north through the Poynings gap. To the west is the mound of the Dyke tumbling down to its wooded fringe. Northwards is the tower of Poynings church amongst the trees, with the Weald behind. To the north east is the flank of Newtimber Hill, and — further east — the West Hill ridge. All the bushy pastures you see are ancient — much older than Poynings' six hundred year old church tower.

It is a view that would have been familiar to many centuries of shepherds and travellers. Details have changed (for the hills would have been bare of bushes and trees till the last seventy years; the Saddlescombe quarry would have been much smaller; and the road along Newtimber Hill's flank would have been a mere chalk whiteway) but all the broad elements of the landscape have an ancient continuity.

The Devil's Dyke. TQ 260 110.

Wind in your hair,
Kites in the air,
Ice creams dripping,
Grandparents tottering,
Children skipping…

The best in life is here.

WHAT a robust place the Devil's Dyke is! Ancient Down pasture is a tough and hardy ecosystem. It can survive a real pounding. It's had to. For here, in the last two centuries, there have been an amusement park and pleasure gardens, a hotel, three railways (the railway up from Hove; a funicular railway down the north scarp slope; and a cable car across the Dyke Valley), golf courses, and a zoo. The funicular, the cable car, and the women's golf course were short-lived enterprises. So was the zoo, which was created by an entrepreneur in the 1960s within the windswept ramparts of the Iron Age camp topping the Dyke. It housed forlorn Antelope, Cranes and other shivering livestock. On more than one occasion I remember coming across lost Cranes standing bemused amongst the grass of the Dyke Valley, waiting to be recaptured and returned to their paddocks.

The Devil's Dyke and The Devil's Punchbowl from the Saddlescombe Road.

Despite all that human activity you can take a few minutes walk from the car park and be amongst Sussex Rampion and all the other Downland wildflowers, and a quick stroll in June to the steep slope at the head of the Dyke valley will show you Adonis Blue butterflies in plenty, Brown Argus and the shining irridescent green of day flying Forester moths. You can find orchids and butterflies, blackberries and raspberries, cowslips and cuckoos all in their seasons.

The Hill has, in a sense, always been a public landscape. It was a common up until about 1805 when the Crown Estate and their new leaseholders began to exploit it more intensively, dividing the common up into a new farm — the present Devil's Dyke Farm — and a recreational landscape around a new Dyke Inn. It was, though, already well known as a holiday destination, and Gilbert White, the famous 18th century naturalist, visited it.

Its qualities as a recreational wilderness were in uneasy conflict with its potential as an entertainment resort right up to the 1960s and the dawn of modern consciousness of conservation issues. In the 1920s came a threat to build a 300 bungalow settlement, scotched by the combined intervention of the new Society of Sussex Downsmen and Alderman Herbert Carden of Brighton, who bought the Dyke and transferred it at cost price to Brighton Council in 1927.

In the 1960s the Dyke Hotel's leaseholder planned to build a giant replica of the Nile Valley's Temple of Abu Simbel on the side of the Devil's Dyke Valley. Inspired, no doubt, by the imminent inundation of the real Temple by the rising waters behind Nasser's great Aswan Dam, the hotelier's plans stirred a hornet's nest of controversy. The temple plan was dropped.

The whole of the 'Devil's Dyke Estate' was owned by Brighton Council from 1927 until 1995. After decades of Conservative neglect, the election of a Labour Council in 1987 brought a twitch of new life to the management of Brighton's huge Downland estate. Systematically the estate was surveyed for its wildlife. Scrub clearance was initiated and sheep grazing was re-introduced. Then, out of the blue, in March 1995 the Dyke and Saddlescombe Farm was sold on again, for £887,000, this time to the National Trust.

Given that the Dyke Estate had been "dedicated to the use of the public

The Devil's Dyke and Newtimber Hill

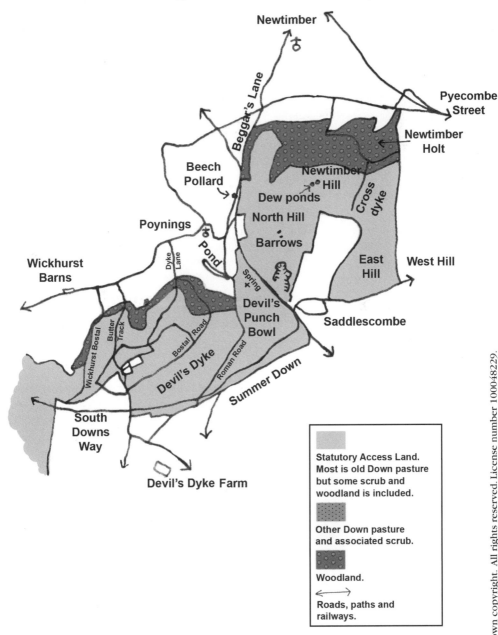

Newtimber

Pyecombe
Street

Beggar's Lane

Newtimber
Holt

Beech
Pollard

Newtimber
Hill

Dew ponds

Cross dyke

North Hill

Poynings

to Pond

Barrows

Dyke Lane

East
Hill

West Hill

Wickhurst
Barns

Spring

Devil's
Punch
Bowl

Saddlescombe

Wickhurst Bostal

Butter Track

Bostal Road

Devil's Dyke

Roman Road

Summer Down

South
Downs
Way

Devil's Dyke Farm

Statutory Access Land.
Most is old Down pasture
but some scrub and
woodland is included.

Other Down pasture
and associated scrub.

Woodland.

Roads, paths and
railways.

forever" in 1928, as the stone memorial seat at the Dyke testifies, and given that Brighton's Downland management was at last "coming good', the sale was a serious betrayal. The National Trust launched a big appeal for £800,000 to complete the purchase and for management costs. They got it, of course. What most donors to the Trust will not have realized, however, was that they were indirectly giving part of their money *not* to save a threatened countryside asset, but to secure for Brighton the cost of re-wiring the Brighton Conference Centre, repairing the balustrades of Marine Parade, and the copper roof of the Dome Leisure Centre!

At around the same time, another iconic part of the South Downs scarp near Amberley came onto the market, and the National Trust decided against involvement in purchase. The price was too high. Thus, nearly one million pounds was wasted on buying an asset already safe in public ownership, whilst other top quality Downland was left to be purchased by rich landowners primarily interested in its pheasant shooting potential.

The Iron Age Hillfort. The crown of the Dyke Hill is surrounded by the well-preserved ramparts of an Iron Age hill-fort on all sides, which meander along its contours. The tallest ramparts guard the vulnerable entrance-way on the plateau to the south west, through which the modern entry road still passes. It's a large enclosure — of 37.5 acres — only exceeded in size by Cissbury Ring. There was an Iron Age settlement outside the ramparts to the south west, excavated in the 1930s. That was also the area occupied by the Edwardian women's golf course, and you can still make out gentle corrugations under the cattle pasture which must be the old bunkers. We can tell very little about the hillfort's usage, for it has not been excavated in its own right. The 'Devil's Dyke' was originally one of the old names for the hill-fort ramparts, but the name migrated in modern times to describe the deep dry valley. The ramparts were also called the 'Poor Man's Wall'.

The tall south western ramparts still retain an aboriginal flora and fauna with Sussex Rampion and the tiny Scree Snail. The area within the ramparts has a more acidic soil and much of its grassy sward has been improved, but the acidic turf just outside the ramparts at the north east end of the promontory is flowery, with much Tormentil.

Like a huge tsunami rolling over the Weald. **Probably the most iconic view of the Brighton Downs: the scarp from the Dyke Hotel.**

The north scarp slope. Beautifully flowery, with well-developed cattle terracettes in parts, making traversing its extreme steepness easier. Looking westwards from the ramparts in the evening sun I counted a ladder of 115 cattle terracettes on the slopes around Wickhurst Bostal. The scarp slope has old anthills, lots of Rockrose, orchids, and lots of Wayfaring Tree, with a population of Orange-tailed and Yellow-legged Clearwing moths.

The Dyke Valley, TQ 263 110. This is the grandest dry valley on the whole South Downs chain, scarcely rivalled by its nearest competitor at Butser Hill on the Hampshire border. The two sides of the valley are very different in character. **The north slope** is much hotter because it catches all the sun. It has only skeletal soils with much white chalk showing through. Horseshoe Vetch is abundant, with Mouse-ear Hawkweed, *Hieracium officinarum*, Knapweed, and Rockrose. It's a great place for the Blue butterflies. Mixed scrub has developed at the slope top at the eastern end of the valley, but some of it, including a few Juniper bushes and Scots Pine, was planted by the Brighton Council Parks Department back in the 'sixties. **The south slope,** by contrast, is mossy and cooler and has less bare ground. In late summer it is blue with Devil's-bit Scabious, appropriately for a valley with a Devilish reputation. It's called Devil's-bit because the rootstock has a bitten-off look. It becomes noticeably less flowery as you climb from bottom to top as the influence of soil leaching and clay-with-flints deposits shows through.

Bostal paths. There are a number of ancient bostal paths down from the Dyke top. The most varied and interesting route to take is **The Bostal Road**, a bridlepath, which runs along the Iron Age ramparts above the Dyke Valley before curving down through the woods and into Poynings. **The Wickhurst Bostal,**

descending to Wickhurst Barns, is on the Devil's Dyke Farm ground to the west and tops at the junction with another bostal down to Fulking. Near its base is a tiny chalk quarry, TQ 255 110, with a Victorian limekiln still intact. The quarry has lots of butterflies and moths, including Chalk Carpet, Brown Argus, Small Copper and Black Pyrausta. From the Dyke Pub a footpath, which was called the **Butter Track** two centuries ago, takes you steeply down due north. Another steep and narrow footpath takes you down north eastwards across the Dyke promontory to the back of Poynings Village. In the woods at its base is another derelict chalk pit and extant limekiln. There is an ancient **terrace way** (now a bridleway) that tracks down and across the south slope of the Dyke Valley from its head to its mouth. This is probably part of the Roman route starting at Southwick, on the coast, and joining the Roman road now called the Greensand Way south of Hurstpierpoint.

The woods on the eastern base of slope of the Dyke promontory, TQ 263 115, have old Hazel coppice and many Bluebells in spring. As a boy I collected unripe green hazelnuts (they have to be green) from these woods and made hazelnut bread. The fragrance was ambrosial! In late summer there's lots of Nettle-leaved Bellflower. Below these woods and overlooking **Poynings Pond, TQ 265 117,** (an old mill pond) there's a bushy slope we used to call **"the orchid bank"**, TQ 264 117, that used to have Fly Orchis and lots of other orchids and good flowers. It may have still. It's rapidly being lost to scrub just in the last decade.

Summers Down. TQ 267 110. Has beautiful views through the Poynings Gap. It has bushy acid grassland with lots of sheltered places for picnics. South of the road and the National Trust car park two Bronze Age bowl barrows are still upstanding, both with their tops dug out by treasure seekers in the past — like scotch eggs with the egg bit picked out. The place also has a pagan Saxon cemetery, the site of an old windmill, and a small cross dyke, but the rank grassland and scrub and modern disturbance will not let you see these subtle corrugations of the land surface. You can, however, follow the old braided trackways either side of the tarmaced modern road down to Saddlescombe.

The Devil's Punch Bowl, TQ 267 114, and the Poynings springhead, TQ 267 116.

T H E Devil's Punch Bowl is the little rounded hill between Saddlescombe and the mouth of the Dyke Valley. It's a peaceful place and its steep northern slopes are covered in Cowslips in spring and Fragrant Orchis in early summer. The Poynings springhead lies to its north, with a little modern pumping station hidden in a lush gill wood. It's all as green and cool as a summer salad.

Poynings. TQ 264 120.

P O Y N I N G S church is a real 'cathedral of the Downs'. It's just like Alfriston church only without the spire. Probably had the same master mason architect. Till Chaucer's time there would have been a big baronial manor house and a little church. Then Michael de Poynings willed the building of the present church. Over the next five hundred years the de Poynings family disappeared and their stately home crumbled, till all that's left of it is a forlorn pillar of masonry in the back garden of the adjoining Poynings Manor Farm.

The church is the de Poynings real memorial and its tower is like a bit of a baronial castle. The church has an echoing empty interior and scant signs of the wealth of the donor family. There are only the smallest fragments of fourteenth century glass surviving in the plain glass windows. It's like a house that the owners have just driven away from with all the fittings.

With its big, centralized, empty interior it feels more like the clean space of a grand old mosque than like the homely eclectic busy-ness of many medieval parish churches.

Saddlescombe. TQ 272 114.

T H E nicest farming hamlet on the Brighton Downs. National Trust since 1995, but long managed sympathetically by Brighton Council and their farm tenants. The white ducks were paddling on the pond in 1960 and they're still there! We counted 30 and more Swallows gathering on the wires in early August. Glow-worms on the grassy tracks out from the hamlet. Chickens a-wandering. A couple of old waggon barns and a part-tudor manor house with lovely walled gardens. A scattering of old cottages, from one of which you can buy eggs and marrows and even a few second hand books. Several cow byres, old pig pens and an outhouse with an ancient door covered in generations of old iron work. Big shady Sycamores, and an old Hornbeam pollard on the disused trackway to the Brighton road.

Saddlescombe was one of the two manors of Newtimber Parish. It was a manor of the Knights Templar till they got closed down. The ancient covered well is probably the only visible relic of their tenure. The donkey wheel above it that wound up the hamlet's water is still intact. Notice the rusting iron oxen shoes tacked to the old doorway.

Newtimber Hill. TQ 27 12.

T H E **Hill's western slopes.** Walking its flanks never fails to lift the spirits. There's a view all along the ocean wave of the chalk scarp to Hampshire, and across the dim blue forest goodness to Blackdown on the Surrey border. You could find tiny Frog Orchids and a funny late-flowering form of Burnt-tip Orchis in its turf. There's a ribbon of Tormentil where the chalky slopes break to meet the acidic plateau top. Lots of anthills and cattle terracettes. Dark Green Fritillary if you're lucky. Nowadays the Silver-spotted Skipper butterfly — an erstwhile great rarity — is one of the commonest butterflies on the western slope. There's one of the biggest Glow-worm populations I know.

Down by the road — both above it and below it — are its other disused braided trackways. They used to be called the 'Devil's Stairs'. These trackways are the location for East Sussex's only remaining Juniper population. Some years ago the National Trust folk discovered more Juniper bushes lost amongst encroaching thorn scrub on the slope below the road. That part of the slope was open pasture till the 1960s but road traffic cut it off from the higher slopes above the road and it scrubbed-up. The National Trust and the Sussex Wildlife Trust are now bravely restoring the Juniper's old Down pasture habitat.

Saddlescombe chalk quarry. TQ 270 116. Very steep, but lovely for clambering over. Too steep for kids, though. The old limekilns are still there under some big old bushes.

Nice chalk-loving mosses, waxcaps and earthtongues on the terracettes. Adonis Blue is still there enjoying the hot micro-climate, This used to be one of the last Downland sites for the Grayling butterfly, but use of the quarry floor for cattle feeding eliminated it. Now the Grayling has one last Downland redoubt — at Deep Dean behind the Long Man of Wilmington.

The Hill's plateau top. A century and more ago the top of the Hill was bare of scrub and covered in a mantle of purple heather and old acidic grassland. A combination of dereliction and fertiliser use eliminated this chalk heath, so that most of the hilltop grassland is now botanically poor. The glades and scrub thickets are still excellent places for chilling out. I once watched a roding Woodcock go round and round its circuit there.

Two small good patches of acid grassland do survive. On the **top of North Hill, TQ 270 120,** there is an island of old acid grassland around two prominent Bronze Age barrows. There's Betony, Eggs and Bacon, Tormentil and Knapweed, and in autumn (in a good year) a real cornucopia of colourful waxcaps, fairy clubs and earthtongues, including several good old pasture indicator species. The barrows themselves have both been robbed, but finds of pottery vessels, a skeleton and a dagger were made. The

The upturned boat of Newtimber Hill, seen from the Dyke Hill.

banks of the dried-up dewpond, TQ 272 123, on the top of Newtimber Hill (as opposed to North Hill) can also be colourful with waxcaps. There's a restored dewpond next to it with good pond life.

South of the dew ponds the plateau descends by a staircase of medieval strip lynchets to the combe of sheltered Saddles*combe*. The lynchets are chalky in character with nice flowers and old meadow fungi.

There's a cross dyke, TQ 275 124, between West Hill and Newtimber Hill, along the line of the bridlepath.

The West Hill slope, TQ 276 120, down to Saddlescombe, is good old chalk grassland with an up-slope fringe of scrub. It has some Dyer's Greenweed up-slope, too, as on the slopes of Varncombe Hill, to the south.

Newtimber Holt. TQ 277 126. A rich ancient woodland with a history possibly going back to the wildwood. The Holt is in two very steep combes on the Hill's north eastern corner, but most of the rest of the Hill's northern slope has also grown over into Ash, Beech, and Hazel secondary woodland since Victorian times. The Holt is bounded on its south side by the rising bostal bridlepath. There's a big old Beech boundary pollard half way up the bostal. The Holt doesn't have Large-leaved Lime anymore, but it does have some very tall Large-leaved / Small-Leaved hybrids. The good representation of other trees and shrubs is indicative of the Holt's age. There's Wych Elm, Maple, lots of Hazel coppice, large old Beech, a big Oak, Holly, Ash and even Midland Thorn (usually found on the Wealden Clay). Charlie Cain, the National Trust's manager, says that some big Whitebeam may mark the now-lost coppice compartments of the Holt. Sycamore is invading more and more of the wood and may change its whole character over time.

There's lots of Bluebell, with some Wood Anemone, Goldilocks buttercup, Yellow Archangel, Early Purple Orchis, damp-loving Polypody Fern, Redcurrant, Nettle-leaved Bellflower and other indicator herbs and grasses. In May you could find both species of red Cardinal Beetle sunning themselves on fallen beech boles, for there is an excellent abundance of dead wood. The rotting timber hosts many interesting fungi and slime moulds in autumn.

Roe Deer enjoy the deeper parts of the Holt. Bird song fills the air at dawn in springtime, and you may disturb a sleeping Tawny Owl — that is, if the small birds have not mobbed it away first.

It would be interesting to know how affected the song birds are by the noise of the nearby A23. For all the Holt's beauty that loud din means it is no longer a wholly tranquil place.

Beggar's Lane, TQ 267 126, runs round the north west corner of Newtimber Hill. It's a lovely sunken woodland lane with stately Beeches shading it — a haven from the busy lanes it joins at both ends. We used to find White Helleborine orchis on its banks and it's probably still there. There's Wood Millet, *Milium effusum*, and Wood Melic and other ancient woodland plants. It's only one part, though, of the likely Roman Port Way which came down off the Downs by the Dyke Valley terrace way and continues northwards up Newtimber's Church Lane.

At its southern end Beggars Lane joins the Saddlescombe road, but that is not its original course. Just a few yards to the west of that busy lane back to Poynings, on a wooded terrace below it, is the old Roman path. That lost route is still the parish boundary between Poynings and Newtimber. Just after joining that old green way you will come across the hugest old Beech pollard, TQ 266 123. A real monster of a tree. I can't imagine how we could have walked the Saddlescombe road so many times over nearly a half century and not noticed this giant. It deserves our respect.

7 : THE WATERHALL AND SADDLESCOMBE VALLEY

T H I S is a landscape of wide scrub thickets, golf courses, new cattle and sheep pastures and fragments of ancient Down pasture. It is dominated at its southern end by the roar of the Bypass, but away from the road there are some delightfully peaceful and remote spots. It is an easy walk to the Devil's Dyke, Saddlescombe and Newtimber.

There's more Downland south of Patcham that has been built on than there is Downland north of Patcham that remains open.

Red Hill, The Green Ridge, Patcham Windmill, and Coney Hill.

I F you stand on the **Green Ridge open space, TQ 290 085**, by Patcham Windmill, and look south, there is a good view across two and a half miles of built-up Downland to the two great semicircular canopy arches, built in 1882, at the mouth of Brighton Station. **The windmill** is younger than the railway station canopy! It was built in 1884-5 and was the last windmill to be built in Sussex.

This narrow strip of meadow, hedgerow and pond south of Mill Road has had much love devoted to it by local residents in the Friends of the Green Ridge. The gardens of The Green Ridge back on to the most northerly portion of the millennia old Long

Hedge boundary, which separated West Blatchington from Patcham parish.

The hilltop at the junction of the Devil's Dyke Road, the Bypass and Mill Road is called **Red Hill, TQ 284 082**, because of the large clay-with-flint deposits there, which attracted flint workers right through Mesolithic and Neolithic times into the Bronze Age. The Hill has one of the largest Mesolithic flint assemblages to have been recovered from the South Downs[1]. It was possibly a seasonal hunting camp. The Hill has recently been a tolerated site for travelling peoples' summer encampments. Modern travelling people are often pushed onto such places — on windy hilltops and by roaring roadsides.

The woodland on the north side of **Coney Hill, TQ 295 089**, has plenty of interest despite the traffic noise. Good numbers of fallen trees from the '87 and '92 gales make excellent habitat for fungi and those weird half animal / half plant life forms called 'slime moulds', (*myxomycetes*). On a couple of early spring visits I saw Scarlet Elf Cup fungus, *Sarcoscypha coccinea* (which normally likes damper places than this), Eyelash Fungus, *Scutellinia scutellata*, on rotting wood, and Dead Man's Fingers, *Xylaria polymorpha*. I counted seven species of slime mould hiding in the damp recesses of the rotting tree trunks. Some of them were brightly coloured — pinks and yellows and white.

Waterhall. TQ 284 087.

WATERHALL is made up of two valleys, one short valley south of the golf course clubhouse, and one long valley north of the clubhouse, coming together in a wide valley suitable for sports pitches. It has a mixture of scrub thickets and golf fairways, but, in between, there are neglected roughs where you can find ancient Down pasture and all its wildlife. There's still a good population of Adders, so dog walkers need to exercise care and help protect these beautiful and unaggressive creatures.

The flat floor of the Waterhall valley just north of the Bypass was long used as a municipal waste tip. It has been a very contested area in recent years, as sports lovers have jockeyed with travellers' encampments for use of the ground. The Rugby Club, with friends in high places, succeeded in sorting things to their own advantage, getting a floodlit pitch (with *twelve* masts), tall excluding fencing like a prison exercise yard and a litter of advertising banners all around the perimeter.

By the bridlepath just downhill of the Clubhouse there are the damaged remains of a **Bronze Age round barrow, TQ 283 087**, which has long acted as a marker on the old parish boundaries. On my last visit a shining Adonis Blue butterfly was flying over the little tump, which still has Harebell, Scabious and Horseshoe Vetch.

The **short southern valley's south facing slope, TQ 284 086**, has the best surviving fragments of old Down pasture. It also has a large thicket of old Gorse, which is scarce nowadays. The Down pasture fragments on the slope and fairway edge are very colourful and have Cowslip, Rockrose, Betony and Devil's-bit. There are large old anthills and Chalkhill Blue and Brown Argus are still present. To my surprise (for I have not seen them here

before) I recently saw two Adonis Blues on these roughs. Adonis is a butterfly that, until now, has only been able to survive on old Down pasture where the turf is less than three centimetres tall, for only such short turf could provide the heat the caterpillars need. It seems, though, that global warming may be enabling the butterfly to tolerate taller grasslands, as is happening with the erstwhile very rare Silver-spotted Skipper.

The **west slope of the long valley north of the clubhouse, TQ 282 093** has several large roughs which retain their aboriginal grassland, though they have been left unmown or grazed for many years. You can find Spotted Orchis and still see good displays of Sussex Rampion. Little Blue was certainly present a few years ago.

Much of these two valleys have now grown over into dense Hawthorn scrub. For the present, though, you may see Glow-worms there, and many old grassland moths and butterflies. It is remarkable that so much clings on. It needs much better care soon, or it will be too late.

At the corner of the Saddlescombe Road and the turn-off to the golf clubhouse there is a **sarsen stone, TQ 278 090**, of the same sort as the Goldstone, marking this point in the medieval boundary between Patcham and West Blatchington parishes. On the crown of the hill, TQ 276 091, above the gas relay station I have found pieces of fire-cracked flint and flint working flakes — and a 'shepherd's crown' fossil sea urchin. There must have been activity there in prehistoric times.

Sweet Hill is a lovely spot, though noisy. It's lost its ancient pastures, but there is a nice flowery bank on its **western slope, TQ 286 091**, a bushy lynchet along its brow and an old dewpond site on its top.

The Saddlescombe valley and the slopes of Varncombe Hill.

THE Saddlescombe Road was a quiet lane in the 1960s. You could walk or cycle along its whole length and be passed by only one

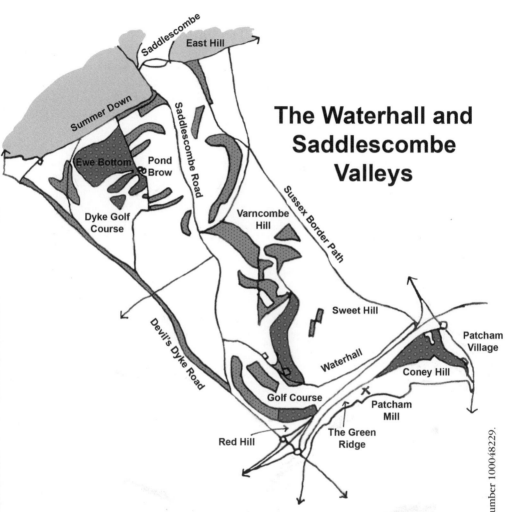

The Waterhall and Saddlescombe Valleys

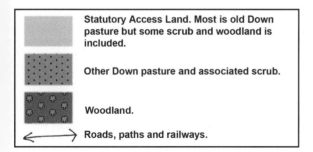

Statutory Access Land. Most is old Down pasture but some scrub and woodland is included.

Other Down pasture and associated scrub.

Woodland.

Roads, paths and railways.

or two cars — maybe none. Now it has become a dangerous place.

Walking the valleysides to the west and east of the Saddlescombe Road about a decade ago I came across a small bush of Catmint, *Nepeta cataria*. This rare herb really stinks, and cats go bonkers for it. I searched for it again in subsequent years in this valley without success. Then, in 2007, it turned up again, this time on the other side of the valley half a mile away. Where will it appear next?

The **south-west facing slope of Varncombe Hill, TQ 280 099**, is a bosky place with lovely old pasture glades. Rockrose is one of the commonest flowers here, with some of its associated fungi, but there's an odd absence of some old pasture flowers, like Sussex Rampion and Horseshoe Vetch. These are undoubtedly ancient pastures, though.

The **west facing slopes of Varncombe Hill, TQ 279 105**, were sold by Brighton Council with the rest of Saddlescombe Farm to the National Trust, but the Trust did not dedicate them as Access Land, though they should have done. They have, however, done much excellent scrub clearance and have reintroduced grazing on the derelict southern part of the slope.

These slopes are a lovely diverse place, with old scrub thickets along the top and beautiful old pasture below. There are Cowslips and Pyramidal and Bee Orchids, Purse-web Spider, Heath and Forester moths and Adonis Blue. I watched a Humming-bird Hawk-moth nectaring on tall herbs there one August. You may spot these moths nowadays in gardens in Brighton, but out here in this gorgeous place it was doubly special.

Along the scrub edge you may find Dyer's Greenweed, for this sub-shrub likes the nearby presence of clay-with-flints on the hilltop.

Along the top of these slopes ran the minor Roman road from the Clayton Hill pass south-westwards towards Shoreham harbour. No doubt the ancient parish boundary which tracks this same top break-of-slope was placed here because the Roman road was a sufficiently significant feature to follow.

Ewe Bottom and the Dyke Golf Course.

E w e **Bottom, TQ 267 106**, is a good place to practice survivalism. You could hunker down amongst those dense thorn thickets and not be spotted for days or

Varncombe Hill's western slope: Dyer's Greenweed and Adonis Blue butterflies in summertime.

weeks! I reckon some folk already do, for you may find the odd mouldering sleeping bag or scatter of sodden porn magazines in those jungles.

Till Victorian times Summer Down, Ewe Bottom, Pond Brow and most of the golf course were part of Saddlescombe's sheep pastures — except for the area west of the bridlepath, which was part of Poynings' pastures. Ewe Bottom was left derelict by the golf course and the Gorse and thorn on its valleysides spread across the entire valley. Now the valleysides are growing over to Ash woodland in the next stage of this long succession. There are huge old Hawthorn bushes in these thickets. Some of them can be seen along the footpath on the **south-east perimeter of the golf course, TQ 270 100.**

Pond Brow, TQ 271 105, has two beautiful peaceful old dewponds which watered these great pastures, which were known as West Down. Now they are fenced off from the golf course and are used by the sheep on the ex-arable land below. The ponds' watery eyes are fringed with Flote Grass, *Glyceria fluitans*, shaded by Gorse and thorn draped with Honeysuckle.

The valleysides south of Pond Brow were also past of West Down and tiny fragments of old flower-rich pastures survive on the steepest parts. Where those pastures met the road, TQ 275 103, the verges are still colourful with old Downland herbs including swarms of Spotted Orchis. One early summer I counted eight vetch and pea family herbs along the roadside, including Grass Vetchling, *Lathyrus nissolia*, with flowers like gorgeous crimson droplets.

The **Devil's Dyke Golf Course, TQ 265 103**, was founded in 1908, though the women's course pre-dated it. It was badly damaged in the Second World War when it was used for tank training, but Brighton Council rescued and rebuilt it, though it is now on a long lease to the Club.

The course has lost almost all of its old Down pasture flowers, but — remarkably — many of the old meadow fungi seem to have survived, as we discovered in the autumns of 2004-5. We found Meadow Waxcap, *Hygrocybe pratensis*, Golden Waxcap, *H. chlorophana*, and Scarlet Hood, *H. coccinea*, and the little Fairy Club known as White Spindles, *Clavaria vermicularis* — 14 old meadow species all in all, in a place I had always thought so unpromising.

East of the bridlepath there is a spot, now largely forgotten, which used to be called **Beggar's Haven, TQ 266 104**, where a curled up skeleton[2] was unearthed in Victorian times with a necklace of beads of lignite and tubular beads of bronze. Accompanying it was a decorated pottery 'beaker' nearly five inches wide of a type found at several sites on these Downs. Probably a burial mound once rose above this early Bronze Age burial, but it isn't there anymore.

Part of Summer Down, TQ 272 111, is fenced off from Summer Down road on its south side, though it is scored with the deep-cut braided paths of that road. Centuries of passage by pack horse trains, carts and flocks, have cut tracks up to ten feet deep — deeper than the ditches of the Devil's-Dyke hillfort. I counted three main braids and four minor ones, all with a fine old Fescue turf on their crests and a mess of nettles in their cuttings.

Footnotes

1   *Downland Settlement and Land-use: The Archaeology of the Brighton Bypass*, edited by David Rudling (English Heritage, 2002). Section Five, by Luke Barber and Maureen Bennell, page 102. *Prehistoric Sussex* — Miles Russell (Tempus, 2002), page 36.

2   *The Archaeology of Sussex* — E. Cecil Curwen (Methuen, 1937), page 159. Also the *Sussex Archaeological Collections*, Vol. 72, page 39.

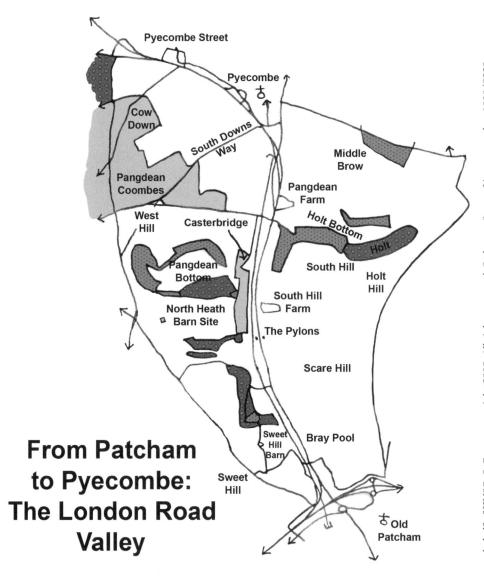

Pyecombe Street

Pyecombe ↑

Cow Down

South Downs Way

Middle Brow

Pangdean Coombes

Pangdean Farm

West Hill

Casterbridge

Holt Bottom

Holt

Pangdean Bottom

South Hill

Holt Hill

North Heath Barn Site

South Hill Farm

The Pylons

Scare Hill

Sweet Hill Barn

Bray Pool

Sweet Hill

Old Patcham

From Patcham to Pyecombe: The London Road Valley

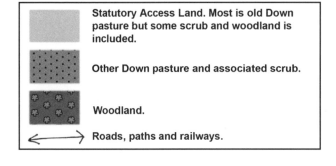

Statutory Access Land. Most is old Down pasture but some scrub and woodland is included.

Other Down pasture and associated scrub.

Woodland.

Roads, paths and railways.

8: FROM PATCHAM TO PYECOMBE

— THE LONDON ROAD VALLEY

MOST Brighton people and millions of visitors will have driven up this valley, with its two stone 'pylons' (or gateway towers) by the roadside marking the beginning of Brighton City's territory. Yet very few have explored its valleysides. That's not surprising — for only in its north western quarter is there any Access Land, where the South Downs Way crosses the valley, and there are no footpaths or Access Land at all on the eastern valleyside. Yet much of the valley is in public ownership.

The deep combes to the west and east of Pangdean Farm are lovely places where the din of the road quietens and ancient woodland and ancient flowery pastures still survive.

Old Patcham. TQ 301 090.

OLD Patcham retains much from its agricultural past. It has many old flint cottages, big allotment sites, and winding twittens. There's Patcham Place and Park. The best cluster of buildings, however, comprises its Norman church (which has kept part of its medieval wall paintings — a scene of the Last Judgement) and the old buildings of Patcham Court Farm, with a 17th century flint farmhouse and dovecot.

My personal favourite is the giant barn (next to the church), like a beached whale, 250 feet long and the biggest in Sussex. It's now converted into houses, but the eastern end is still internally open and functions as the church hall. Go and peer through its windows at that end. Its huge timber beams and high rafters are like a cathedral.

Patcham was one of the bigger settlements in Sussex at the time of Domesday, with ten shepherds and six slaves. It produced a medieval Archbishop of Canterbury. More memorably, it was the home of one of the 'regicides', those brave folk who challenged a millennia of monarchy and signed the death warrant of 'the man of blood' King Charles 1st in 1649. Anthony Stapley was lucky to die naturally before the monarchy returned in 1660.

Sweet Hill. TQ 290 100.

SWEET Hill just escaped development as a 'plotlands' estate after World War One, when homeless ex-servicemen utilized old army huts to start a new community. Brighton Council won the right to compulsorily purchase and clear the colony, fearing a threat to the town's water supply (and Downscape) from a polluted chalk aquifer, and soon after commenced a major council house-building programme, closer to the town centre on more rational lines. Now only two homes exist on the hillside to commemorate the colony, but they are hacienda-type modern dwellings with electronic gate security and bear no resemblance to the plotlanders' shacks.

One wall of the 150 year old Sweethill Barn, TQ 291 097, stands alone on the valley slope, like some lost bit of theatrical scenery.

The eastern slopes of Sweet Hill have dense thorn scrublands growing over into woodland. Back in the 'fifties and 'sixties these were well-known places to listen to Nightingales. To be attractive again to those songsters they'd need to be coppiced to encourage a denser undergrowth. Would the birds come and would we hear them if they did, now, for the roar of the traffic on the A23 is relentless all up this valley?

The drove road along the top of Sweet Hill is wide and many-tracked. It's like a linear nature reserve. The modern pastures all around have many barbed wire fences, though. Even the restored — but again derelict — dew pond has barbed wire all around — no use for cattle, sheep or humans.

'Casterbridge'. TQ 290 110.

ALONG the western side of the railway opposite South Hill Farm there is a lovely old Down pasture smallholding known as 'Casterbridge'. It is very colourful, with much Marjoram, Rockrose, Devil's-bit Scabious and other herbs. It has a line of Gorse at the slope top. You can see Chalkhill and Common Blues, Silver-spotted Skipper and Brown Argus. The Rockrose has Lurid Bolete accompanying it. In autumn there is Chalkland Waxcap fungi.

It is not grazed and the sward is increasingly dominated by Tor Grass. Scrub encroaches. This is a vulnerable and neglected site and has been threatened in the recent past by trail bike riding.

Pangdean Bottom. TQ 285 113.

THIS grand combe is a half mile long and a third of a mile wide. It takes you from the blaring noise of the A23 into green tranquility. There were two Buzzards circling when I last visited. The coombe is owned by Brighton Council, but is almost wholly unknown to the public — or to the Council! When I took a Brighton Council Ranger there more than a decade ago he was amazed to discover its existence and immediately made a mobile call to his Countryside Manager to express his astonishment.

With such flimsy Council control it is not surprising that severe damage has been done to the integrity of the ancient chalk grassland slope by the game shoot that uses the valley. More than a decade ago the north slope was chopped up into compartments and sealed off along the top by fencing in scrubby patches. Pheasants, you see, need scrub and woodland. The result has been to further fragment the chalk grassland, though it was already fragmented by scrub and tillage. Yet butterflies like Adonis Blue — which is present — have minimal powers of dispersion and find even hedgerows major obstacles to their spread.

The grazed pasture islands still have fine chalk grassland. The valley's north side has one of the largest populations of Autumn Ladies Tresses I have seen. There are many hundreds of the tiny woolly flower spikes in late summer. There is also a large population of the white variety of the normally violet Self Heal, *Prunella vulgaris*. It looks like quite a different flower.

The scrub at the head of the valley is old and diverse, with Wayfaring Tree, Old Man's Beard, Honeysuckle, Hazel, and Gorse.

The south slope has developed an Ash wood over old scrub and there is now a large Pheasant rearing pen in the middle of it.

The Pangdean Combes: 'Constablewick Down'. TQ 282 118.

'CONSTABLEWICK **Sheep Down'** is the older — and better — name for the Downs around the South Downs Way here.

Two combes owned by the National Trust lie one to the south and one to the north of the South Downs Way as it descends to Pyecombe from West Hill. The contrast with Pangdean Bottom (above) is telling. The National Trust has pursued drastic scrub clearance and control of rank vegetation, so that the **south combe**, which you could scarcely cross a decade ago for nettles and scrub, has become again a delightful place with a revived old Down pasture flora, especially on its north side. It's a tribute to Charlie Cain and his fellow National Trust workers.

The **north combe** has quite deep soils so there are lots of the old pasture species of less chalky soils, like Dyer's Greenweed, Devil's-bit, Betony and Crosswort. There is lots of Tor Grass and Rockrose, and sometimes very large numbers of Brown Argus butterflies. The old Hazel scrub at the slope top has a lovely Bluebell display in spring, with Yellow Archangel and Moschatel. It's a good example of the well-established thickets that you sometimes meet on the clayey tops of the Downs. Oddly, I've seen Bearded Couch, *Elymus caninus*, there.

Alongside the South Downs Way half way down the hill there is a good **section of the ancient braided pathway, TQ 284 119.** There are five deep-cut braids, and they have a good flora, with Sussex Rampion, Fragrant and Spotted Orchids. The braids have been truncated by ploughing at the top and bottom of the section.

Back in Mesolithic times (about 7-8000 years ago) folk used West Hill a lot for making tools out of the good quality flint you find with the clay-with-flints soil. Field walkers have found over 1200 flint artefacts[1] — scrapers, microliths,

axes, adzes and debris — there. In the Bronze Age a barrow was built, which was recently excavated.

The Cow Down. TQ 281 123.

THIS site was one of the three commons of Pyecombe till enclosure in 1872. It is good that the public dimension is once again recognized by its designation as Access Land. The best bits are on the steeper slopes between the scrub thickets and they have been restored by recent cattle grazing. There are old anthills, much Marjoram, *Origanum vulgare*, Knapweed, Betony and Devil's-bit, and Common Blue and Small Copper butterflies.

Pangdean Farm and Pangdean Holt. TQ 300 112.

Pangdean is likely older than Pyecombe. It appears in the Domesday Book, whilst Pyecombe doesn't. For most of its history there was scarcely any road down this valley, where the London Road runs, for the roads went over the hilltops to east and west, and the valley bottom was given over to meadows and corn. Now the Farm is walled off from the London Road. Living there otherwise would be intolerable because of the dreadful noise.

The **steeper slopes of South Hill**, just south east of the farmstead, have good chalk grassland. The **west slope (TQ 293 113)** has lots of Rockrose, though it is very tussocky with Tor Grass. There's Sussex Rampion, Orchids, Tormentil and Autumn Gentian. The **north slope (TQ 296 114)** has lots of Cowslips and Yellow Rattle and Spring Sedge.

The main delight of Pangdean is the ancient **Holt (TQ 300 112),** up the valley east of the farmstead. It was woodland 700 hundred years ago, which means there's a fair chance it's been woodland since the days of the wildwood. The Saxon's called woods dominated by a single species 'holts' and Hazel is the main woody species at Pangdean Holt.

Pangdean Holt, a lovely ancient woodland survival, full of birdsong and bluebells.

I love it best in spring, and on our last springtime visit it was full of birdsong. No sooner had we entered the wood than we found big wrinkled plates of the chocolate-brown Bleach Cup fungus (a cousin of the Morels) with Primroses and Bluebells at their best. All in all I've found ten plant species indicative of the Holt's antiquity. That might not sound like a lot, but the wood is only little and it's on a steep slope, and, in the circumstances that's a good total. There's Redcurrant and Pignut, Early Purple Orchis, Sanicle and Early Dog-violet. The richest area of the wood is at the slope top.

You may find Wild Strawberries, Raspberry and Gooseberry (though not in quantities to wet the appetite) and pretty Germander Speedwell, *Veronica chamaedrys*, and False Oxlip, *Primula vulgaris x veris*. There are several big old Ash trees that have nice lichens and liverworts.

The wood has two Pheasant rearing pens, one of which is derelict, and there are big quantities of spent shotgun cartridges in places. So a wood that for centuries provided Hazel for building, for sheep hurdles, for tools, and for thatch now just shelters semi-wild pheasants to be slaughtered for the pleasure of it.

South Hill, Holt Hill and Scare Hill. TQ 29 10.

THREE names for different bits of the same hill — four if you count in Ewebottom Hill.

I've seen Lapwing frequently on Holt Hill. They're rare on the Downs now. There's no chalk grassland on this ridge anymore, sadly.

The brave folks at the South Hill Farm smallholding deserve our praise for putting up with living next to that road. It's more than I could do.

Footnotes

1   Article by Robin Holgate in *Archaeology of Sussex to AD 2000*, edited by David Rudling (Heritage Marketing and Publications Ltd. 2003), page 33.

9: WOLSTONBURY HILL AND CLAYTON WINDMILLS

Wolstonbury Hill. TQ 28 13.

WOLSTONBURY, around 1963, was where I first discovered the old Sussex Downs my mum and grandparents had described. The turf was as short and soft and clean of hedge or tree as they had described. It stretched up skywards towards the ancient camp, and mantled path-side banks, long-deserted chalk pits and ant mounds alike with its velvety nap.

They had been able to take that landscape for granted. I felt I had to race to hunt out its relics before they disappeared.

And it still remains, though 45 years have passed since then. To be sure, the turf has lost some of its velvety sheen as coarse Tor Grass has advanced; some parts look unshaven with young scrub growth; more ancient turf on gentler ground has been lost to the plough; and the roar of the London Road now cannot be ignored. It batters into your consciousness. For all that, the Hill's pastures would still be recognisable to the shepherds who walked this Hill for many centuries.

On one of those boyhood walks I took a photograph of an old horse drawn haywain, piled high with bales, that had been pulled to the top of the Down to provide winter feed to grazing cattle. I took a note of the name on its side. It was one of Albourne farmer Sidney Hole's waggons. (Older Hove folk will remember 'Holes and Davigdor' the dairy firm he owned). One blustery late summer afternoon last year we came across the remains of that same haywain lost amongst the tall grass near the cross dyke and barrow that mark Wolstonbury's saddle. Its ironwork, sturdy oak frame and axles were still recognizable as it collapsed in upon itself.

Close by, rabbits had scuffed the side of the **round barrow, TQ 285 133**, down to bare earth and chalk, and, looking close, I picked up a 'shepherd's crown' fossil sea urchin. Had it just been amongst the earth used by the ancient people to mound up their funeral monument, or was it a special object placed with the dead to accompany them into the after life?

A year or so earlier, on the **adjacent cross dyke**, I came across a large cluster of Crimson Waxcap, its lubricious blood-red caps and yellow gills bringing summer colour to the drab of late December.

Looking downhill from the cross dyke there is a modern barn called **Chantry, TQ 282 132**, on the site of an older barn. Back in 1849 there was a serious outbreak of cholera in the cottages of Pyecombe Street below. The Chantry Barn was requisitioned as a hospital and a large tarpaulin screen

The prow of Wolstonbury with Jack and Jill windmills.

was rigged up across its middle to separate the sexes, before the patients arrived. When the doctor came the next morning the screen had been pulled down and the sexes intermingled![1] **Pyecombe Street, TQ 284 129**, has some nice old cottages. It is said to be located half a mile from the church because the inhabitants removed there from the older site after an outbreak of plague.

Things happen on Wolstonbury. One hot afternoon in June, 15 years ago, I was traversing the steepness of the Hill's northern slope when I came across a walker — an ordinary seeming bloke — sitting on the grass in front of me. "I've just seen a Roman soldier clambering up the Hill", he said. I'd just seen an Adder basking in the sun myself, but my sighting was no match for his revelation. "He was dressed in army gear with a helmet, short shield and sword, and he climbed past me and disappeared over the top". What could I say? I listened and hid my scepticism. On that still and sweltering afternoon in that ancient place I wasn't wholly sure that he hadn't seen something.

Wolstonbury is capped by its **Late Bronze Age hillfort, TQ 283 138**, which is unusual in having the ditch inside the rampart, as 'henges' had. Inside the fort the soil is clay-with-flints and the vegetation is an acid grassland with Field Woodrush, Sweet Vernal-grass and Tormentil. There are many old meadow fungi in season. The humps and dips are due to 18th and 19th century flint digging. The view from the top sweeps from the far scarp of the Hampshire Downs to the Surrey Hills, Ashdown, and south to Patcham Mill. Brighton's white skyscrapers also push their way into view.

The **old chalkpits, TQ 282 138**, on the north-west spur of the Hill have a fine flowery sward. You could see Chalk Carpet moth, or Dark Green Fritillary in season, and the tiny Blind, Moss, and Scree Snails are present.

Wellcombe Bottom, TQ 286 136, is a natural amphitheatre. It has the butts of an old rifle range at its head. Its cool, damp grassland is free of scrub and has drifts of Devil's-bit Scabious. You may find Dyer's Greenweed, or bits of Angelica, *Angelica sylvestris*, Valerian, *Valeriana officinalis*, or Marsh Thistle, *Cirsium palustre*, alongside the ordinary chalk species. There's a rabbit bury halfway upslope with tall Mullein spikes that look like termite towers in the African bush.

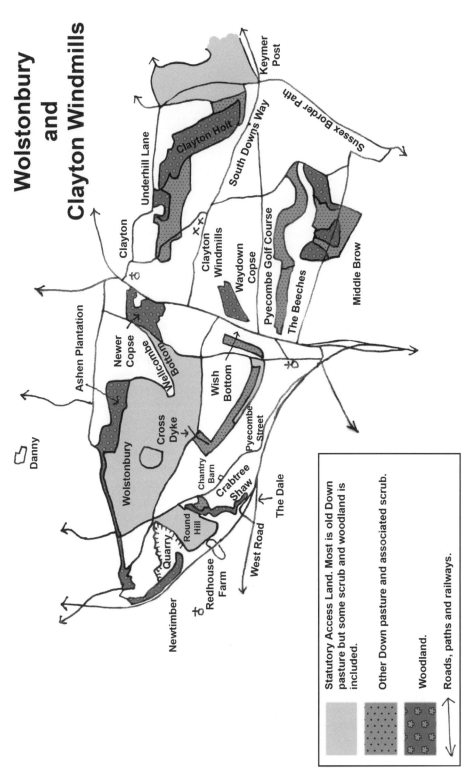

Wolstonbury and Clayton Windmills

Underhill Lane

Clayton Holt

Clayton

Clayton Windmills

Waydown Copse

South Downs Way

Sussex Border Path

Keymer Post

Pyecombe Golf Course

The Beeches

Middle Brow

Ashen Plantation

Newer Copse

Wellcombe Bottom

Wish Bottom

Pyecombe Street

Danny

Wolstonbury

Cross Dyke

Chantry Barn

Crabtree Shaw

The Dale

Quarry

Round Hill

Redhouse Farm

West Road

Newtimber

Statutory Access Land. Most is old Down pasture but some scrub and woodland is included.

Other Down pasture and associated scrub.

Woodland.

Roads, paths and railways.

Round Hill's slopes with Newtimber Hill's woods behind.

Round Hill's slopes, TQ 277 134, above the London Road, have fascinating contrasting aspects. I counted nine mosses and a lichen I could name (I'm no expert) on its shadier north-west facing slope, but mosses are replaced in the skimpy turf of its hot south-east facing slope by Stripe-winged Grasshopper, Adonis and Chalkhill Blues and spikes of Viper's Bugloss.

Wish Bottom, TQ 292 130, and the **south boundary of the old Tenantry Down, TQ 290 128**, have chalk grassland sites of interest, too. Purple Bar, *Cosmorhoe ocellata*, and Purple Pyrausta, *Pyrausta purpuralis*, moths are present on the south boundary and I found the green grub-like caterpillar of Adonis Blue there, once.

Wolstonbury is noteworthy for the scatter of old woods around its base. Little **Newer Copse, TQ 294 137**, is remarkably rich in wildlife for its size. **Crabtree Shaw, TQ 279 132**, is good, too, despite the road noise. The long **rew woodland, together with Ashen Plantation, TQ 284 142**, along the base of its north slope has unvisited, tangled chalk pits like little lost worlds, with Ent-like giant Beech. There is an old Large Leaved Lime coppice stool at the crossroads, TQ 285 142. You may find White Helleborine orchis, and in autumn you will certainly find many bizarre fungi on the rotting trunks felled in the '87 and '92 gales. One *Tyromyces* species looked and smelt like very ripe cheese.

Pyecombe Church, TQ 291 126, is a lovely Norman structure, peaceful against the madness of the London Road below.

Opposite it is the old forge, which was long famous for the shepherd's crooks made there, not just for shepherds but for bishops world-wide, who use them as symbols of office. (Bishops are meant to be 'shepherds of men').

The Roman road[2] from Southwick harbour passes by The Plough Inn (after descending West Hill), rises due north past the church and little council estate, then becomes a green lane above the steep slope of Wish Bottom before descending past Newer Copse to Coldharbour Farm and away northwards across the Weald. It used to be called The Noor Track, (corrupted to 'Newer' in the copse name), and its high point, where the east-west ridgeway track along Wolstonbury forms a crossroads with it, was called Balcombe Cross. This is probably a memory of the Saxon use of this road by the peasants of Pangdean to access their manorial swine pastures out in the Weald at Balcombe.

Clayton Windmills, Tunnel and Church.

A s kids coming home to Brighton from family trips to London on the train we'd always be told to look out for **Jack and Jill windmills, TQ 303 133**. Then the train would whoosh into **Clayton Tunnel** as we strained for a glimpse of its castle turrets and the little house over its entrance. The Tunnel, built in 1840, is older than Jack, built in 1876, and almost as old as the daintier white Jill, built in 1821 and later hauled to Clayton Hill from the

Dyke Road. Several of the brick towers of the Tunnel's airshafts can be seen along its 1.25 miles between Clayton and Pyecombe.

Clayton has far older things, though. The little **Saxon church, TQ 299 139**, is a gem. Its elegant Norman frescoes, narrating the Last Judgement with Christ in Glory over the Chancel arch, are extremely moving. Next to the church I went to in my childhood — St Helen's, Hangleton — I love this church the most. Its paintings are amongst the earliest medieval murals to survive in England and, with those of Plumpton, Coombes and Hardham, are the product of a single workshop active between c. 1080 and c. 1120. I was myself a mural painter for a decade. If I could paint with just half of that simplicity and power I would be proud. Bats had left droppings on the window sills a few years ago. Lets hope they still find a home there.

Clayton Holt, TQ 310 134.

THE Holt can claim an antiquity far greater than church or mills, for it may descend directly from the days of the wildwood. It is full of old, deep time. Spring is the best time to see it, for its floor is dusted with Bluebells, and patches of light brighten it before the leaves of the Hazel coppice expand. You may find Primrose and Early Purple Orchis, or even Fly and Butterfly Orchids. Green-veined White flitter about. It has some grand old Beech at its northern end and along the base of slope, and Borrer[3] recorded, in 1838, the presence of the wildwood indicator Large-leaved Lime. Now, only a couple of the Lime hybrids are still present. The Holt's steepness means that the soils are thin, so the fungi are mostly found along the base of slope or on the rotting trunks of fallen Beech. Under the Beech there are several Earthstar, **Geastrum spp.**, swarms, appearing first like brown puffballs, then bursting into leathery flowers, puffing spores at a touch.

Clayton Down. TQ 305 136.

As you step away from the Windmills, down the slope of **Clayton Down**, the sward is bland and improved. Do not be deceived, though, for as the Down gains steepness it gains richness, too. It is a lovely place, with several small combes, velvety-turfed chalk diggings and steep bostal sides, and a gathering sense of wildness as you walk eastwards towards the Holt. There is much rank Tor Grass, which the grazing sheep do not tackle, but the slopes are very flowery, despite that. I counted 18 woody species in the pockets of scrub, with at least three Rose species. The grassland is damp at its base, with Hairy Sedge, *Carex hirta*, and odd tufts of Rush, *Juncus x diffussus*. A pair of Buzzard and a Kestrel flew above on my last visit.

Waydown Copse, TQ 297 131.

THIS puzzling Copse lies midway along the line of the Clayton Tunnel. It is a classic coppice-with-standards wood, with fine old Oaks over Hazel. In spring the Bluebells make a magnificent carpet. Yet, apart from tiny bits of Anemone and Moschatel I have seen no other plants of ancient woodland. It must have been planted on the open Down, perhaps two or three centuries ago.

Pyecombe Golf Course and The Beeches.

PYECOMBE **Golf Course's site, TQ 303 123**, was well chosen. Constructed in 1894 on an exhilarating area of ancient Down pasture and chalk heath it included Rag Bottom — remote enough to be a cock fighting venue[4] before the coming of the golfers — and the windy Middle Brow. The South Downs Way passes through its northern side.

It was lucky the Club did come, for in the next century all the surrounding tractor-accessible Down pasture was ploughed out. Yet the Club's members are golfers, not nature conservationists, and gradually the ancient grasslands of

The dark smudge of Clayton Holt against the western sky.

their roughs became rank and overgrown with scrub. After 113 years of this benign neglect it is remarkable that any of the original chalk grassland and chalk heath survives, but it does — just.

It will not survive for more than a few years further if things do not change. When I last went there, in September 2007, only one small tuft of Dwarf Gorse, *Ulex minor*, was in flower on Middle Brow's chalk heath. This is its sole surviving site on the entire chain of the Sussex Downs. Yet when I went there ten years ago I described it as 'common' on Middle Brow in my notebook. Ten years ago there was a mown sward of Ling Heather at that spot, like parts of the heath on Piltdown Golf Course. Last September I found only one surviving bush in flower. And I could not re-find the scattered senescent Ling bushes that were still present a decade ago on several places on the course.

This still-lovely place fills me with anxiety. I hate that feeling — the feeling that I am witnessing the extinction of a vegetation community that has existed on these Downs for millennia.

Pyecombe Golf Course has the only substantive chalk heath site on the Brighton Downs. *True* heath survives at Peacehaven Golf Course, but *chalk* heath — mixing chalk loving and chalk hating plants — survives only here. On Middle Brow I have found Heath Bedstraw, *Galium saxatile*, Heath Speedwell, *Veronica officinalis*, Slender St John's-wort, *Hypericum pulchrum*, Tormentil, Dyers Greenweed, and many other calcifuge plants, alongside Fragrant Orchis, Rockrose, Harebell, Betony and Yellow Rattle. I found the rare Eyebright, *Euphrasia pseudokerneri*, a decade ago. It is probably still there. It is known at only one other Brighton Downs site.

In autumn on Middle Brow there can be colourful Waxcap displays. I counted ten old meadow fungi in just one visit, including seven Waxcaps.

Elsewhere on the golf course, especially in Rag Bottom, scallops of old grassland, rough flowery slopes and banks survive.

The golf course and the rangers have done some work. Sadly, it has not been nearly enough and the loss continues.

The Beeches. TQ 296 126.

THIS south facing site has a peculiar mix of wildlife-rich Down pasture, scrub and clusters of ancient Beech. One grand old Beech pollard must well-exceed two hundred years in age.

"Ungrazed and unloved" were the words I scribbled in my notebook on my last visit here. Scarce anyone visits. Soon no-one will be able to, for the scrub thickets have now almost surrounded the derelict chalk grassland glades. Till a few years ago there was some horse grazing. Now there is none.

If there were justice in this world this site would be confiscated and given to a public organization. It lies only a few hundred paces from the South Downs Way. A local gamekeeper told me that his syndicate bought the slope. He encouraged the site's bushiness because it reminded him of his native Kentish Downs. Such neglectful whims will likely see the end of its specialness.

I first properly visited in June eleven years ago. The Down pasture was dominated by a colourful mixture of Dropwort, Rockrose and Dyer's Greenweed. It had abundant Bastard Toadflax. There were Heath Moth and Purple Pyrausta, large old anthills, and Blind, Grass and Moss Snails. Pyramidal Orchids were in bloom. Now the rank Tor Grass is difficult to struggle through and the Blackthorn stabs you as you struggle through the scrub.

Shame on those rich enough to buy this site but too poor in spirit to preserve it.

Footnotes

1   *Sussex in Bygone Days: Reminiscences of Nathaniel Paine Blaker* (Combridges, 1919), page 104-5.

2   'The Course of the London to Brighton Roman Road south of Burgess Hill' — Glen Shields. *Sussex Archaeological Collections* 137 (1999), page 86.

3   'Large-leaved Limes on the South Downs' — Frances Abraham and Francis Rose, *British Wildlife*, Vol. 12, No. 2 (Dec 2000), page 87.

4   *From Pyecombe to Cuckfield* — Mark Dudeney and Eileen Hallett (Mid Sussex Books, 1999), page 10.

From Patcham's Ladies Mile to Ditchling Beacon

Ditchling

Watershed Path

Burnhouse Bostall

Ditchling Old Tenantry Down

Ditchling Beacon

Keymer Post

Dencher Bottom

Hogtrough Bottom

Rocky Pond

North Bottom

Standean

The Chattri

New Barn

Deep Bottom

Ewe Bottom

Ewe Bottom Hill

Barrows

Tegdown Hill

Ditchling Road

Eastwick Field System

Old Patcham

Ladies Mile

Statutory Access Land. Most is old Down pasture but some scrub and woodland is included.

Other Down pasture and associated scrub.

Woodland.

Roads, paths and railways.

10: FROM PATCHAM'S LADIES MILE TO DITCHLING BEACON

THIS is the landscape of the Ditchling Downs and the long Standean valley, which snakes south from Ditchling Beacon to Withdean. The Saxons were so struck by its surface scattering of big sarsen stones that they named the valley after them — 'Standean': 'stoney valley'.

The area's Down pastures were very heavily damaged by pre-war dereliction and post-war intensification. Now only scattered fragments of the aboriginal turf survive, though much of the surrounding arable has thankfully been returned to permanent pasturage.

The scarp slopes around Keymer Down and Burnhouse Bostal survived better and — with Dencher Bottom — remain top quality. However, Ditchling Beacon's slopes and archaeology are still a wretched mess, despite the continuing valiant efforts of good folk.

Ladies Mile Down. TQ 318 093.

A TRULY remarkable survival of plateau chalk grassland on Downland where almost all such flattish sites have been destroyed by farmers. The ancient turf has preserved lots of odd linear banks and a grassy tump at the eastern end. The banks are surviving fragments of an Iron Age and Romano-British lynchetted field system which stretched across the line of the bypass, beyond which one or two more fragments also survive. The low tump is a Bronze Age burial mound. The Down is now a Local Nature Reserve.

Try to ignore the din of the bypass. Notice instead the Harebells and Sussex Rampion flower, the purplish Devil's-bit Scabious and the powder-blue Lesser Scabious, the Rockrose and the Yellow Rattle. At midsummer there are still good numbers of Glow-worms here. Adonis and Chalkhill Blue butterflies have been lost, though, to the sites gross under-management, for although the flattish areas are mown, the steep slope has been choked by rank grassland and thorn scrub. The windblown scrub oaks on the plateau mark its deeper soils.

The view from Ladies Mile stretches from wooded Withdean to the Devil's Dyke and Ditchling Down. ASDA and the rest of the Hollingbury Industrial Estate, though right alongside, are almost hidden. That didn't stop the National Park Inspector recommending the exclusion of this place from the National Park.

If you walk across the bypass bridge and take the field path up to Stanmer Park Upper Lodges you will see a high field bank tracking away northwards, just below you and parallel to the Ditchling Road. That bank dates right back to the Saxon Dark Ages, and has probably always marked the western boundary of Falmer parish.

Tegdown Hill's barrows. TQ 313 101.

A L L of the three hills to the north and east of old Patcham were marked by prehistoric barrows. Ploughing has destroyed all sign of the Ewebottom Hill cluster. One of the two barrows on Ladies Mile Down survives. On Tegdown Hill, however, a remarkable 'ring barrow' survives, together with the slight mounds of two other bowl barrows and the sites of two more. Grinsell, the great expert on prehistoric barrows, described the Tegdown ring barrow as "probably the best of this type in the county".[1] It consists of a circular bank about 45 paces wide with a ditch and a flattish interior (marked by some smaller humps). It lies just south of a big dried up dew pond. The Hill has lost its ancient turf, but permanent pasture has been restored there and cattle roam.

From Tegdown you can see the three Iron Age camps of Hollingbury Castle, Ditchling Beacon and the Devil's Dyke.

Ewe Bottom, Deep Bottom and The Chattri

A s you walk from Patcham and descend the hill into **Ewe Bottom**, you will see a steep slope of bushy old pasture on your right, **TQ 305 101**. It's the only bit of the old Tegdown pastures which are still intact. Often the cattle graze off the flowers, but if you're lucky (as I was one afternoon three summers ago) you can see this slope in its glory…mantled violet-blue with Devil's-bit and dotted with red-purple Betony and deep blue Rampion flower. Burnet Saxifrage, Autumn Gentian and clusters of Harebell add their hues to this pointillist fabric of colours.

Opposite this slope is the mouth of **Deep Bottom, TQ 303 105**, which will

The Chattri — Old India takes to Sussex Downland

lead you via a scramble through a thicket up to **The Chattri, TQ 304 110**.

The southerly slope of Deep Bottom is a lovely and colourful old pasture site. Abundant Rockrose brings several interesting dependant fungi, including two Boletes. There's Spring Sedge and Brimstone butterfly in spring and several old meadow Waxcaps and a Fairy Club fungus in autumn. On the slope below The Chattri is an old scrub thicket with much Hazel, and Holly, Oak and Sallow.

The Chattri is the solemn place where the bodies of First World War Indian Sikh and Hindu soldiers who died from wounds whilst being nursed at the Brighton Pavilion "passed through the fire", for this was their 'ghat', or place of cremation. Its white Sicilian marble dome is in good condition, but the surrounding memorial garden is rough and unkempt (August '07).

Standean Farm. TQ 31 11.

THE valley is a peaceful place, though the ridges to west and east are not, for they suffer much from the traffic noise of the A27 bypass, the London Road and Ditchling Road.

The medieval landscape of sheep and corn around Standean Farm was gentrified in the eighteenth century with many small plantations, which aped the aristocratic fashion newly set by neighbouring Stanmer Park. The new names were redolent of modern pleasure landscapes, like Wonderhill Plantation and Blackberry Shaw, Nightingale Wood and Alpha and Beta Cottages.

Sadly the older flint cottages and farmhouse did not survive their treatment by Canadian forces during the Second World War, but several old flint barns and barnyards do survive, including New Barn and its two hovels up on the eastern hillside. The two new post-war farmhouses, at Lower Standean and Mid-down house, continue the theme of gentrification, and would look well in Surrey's stockbroker countryside.

The Farm's Down pastures did not survive the post war decades and there's only one intact fragment left — on **the valley's west side between Lower Standean and North Bottom (TQ 318 117).** No designated Access Land exists on the farm despite its long ownership by Brighton Council and the large quantities of public subsidy that such farms receive. If you walk over the stubbles by New Barn or Mid-down House you could start dozens of pen-reared, corn-fed Partridge cossetted for slaughter by a shooting syndicate. Yet the City Council's own policy is to oppose all blood sports on its Downland estate.

A small part of the valleys' most ancient heritage does survive, however, in two clusters of sarsen stones. Many of these megaliths have been removed from the farmed land and now form a rockery in the private garden of Standean Farmhouse.

One cluster survives in situ at **Rocky Pond, TQ 315 120,** on the high slope north of Lower Standean, though the pond is surrounded by barbed wire, has dried out, and is rapidly growing over into thick scrub. The big stones are still impressive.

Two Beautiful Bottoms: Dencher and North Bottoms

TILL the end of the 1950s all of the dry valleys and tops south of Ditchling Down and Beacon retained their primeval heathy grasslands, with much chalk heath and gorse. **Dencher Bottom, TQ 317 125,** is still completely delightful. There is the scarce Chalk Milkwort, much Devil's-bit, Purse-web Spider and Boxing Gloves Spider, Alopecosa cuneata. The large old anthills which pepper the slopes demonstrate these grasslands great antiquity. Dencher's unimproved Down pasture has two aspects: a shadier western slope and a hot south-facing slope. The south facing slope can feel Meditteranean — dry and topped with a fringe of colourful gorse, and with Chalkhills and Brown Argus bobbing and dancing. The cooler, western slope is better for old meadow Waxcap fungi, and I counted twelve species in one October visit, with Fairy Clubs and Pink Gills. The south-facing slope is better for the Boletes and Amanitas which take advantage of the sun loving Rockrose.

North Bottom's north slope, TQ 323 119, also retains its soft and ancient Sheep's Fescue turf, with Spring Sedge and Cowslip in spring and Carline Thistle, Rampion and Autumn Ladies Tresses orchis in August and September.

Ditchling old Tenantry Down, TQ 326 126.

THE plateau which runs for over a mile south from Ditchling Beacon (and the scarp to the north) used to be one of Ditchling's two old commons. (See map of commons and enclosures). The common included most of the Iron Age hillfort and the heads of three dip slope dry valleys, two of which retain their rich old Down pastures. In 1978 the plateau part of the common was stripped of its common land status and is now privately owned. To be sure, the more tractor-accessible parts had long been ploughed out, but common land status did at least confer the sense that there was a public interest in the land, and since the passing of the Countryside and Rights of Way Act in 2000 all commons have a right of public access. The fragments of old Down pasture which survive there were not designated as Access Land, though they should have been.

The **upper part of Hogtrough Bottom, TQ 326 126,** is one of the fragments of the ex-common to have survived. It is superb. Juniper was still here at least till the 1930s and Ling Heather is still present at the top slope, though it risks being swamped by surrounding Gorse. Dyer's Greenweed — that other signifier of these clay-with-flints soils — can also be found at the slope top and there is much Tormentil. In spring the hillside is tinted with Early Purple Orchids and Cowslips.

Dark Green Fritillary can be seen, with Small Heath and Small Copper butterflies. Dry grass bends before the breeze and Betony, Harebell, Rampion and Hawkbit colour-up the ground like a Turkish carpet. You may see Hares if you are lucky.

The **upper part of North Bottom, TQ 327 117,** shows the boney ridges of an old field system beneath its turf. On its north side you may see Chalkhill Blue butterflies and there is Rockrose, Horseshoe Vetch, Spring Sedge and Early Purple Orchis. You may find Waxcaps in autumn.

The High Top and the Scarp Slopes.
DITCHLING **Beacon. TQ 331 130.** Here you are on top of the world. There are superb views in all directions, but particularly to the east, where you can see the prow of Firle Beacon, Kingston Hill, the cliffs at Seaford Head and the start of the Seven Sisters. The **Iron Age hill fort ramparts** are detectable on their north and east sides (e.g. **TQ 332 131**), though the rank vegetation and fences makes it difficult to walk them in parts. The eastern ramparts bound a fragment of derelict chalk heath, which is disappearing

Ditchling Beacon in the 1880s — smooth as a baby's bottom!

The Ditchling Down scarp, looking west to Clayton Holt and Wolstonbury.

under scrub and rank grassland. Alone Ling Heather bush tries to keep its head above the tussocky mess, like a drowning swimmer. Yet this is a Brighton Council-owned site. For many years, till recently, the farmer-owner of a large chunk of the western part of the hill fort ploughed over the remains. They're just crop marks now.

There are **three bostals** down the scarp, the middle one of which carries the motor road, for this was a major route in ancient times. Ditchling Beacon is the highest point on the eastern Downs, at 813 ft, so no traveller could mistake their directions here. In prehistory people descended the scarp by the lower bostal to go north across the Weald because this route kept their feet somewhat dryer, following the **watershed route** between the Adur and Ouse catchments. It went north past The Nye, over Lodge Hill, Ditchling (with its round barrow), past Oldlands Windmill and over Broadhill. It was a route free of soggy fords or wonky clapper bridges. In early medieval times the swineherds from Patcham, Withdean, Stanmer and probably Brighton drove their pigs down these bostals to their swine pastures at Wivelsfield and beyond to Worth Forest.

Now, though, the road traffic on the middle bostal road is a curse, threatening the safety of every walker and cyclist of the South Downs Way and providing a major rat-run for surplus traffic from the improved A23 trunk road. The traffic long ago stopped the proper grazing of the scarp slope, for it remained as common land and thus could not easily be fenced. As a result the scarp has lost all of its smooth, bare beauty of a half century ago, and the mosses and tiny wild flowers for which it was renowned are threatened. Boring Ash woods creep across its slope and the top break of slope is tangled with Hogweed and Mugwort.

People do not use the Beacon as they use its sister site the Devil's Dyke — scrambling excitedly up and down the slopes — for the Beacon's slopes are broken up by thickets, rank vegetation and barbed wire and most people would not even notice the higher and lower bostals, which give easy access. Yet, most of the land around the Beacon is in public ownership or leasehold and Brighton Council bought their chunk in the same year they bought the Devil's Dyke, to provide a twin 'honeypot' site for Brighton visitors.

Now the Sussex Wildlife Trust is doing good scrub clearance work. May it continue and expand and may Brighton Council emulate them on their adjacent land.

The Traffic Authority has resisted traffic calming — leave alone road closure — and every year it increases.

Barrows. The pastures west of the Beacon, on the top of **Ditchling Down, TQ 323 131**, are open and unfenced to the south, like the old Downs. There's a lovely bare dew pond and a cluster of round barrows along the South Downs Way, TQ 323 131. I count about seven, though that's optimistic. Some are obvious and round, with the characteristic 'pillage dimple' in the top, and some are scarcely detectable. There's also one by the fenced dewpond. Ditchling Tenantry Down has a barrow, TQ 325 132, which you can make out amongst the rank vegetation. Two more big barrow clusters around Keymer Post, TQ 315 129, have been ploughed out.

Keymer Down scarp, TQ 315 133, due south of Keymer church, is one of the very best Brighton Downs sites.

We had a picnic there one evening in early August, amongst the humpty-tumpty velvety turf of the old quarries, looking west to the dark leaf greens and Prussian greens of Clayton Holt, in shadow. A Buzzard mewed somewhere down in the coombe. Everything was tinged with gold… the yellow gold of the mown hay fields, and the gold-edged olives and tarragons of the Wealden woods. Rooks cawed. A Yaffle mocked. Far away was the grey-blue bulk of Blackdown under a sky of luminous watery yellow with red-grey, gold-edged clouds. Harebells and tall grass shivered in the breeze. When we descended we counted five Roe Deer in Coombe Bottom and startled a foraging Pygmy Shrew.

One spring we found 38 fat larvae of the Large Bloody-nosed Beetle — all iridescent green-black — scattered along a hillside path here, enjoying the abundant Bedstraws.

In spring a dwarfed version of Field Fleawort grows on the short turf edge of the quarries and there's Chalk Milkwort. You may find Bluebell amongst the old Gorse scrub, though Juniper has been gone for more than a half century, and Heath Snail, too, was recently lost.

In summer there's Dark Green Fritillary, Chalkhills, Chalk Carpet moth on the scree slopes and Marbled White on the tall grass. In winter the quarry slopes host rare mosses and lichen.

Burnhouse Bostal and Ditchling Down scarp. TQ 320 133.

THERE'S much tussocky Tor Grass on these slopes, but they're still walkable,

The old chalk pits on Keymer Down. A very special place.

with many terracettes. To the east of Burnhouse Bostal is the National Trust's recently-acquired Ditchling Down. It's a lovely place. The small quarries have grassed over and their skeletal soils support a specialist wildlife. There's Musk Orchis. The tiny Black and Purple Pyrauster micro-moths zip about, with the iridescent coppery-purple longhorn moth *Nemophora fasciella*. There's Chalk Carpet moth and Silver-spotted Skipper. Golfinches twitter.

Cotoneaster is beginning to take hold, though, and will eventually wreck the slopes unless it is controlled.

Don't light fires. This place is too special for such invasive activity.

The linear rew woods at the base of slope have Bluebell, Wood Anemone, Primrose and Early Purples in spring. There's much Whitebeam.

Footnotes

1   'Sussex Barrows' — L.V. Grinsell. *Sussex Archaeological Collections*, Vol. LXX 75 (1934), page 224.

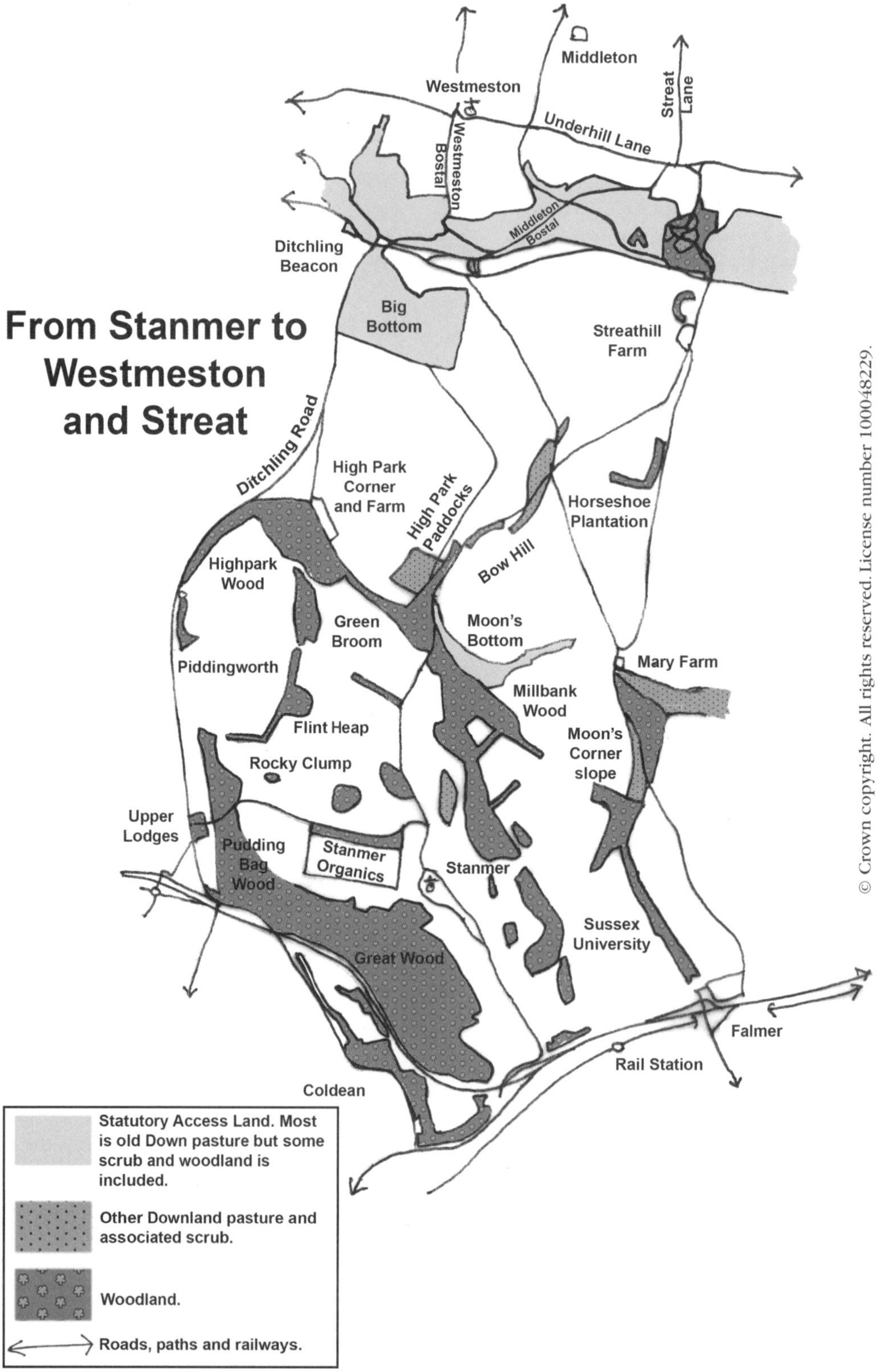

From Stanmer to Westmeston and Street

Westmeston

Middleton

Streat Lane

Underhill Lane

Westmeston Bostal

Middleton Bostal

Ditchling Beacon

Big Bottom

Streathill Farm

Ditchling Road

High Park Corner and Farm

High Park Paddocks

Horseshoe Plantation

Highpark Wood

Bow Hill

Green Broom

Moon's Bottom

Piddingworth

Mary Farm

Millbank Wood

Flint Heap

Moon's Corner slope

Rocky Clump

Upper Lodges

Pudding Bag Wood

Stanmer Organics

Stanmer

Great Wood

Sussex University

Coldean

Falmer

Rail Station

Statutory Access Land. Most is old Down pasture but some scrub and woodland is included.

Other Downland pasture and associated scrub.

Woodland.

Roads, paths and railways.

11: FROM STANMER TO WESTMESTON AND STREAT

THIS landscape moves from the aristocratic woodlands of Stanmer to the high scarp slopes between Ditchling bostal and Streat Hill bostal — which have some of the best chalk grasslands in East Sussex. In between lies the open plateau of High Park Farm, Stanmer Down and Streathill Farm, badly damaged by agribusiness, but with good fragments of ancient Down pasture surviving.

The landscape has many visible layers of history. In the slanting light of late afternoon bony prehistoric and medieval lynchets show up on the slopes of High Park, Mary Farm and Piddingworth. Round barrows pepper the line of Western Brow, and the bumps and house platforms of Stanmer's deserted medieval street are plain to see in the horse pasture opposite the village teashop.

Stanmer village. TQ 33 09.

THE old village has many delights. The huge timber barn which dominates the lower village street is 17th century, and was built after engrossing landlords had acquired all the medieval peasant holdings, with their own little barns, crofts and orchards, and consolidated the larger village into its present form. The upper village street has 18 beautiful flint cottages,

with colourful gardens. They were lovingly re-built by Brighton Council after being largely destroyed in the Second World War during military training, for the Council had boldly acquired the whole 6000 acre estate from the cash strapped Earls of Chichester in 1947. The pretty church is also a reconstruction, though earlier, being a rebuilding of 1838 of its medieval predecessor. The two huge and knotty Yews in the churchyard amply pre-date it. Next to the church is a sour-looking pond. Its origins may be very ancient, however, for Stanmer was probably named after it. ('*Stan mere*': stony pool). Between the church and the barn is a flint well-house containing a Tudor well 252 feet deep and a wooden donkey wheel, like that at Saddlescombe. It was in use till mains water was installed in 1900. It is opened in summer by the Stanmer Preservation Society who also run the wonderful village museum on the lane to the City Nurseries, behind the House.

Across the lawn from the church is the 18th century mansion house. It long lay unoccupied and would have provided the perfect headquarters for the coming South Downs National Park Authority. What a missed opportunity! Instead, it's been leased to a millionaire who currently (2007) uses the ground floor for corporate functions and weddings. That bit is open to the public sometimes, but is largely empty except for a few bad paintings and big TV screens in the rooms. The millionaire has stuck a painfully bad oil-type painting of himself near the entrance so's we know how important he is.

With such constant reminders in the Stanmer landscape of the power of very rich people it is good to remember the example of one prominent son of Stanmer who showed real moral courage. He was William Goffe, the son of a rector of Stanmer, who rose to be a Major General in the Parliamentary army in the English revolution, commanding Cromwell's own regiment. His courage steeled him to be one of the signatories to the death warrant of King Charles in 1649, like his comrade Anthony Stapley of Patcham. At the restoration of the monarchy in 1660 he had to flee to America, where he hid for some time in a cave in Connecticut. He was lucky to escape with his life. The royalists' revenge was so mad they even dug up Cromwell's body and 'executed' it. Those signatories who couldn't escape were hung, drawn and quartered. Goff's grave in America is unknown.[1]

Stanmer Park

STANMER was transformed in the 18th century after the Pelhams, later Earls of Chichester, had bought it. A circle of woods was planted along the hill-tops surrounding the dry valley in which the village lay and more shaws and clumps were scattered within. Much of the planting was Beech, though Oak and other species were occasionally used.

Three quarters of Stanmer Parish, together with parts of Ditchling and Falmer, were enclosed in this giant park — two miles by one and a half miles across.

The City Council took the initiative after the recent retirement of the Park's farming tenant and opened up all the closed woods and pasture fields to public access, and folk are using this new freedom to explore more widely than they have ever done before. The paths, gates and benches the Council made are excellent. The land, though, has not so far been designated as *statutory* Access Land, though it should be.

The open Park has been one of the few places where travellers can camp in relative peace. There are nearly always one or two van dwellers vehicles somewhere there. New parking fees and bunding threaten to finally tidy these people out of the way of those who can't bear to accommodate their cultures. The new parking regime also threatens the usage of the Park by Brighton people who are poorer but still car-dependant.

West of the village, on part of the site of the old Stanmer Nurseries, **TQ 332 096, Stanmer Organics** embrace a series of excellent experimental businesses running tree nurseries, herb gardens and organic horticulture. The Council's walled Nurseries are also open to the public part of the week.

The **Great Wood, TQ 335 090**, is now 250 years old and has acquired many of the plants of ancient woodland, often by planting, though many species have made their own way there. Under Corporation control there has been much imaginative new planting. "The trees are laid out alphabetically, with *Acer* and *Betula* at the lower east end and *Ulmus* and *Zelkova* high up to the west."[2] On the lawns behind the House is a gigantic Blue Atlas Cedar, *Cedrus atlantica*, with several slighter companions.

The Great Wood also has a damaged round barrow and well-preserved **cross dyke, TQ 331 092**, and **Pudding Bag Wood, TQ 326 096**, next to it, harbours a couple of round barrows and a cross dyke.

The gales of '87 and '92 brought down many of the big veteran trees and the survivors are now scattered unevenly through the woods. Good lines of mature Beech run along the main north-south footpath through Pudding Bag Wood. The gale was not uniform in its effect. Some places have every pre-'87 tree flattened and other spots — even on the highest ground — were miraculously spared.

The parts of Great Wood and neighbouring areas which face the Bypass suffer badly from its noise pollution. There's a massive din.

In the upper Stanmer valley the path through **Flint Heap** and **Green Broom, TQ 330 110**, is blessedly sheltered from that noise. Flint Heap still has fine old beeches and much splintered huggle-muggle of fallen giants. Walking there recently we found a wasps nest bigger than a football on the side of a rotting Beech bole. The wary workers came to check us out, but we showed them plenty of respect and walked on. Green Broom has some grand old maiden Oaks and Sweet Chestnut.

The fallen trees do provide much of interest in their own right, of course, and their fungal assemblage is probably the best to be found in these woods. The very rare Lion's Mane or Bearded Tooth fungus, *Hericium erineus*, has been found in at least two places. On one foray recently more than four fifths of the species we found were dependent on rotting wood for their sustenance. There was the embarrassing-looking Dog Stinkhorn, *Mutinus caninus*, the distinctive smell of the ordinary Stinkhorn, *Phallus impudicus*, as well as Bird's Nest fungus, *Cyathus striatus*, Yellow Stainer, *Agaricus xanthodermus*, lots of Turkey Tail, *Trametes versicolor*, and many others.

Near to **Granny's Belt, TQ 334 105**, there are reports that a sarsen stone circle existed till the 19th century. This was probably a modern folly, of sorts, for farmers collect and pile up sarsens exposed by the plough. The bridleway nearby has small sarsens in its surface and there are re-located sarsens all around Stanmer on road, path, wood and pond sides used as decorative features.

There must still be many sarsens in situ, though, and one huge stone was exposed by the excavations at **Rocky Clump, TQ 328 101**, on the site of the likely pagan Saxon temple known as '*Paeccel's Weoh*' — '*weoh*' being Saxon[3] for 'sacred place', or even 'temple'. That name was corrupted to Patchway, which became the modern name for the whole Ditchling Road ridge between Upper Lodge Wood and Hollingbury Hill. Saxon skeletons were dug up and much activity obviously took place at Rocky Clump. The place remained important into Christian times because the parish boundary is aligned through it and the Saxon charter of 765 AD actually names it.

Moon's Bottom. TQ 340 106.

MOON'S Bottom has a cool and mossy slope lying under the shade of Millbanke Wood. There are cowslips in spring and in late summer it has a sky-blue dusting of Small Scabious. Some parts of it have a slightly acidic soil chemistry, with Tormentil, Sweet Vernal-grass, *Anthoxanthum odoratum*, and Field Wood-rush. Agro-environmental support has come to its aid, and it has been transformed from its earlier derelict state by good scrub control and cattle grazing.

On the flat ground above the eastern end of this slope is a scrub-covered round barrow, TQ 343 106. The open ground between Moon's Bottom and Moon's Corner slope (next) has the lynchets of perhaps Iron Age cultivation visible.

Moon's Corner slope. TQ 348 100.

THIS delightful little slope lies below the lane to St. Mary's Farm, and, judging from the bottles and cans I've found there, some University students already appreciate its charms. On a hot spring day I sat and watched a Bee-fly, *Bombylius major*, hovering over patches of bare ground and releasing its eggs one-by-one each with a flick of its tail. The place buzzes with

Moon's Corner slope, north of Sussex University, framed by Moon's Plantation.

insects in summer, and Chalkhill Blue butterfly was still there a few years ago, with Brown Argus and Marbled White. In autumn there's Chalkland Waxcap.

Bow Hill and Stanmer Down.
TQ 34 11.

THE whole of Stanmer Down survived unploughed till a generation ago, but dereliction turned large areas of it to scrub. It was then cleared and cultivated except for islands of scrub kept for pheasant cover. The valley on the west side of Bow Hill, where the bridlepath runs, was a magical old Downland spot before its 'improvement'. Now only the steep slope survives.

The Down used to be covered with prehistoric field systems, and on the top of Bow Hill there were perhaps as many as nine barrows in two clusters. Now the visible signs of the ancient peoples have gone, except when the shadows are long and sharp.

Of late the **bridlepath slope, TQ 342 116**, has been managed better, by cattle grazing and mowing. There's a scatter of thorn and Gorse and you could see Small Copper, Small Heath and Common Blue butterflies, and a few Wild Strawberries and Harebells — Cowslips, too, in spring. At its northern end, over the fenceline, there's a tiny-but-beautiful fragment of Down pasture on the **downslope edge of the thicket, TQ 344 120**. It has survived in

isolation, surrounded by arable, for as much as 150 years, perhaps by rabbit grazing.

High Park Farm paddocks.
TQ 335 112.

THESE paddocks have several prehistoric lynchets making giant steps down the valley. Much of the grassland has been improved, except at the bottom of the valley on the steepest slopes, where you can find Harebell and Quaking Grass, Common Blue and lots of Restharrow below the scrub.

High Park and Streathill Farms were carved out of the ancient sheep pastures in the mid-19th century corn boom. Now the whole of Streathill and two thirds of High Park have been put back down to pasture. In an excellent initiative Brighton City Council has swopped land with its High Park tenant farmer to re-create a corridor of publicly accessible pastures between Big Bottom and Stanmer Park.

Till the last war **High Park Corner, TQ 329 116**, by the farmstead, was a favourite site for gypsy encampments, for it was on level ground and on common land. Something like twice a year a posse of farmers and other thugs, organized by the Ditchling Constable, would use frightening violence to evict the gypsies, who must have included many small children. Charles Yeates[4] records one vigilante attacking the gypsies with a lead-filled bamboo cudgel and nearly killing one of his own mates in the process.

...I recently counted at least five caravans being stored at High Park Farm in barns and on hard standings... One law for some, and one for others.

Big Bottom. TQ 335 125.

IN 1925 one writer[5] described the Downs around Big Bottom as follows. *"In July, or the beginning of August, one could stand for hours to drink in the beauty of it all — heather and ling in its purple-pink mantle, and the furze with its golden bloom and sweet scent. The hum of insects fills the air — the Dark Green Fritillary flashing in the sun, with the brilliant Adonis Blue and many others making a picture that my pen is quite unable adequately to describe."*

It's still a lovely place, though the heather on the hill brows has long gone and I have never seen the Fritillary or Adonis there in my time. Big Bottom still has a fringe of Gorse, and three of its four slopes are still lovely with Downland flowers. The western slope has been lost to thorn scrub. Recently I almost stepped on a Brown Hare snuggled deeply down in its form in the Tor Grass, which has spread widely now. There has been no official scrub control for well over a decade (though the 'Phantom Conservation

Volunteers' did a bit of unofficial clearance a while back).

The valley is still very under-grazed. Typically, last summer the ex-arable land to the south was heavily grazed by a large sheep flock, whilst the Bottom grew rank grass and benefitted from a mere week or so of cattle grazing.

Though Big Bottom, like the rest of High Park Farm, has been owned by Brighton Council since 1927, it was off-limits — till the recent coming of the statutory Right to Roam — to the thousands of walkers on the South Downs Way, just over the fence.

Despite now being Access Land few people visit. I think Badger digging has taken place in the past. I found a Badger scalp there some years ago and we found a frightened Badger cub hiding under a bush one morning next to a dug-out sett.

Home Brow, Western Brow, Streat Hill and the scarp slope.

EAST of Ditchling Beacon the scarp brow gently decreases in height and opens up easterly views of the Vale of the Brooks, south of Lewes, the chalk sea cliffs, and the east Sussex Weald.

The scarp slope north of Home Brow and Western Brow is 'Cowslip heaven'. I have never in my life seen such astonishing

Westmeston Bostal: Cowslips and sheep terracettes.

displays of Cowslips as I have seen there. The hillside can be yellow with them in May-time. There are lovely displays, too, of Early Purple Orchis and, in August, Devil's-bit. There was a large Heath Snail population where a spur turned to face south, TQ 333 132, but their numbers had drastically dwindled when I last looked. There is little scrub.

The rew woodland to the west and east of Westmeston bostal is rich with vernal wildflowers, and it shelters a huge old ash pollard at TQ 340 130. There are old limekilns in Westmeston chalkpit and the chalkpit south of The Gote, TQ 348 132.

These slopes have well-formed sheep terracettes and the bostals and old parish chalk pits have carved deeply into the chalk. The **old Middleton bostal, TQ 343 130**, used to connect at its top with the **Westmeston bostal, TQ 338 130**, but it has long been wired off from the latter and is now becoming overgrown with scrub and has lost its public path status.

Where the two bostals cut a joint cleft in the brow of the scarp, like a hair parting, between Home Brow and Western Brow, they divide a **large cluster of round barrows, TQ 339 128**, distinctive on the western side, but less easy to trace on the eastern side. There were other barrows on Streat Hill, but they are scarcely visible, now. The ground along the route of the South Downs Way has lost its old Down pasture flowers, replaced with nitrogen green 'improved' pastures.

On Underhill Lane is the medieval church of **Westmeston, TQ 338 136**, which is part-Norman, though badly treated by Victorian restorers. It is of the small size most of these churches were in their original building. It used to have fine Norman wall paintings from the same workshop that painted nearby Clayton and Plumpton, but they were destroyed after their Victorian uncovering.

Streat Hill bostal, TQ 351 130, has long been fenced off from the surrounding Down pastures and is rapidly turning into thorn scrub and woodland. Despite that it has islands of very rich turf on its deep cut sides. It is still a lovely place, but will not be for much longer. It has Green Hairstreak, Dingy Skipper and Wall Brown butterflies, and Orange-tailed Clearwing, Purple Bar, Black Pyrausta and Burnet Companion moths. The mossy turf has the moss species *Neckera crispa*, *Ctenidium molluscum*, and *Dicranum scoparium* looking very like *D. majus*. It also has the Scree Snail. In the colourful scrub I have found Wasp Beetle, *Clytus arietis*, several times.

To the west of the bostal there is the **Queen Victoria Jubilee 'V'-sign plantation, TQ 348 130**, on the middle of the bare scarp slope. Six species were planted out, including surprisingly healthy Pine. *'Fingers' to you, too, Madam!!*

Footnotes

1   *Hovel in the Wood: The Pageant of Stanmer Parish* — Charles Yeates (Stanmer Publications), page 42-3.

2   *The Sussex Tree Book* — Owen Johnson (Pomegranate Press, 1998), page 91.

3   *The Place Names of Sussex* — Mawer, Stenton and Gover. (English Place-Name Society, Reprinted 2001), page 310.

4   *Hovel in the Wood* — Charles Yeates (Stanmer Publications), page 32.

5   *Round About Sussex Downs* — Frederick F. Wood (Duckworth, 1925), page 24.

12 : FROM BALMER TO PLUMPTON

THIS landscape is one of the islands of true tranquility on the Brighton Downs, counted as 'remote' in a recent study.[1]

It is a prehistoric landscape of the first importance. Wild and windy Balmer Down and Plumpton Plain are so crowded with signs of the past that they remind one of the Wessex Downland, made more famous by Stonehenge and Avebury. Here you can see the fossilized fields of Bronze Age, Iron Age and medieval peasants, spanning perhaps 3000 years of pre-modern farming. Agri-business has done massive damage in the last sixty years and the old pastures and scrub thickets that protected the marks of the ancient peoples have been eradicated, but the network of sites that survive are truly extraordinary.

Exploring **Horseshoe Plantation, TQ 349 117**, near Streathill Farm, recently I came across a circular embankment, partly ditched on its outside and raised in the middle. Scattered on its banks were dozens of struck flint flakes, pot boiling fire-cracked flints and a possible flint tool. Is this a previously un-recorded Bronze Age barrow, or a round house enclosure, like those across the valley on Plumpton Plain? We shall have to wait and see, but it is only one of many sites in this landscape that await investigation.

Housedean Farm, TQ 369 092, which manages part of Balmer Down, was one of the last on these Downs to use an ox team for tillage, only giving up in 1914.

You may approach Balmer Down via **Balmer Farm, TQ 358 099**, which lies on the site of the Saxon hamlet of *Bergemere* (the pool by the 'burh'). It was sufficiently important at Domesday to have two slaves, a manorial church, swine pastures in the Weald at Horsted Keynes and Birchgrove, and brookland meadow south of Lewes still called 'Bormer Brook'. The church has long gone but you can still trace the outlines of the hamlet green under the mess of modern farm clutter. Big Blackthorn hedges mark the bounds of the medieval open fields of the hamlet, which drop away southwards from the farmstead, TQ 357 096. They went under the evocative names of Lanthorne Lane, Church Laine and Barren Laine.

West of Balmer Farm there is a track to the derelict **Ridge Farm, TQ 350 099**, north of Falmer. It was the start of the route of the biggest of the mass trespasses that marked the Sussex campaign for the right to roam in 1998-9.

Balmer Down and Buckland Hole. TQ 367 110.

STANDING on Balmer Huff and looking down into Buckland Hole you will see that the whole valley is filled with a pattern of rectangular banks, often topped with Gorse or thorn. They surround the fossilized fields of two Iron Age and Romano-British villages. They look a bit like the tiny fields you can still find in the west of Cornwall or Ireland. You are looking at the lineaments of the farmed landscape of people who lived and breathed two thousand years ago and more. The two villages lay opposite one another — one on the spur of the Huff and one across the Hole on the ridge where the South Downs Way now runs. At the head of Buckland Hole lay their cemetery, a circular platform of flints and soil some 60 yards across, that yielded up more than a score of funerary urns when it was excavated in 1849.[2]

You cannot now make out their banked roadway, or the strange enclosure that has been called their circus or moot, or many of the subtleties of pits and platforms that used to be found in their fieldscape, for this landscape was ruthlessly ploughed in recent decades and these signs eroded, till the coming of the ESA scheme encouraged the re-conversion of this Scheduled Ancient Monument back to pasture. Even that did not end the damage, for a modern surfaced gallops was carved through some of the most sensitive area near the South Downs Way. To be sure, it was removed after enforcement action from the authorities, but more damage had been done. The steeper parts of the valley that escaped the plough in modern times still lost their old Down pasture vegetation to modern agribusiness sprays. Now only the occasional steep lynchet retains a smidgeon of that old flora.

For all that, there is still enough here to fill you with wonder and delight. On one blustery afternoon on the cusp of September and October we walked a stubble field overlooking Balmer Down. It was almost silent, save for a distant tractor. In the slanting light we could pick out all the bostals descending Kingston Hill. The visible sliver of Seaford Head cliffs glowed white in the sun. The Vale of the Brooks was laid out from end to end. A Hare started up, the black tips of its ears helping us see it as it ran across to the Huff. There was a scatter of sarsen debris

Mass trespass crossing Balmer Down in the summer of 1998, campaigning for the right to roam.

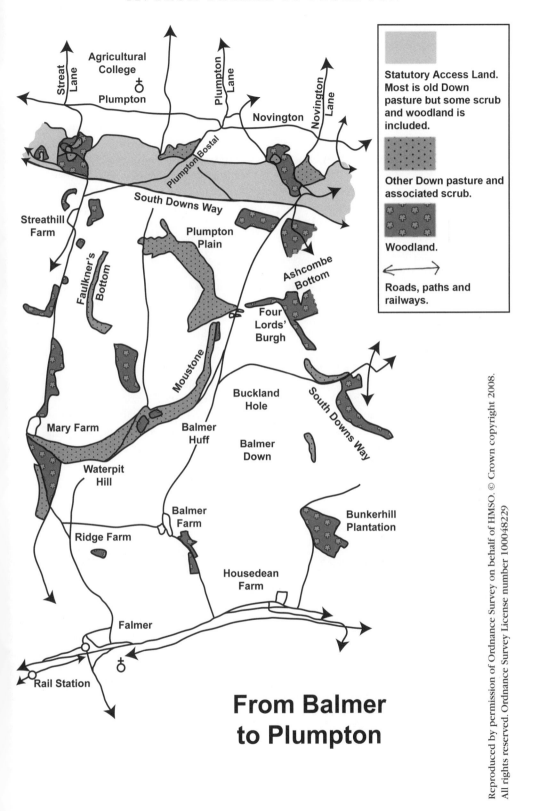

Statutory Access Land. Most is old Down pasture but some scrub and woodland is included.

Other Down pasture and associated scrub.

Woodland.

Roads, paths and railways.

From Balmer to Plumpton

all around — both the 'puddingstone' kind and pure sandstone. There were scraps of iron and even the fins of a Second World War bomblet. Then we found a 'shepherd's crown' fossil sea urchin — whoopee!! We continued looking. We found much yellowed flint, characteristic of hilltop clay-with-flint. Then we found a second sea urchin, bigger than the first and the best of my collection — with many of the big spine sockets intact. We found a fossil sponge, *Siphonia koenigi*, with all its wiggly interior still there. We took it to be a piece of bone till close inspection. We found a piece of abraded Romano-British pottery. I counted the cornfield flowers growing amongst the stones. There was *Common Field Speedwell, Green Field Speedwell, Field Pansy, Scarlet Pimpernel, Black Bindweed, Knotgrass, Field Madder and Common Orache*. Lovely.

Waterpit Hill. TQ 352 105.

B A L M E R Huff presides over a mile and a quarter long sub-scarp between Waterpit Hill and the Moustone. The north-facing slope of Waterpit Hill is one of the most attractive old Down pasture slopes on the Brighton Downs plateau. There is little scrub, except at its eastern end, and much colour — Cowslips and Orchids, Harebell, Yellow Rattle, Devil's-bit, Carrot and Picknicker's Thistle. There are Chalkhill Blue and Marbled White butterflies and Burnet Moths. The northerly aspect brings *Neckera crispa* moss and the scarce Scree Snail, *Abida secale*, in places. It is well-managed at present. It is bizarre that it was not designated as Access Land.

The Moustone. TQ 361 110.

T H E sub-scarp continues eastwards with the Moustone slope. The Moustone was an independent farm back at Domesday, but is now part of Balmer. It's a lovely lonely place of Roe Deer, Hare and Windhover. The slope's turf is more acidic than Waterpit, with more Tormentil and bits of Wild Strawberry, but most of the old Down pasture herbs are there — Dropwort and Spring Sedge, Cowslip, Rockrose and Basil, Hairy Violet and Devil's-bit.

The Four Lord's Burgh. TQ 365 116.

A T the point where the South Down Way turns south-easterly there were

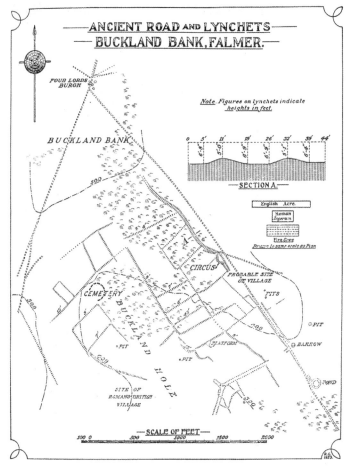

—ANCIENT ROAD AND LYNCHETS—
— BUCKLAND BANK, FALMER.—

FOUR LORDS BURGH

Note. Figures on lynchets indicate heights in feet.

BUCKLAND BANK

0   5'   11'   19'   26'   32'   39'   44'

—SECTION A.—

English Acre.

Roman jugerum.

Five Gyves

Drawn to same scale as Plan

BUCKLAND HOLT

CIRCUS   PROBABLE SITE OF VILLAGE

CEMETERY   PITS

·PIT   PLATFORM   ◦PIT   ◦BARROW

·PIT

·PIT   ○POND

SITE OF ROMANO-BRITISH VILLAGE

—SCALE OF FEET—
100 0   500   1000   1500   2500

about five round barrows, named the Four Lord's Burgh because at this point four manorial (now parish) boundaries came together. (Each manor had a 'lord'). Boundaries were often aligned on such prehistoric features. Only the two barrows over the fence on the western side of the north-south track still exist as slight tumps. The rest have been ploughed out.

Due west of Four Lord's Burgh lies a **triangle of wood pasture, TQ 362 117**, of the most delightful character. It was sunk under dense scrub, but much clearance has been done and the site is now grazed by Sussex cattle. It lies over the boney lynchets of the field system of the Iron Age and Bronze Age people of this landscape. In August it is gloriously colourful, with Harebells everywhere, Rockrose, Red Clover, Eggs and Bacon, and Scabious. There is much Bracken on the western side, and shady Sycamore and Oak and occasional Gorse. It has a parkland flavour.

Plumpton Plain.

PLUMPTON Plain was the home of several hamlets of Bronze Age farmers. That was a long, long time ago — between about 3600 to 2900 years ago. They cleared and tilled their fields, piling up the stones in little cairns, and built enclosures within which they placed their round houses with conical thatched roofs and little house ponds — a bit like African kraals in modern times. Most of their landscape has been ploughed out, but, at the top of a **gentle valley, TQ 357 121**, about a quarter mile south of the South Downs escarpment you can step back across the centuries to walk the fields and paths they walked and sit in the enclosures they used. This place is a truly remarkable survival, where tiny bumps and hollows may mark a house site, a farm path, and even the earliest 'ridge and furrow' cultivation traces to be found in southern England. If those folk were to return before

us now they would be able to recognize and point out every place in their domestic lives that was significant to them.

They were the first people in Britain to organize a settled agriculture, based on the use of the ox plough, with sharp land divisions and long-lived nucleated settlements[3], in a Downscape where widespread woodland clearance had been achieved. They traded internationally, importing pottery from the Continent, and made bronze tools and weapons, bits of which have been found.

One enclosure lies to the west of the bridlepath running southwards from the South Downs Way. It is still covered in scrub. The four enclosures to the east of the bridlepath are under pasture, though, and quite plain to see with the use of a site plan, as are the field paths and banks. On the now-wooded valley sides to the south east there are other house sites and field lynchets, and, about a quarter mile in that direction lay their successor settlement, now mostly ploughed out. Even on the surrounding modern ploughlands of the Plain, though, you can still easily find pieces of struck flint flake. David McOmish, the co-author of the latest field investigation, found a beautiful Neolithic flint axe, over 10 inches long, whilst walking these arables.

The remarkable survival over the millennia of this settlement site may be due to the outward spread of woodland from neighbouring Ashcombe Bottom (perhaps never cleared) after the abandonment of the settlements. This woodland cover safely sealed the remains until the middle ages, when, after its clearance, sheep pasturage similarly cloaked and protected it.

The little wooded valley south east of the main settlement is still pregnant with a sense of wilderness. When I walked up there one August three years ago all was silent, save the rustling leaves, when a most awful caterwauling broke out amongst the trees — screeching and squawking and branches shaking. My heart thumped — till out of the branches broke a Sparrowhawk closely pursued by a Green Woodpecker and a posse of small birds.

Faulkner's Bottom. TQ 352 116.

T H E field systems of neighbouring Bronze Age settlements spread across Faulkners Bottom and south across Bow Hill. Most of the visible signs of those people have been ploughed out, but on the west side of Faulkner's Bottom two Bronze Age enclosures survive (plus the possible one I found in Horseshoe Plantation), as well as — at the head of the valley — an undated 'valley entrenchment' crossed by a

terrace way, TQ 352 125. This rectangular enclosure is an atmospheric place, long-covered with old thorn bushes, Bracken and Rosebay glades, and with some scrub Oaks.

Only a long strip of steep eastern valleyside survives from the old Down pastures of Faulkners Bottom. Still nice, though, in a scruffy way, with Orchids and Dropwort amongst much low Bramble, with Lousewort, Centaury and Hogweed testifying to little management and occasional cattle grazing.

The wider valley has now (2007) been returned to pasture, and the **scrubland, TQ 355 112**, at its southern end planted up with Laurel, Spruce, Pine and Cypress, presumably to keep the Pheasants reared there happy. We saw a Hobby scooting across the valley last autumn, preparing for migration in tandem with the gathering Martins. A short time after, we spotted two circling Buzzards and a Kestrel.

Plumpton and Novington scarp.

T H E R E are three clusters of round barrows on this section of the scarp, one on each of the three main spurs that jut forward. Most of them are so low that they have to be looked for, though there is one on the arable just south of the South Downs Way and just west of Novington Plantation that is a yard tall, TQ 364 125. Most of them have 'pillage dimples' in their tops. They were probably built by the ancestors of the Bronze Age farmers who built the Plumpton Plain enclosures.

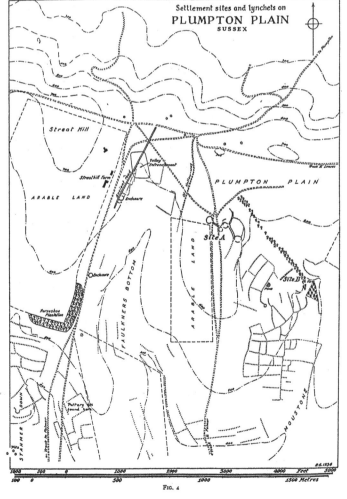

Settlement sites and lynchets on
PLUMPTON PLAIN
SUSSEX

FIG. 4

The **Plumpton bostal, TQ 360 128**, rises from the Half Moon Inn. It was an army road in the Second World War taking vehicles to the training grounds on the plateau, so it has been concreted. It looks down over a stretch of scarp which is still owned by Brighton Council, though leased to Plumpton Agricultural College. It has a good assemblage of Down pasture flowers. At the base of the scarp the rew woodland is relatively rich in species, with Bluebells and Ramsons.

On the west side of **Novington bostal, TQ 370 128**, a wood was planted in the nineteenth century called The Beeches, which has spread more widely. It is now creeping over the Novington chalkpit. The field opposite the Half Moon was known as the Brighton Laine, perhaps because it marked the beginning of the Downland route to the town.

Norman wall paintings by the same workshop as those of Clayton church were uncovered fifty years ago in **Plumpton's lovely church, TQ 356 135**. Made five hundred years before Michelangelo painted the Sistine Chapel, and by the same technique, they include a picture of Christ enthroned in Paradise amongst flowers.

Footnotes

1   'Tranquil Areas of the South Downs' for the Sussex Downs Conservation Board, by The ASH Consulting Group (March 1997).

2   *Downland Pathways* — A. Hadrian Allcroft (Methuen, 1924), page 111.

3   'Plumpton Plain, East Sussex' — David McOmish, Cathy Tuck and others. Archaeological Investigation Report Series A1/08/2004. (English Heritage, 2004) ISSN 1478-7008

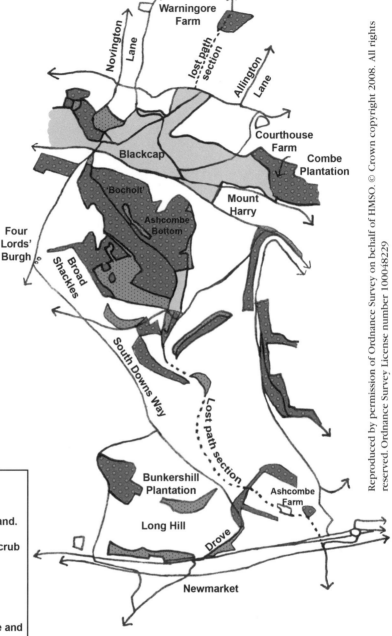

Warningore
Farm

Novington Lane

lost path section

Allington Lane

Courthouse
Farm

Combe
Plantation

Blackcap

'Bocholt'

Mount
Harry

Ashcombe
Bottom

Four
Lords'
Burgh

Broad Shackles

South Downs Way

Lost path section

Bunkershill
Plantation

Ashcombe
Farm

Long Hill

Drove

Newmarket

Statutory Access Land.
Most is old Down
pasture but some scrub
and woodland is
included.

Other Down pasture and
associated scrub.

Woodland.

←——→

Roads, paths and
railways.

Blackcap, Mount Harry
and Ashcombe

13: BLACKCAP, MOUNT HARRY AND ASHCOMBE

THIS landscape is centred on the 2.5 mile long Ashcombe valley rising from Ashcombe Farm, just off the A27, to the twin peaks of Blackcap and Mount Harry. It is tranquil and remote once you've walked north behind Long Hill, which acts as a wall blocking the blare of road noise.

Though this valley of Ashcombe was encircled by a string of round barrows on its surrounding high places it is itself, in its northern upper reaches, remarkably free of visible traces of an ancient human presence. Perhaps this is because it always remained under woodland cover, as it does today. The continuity of that woodland cover may — or may not — have been broken in the 19th century. It's a bit of a mystery. Perhaps its wildwood character was the reason why Mount Harry became a pagan shrine in the Saxon Dark Age? …Ashcombe provokes many questions.

No village is attached to this landscape, though it was divided amongst four Domesday manors that remain just as farms today — Warningore and Allington, to the north, Hamsey, by the River Ouse, and Ashcombe, to the south.

Long Hill, TQ 376 093.
An **ancient terrace way,**[1] TQ 381 092 — now a public footpath — rises from the A27 opposite Newmarket to the top of Long Hill above Ashcombe Farm. It forms a fine corridor of ancient turf, though now somewhat undergrazed (September '07). On a fine June evening we found Mullein Wave moth, *Scopula marginepunctata* and Large White Plume Moth, *Pterophorus pentadactyla*, like two little white ghosts amongst the luminous grass and herbs. There was Pyramidal Orchis, Crested Hair-grass, Hairy Rock-cress, *Arabis hirsuta*, Milkwort and Sussex Rampion. Sadly, Heath Snail, present ten years ago, is now extinct there.

The **south face of Long Hill, TQ 375 092**, is not rich in old Down pasture herbs, but is still flowery in parts. The **top of Long Hill, TQ 378 094**, was tilled ground till recently, and in 2004 I re-found the rare arable weed Fine-leaved Fumitory, *Fumaria parviflora*, there. This little flower had not been seen in Sussex since 1996. The field is now back in permanent pasture and the flower is gone, but that is of no great concern, for the seed can lie dormant for many years.

The **north face of Long Hill, TQ 377 095**, has a delightful flowery Down pasture. Standing there in peace after climbing from the din of the A27 corridor is happiness enough, but the slope has many treats to enjoy: Fragrant, Pyramidal and Spotted Orchids, Cowslips, Chalk and Common Milkworts, Heath Speedwell, Betony, Devil's-bit, Lesser Scabious, Rockrose, Ox-eye Daisy and Rampion flower. Gorgeous.

Ashcombe Farm, TQ 385 095, is beautifully folded in the shelter of 18th century plantations. It has some lovely old barns, cottages and flint walls. Its handsome Georgian manor house is, alas, no longer owned by the University of Sussex.

Bunkershill Plantation. TQ 372 097.

THIS wood, alongside the South Downs Way, is a place of contradictions. Though perhaps 230 years old (planted after the British victory at Bunkers Hill in the American revolutionary war) it has scarcely acquired any of the plants of ancient woodland, such as Bluebell. It exemplifies the limitations of the argument that ancient Down pasture is not worth saving, because diverse woodland can be developed in its place. We'd have to wait a long time. Yet it is a place of profound peace and dignity.

At its heart there is a huge pollard beech, three of my arm-spans in girth, which rises majestically skywards, like a high roof, and commands a temple-like open space below. And there are other good old Beech nearby, at the base of slope. The centre of the wood has much Hazel, whilst around the edges Sycamore dominates. I found the rusting fin of an exploded bomb there, yet nowadays Buzzards call overhead and Squirrels play as though they own the place.

Ashcombe Bottom. TQ 37 11.

ASHCOMBE Bottom is now a place of Brackeny thorn thickets and scrub-grown Oaks, of tall Ash and nut-laden woods of Hazel, and of tangling Bryony skeins, Rosebay Willowherb, berry-laden Spindle and Honeysuckle. It is a wild place. Till recently you could still hear Nightingale

in May-time. You may see Muntjac deer at dawn, and in winter you may get lucky and see Hen Harrier or Long-eared Owl.

In early May, after sunrise, I walked up Warningore bostal to Blackcap, and over into Ashcombe Bottom. I crept through the woods doing my best Indian tracker imitation. The bracken fronds were only just beginning to unfurl, so the walking was easy, and everywhere the leaves were the freshest new-growth greens. Chiff Chaff and Chaffinch were belting out their songs, with Great Tit and Blue Tit harmonies. There was Whitethroat jangling on the thicket edges, lovely Blackbird music, and raucous Jay and Pheasant. And…there it was…the soft cat-purring of Turtle Dove down-slope. In the next hour or so I heard them often in the background. I heard no Cuckoo, though they've often been there, but Blackcap showed itself, Willow Warbler sang, and the drilling of Great-spotted Woodpecker echoed. In a tangle of clematis I spotted a Long-tailed Tit's nest, and retreated hastily before I disturbed the parents. A Sparrow-hawk shot through. I nearly stepped on a wandering Glow-worm larva.

The western valley side has the older woodland and here you can find patches of Bluebell, with Early Purple Orchis, Barren Strawberry and Primrose, though the flowers of the woodland floor are not abundant. You could find the rare Thimble Morel, or Ribbed Stalk-cup fungi, *Helvella acetabulum*, near the old thorn. There are sometimes big crinkled dinner plates of Bleach Cup fungus — all cinnamon, burnt sienna and umber on the inside, like studies in tints of brown.

In the hot stillness of a July day there are White Admiral butterflies, *Limenitis camilla*, on the rides of the western plateau woods, and its commoner cousins — Red Admiral, Peacock and Comma — will certainly be there.

Beech is now scarcely found, though it must have been dominant in Saxon times, for Ashcombe Wood's old name was 'Bocholt' or 'Boxholt'. *'Boc'* was Saxon for Beech.

That names usage probably died in late Victorian times, but it is not clear whether the last fragments of the ancient valley wood finally disappeared then, or if there is a thread of continuity with the present wood. The Victorian map evidence is ambivalent, showing what may have been Hazel coppice surviving along the valley bottom — where it can presently still be found. And there are several tall Ash trees which stand close together on the parish boundary in the upper valley. You don't notice their affinity at first, but then you do a double-take and look again…They are not separate trees, but linked in a part-circle by their roots. They are the outgrowths of a truly gigantic old coppice stool that must have marked this boundary for centuries. There, at least, is some ancient woody continuity.

The valley bottom soils are deep, like woodland soils, and Dormice are present in the woods. Those golden-haired, black-eyed little beauties usually depend upon nut and berry-rich woods, so that argues for continuity of woodland. There are no open growing veteran trees above ground (despite that Ash stool's ancient roots) so we cannot expect to find old forest epiphytic lichen and mosses, which depend upon such veterans, to give us clues. Perhaps the mycorrhizal fungal community — the Knights and Amanitas, Brittlegills, Milkcaps and Webcaps — would provide the most convincing evidence of woodland continuity. We will have to see.[2]

The Bocholt is said to have acted as cover for Simon De Montfort's troops waiting to commence the Battle of Lewes in 1264, and later to have been a place of attempted refuge from the slaughter.

Whether or not the Bocholt survived, Ashcombe was always a bushy place, and scrub spread widely during the agricultural depression a century ago. In the last half century there were attempts to cultivate the tractor-accessible parts, but they were not vigorously pursued. Such desultory activity and inactivity has left us with a mosaic of old and young scrub and woodland, ancient chalk grassland fragments and areas of recovering chalk grassland.

The best surviving chalk grassland is strung out along the eastern valleyside, especially at its southern end, where part of it is designated as statutory Access Land. The older fragments, for instance, the **bridle path crossroads slope, TQ 377 112**, are dominated by a soft mat of Rockrose, with dustings of Cowslip in spring and Devil's-bit in late summer. The **gentle slope opposite, TQ 372 113**, descending from Broad Shackles, is recovering beautifully from an episode of ploughing before the National Trust took over. It has much Basil, and Autumn Ladies Tresses orchis and Devil's-bit are present. The Rockrose there has fairy rings of a large golden-tawny Web-cap fungus, *Cortinarius*, in autumn.

Around 1870 a primeval cavern — 10 foot across[3] — broke open in Ashcombe's hillside, which was found to contain two urns, one wheel-thrown and the other hand-moulded.

Blackcap and Mount Harry.

THE ridgeway that connects these two peaks is unfenced and open, as the old Downs were, and under the National Trust's ownership the Down pasture is recovering from past damage. Cattle and sheep wander freely in their aimless-seeming ways. The scarp top is remarkable in still retaining some rich ancient grassland fragments, especially where the slope begins to tip northwards. You could find Frog or Bee Orchids and there are tiny fragments of heathy grassland. Ling Heather was certainly there a few years ago. In autumn the Waxcap fungal flora can

be spectacularly colourful. We counted 21 old meadow species, and there must be many more.

You are on the top of the world here, and the view encompasses Ashdown northwards, Mount Caburn, Windover Hill (home of the Long Man), Firle Beacon, Seaford Head, Newhaven's Rushy Hill, Kingston Hill, Hollingbury Castle, and — sadly — Brighton's high-rise towers. We will scarce-ever uninterruptedly be allowed to enjoy nature on these high places near that city. There will always be a high-rise intruder 'peeping round the bedroom door'.

Mount Harry's name probably indicates that it was used as a pagan shrine, or *bearg*, in early Saxon times, like the Harrow Hills in West Sussex and Middlesex, though the name was first recorded only in 1610. On Blackcap, next to the top of the Warningore Bostal, are a cluster of 12 smallish round barrows, each one with a 'pillage dimple' in the top, but otherwise well-preserved.

Crows caw, Jackdaws squark, clouds pass, peace still reigns in this old-fashioned place.

Warningore Bostal. TQ 375 127.

THIS ancient swine pasture drove 'takes the biscuit' for almost mountainous drama. At one point it cuts 20 feet deep into the slope and its sheer sides cut you off from the surrounding views. At its base it pans out, delta-like, into at least five braids, each mossy and colourful with flowers. It took Falmer's swine herds north to Chailey, East Grinstead and Horsted Keynes.

In autumn the Whitebeam makes fat berries — all orange and scarlet — and the thorn is laden with red haws on its sunny, southern side. There are Dewberries, too, sharp and watery — good for the thirst.

The top of the Bostal is 'butterfly heaven' and we counted Brown Argus, Chalkhill, Common Blue, Small Heath, Browns, Skippers and Whites. In late summer Long-winged Conehead bush-crickets, *Conocephalus discolor*, jitter the grass

Black Cap from Mount Harry.

Footnotes

1   *Downland Pathways* — A. Hadrian Allcroft
    (Methuen, 1924), page 107.
2   'Ashcombe Bottom: The Study of a
    Downland Combe' — Glen Redman (the
    National Trust warden). Landscape Studies
    Degree Dissertation (1995)
3   *Sussex Archaeological Collections*, Vol. 22
    (1870), pages 192-4.

around your picnic spot. The place is alive, at that time, with hover flies — the little Pinocchio-nosed *Rhingia* flies, with their red bottoms, the yellow-and-black-pin-striped *Helophilus* flies, and Drone-flies, *Eristalis*. You can watch the males doing their courtship display, hovering perfectly still an inch above the nectaring females. Better than break dancing!

Much of the scarp slope between Blackcap and Mount Harry is terribly invaded by scrub, and the lower slope pastures are separated from the crest by large thickets, making access both along and up the slope difficult — sometimes impossible. Few people use the lower slopes. At least till recently, there has been a puzzling contrast between the dynamism with which the National Trust have tackled scrub invasion at the Devil's Dyke and their occasional and small-scale efforts here. These lower grasslands are very under-grazed, too, in contrast to the plateau. For all the Trust's worthy efforts, these scarp slope Down pastures remain at high risk.

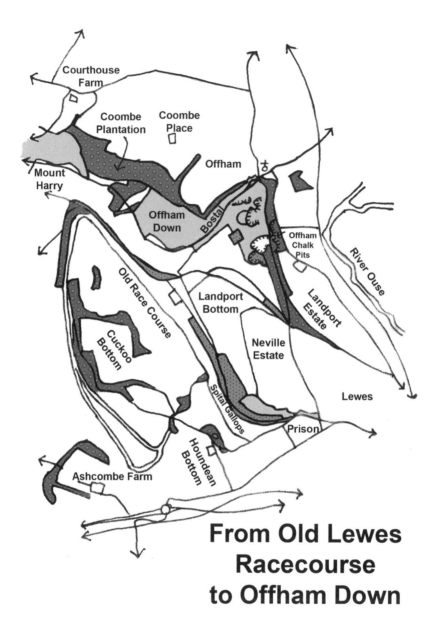

From Old Lewes Racecourse to Offham Down

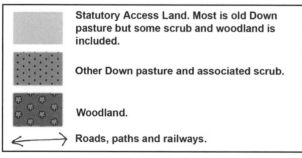

	Statutory Access Land. Most is old Down pasture but some scrub and woodland is included.
	Other Down pasture and associated scrub.
	Woodland.
← →	Roads, paths and railways.

14: OLD LEWES RACECOURSE, THE CHALK PITS, AND OFFHAM DOWN

A BATTLE took place over this landscape that challenged the power of the feudal monarchy and gave birth to the first Parliament. The Battle of Lewes, in 1264, saw the first major involvement of urban forces — the levies of the City of London — in the bloody politics of feudalism. After the defeat of the king the popular forces gained strength and squeezed the power not just of the monarchy but of the big barons as well. Scattered across this landscape and on the edge of Lewes are the burial pits of fallen soldiers. Many were thought to have been buried under barrows on Mount Harry and one soldier's grave was found below the scarp near Mount Harry House.

A modern battle took place in 1997, when 250 people from Lewes, Brighton and all around took part in the 'un-ploughing' of the damaged SSSI chalk grassland on Offham Down in a critical dispute for nature conservation.

Though that battle was won, most of the old wildlife of this landscape has been lost, and much of what remains is disappearing before our eyes.

There is something truly tragic about the fate of the Lewes Downs.

Old Lewes Racecourse. TQ 39 11.

THE old racecourse — preserved as a training gallops after its closure in 1964 — runs in a giant loop from Lewes Prison up the Spital ridge almost to the scarp, then runs south along the next ridge, above Ashcombe. It embraced giant Down pastures covering Cuckoo Bottom and Offham Down, and most of Houndean and Landport Bottoms. Now, well over 90% of its original wildlife has gone.

The **Spital gallops, TQ 398 103**, have the last significant fragments of these ancient steppe grasslands on the racecourse landscape. By ten years ago they were in a wretched state. Most of the grass was rank, and scrub was invading. Only along the worn tracksides and on one of the barrows did a significant old Down pasture flora survive. One of the Bronze Age barrows still had the rare Bastard Toadflax, with Horseshoe Vetch, the lichen *Cladonia rangiformis*, Autumn Gentian and Thyme, and the tracksides had a Sheep's Fescue turf, with Sussex Rampion, Salad Burnet and Thyme.

Now — try as I have — I cannot find the three extant barrows at all, so sunk are they under a mess of bramble and scrub.

And the scrub has spread to such an extent that large thickets are beginning to form. Only on the much-enlarged mown gallops do significant areas of good quality chalk grassland survive, and they are vulnerable to 'improvement'.

I am told that some years ago Lewes District Council turned down an application for the fencing of this site for the introduction of ESA grazing. If they did, then most of the blame lies with them for this mess.

To be sure, if all we want is fresh air and somewhere to walk our dog then we shouldn't mourn. On my last visit there were Swallows hunting low, and high-stacked clouds and gorgeous views of the Vale of the Brooks, of Malling Downs and of the course of the Ouse.

Lewes Council bought 110 adjacent acres of ex-arable in **Landport Bottom, TQ 397 110**, and are to be praised for that. It was done principally to stop soil erosion from irresponsible winter ploughing. These acres do not compensate for what is being lost, however. On this property, **at Landport Fork, TQ, 401 110, there are three fine barrows.** The most westerly

one looks like a slightly mummified flying saucer out of some 'fifties comic! I'd rate it as the most evocative and sculptural of all the ancient barrows on the Brighton Downs. It's also amongst the biggest surviving. At 31 paces across it's not as wide as the Tegdown platform barrow (45 paces), and at 3ft high it's not as tall as Thundersbarrow (6.5 ft) or one of the Kingston Hill barrows (6 ft) — but who cares, for you can feel the millennia drop away as you gaze at it.

The barrows are a mess, though. They are un-mown and un-grazed and are sunk in rank grass. One of them is planted up with some kind of honeysuckle. One of the delights of the barrows and camps of the Downs is the way that they often preserve the highest quality ancient turf, spangled with tiny herbs. Not here, though…

To the west of the old racecourse buildings lies **Cuckoo Bottom, TQ 388 107** — a mile long by half a mile wide. It is now a bleak arable wasteland, as bad as anything in East Anglia. There are patches of scrub on the steep places, but they are species-poor and growing over to poor quality woodland. In **Houndean Bottom,**

The 'Offham Alps': behind the Chalk Pit Inn. The turf in the foreground is very flowery.

TQ 396 099, the sole, tiny patch of chalk grassland in this whole valley is in the final throes of being over-whelmed by scrub. A large notice on the gallops nearby warns you not to stray: "Danger. Racehorses in training. Risk of fatal injury. Private gallops. Please Keep Off".

As some small compensation I came across a Crab Apple tree on my last visit. Its clustered yellow fruit were gathering a sunset-orange bloom on their outer branches. Nature still offers us its beauty even as we destroy it.

There is no better argument than the fate of this place for the democratic public ownership of our Downs.

By contrast, on the Council-owned Brighton Racecourse Downs, there are no prohibiting notices, despite the presence of racehorses in training, and the old arable fields have long been turned over to nature conservation and public enjoyment.

The Offham Chalk Pits. TQ 400 116.

THERE is a chain of disused chalk pits along the Ouse river cliff and around the spur of Offham Hill. Most of the chalk pits are pre-industrial in origin and long-grassed over by a fine Sheep's Fescue sward. The pit which contains the Chalk Pit Inn, was, by contrast, active in the first third of the nineteenth century. The Offham Road, outside the Inn, bridges a steep chute which took chalk from the Pit down to barges moored on the Chalkpit Cut.

That late Georgian pit is very different in character to the older quarries. It is alpine in its cragginess. The chatter of Jackdaws echoes, and sun lights up parts of its shady glooms.

The older pits are far softer, melding into the adjacent Downland at their northern end, whose rich Down pasture wildlife they acquired. They were always grazed as part of those Down pastures. Twenty years ago there was Musk Orchis. Perhaps it is still there. Bee, Pyramidal and Spotted Orchids are still certainly there, though, with Viper's Bugloss, Devil's-bit and Small-flowered Sweet-briar. Much of the turf is very mossy and the moss *Pleurochaete squarrosa* and the scarce lichen *Cladonia pocillum* are probably still there.

The southern-most of these older quarries, TQ 400 113, south of the Chalk Pit Inn pit, may be one of the oldest, for it has the indicator species Bastard Toadflax, Horseshoe Vetch and Rockrose, and Chalkhill Blue, Brown Argus and Common Blue butterflies. The thin open sward enables Blue Fleabane, *Erigeron Acer*, Autumn Gentian, and Wall Brown butterfly to thrive.

Enjoy it now, though, for, year on year, a sea of Cotoneaster, Privet, Sycamore, Ash, and other scrub species takes over more of the ground. Already the whole of the river cliffs and the brow of Offham Hill, which were open turf till 80 years ago, have grown over into dank woodland. When this process finishes the kids on mountain bikes, the picnickers, the courting couples and all those who like flowers, sun and peace will have nowhere to go.

Yet, just over the fence to the south, sheep graze intensively on the Council's dull land. As so often, the medicine is given where it is not urgently needed and the sick go un-succoured.

There is half of a **Neolithic causewayed camp, TQ 398 117**, on the spur of Offham Hill, (though there is no sign of it above ground now). The chalk pit dug away the rest. There are also three surviving barrows between the camp and the covered reservoir, but they are becoming difficult to see under tangled vegetation. The covered reservoir, like so many, had a good Down pasture flora with Rockrose, Cistus Forester moth, and old anthills, when I last looked a decade ago.

Landport Farm, TQ 403 113, down by the brooks, ran the grazing of the racecourse Downs till 1928, when the last big farming tenant sold up. The farm buildings, though, are still very attractive, and have been sympathetically converted. The farmhouse is now council flats.

The greenway at the base of the river cliff is extravagantly picturesque. The romantic nineteenth century watercolorists would have loved it. Cattle-grazed reedy brookland is embraced by wooded Downland in a curved sweep from Offham church spire to Landport Farm, whilst the Lewes church of St John's Sub Castro guards its southern end.

The woods of the Landport river cliff are home to thousands of toads. Every spring the Offham Road has to be fenced on the up slope side to stop the migrating Toads hopping to their doom under motorists wheels on their journey to breed in the Pells brooks.

Offham Combe and Down.
TQ 392 117.

THIS place is breathtakingly beautiful and peaceful. It has not changed that much in the 45 years since I first walked there as a child with my family. It would have changed drastically, though, if people had not taken bold action a decade ago, in 1997. It was a close-run thing.

Though it is part of an SSSI the farmer wished to plough much of the tractor-accessible ground to grow Flax, which was then attracting huge EU subsidies even on such protected sites. English Nature, as usual, failed to use their powers and the farmer commenced ploughing. Nature conservationists attempted to block the plough, but the farmer returned at night. The struggle then escalated and

conservationists demonstrated, set up camp on the land and started to organize its 'unploughing' — turning over and re-fitting the sods. Local people (for whom this was 'Happy Valley') turned out in force. Luckily the battle took place during the general election, so the Conservatives and Labour competed to show their conservation mettle. We won that time.

The most attractive approach is via the peculiar two-track bostal which rises up the valleyside from Offham. The bostal is flowery (with Harebells and orchids) and mossy (with *Neckera crispa*). Orange-tailed Clearwing moth and Chalkhill Blues live there.

Up this bostal — and up the spur across from it, which Coombe Plantation now partly covers — the London troops under Simon De Montfort must have sweated in the dawn of the day of the Battle of Lewes, after a hard march from Fletching. They formed the left flank of the rebel army. Poorly armed and trained they were swept away back down the scarp by the royalist cavalry. Those hot-heads over-reached themselves, though, and De Montfort's other troops battled down into Lewes and victory.

The valleysides are good in all seasons. In spring they have Milkwort, Cowslip and Lesser Dandelion, *Taraxacum erythrospermum*. At midsummer there are Glow-worms and Bastard Toadflax. In high summer there is Sussex Rampion and, later, sheets of Devil's-bit. On the higher land,

Offham Down 1987 with its top part-ploughed.

Offham Down 2007 with its Downland turf restored.

where the soils are more acidic, there may still be Heath Dog-violet, *Viola canina*, and there are nice mosses like *Bryum rubens* and *Pleurochaete squarrosa*. In autumn the old meadow fungi are superb. We counted 12 Waxcaps, two Earthtongues, two Fairy Clubs and a Pink Gill in one visit.

There is an evocative group of 10 pagan Saxon barrows on the short turfed, flatter ground of the spur, but the barrows further uphill are either destroyed or sunk in tangled scrub.

Some other things are lost for good. The purple heather on the crown of Offham Hill gained it the nickname 'Little Scotland' in Victorian times. It is secondary woodland, now.

Coombe Plantation. TQ 386 122.

THIS wood, perhaps 250 years old, has a cool and lofty interior of tall Ash, Sycamore, surviving Beech and occasional Horse Chestnut. The biggest trees are along the lower boundary, though many were smashed in the '87 and '92 gales. In places, particularly at its eastern end, the fallen gale-thrown trunks lie as thickly as the slain soldiers of de Montfort must once have lain. The vernal flowers are best along the line of the original rew at the base of slope. Elsewhere things like Bluebell are scarce, though there are lovely swarms of Early Purple Orchis upslope. Fly Honeysuckle, a relict species of the Downland wildwood, occurs at one spot on an upslope path. In the shadier parts, such as along the bostal, there are profuse growths of Hart's Tongue Fern. The names of the fungi on the rotting Beech carcases have a vaguely culinary poetry: *Green Stain, Bitter Bracket, Turkey Tail, Liver-brown Polypore, Tripe Fungus, Peeling Oysterling, Lemon Disc, Beech Jelly Disc, Jelly Rot, Beech Wood-wart, Porcelain Fungus and Dryad's Saddle.* Collared Earthstar is here amongst the leaf litter. In spring there are warblers and tits all in song.

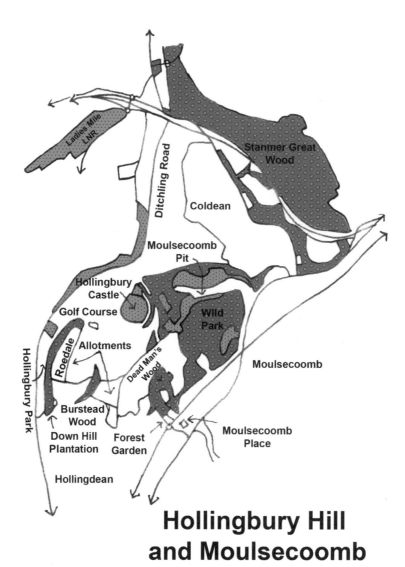

Hollingbury Hill and Moulsecoomb Wild Park

Labels within map:
- Ladies Mile LNR
- Stanmer Great Wood
- Ditchling Road
- Coldean
- Moulsecoomb Pit
- Hollingbury Castle
- Golf Course
- Wild Park
- Roedale
- Allotments
- Dead Man's Wood
- Moulsecoomb
- Hollingbury Park
- Burstead Wood
- Down Hill Plantation
- Forest Garden
- Moulsecoomb Place
- Hollingdean

Legend:
- Statutory Access Land. Most is old Down pasture but some scrub and woodland is included.
- Other Down pasture and associated scrub.
- Woodland.
- Roads, paths and railways.

15 : HOLLINGBURY HILL
AND THE MOULSECOOMB
WILD PARK

HOLLINGBURY Hill is by far the tallest hill within the skirts of Brighton. It stands proud of the lesser hills around it. It is an island of open Down country rising above a sea of built development. From its height we can scan westwards across the Bay of Sussex to the Isle of Wight, to Selsey, Worthing and Cissbury. From the Downs to the east the built development that almost encircles it is invisible and it still looks just like another landmark hill of the open Downs, topped by its ancient hillfort.

Moulsecoomb Pit — the core of the Wild Park — drops steeply from the east side of the hillfort. It was famous 150 years ago for its profusion of Down pasture butterflies and moths. It clings still to some of that richness, but it cannot cling much longer without our rescue, for scrub and woodland has a stranglehold that tightens ever harder.

Hollingbury Castle — The Hillfort.
TQ 322 078.

THEY chose this site well, those ancient people, but the Iron Age folk who built the square hillfort's rampart and ditch some 5 or 600 years before Jesus were not the first to make this place special. Nearly a millennia earlier the people of the Bronze

Age had made this place sacred with the mounding of four round barrows. They still stand amidst rough grass, Bramble and Gorse, though all have been robbed of their grave goods.

Not long ago a group of us stood on the ramparts and barrows as the setting sun flamed up the western sky all orange, crimson and purple. It set where the Bay of Sussex met the horizon. To the east, as we turned, the moon rose, huge and harvest yellow against a blue-grey gathering darkness. This moon was different, though, for out of its top a great bite had been taken. We watched, and peered through telescope and binoculars as she rose slowly and the bite receded.

The ancient people will have been attuned to many more such astral events as that eclipse. The fort itself may be aligned through its eastern and western gateways with a solstice dawn rising in the gap between Caburn and Firle Beacon, to the east. It may be, too, that the later Roman occupiers built a temple in these precincts, for potsherds have been found from those times.

Certainly the fort was lived in, for five round houses have been excavated within it, near its southern rampart, in that small part of the fort that has been investigated. Certainly it was defensible, for the fortifications were sturdy, with six feet deep ditches and a timber boxed palisade up to 9 feet high above. The post holes of the strong eastern gateway can be seen, marked by concrete filled iron cylinders. Hollingbury Castle was a place of much prestige and military capacity.

It is still a wild place. The thickets of Gorse shine yellow in spring. Linnets love it. You can sometimes see good flocks of them there. Stonechat is a familiar bird, too, and the rarer Whinchat has been seen. The soil within and around the camp has a layer of superficial acidity, with Sorrel, Bent-grass and Tormentil. Till recent years Ling Heather clung on just north of the fort's ramparts, and within them Waxcap fungi seem to thrive. One November morning a foray there found eight species and a Fairy Club. Children raced around, their sharp eyes spotting the glistening golden caps within the tangle of grass and low Bramble.

For me, late April is the finest time, for then you may see a glorious show of Early Purple Orchids both within the fort and in the scrubland and golf course edges to its east. That is a magnificent sight. Do not pick them. Leave them for others to enjoy.

The Ditchling Road ridge. TQ 323 087.

THERE is a causeway of open Downland between Hollingbury Castle and the A27 bypass. It is an extension of the archaeological landscape of the hilltop. The eastern slope still shows the lynchets of a prehistoric field system, best seen from Coldean.

The widening of this section of the Ditchling Road in 1921 revealed three Bronze Age burials, one of which lay under a platform barrow, as well as an Iron Age or Romano-British oven. In 1950 a Bronze Age bowl barrow on the hillside to the east was excavated, revealing three burials, urns and flintwork.

Excavations[1] in the path of the coming bypass, just north of Coldean, revealed a Bronze Age farming settlement that may have lasted for six hundred years, with round houses and fire pits and evidence of cattle herding and woodland management. No graves were found, so maybe the Ditchling Road ridge, Stanmer Great Wood and Pudding Bag Wood, where barrows survive, was where they took their dead.

Moulsecoomb Wild Park. TQ 327 080.

MOULSECOOMB Wild Park is in a scandalous mess. Visit it now, for its special attractions will soon be gone, at this rate.

Back in the 1850s Moulsecoomb Pit, then known as Hollingbury Coombe, was one of the most famous of Sussex sites for lepidopterists (butterfly and moth experts). "Collectors[2] visited from far and wide. The main attractions included vast numbers of Dark Green Fritillary and the presence of Forester moths, whilst Silver Spotted Skipper used to fly 'in the utmost profusion'."

In 1925, when the Wild Park was opened, it was still a fine area of ancient grassland with some old scrub, ideal for children's free play. In the last 80 years, however, its slopes have been continuously neglected and the Park now has a wooded aspect, the old grassland reduced to

Moulsecoomb Wild Park: This is the 'combe' that Moulsecoomb is named after.

shrinking glades and mown strips. When I planned to take a party of children from Moulsecoomb Primary School to the slopes opposite their school in July 2007 I found access blocked by bramble and bushes and had to hack an entrance way through before it was fit for their visit. Yet the Park was created for such children.

For all that, the wildlife of the old pasture fragments has shown a remarkable resilience. You may still see Glow-worms on the slopes of the Pit at midsummer. On the north slope of the Pit you may (just) see Adonis, Chalkhill and Common Blues and Brown Argus, and global warming has seen the remarkable return of the Silver-spotted Skipper. In spring you may see the gorgeous Green Hairstreak and Orange-tip butterflies or find the wacky Small Bloody-nosed Beetle.

Children could learn so much about nature and have such fun there, with the guidance of teachers and properly resourced rangers and other wildlifers. One spring I watched two Gold-fringed Osmia bees, *Osmia aurulenta*, making their nests in old snail shells. They'd both provisioned their nurseries and were finishing off their work by sealing the shell entrances. One was cementing a door across using tiny beetle wing cases it had found. Another was using a sort of green 'spinach-concrete' to make its seal.

The flowers are still lovely, and you can find orchids and Harebells, sheets of Rockrose, Sussex Rampion, Devil's-bit and Carline Thistle. Great Blackberries, too!

The parts of the scrub that have not succeeded to Sycamore woodland are rich in diversity, with old Gorse and Wayfaring Tree, which has a rare colony of the Orange-tailed Clearwing moth.

Most of the southern part of the Wild Park has now grown over into woodland and much of this is way beyond a return to its old condition, Children and their parents have made good trail bike rides, tree swings and woodland slides. Very

gradually more plants and animals are colonizing. Penny-bun Bolete, *Boletus edulis*, has appeared, as well as Collared Earthstar, Stinkhorn, and Shaggy Inkcap, *Coprinus comatus*, fungi.

There is a welcome café in the Wild Park combe, which serves sausage sandwiches, tea and cold drinks, and you can read the newspaper there or bask in the sun on their terrace.

Dead Man's Wood and the Moulsecoomb Forest Garden. TQ 324 071.

WALK under the railway bridge next to Moulsecoomb Station. From the noise and busy-ness of the Lewes Road you will enter another world. All around you will be green trees and birdsong. In front of you, encircling Queensdown Special School, the whole combe is filled with woodland. That is **Dead Man's Wood**.

One afternoon one of the friends of the wood was walking his dog there when he came across a woman sitting on a log, her head in her hands. Fearing she was in distress, he quietly approached and asked her if she was alright. "I'm OK, thanks," she said. "I'm a teacher at Queensdown School down there…I'm just taking some 'time out'"…That's what these woods do…make a refuge so close to our everyday lives, but so separate, too.

If you turn sharp left after walking under the railway bridge you will after a few yards come to the entrance to the **Moulsecoomb Forest Garden**. What a grand place this is! If you walk past you'll often see groups of children there helping out and having fun. Don't just walk past, though. They often have open days, so you can say 'hallo' and have a cup of tea, if one is going. The Garden offers an open house to all local people and to many troubled local children, who find a space where they are welcomed and not judged and can relax and maybe learn, too. It's made up of a group of cooperatively run allotments.

The gardeners use permacultural principles, and their tapestry of bushes, trees, flowers and vegetables tumbles down the hillside from Dead Man's Wood.

One spring recently we found three species of Morel fungi in the Wood and on the allotments, including the rarely appearing Thimblecap, (but not the edible Morel, so don't expect to find that there!) You may see Twayblade orchis and Celandine and Wild Arum. The Wood is a shady place and there is much Hart's Tongue fern and even Polypody fern. Much of the canopy is Sycamore, draped in Ivy, but there is Ash, Hawthorn and Hazel, too.

We systematically searched for bird's nests that spring, too. We found Dunnock, Blackbird and Robin's nests, and watched a pair of Carrion Crow's on their nest. Hidden deep in the Ivy round a trunk we saw a Wren's nest, with four eggs in it. In the canopy of an old thorn tree we watched a Wood Pigeon quietly incubating her white eggs. These are great things to see. They fill you with wonder and delight.

Above the Wood is a large field now managed as rough grassland, where Skylark's nest (just surviving the attentions of the many local dogs). From there you can survey the long Lewes Road valley, down to the sea. The whole history of Brighton is opened up before you, from the houses built along the strips of the medieval open fields, down in Hanover, to the Victorian Workhouse on Whitehawk Hill, now the General Hospital, and the model homes and allotments of the pre-war Moulsecoomb council estate.

Moulsecoomb Place. TQ 326 069.

THE 220 year old Moulsecoomb Place is now stranded by the Lewes Road and separated from the open Downs. It is a fine Georgian manor house, and behind it is a gem — a late medieval timber-framed cottage, which is one of the oldest secular buildings in Brighton.

Hollingbury Park and Woods. TQ 314 075.

HOLLINGBURY Park, alongside the Ditchling Road, was originally part of the Golf Course. Its Edwardian pavilion was the original (circa 1908) Clubhouse. East of the Park is the two century old **Down Hill Plantation**, now full of the rotting carcases of Beech giants toppled in the '87 gale. It is fine place, with good Fittleworth Stone walks, glades and benches. It has received the loving care of a local 'Friends' group for many years now. On my last visit I saw a black Rabbit hopping through the undergrowth. I was not hallucinating — honestly…

Roedale. TQ 315 075.

BLACK Rabbits are not the only thing to make you doubt what you see in this place, for, just to the east of Down Hill Plantation, is a tiny *Shangri-la* — a hidden valley dropping away southwards towards the sea, like a little piece of Tolkien's Shire, busy with the workings of more than 200 allotments, all growing and building and harvesting, so far and yet so near to the heart of the City. It is a magic place!

Footnotes

1 *Downland Settlement and Land-use: The Archaeology of the Brighton Bypass* — David Rudling. (English Heritage, 2002), Section 7, pages 141-201.

2 *A Revised History of the Butterflies and Moths of Sussex* — Colin R. Pratt. F.R.E.S. Compact disc published by Brighton and Hove City Council, The Booth Museum of Natural History (1999), page 23.

16: THE BEVENDEAN AND FALMER DOWNS

THE valley slopes at Bevendean, Hog Plantation and Loose Bottom are colourful fragments of the old Downscape. The hilltop paths over Falmer Hill to Newmarket Hill will take you high up above the world! Ignore the noise of the Falmer Road and the A27. Enjoy the Skylarks instead...

Back in the 'thirties folk from the new Bevendean, Moulsecoomb and Whitehawk estates wandered widely over these Downlands. Beyond the Falmer Road there were vast areas of heathy grassland and Gorse to explore. Then came the wartime 'Dig For Victory' plough-ups and the decades of post-war productivism. Now, some of this landscape is being restored and you can wander more freely than for many years.

Still-lovely Falmer village is at the centre of this Downscape. Its thatched manorial barn is one of the best buildings on the Brighton Downs.

Bevendean valleysides. TQ 33 06 and around.

A CENTURY ago 'Bevendean Down' — the dean's hot, south-facing slopes — was famous amongst butterfly hunters. These slopes are still lovely, due to the care of local people in cooperation with the tenant farmer and the Council rangers.

Hogtrough Bottom, TQ 340 070, is the very best. There is a mixture of taller grassland, short Sheep's Fescue turf, and scrub. On the shorter turf you may find large swarms of Autumn Ladies Tresses orchis, and flutterings of Chalkhill Blue butterflies. There are lots of scarce species — Bastard Toadflax, Waxcap and Web-cap fungi, Four-spot Orb-weaver and Purse-web spiders — but the tapestry of summer colours is the main delight — purple Knapweed and Felwort, blue Scabious, yellow Hawkbit and Rockrose.

The grasslands and thickets of Hogtrough Bottom continue westwards above **Heath Hill Avenue, TQ 335 066.** You may find Apple wildings and odd garden species in places close to Adonis Blue and Sussex Rampion. It's a great place for Lizards and birdsong.

Far up the dean, beyond the Primary School, a wood tumbles down the slope between Norwich Drive and Heath Hill Avenue. Within the wood is a remarkable **secret glade, TQ 342 066**, that the Victorians called **Bevendean Bank**. Local conservationists guard its precious turf, mowing and pushing back the ever-encroaching wood. There are lots of old grassland flowers and butterflies. It has a large population of Purse-web spider. Once I found a dozen of the tops of their silken webs — like the fingers of little gloves — swiped off by the passing mower. It would not take them long to darn them up again, I expect. Those spiders must understand the dilemma…either we mow and they receive some collateral damage, or we don't mow and their homes are lost in a tangle of woodland!

Both the bank and Hogtrough Bottom had populations of the rare Heath Snail till recently. They're extinct now, probably through a lack of the cattle grazing they need.

The **south side of Bevendean Valley** is a place of horse paddocks and scrub thickets, old allotment sites and cattle grazing. At the eastern end **Upper Bevendean Farm, TQ 350 062**, looks down from the higher slope. From early beginnings as an outlier of the old Bevendean Manor, which nestled in the valley where the Primary School now is, it has become the only farm in the valley.

As its name implies **Heath Hill, 342 060**, was once a place of Heather and Gorse. On its western side at the base of slope against The Hyde Industrial Estate a sliver of old Down pasture survives, TQ 340 060, where you may find Great Green Bush-cricket in high summer.

On Race Hill the paddocks around the **Southdown Riding Stables, TQ 335 058**, receive no agro-chemicals and have gathered a rich wildlife in the past half century, though parts are heavily over-grazed. It's all down to horse dung! Swallows and Swifts, Bats and Dung Beetles, Rooks and Yaffle and the troll-like Hornet Robber-fly, *Asilus crabroniformis*, all rely on the rich supply of insects attracted by the pony dung.

Hog Plantation combe TQ 342 077.

THIS combe, behind East Moulsecoomb and Falmer School, is another of those 'secret' sites used only by neighbouring residents, which deserve far wider recognition. One August afternoon four

summers ago I visited the hot, south-facing slope and scribbled in my notebook: "the whole site is absolutely dancing with Chalkhill Blues. Amazing". It doesn't happen every year, but when it does it gives us a glimpse of an abundance we have almost lost.

Though the combe was long left derelict and nibbled by the plough it may be on the edge of a renaissance. The new grazier, with the Council, has done massive scrub clearance and re-fencing and sheep have returned.

The slopes have a top fringe of Gorse and thorn and there's Scarce Forester and Yellow Shell moths, *Camptogramma bilineata bilineata*, Adonis, Silver-spotted Skipper and Marbled White butterflies. The funny Bishop's Mitre bug, *Aelia acuminata*, is there in summer. Burnet Rose was still present a few years ago.

Falmer Hill. TQ 365 076.

FROM the Hill there are great views across to Hollingbury Castle and Stanmer Park and the higher Downs beyond. The din from the A27 is dreadful.

The Hill's top remained unploughed till the last World War. It had a cluster of about ten probably Saxon barrows and a couple of round barrows. Nothing remains now except white smears of chalk and flint on the ploughed earth, where the barrows were. I've picked up a couple of struck flint flakes.

Falmer old village. TQ 354 087.

THE grouping of pond, flint cottages, church and giant thatched manorial barn is still delightful. Unlike almost all Downland ponds this one is natural, and the village is named after it. ('*Fealu mere*' = '*dark pond*'). The flint walls of the cottages have lots of sarsen and pyrites boulders included in them, for the village lies on locally rare Tertiary rocks. Other sarsens are scattered round the pond and in the farmyard, and the surrounding fields have

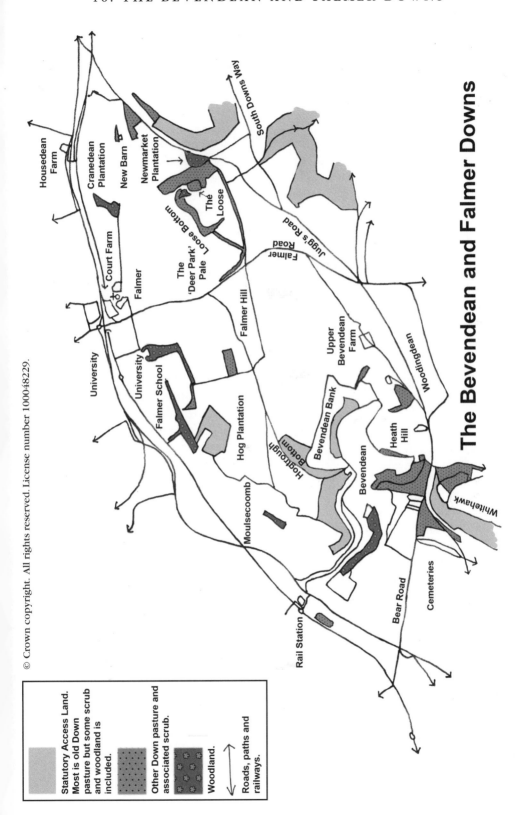

The Bevendean and Falmer Downs

Statutory Access Land. Most is old Down pasture but some scrub and woodland is included.

Other Down pasture and associated scrub.

Woodland.

Roads, paths and railways.

Newmarket Hill in the 1940s. Fred Netley (the Whitehawk tenants leader — seen here) and his mates wandered this Downland as kids. Later, most of it was destroyed by ploughing.

much sarsen debris. The flint work of the Victorian church is superb. Look closely at its careful craftsmanship.

The village was split by the widened A27, but has kept much of its character. Old barns and little paddocks survive in nooks and crannies, and the Swan Inn is now bypassed by the new road.

The thatched barn is one of the best vernacular buildings surviving on the Brighton Downs. In cultural terms it is far more worthwhile than somewhere like Stanmer House, whose future has been so publicly debated. Yet scarce anyone in Brighton has visited it, despite it being sited on a Council-owned farm, for the farmyard gate tells you to keep out of this private place. In 2006 the barn and Court Farmhouse were quietly sold by the Labour Council to the tenant farmer, who promptly sold it on to a property developer. Conversion to an entertainment centre for corporate and private functions is planned.

Only a few years ago we lobbied for the barn to be taken over by the Wildlife Trust as a countryside educational centre. Now it is privatized. Thus are the public purposes of our Council-owned Downland and the coming National Park frustrated. If Brighton folk had been able to enjoy this building they would not have let the Council behave like that.

Loose Bottom and Newmarket Hill.

L O O S E **Bottom, TQ 362 080**, is tranquil, beautiful and rich in wildlife. It is much seen from the Falmer Road, but scarcely visited. Though the heathy Down pastures of Newmarket Hill were bulldozed for corn the slopes in Loose Bottom were saved by their steepness. It takes its name from an ancient stock enclosure ('*blose*', in Saxon) whose grassy bank-and-ditch takes a serpentine course across the valleysides of its remotest combe, TQ 365 080. Another earthwork tracks alongside the Falmer Road before dropping into the head of the

Loose Bottom (don't laugh).
The bit of Falmer's Downland that survived the plough.

valley. Allcroft[1] suggested it was the edge of an old deer park. Both the 'deer park' bank and the Bottom slopes have scattered clumps of Burnet Rose.

The fragments of surviving Down pasture have been fenced back into a restored pasture block covering the same ground that was lost to the plough in the past seventy years, and they are already improving. There's Cowslip and orchis, Devil's-bit and Betony, Rampion flower and Chalk Milkwort. There's Adonis Blue and Emperor moth. Cuckoo and Green Woodpecker haunt its Gorse and thorn thickets, and Meadow Pipit and Skylark its pastures. It's a more hopeful place, now.

On the slopes of **Newmarket Hill, TQ 359 073**, an old concrete dewpond still holds water. There was a well-known barrow on the Hill's top. It's gone, now.

Newmarket Plantation. TQ 367 080.

IT lies on the South Downs Way, next to the Newmarket bostal. The wood has been made much easier for visitors after the chaos of the gales, and mown paths now circle its interior. It is still a place of big upturned rootplates, though, that Robins and Wrens love for nest sites. There's Beech, Ash and Sycamore and new plantings.

Cranedean Plantation. TQ 363 087.

ACROSS the flinty cornland to the east of Falmer lies the old Cranedean Plantation. It has some fine Beeches, particularly at its north end, though the wood is strewn with tumbled hulks from the gales 20 years ago.

The name 'Cranedean' is a corruption of *'Crane Down'*. Cranes, though, are wetland birds and would not be seen on these hills. Could it be that the name refers to Bustards, which are close relatives of Cranes, look fairly similar, and feed in a similar fashion? 'Bustard' is an old French name, whereas 'Crane' is a Saxon name, so shepherds and ploughmen may have used the latter term in medieval times. The Bustard would certainly have lived around this place.

The New Barn valley. TQ 369 087.

THIS valley is full of peace. Crows caw and cattle graze. The spur behind shelters it from the noisy A27 corridor.

New Barn was built in 1845 on the edge of ground only recently 'broken' for corn crops from the old Down pastures. It has two yards and a shepherd's room, complete with blackened fireplace, so he could attend the sheep round-the-clock during lambing.

There are several tumps that look like possible barrows at the top of the slope, TQ 371 085, south of the barn, next to the South Downs Way. The bank behind the barn has the flowers and insects of old Down pasture.

Footnotes

1   *Downland Pathways* — A. Hadrian Allcroft (Methuen, 1924), page 105.

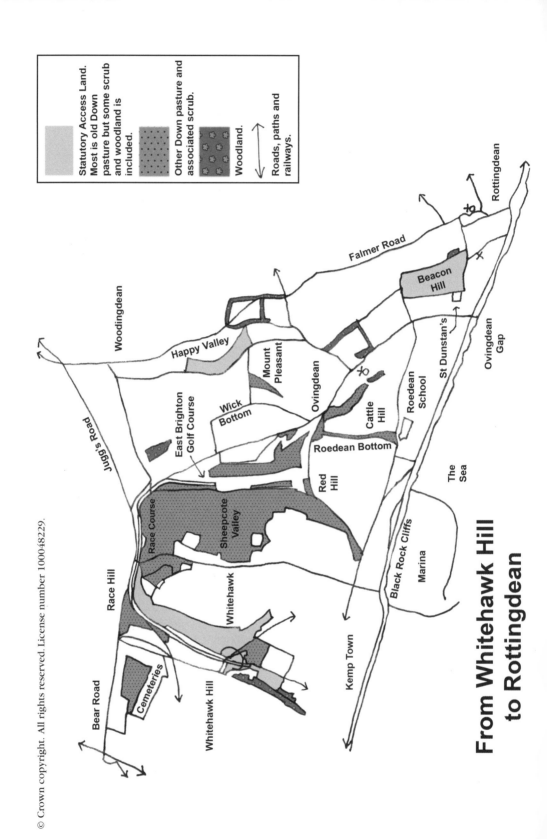

Statutory Access Land. Most is old Down pasture but some scrub and woodland is included.

Other Down pasture and associated scrub.

Woodland.

Roads, paths and railways.

Woodingdean

Happy Valley

Mount Pleasant

Ovingdean

Wick Bottom

East Brighton Golf Course

Cattle Hill

Roedean School

Roedean Bottom

Red Hill

Race Course

Sheepcote Valley

Jugg's Road

Race Hill

Whitehawk

Bear Road

Cemeteries

Whitehawk Hill

Black Rock Cliffs

Marina

Kemp Town

The Sea

St Dunstan's

Ovingdean Gap

Rottingdean

Falmer Road

Beacon Hill

From Whitehawk Hill to Rottingdean

17 : FROM WHITEHAWK HILL TO ROTTINGDEAN

So close to the heart of Brighton, yet so close to its own ancient past, to the sky, to the sea, and to nature, Whitehawk Hill is a very special place. Peaceful Sheepcote Valley, to its east, proves that we can heal the wounds to nature that we have caused. Till recently a noxious wasteland, it is now a place of Skylarks, Short-eared Owl and Bee Orchids. Beyond this racecourse landscape Ovingdean's smooth hills drop down to the chalk cliffs. Though modified by coastal engineering these cliffs are still a place to meet nature at its wildest.

The ancient character of this Downscape is challenged repeatedly by spreading suburbs, neglect, roads and egotistical giant buildings. Whether its values survive is in contention. It is up to us.

Brighton's Racecourse Landscape

ONE summer night we sat on the crown of Whitehawk Hill, just south of the Stone Age encampment. Our generator whirred and big Elephant Hawk Moths crashed into our glowing moth trap. Below us the lights of the Palace Pier and its wind-milling rides and carousels glittered and their music rose to us on the breeze.

One pearly springtime dawn we met to walk the gorsey brakes and evergreen hedges of Race Hill and Whitehawk Hill. The yellow sun strained to burst through the white mist. Linnet and Stonechat, Dunnock, Whitethroat and Blackcap filled the air with their songs and alarms, sweet, melodic, jangling and rattling. They sang as though they owned this world…and in those dewy, peaceful, days' beginnings they still do.

One midday in May I walked along the terraces at the base of Whitehawk Hill's steep slope. Horseshoe Vetch dusted the hillside yellow. A Grizzled Skipper sunbathed and Small Copper and Dingy Skipper were out, too. Little Two-coloured Osmia bees were busy. Then, up above me on the hillside I spotted a Fox. She was watching me. She yawned and scratched once or twice. She was in full view of the whole of Whitehawk's suburb laid out below her. She did not care. A thorn thicket lay close by. This was her world.

One afternoon in high summer I walked the broad shoulder of Sheepcote Valley below the spine of Red Hill. There were Larks and Meadow Pipits making their sky music. Stretching far in front of me was a glaze of blue-violet Creeping Bellflower — tall spikes clustered with hanging flowers. Above me their blueness covered the ground till it met the sky and below me they ran down to the bushey border of

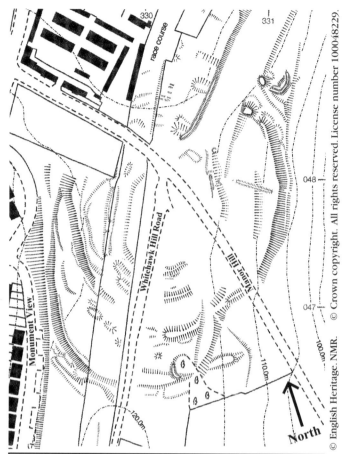

Older than Stonehenge: the surviving banks of Whitehawk's Neolithic causewayed camp.

Weather, wild things, peace, conversation, solitude, earth, growing things, sea, new thoughts, old worlds. They are all here. On our very doorsteps.

Whitehawk Hill. TQ 330 047, has Brighton's oldest building. The encampment whose faint ramparts circle the saddle between Race Hill and Whitehawk Hill was built by Neolithic people some 5000 years ago, long before Stonehenge. There is little sign of warfare here, despite the four, maybe even five, embankment lines. These ramparts, after all, had many openings — called 'causeways' — left in their circuits. They were not meant for defence. The camp's position, too, was not chosen for defence. They would, instead, have used the hilltop if that had been the builders' intent. They chose this place for its sacred qualities — perhaps because it was already a sacred place, for one of the banks incorporates what may be an earlier long barrow.

Before Manor Hill road was built in the 1930s archaeologists excavating its alignment found four skeletons and the charred remains of many more. One of them was the curled remains of a young mother and her new-born child complete with chalk pendant 'jewelry' and fossil sea-urchin 'charms'.

The 'causewayed camp' may have been a place of the dead, like the burning Ghats of Ganges side or the Towers of Silence of the Himalayas or old Persia. The people of the Neolithic may have brought that

the Valley bottom. Sky, earth and sea — all touched with luminous blue.

One autumn dusk I walked that same Sheepcote slope south from Warren Road to the flint pits on Red Hill. The view is vast. The land tips gently seawards. To the west the shadowed bulk of Whitehawk Hill rises again, and across its top the Bay of Sussex all the way to Bembridge's purple-dark cliffs on Wight. There's the sound of seagulls and road noise. The red light before darkness sheets the sky then fades. I hear the sounds of walkers' mobiles. The procession of dog walkers, like some southern summer seaside promenade, continues as darkness encloses us.

mother and her child from their tents and longhouses by the side of Brighton's long-gone river, or from a seaside shingle bank or Downland hutment to this special place to say goodbye to them. Here, whilst Crows and Ravens, Sea Eagles and Kites circled, impatient for the withdrawal of the loved ones, the dead may have been exposed, or the smoke from funeral pyres may have billowed and risen in the wind from off the sea.

There were other reasons, too, for this to be a sacred place, for here the long chain of hills meets the sea and the fertile coastal plain is pinched out. It may have been that the domestic sphere (the coastal plain) here met the sacred (hills). Those people may have placed their funerary monuments on the Hill, their most marginal land, to mark the boundary of high and low: the spirit world of the sky and the hard earth. Or, maybe, the camp was placed for its views of the sea (not the land), that is, the spirit world of voyaging, flux and movement.

Later, a cluster of round barrows was built, perhaps by the Bronze Age peoples, perhaps by the Saxons. It is unlikely we will know their builders for the coming of the Racecourse saw their removal before they could be properly excavated. There are still faint tumps near the racecourse where it bends eastwards on Race Hill. They could be more faint remains of barrows.

In any case there are few signs that people settled here in the whole 2000 year period between the Bronze Age and the coming of the Romans. It seems that Whitehawk Hill remained a sacred place.

In our time it has reclaimed that status, for 150 years ago the north-western slopes of the Hill became again a funerary landscape with the making of the bosky cemeteries around Woodvale.

The Neolithic people brought agriculture to Britain and it was they who cleared the woods on Whitehawk's Downs and brought cereal cultivation and herding of sheep, cattle and pigs. The grassland on Whitehawk Hill's steep slope probably has a continuity right back to those first farmers. In that way its Down pasture is a piece of *living* archaeology. The tiny snails that we can still find if we poke about in the short hillside turf are the descendants of the snails the archaeologists dug up from the camp's ditches. They are their great grandchildren 5000 times removed!!

At its south end Whitehawk Hill is a place of allotments, rough grass, scrub thickets and young woodland. It receives little management from the City Council who own it, but there is a vigorous Food Project on the allotments.

The steep east-facing slope is the core of the Local Nature Reserve. You could see Dartford Warbler in its Gorse thickets and we have started up Sparrowhawk and Woodcock in the winter months. Despite its dereliction this slope is a rich place for old Down pasture wildlife. It has clouds of Chalkhill and Adonis Blue in a good summer. There is a population of Six-belted Clearwing moth on the shorter turf and Fox Moth and Emperor Moth are present. Scarce Forester, Glow-worm and Adder have gone extinct only in the past few decades.

Its colours change with the seasons. In May and June the yellows of Vetch and Trefoil predominate. In June and July there's a mixture of white (Umbellifers), yellow (Hawkbit), and red (Knapweed, Thyme, Clover and so on). Later, in August and September, the old grassland is dominated by blues and purple/reds (from Scabious, Rampion and Knapweed), with a white peppering of Wild Carrot umbels.

The place continually surprises us with its richness. A population of Large Velvet Ant, *Mutilla europaea*, has been discovered in the past few years. This is a very rare and beautiful beastie that depends on the presence of healthy Bumble-bee populations, upon which it is

Whitehawk Hill in the snow. April 2008.

parasitic. The terraces at the base of the slope above the playing fields are home to many tiny and jewel-like solitary bees and wasps, to Waxcaps and to the rare Winter Stalk Puffball, *Tulostoma brumale*.

The highest point lies on Race Hill between Warren and Bear Roads. That place has the richest Waxcap assemblage we have recorded on the Brighton urban fringe so far, though all are at low abundance.

The allotments at the top of Whitehawk valley have been called 'Little Ireland' because of their sheltering evergreen hedges. It is here that Whitehawk can claim national distinction, for the hedges shelter the tiny 'Whitehawk Soldier Beetle', *Malthodes lobatus*, at its only British site. There is also frequent Yellow Vetchling, *Lathyrus aphaca*, and, near the racecourse, the rare Yellow Vetch, *Vicia lutea*.

Sheepcote Valley. TQ 341 045, is a monument to human possibility. For long decades it held a municipal rubbish dump whose smells and blown rubbish irritated local residents. When that purpose was completed, however, a kilometre and more of the upper Valley was terraced with six

giant steps, which have now softened further with the cover of grass and low scrub. They could be the monuments of an ancient civilization for the little sign they show of the Valley's recent past. The valley is large — half a mile wide by a mile and a quarter long — and enclosed, and commands grand sea views. Enjoy them now, for the integrity of this Downscape will be badly mauled by the coming Marina skyscrapers and hyper-development. Like goldfish in a bowl, the valley's walkers will be peered at from the new towers.

Wildlifers know Sheepcote for two main reasons. Migratory birds value the Valley as a major rest and recovery site. You could see anything there: rare Warblers, Wryneck, Redstarts — with great luck even Hen Harrier, Jack Snipe, Redshank or Curlew. Secondarily, its history of cultivation has bequeathed to it a fine assemblage of the plants of disturbed ground, with many special species, including rare kinds of Poppy, Venus's Looking-glass, *Legousia hybrida*, Silky Medick, *Medicago falcata*, and Tuberous Pea, *Lathyrus tuberosus*. Sadly, these species are scarcely now seen, for the Council does not organize the periodic tillage their dormant seeds need to flower.

One April morning we saw three Wheatears and a Whitethroat. In the distance a Short-eared Owl was flapping across the tall grass and dropping, here and there, to investigate possible prey.

On the eastern Valley slope there is a modern carved chalk figure: the 'white hawk'. It looks like a pair of false eyelashes or a corporate logo. Thankfully it scarcely shows.

Sheepcote's lower valley has a fine caravan park where the first municipal site in the country was opened in 1938. There are playing fields embraced by the valley slopes and a good café in East Brighton Park, which has been the start and finish of many a walk and many a game of cricket and football.

The Woodvale Cemeteries. Bear Road, TQ 326 056.

FIVE linked cemeteries cover the western side of Race Hill. They are a profoundly peaceful place of little woods and glades, sunny banks and shady paths. They have become, in the last 150 years, reservoirs for much of the wildlife of the surrounding countryside. Some of the big Beech trees down in Woodvale are as old as the cemeteries. The marbles, limestones, and granites of the memorials are a detective story for geologists. Yaffles call across the trees. The rare Greater Horseshoe Bat has hibernated in the funerary buildings. Badgers pit the mossy turf in their search for earthworms, and violet and celandine cheer the turf in early spring.

East Brighton Golf Course. TQ 346 042.

THE course is still an airy Down, where the Channel wind may stroke your face or wreck your umbrella. Unlike many Downland courses it has not lost its roughs to scrub thickets and woodland. The Short-eared Owls know that its long eastern chalk grassland slope is good hunting for Field Vole. The Club will lose this fine site, though, if it does not start managing it as it should be managed.

There is lots of Sainfoin amongst the matted grass. Is this a relic of the fodder crops that Ovingdean's farmland grew back in the days of horse agriculture? You can find Spotted Orchis, Marbled White and Burnet moths there.

On the top of Red Hill are old flint pits with Gorse, Thyme, moss and bits of Cladonia lichen.

Roedean Bottom. TQ 349 033.

BEHIND the cliffs and miniature golf course there is a Millionaire's Row, and, eastwards, Roedean School, where millionaires' daughters go. Between the two, though, on the east slope of Roedean Bottom there is a little piece of aboriginal Downland turf. Here you can see Autumn Ladies Tresses orchis, Carline Thistle and Hairy Violet. Tiny Moss Snail in the turf demonstrates the site's antiquity.

Further inland this chalk grassland continues by the footpath side, but it is very rank.

Cattle Hill slopes, Ovingdean. TQ 352 037.

THE Hill's eastern slope, looking over old Ovingdean, and its northern slope, between the footpath and bridlepath, retain an old Down pasture sward, though very rough and under-managed at present. Cowslip and Rampion, Sweet Briar and Thyme cling on — just.

Wick Bottom. TQ 35 04.

THIS peaceful dean takes its name from the medieval farm on the Falmer Road, now long-gone. The name 'wick' may denote a far more ancient — perhaps Roman — farmstead.

In modern times it has been a place of cornlands, mostly. The arable stubbles can be good places to walk. Here is a list of the plants I noted there in one October walk: *Henbit Deadnettle, Field Madder, Round-*

leaved Fluellen, Common Fumitory — all lovers of chalkland — and *Field Pansy, Petty Spurge, Sun Spurge, Knotgrass, Fat Hen, Hedge Mustard, Fool's Parsley, Common Field Speedwell, Common Poppy, Bristly Oxtongue, Annual Meadow Grass, Shepherd's Purse, Common Chickweed, Scentless Mayweed, Prickly Sowthistle, Scarlet Pimpernel.*

Mount Pleasant's west slope. TQ 354 045.

LOOKING over Wick Bottom is a small triangle of rich chalk grassland. It's rough and derelict, but its special wildlife clings on. There's big swarms of Rampion, Dropwort, Horseshoe Vetch and Hairy Violet. Stonechat frequent its thorn and bramble. It needs management desperately.

Happy Valley. TQ 357 047.

THE Happy Valley recreation ground is overlooked by a bushy, cattle-grazed slope. It's a lovely place, with old Down pasture herbs, bits of Gorse and thorn. Good for picnics.

Old Ovingdean. TQ 355 035.

THE old core of Ovingdean retains its flint walls, old cottages, barns (converted), and gentry houses. The Norman church of St Wulfran's is a lovely, though shrunken, structure, with lots of surviving early details. The graveyard is crowded with the graves of Victorian Brighton people who wanted Downland burials. North of the church the stonewalled paddock is full of humps and hollows that mark where a Saxon thane had his manor house.

Beacon Hill, Rottingdean. TQ 363 028.

THE iconic windmill and the miniature golf course are what coast road travellers first notice of this Hill. Its landmark quality was important, though, even millennia before the medieval beacon makers used its prominence to warn of enemy fleets or pass great news along the coast. The Neolithic people built two long barrows

on its spine. One remains, and one has gone from its site on the miniature golf course.

When I walk on the Hill I am always left jangling with many competing feelings: *exhilaration*, from the great distances around, the sea, and the Skylarks singing above; *depression*, from the spoliation that the low density suburbs, chaotically set down, have brought to this erstwhile beautiful coast; *anger*, at the thinking that set the gigantic buildings of St Dunstan's and Roedean School down on these cliffs, and *apprehension*, at the prospect of yet more to come — the huge planned towers of the Marina and the City centre beyond.

The Hill is no longer a tranquil place, for the coast road brings a tremendous din. And it has lost most of its historic Down pasture wildlife. The steep slope above the village has been lost to scrub and new woodland, and the top of the Hill has suffered 'improvement' in the past.

There is, for all that, much to love. I went there one hot midsummer day a few years ago. Swallows, Martins and Jackdaws were in the air with the ever-present Skylarks. Along the top edge of the wooded slope I found Forester and Burnet Companion moths and Common Blue butterfly. The Bumble-bees were out in force, and I could find bits of Rampion, Crested Hairgrass, Milkwort and Squinancywort both there and near the old dewpond. Better management should see the site regain further richness in years to come.

The Chalk Cliffs from Black Rock to Rottingdean.

FEELING slightly depressed one blustery autumn day in Ovingdean's tarnished countryside I walked down Greenway Bottom to Ovingdean Gap, through the coast road underpass, and down the cliff steps to the undercliff walk…That's all it took…I could feel my mood lift and exhilaration replace it. The Channel rollers thumped in and returned, noisily rattling and sucking at the shingle as they went.

Creamy flecks topped them way out across the moving ocean. And there at the waves edge I could see a pair of grey, speckled, black-collared birds dodging backwards and forwards, dipping to poke under seaweed and stones, then nipping away from the lunging foam. *Turnstones!*... halfway on their long autumn journey maybe from Greenland and maybe onwards to North Africa. Further west, where the beach was wider a flock of Black-headed Gulls rested and Starlings flew back and forth.

At that time of year the Sea Lavender, *Limonium spp.*, and Sea Stock, *Matthiola incana*, clinging to cliff ledges and crevices were leached of all their high summer purples and blues. In the summer, though, they are quite a sight. Sea Stock is native only on this stretch of cliffs and on the southern cliffs of the Isle of Wight. It received a bashing when the cliff engineering was recently done at Black Rock, but here it is abundant. There's Sea Samphire occasionally, too. Jackdaws and feral Pigeons love the cliffs, and you could see Rock Pipit or the rare Black Redstart.

The cliffs themselves tell two separate stories of deep time.

The oldest is the story of the formation of the chalk itself way back in the Upper Cretaceous, 83.5 million years ago, during the last part of the age of Dinosaurs. In those days this part of the world was at the bottom of a warm tropical sea and the tiny calcium shells of plankton were filtering down over millions of years to form first sludge and then hard chalk rock. If you walk up the cliff path near the eastern arm of the Marina from the undercliff to the clifftop you will be walking upwards through time. Each bed of chalk, flint or marl that you pass has its own assemblage of sea creatures. As you 'get your eye in' you will start to see fragments of coral or sponge, or bits of shell. At the base of the cliffs from Black Rock to Roedean you used to find (and they're still there) hexagonal bits of the shell of a bizarre free-swimming Sea Lily, *Marsupites testudinarius*, an 'echinoid' cousin of starfish and sea urchins.

These cliffs, however, also preserve the 'younger', Ice Age story. At Black Rock the modern cliff face slices across the Ice Age cliff face, which ran in a more northwesterly-southeasterly direction. From the undercliff walk, by Asda, therefore, you can look up at the cliff face and see a cross section of the Ice Age cliffline, the shingle beach below it, and the huge quantities of arctic debris which slurried off the Downs subsequently and covered the old beach up to the height of the present clifftop.

The cross section of shingle beach you see was formed some 210,000 years ago when the sea was 12 metres higher than it is now. From this beach a Paleolithic sea-worn flint axe has been recovered. These Ice Age deposits were called in Victorian times the Elephant Beds because the remains of Mammoth, Woolly Rhinoceros, Wild Horse and other Ice Age creatures were found in them when wells and other deep excavations were made. Now those sediments are called Coombe Deposits, because they fill the bottom of every coombe and dean on our chalk Downs. They appear at Ovingdean Gap, too, where they form lobes of gravel, silt and sand undercutting the *in situ* chalk.

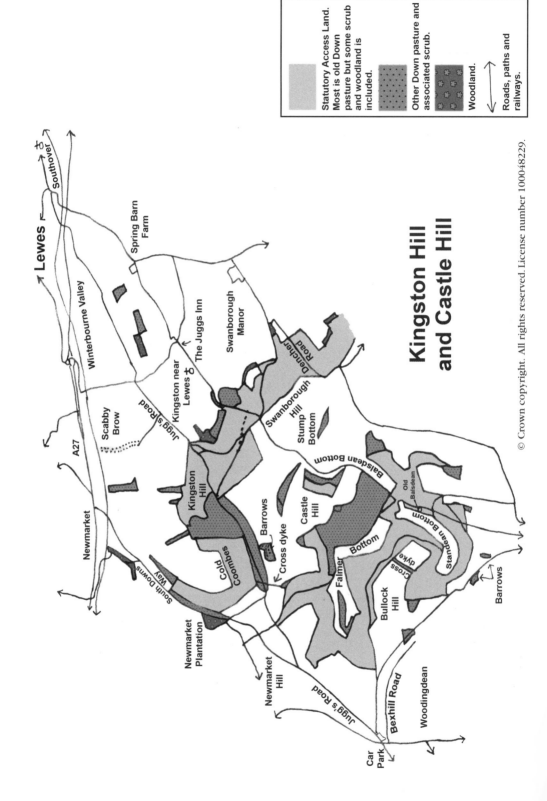

Kingston Hill and Castle Hill

Lewes

Southover

Winterbourne Valley

Spring Barn Farm

A27

Scabby Brow

Jugg's Road

Kingston near Lewes ⚓

The Juggs Inn

Swanborough Manor

Newmarket

Kingston Hill

Cold Coombes

Barrows

Cross dyke

Dencher Road

Swanborough Hill Bottom

Stump Bottom

Balsdean Bottom

Castle Hill

Falmer Bottom

Old Balsdean

South Downs Way

Newmarket Plantation

Newmarket Hill

Cross dyke

Bullock Hill

Standean Bottom

Barrows

Jugg's Road

Bexhill Road

Woodingdean

Car Park

Statutory Access Land. Most is old Down pasture but some scrub and woodland is included.

Other Down pasture and associated scrub.

Woodland.

Roads, paths and railways.

18: THE KINGSTON HILL AND CASTLE HILL DOWNS

THIS block of Downland is one of the brightest jewels of the Brighton Downs. It is our most magnificent survivor from the old landscape. It lies at the widest point in these open hills, crossed by the South Downs Way. And when we walk that Way we follow far older trails — the Jugg's Road of Brighton's medieval fishing folk, and the paths the Stone Age people took, and Romans too, along the ridge top and north across the Winterbourne valley by the Newmarket spur.

This was the last block of the Brighton Downs to retain unbroken its ancient Down pasture mantle — from Woodingdean to Kingston Hill. Only since the 'fifties has the Hill's crown south of the Jugg's Road been put under the plough, but, even with a monk's tonsure, the winding scarp and valley slopes uphold the continuity of *"the wise turf"* and the *"close-bit thyme that smells like dawn in Paradise."*[1]

A mile's walk will take you from the trunk road's roar and the suburb's glare into deep tranquility, where flowers and small creatures flourish — some of them amongst the last survivors of their kind in our islands.

Cold Coombes. TQ 372 077.
THIS is a grand amphitheatre, half a mile wide and often very steep. Much of it faces north away from the sun. The tussocky Tor Grass that has taken hold can make it difficult walking. Yet mountain birds, like Ring Ouzel, fresh from northern uplands, on their way south to escape our winter, may well tarry at Cold Coombes. The gloomy vastness must comfort and remind them of the fells and crags of home.

We struggled up the valleyside one early October afternoon. A Brown Hare started from the cover of Tor Grass. It didn't bother running more than a hundred yards. It knew we weren't going anywhere in a hurry. Then we saw below us, on the fenceline, a party of small birds. They separated and the larger party — Stonechat — flew down the valley. Two birds remained as I hurried to focus my binoculars. Whinchat! — a male with white eye-stripe, and a female, or perhaps a young one. Sitting above and scanning the valley, whilst our thermos tea cooled, we watched a raptor perched on a tall thorn. We watched it glide and return, then move across the valley. Perhaps Honey or Rough-legged Buzzard. Not our Common Buzzard. Sometime I'll take a thermos and sandwiches and sit all day scanning these

Cold Coombes: The pasture on the left of the path is 'right to roam' land, the pasture on the right of the path isn't... Is this daft or is this daft?

slopes. How better to celebrate the coming of autumn?

In August the lower slopes can have great swarms of Autumn Ladies Tresses. Chalkhill and Adonis Blue are here in low numbers, and Hound's Tongue on the disturbed ground. The rare Eyebright *Euphrasia pseudokerneri* was here some years ago, I think. There are large anthills and much Gorse, but it is not a closed thicket and will not stop you traversing the slope.

The Jugg's Road plateau. TQ 375 075.

'JUGGS' was the nickname Brighton fishermen bore in the past. This path was the route they — or their wives — took to market their fish in Lewes. The turf no longer sparkles with old Downland flowers, but more ancient things have survived.

We walked to the high point of the plateau (TQ 374 074, south of the fence) from the east on the same day we saw the Whinchat. A fine white mist stood like a

vcil around the hill, and across the dewy grass a ladder of shimmering gossamer moved before us straight towards the yellow descending sun. On that high point, south of Cold Coombes, sit two fine Bronze Age round barrows and, between them, a scattered swarm of smaller Saxon barrows, like their children. The ancient peoples must have felt their gods were close in this high place. A short way further west the neck of the plateau between Cold Coombes and Falmer Bottom is straddled by a Bronze Age cross dyke, TQ 370 075. The path of the South Downs Way crosses it.

Kingston Hill. TQ 380 080.

THE Hill is the main landmark of this western side of the Vale of the Brooks. Down its face are the partly-healed scars of two descending bostals, and other fainter ones between, like the lines of some forgotten tribal initiation. The top of the Hill is blessedly fenceless, with three dew ponds and a scatter of round barrows and Gorse and thorn. The largest of the barrows now hides beneath a thicket of gorse beside two of the ponds. On one summer morning I walked the bostals hunting for the Chalk Carpet moth. I counted seven kinds of butterfly as well, in that short walk: Marbled White, Chalkhill and Common Blue, Small Skipper, Small Heath, Gatekeeper, and Meadow Brown. There is Frog Orchis here, though I have not seen it.

One Guy Fawkes Night I walked with a friend from Brighton to Lewes along the Jugg's Road to watch their famous bonfire celebrations. We sat in darkness on the Hill's very top to warm ourselves with coffee. Behind us the coastal plain was peppered with squawks and bangs and the air flashed and sparkled with rockets and Roman candles. In front of us Lewes lay silent save for the sound of traffic. Only the glow of street lights marked it out. Such is the discipline of Lewes Bonfire Night that such quietude reigns until the procession begins!

Behind the Hill's brow lies the delightful back slope, all mottled with Gorse and anthills and a patchwork of acidic and chalky soils. It is more tranquil than the outward facing scarp, for, there, peace is tarnished with the low roar of traffic on the A27 trunk road and the valley roads to Newhaven. Few such gentle plateau areas have escaped the plough.

Indeed most of this plateau beyond this backslope was lost, too, amidst angry conflict at the plough's coming. To bring combines up the Hill the southern bostal was bulldozed wide enough for their passage. The round barrow at the bostal's top was clipped. Now, the same farms that damaged such places receive money for environmental management and the plateau is returned to grass and sheep.

Do we pay the embezzler to manage our public accounts? Do we pay the art thief to manage our museums? Yet we pay the landowning wreckers of our countryside to manage its heritage.

Scabby Brow. TQ 384 088.

LOOKING north half a mile from Kingston Hill, below the scarp, there is a great arable field running down to the railway line. This field had two steep slopes that were not tilled. One to the west, TQ 380 088, still retains its cover of old Down pasture. It is a lovely well-tended place, especially on a summer's day, with Cowslips, Fragrant Orchids, Milkwort and Dropwort. Small Copper, Yellow Belle moth and Marbled White dance back and forth.

The slope to the east, Scabby Brow, was different. It had been allowed to scrub up. Whitethroat sang from its bushes and in its glades Pyramidal Orchis, Scabious and Knapweed bloomed. Then the farmer bulldozed the bushes and ripped out what remained of the fences. I feared the worst. The worst happened. The farmer returned and tore up the turf and remaining bushes and burned them in great piles. We complained and DEFRA officials intervened. Too late, though. Now that place is gone.

Kingston village and the lower Jugg's Road. TQ 39 08.

THERE is a kind of ghost, an unseen presence in this landscape. It is the great Cluniac Priory of St Pancras at Southover, by the brooks south of Lewes. From Kingston Hill it used to loom as great as Chichester Cathedral still does in its surroundings. From Kingston Hill much of what we see — Falmer, Balmer, Kingston, Swanborough and Southover — was held in subjection to feed the appetites of the Priory. At the Tudor Reformation it was swiftly demolished, and only cursory ruins remain. Yet those settlements owe their shape and some of their buildings to that presence. Kingston, Swanborough and Hangleton Manors all contain stones pillaged at its destruction.

Kingston church was built and owned by the Priory. Before its building all that village was part of Iford Parish. The church

The back slope of Kingston Hill: gorse pods popping, nodding harebells, plodding cows, skylarks' music.

tower looks too small for the building, for the body of the church was later enlarged, whilst the neat little tower remained as it was. Down the old village street the Juggs Inn has slaked many a Downland walker's thirst.

The Jugg's Road descends Kingston Hill's bostal, then takes you through a posh suburb of the village and out onto a lower ridge into Lewes. Above Spring Barn Farm there is a fragment of old Down pasture, TQ 398 088, around a disused chalk pit. East of Spring Barn lie the farms well-managed brooklands. Snipe, Reed Bunting and Lapwing haunt the margins of its rich ditches, where Sticklebacks, young Eels, Marsh Frogs and Water Beetles thrive.

Castle Hill and its valley: Newmarket, Falmer and Standean Bottoms. TQ 37 06 and around.

WHETHER you approach from Woodingdean, from Rottingdean, from Newmarket on the A27, or from Kingston near Lewes, your first view of the slopes of this long valley under Castle Hill will not disappoint. On all sides they retain their virgin turf, fringed along their crests by Gorse and thorn and dimpled only by gently descending pathways. At morning time and evening the valley will lie part under shadow, and at all times the southern slopes are shadier than the northern. Some parts have deeper soils, some scarce any soil at all. Some have a long sward and some a smooth, fine turf. So there is a place for many ways of living and for many life forms.

Much of the northern slopes are now a **National Nature Reserve, TQ 376 065**, and here you may see hundreds of Early Spider Orchids in springtime, when the Cowslips are still in flower. In June there are, nestling in the yellow heads of Hawkbit, burnished green-and-copper Leaf Beetles, *Cryptocephalus*. In a good summer the hillside is dusted pink with Fragrant Orchis, and Pyramidal, Bee and Spotted Orchids, too, and you can find the small flowers of our rare endemic Early Gentian.

There is so much that is rare and special here: Nottingham Catchfly, Dodder, Field Fleawort — the list is long. The butterflies and moths are superb: Adonis and Chalkhill Blue of course, but so many more: Small Blue, Clouded Yellow, perhaps Dark Green Fritillary, Small Purple-barred, *Phytometra viridaria*, Purple-barred, Forester, Mother Shipton and Burnet Companion moths. There are many rare bees, including some long thought to be locally extinct and only recently re-discovered.

One creature vies with the Spider Orchis in fame amongst wildlifers who know this site, and that is the Wartbiter Bush-cricket. Have no fear, though, for this beastie may be an inch and a half long but it is shy. It is not interested in biting you or your warts! It was estimated a decade or more ago that about 80% of the British population of this locust-sized hopper lived in the Castle Hill valleys. So special is this place for its survival that much of the management of the reserve has been geared to its needs. May it prosper and re-populate its other lost homes. It lives alongside an even grander beastie, the Dark Green Bush-cricket, but that is by no means so rare locally. They chorus on hot summer days with each other and with a host of other grasshoppery creatures, including Coneheads and scarce Stripe-winged Grasshoppers.

The 'castle' on the top of Castle Hill is a small rectangular enclosure with grassy banks. It's not ancient. Perhaps it was used for managing the sheep flocks.

The southern slopes lie outside the NNR, but are all designated as an SSSI, and the farmer manages then well with intense sheep grazing. The wild flowers are more scattered where the slopes are shady, but there's plenty to see. In late autumn you may find Waxcap fungi amongst the Gorse.

Balsdean. TQ 378 060.

S O U T H of Castle Hill, where three valleys meet, lay the ancient hamlet of Balsdean. It had a Norman chapel — used as a barn in modern times — and two farms: Norton Farm, under the slope of Castle Hill, and Sutton Farm, with its Georgian manor house. Now the only buildings to be seen are some derelict post-war barns, for trainee gunners destroyed the hamlet for artillery practice when these hills were a Second World War Army Training Area. All that remains are bumps and hollows in the turf and a grove of Sycamores — the marker trees of many a lonely farmstead. Walking the arable next to the hamlet you can find rusty shell fragments and pieces of tile from those bad times. On the grassy platform where the chapel stood there's a plaque surrounded by sarsen stones, marking the position of its altar.

Balsdean Bottom — 'Partridge valley'. TQ 385 065 and around.

L O U D or soft, distant or close, the sound of this valley is the chucking and clucking of Partridge. When a bush rustles or there's movement in the long grass it will likely be a scuttling bird you see legging it across the slope. From summer onwards, the valley is like a free-range game farm, scattered with cover crops and rearing cages, for the fun of the mass slaughter of these half-tame creatures.

Its slopes have long received a different treatment from the treasured and protected valleys to the west of Balsdean. Till some years ago the remaining Down pasture sites were still being ploughed, sprayed with agro-chemicals, planted with game rearing pens and left to go derelict. One important site is still in steep decline. But there are signs of a change, too, as new agro-environmental support systems kick in.

It's all so sad, for this is also such a place of peace. Away to the south, the sea is visible above the clean line of hills. The sky is huge. The traffic noise from the A27 is reduced to a distant murmur. On the flinty track you may stand and watch the Stonechat upon the fence posts. They flick their tails and dart into the air or down

Castle Hill National Nature Reserve's slopes: 'Keep Our Downs Public' activists on an outing, July 1995. These five people have belonged to the Tory Party, Labour Party, Lib Dems, Green Party and a Trotskyist group — guess which person has belonged to which party…

into the grass — such dainty birds, with orange breast and mottled backs; the males so smart with black heads and sharp white collars.

The valleyside east of Balsdean, TQ 382 058, has a scallop-shaped site on its steepest part which retains its aboriginal vegetation. It has had no grazing for many years now and is rapidly degenerating into a mess of Tor Grass and encroaching thorn. Below its lower fenceline a fragment of old turf is well-grazed by a Brighton tenant farmer. Where the sheep can go, Horseshoe Vetch, Fragrant and Spotted Orchids thrive, and powder-blue Chalk Milkwort — here on the edge of its Downland range.

The eastern slope of Castle Hill, TQ 380 069, just round the corner from the Nature Reserve, is Access Land in its upper part. It holds some of the richest spots for Downland herbs on the East Sussex

Downs.[2] There's plenty of colour amongst the anthills and Gorse and thorn. Recently the fences that divided it and surrounded a rearing pen have been removed and large areas of scrub have been brashed. The ground tilled for a cover crop has been allowed to revert to pasture. The work, though crudely done, is good and hopeful.

The combe north of Castle Hill, TQ 380 072, still has an old flowery slope on its northern side, though a large rearing pen covers part of it. One summer afternoon we sat while a Corn Bunting sung its heart out on a fence post. Opposite us we watched a large 'cat' through binoculars as it approached the rearing pen. It was the size of an Otter, though bulkier, but no Otter, surely, would be walking a valley on these dry Downs?

Stump Bottom, TQ 385 070, was once a fine place. It's been sprayed with agro-chemicals, though, and the old flowers survive only on the steepest bits.

Swanborough Hill, TQ 390 070, is not the 'swan's hill', but the 'herdsman's hill', from the Saxon *'swan'*, as in 'swain'. The hilltop once had a barrow field, including a cluster of small Saxon tumps, but there is little sign of them now.

An ethical crime — though not against any law — was committed here when the scarp slopes of Swanborough Hill were sprayed with agro-chemicals and their ancient vegetation destroyed. In summer, now, Ragwort has taken hold, sometimes in dense patches. A wretched mess.

Swanborough Manor, TQ 400 078, in the hamlet below, was a grange of St Pancras Priory in Lewes. It is a fine building, still with its original hall dating back to circa 1200, and a chapel and gatehouse of the fifteenth century.

Footnotes

1   From Kipling's poem 'Sussex'.
2   *Survey of East Sussex Chalk Grassland*, — Muggeridge and Stevens (English Nature, 1992), page 87.

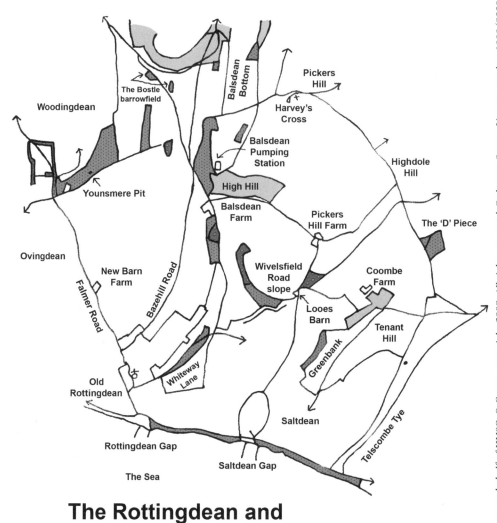

The Rottingdean and Saltdean Downs

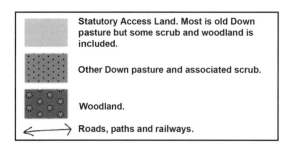

Statutory Access Land. Most is old Down pasture but some scrub and woodland is included.

Other Down pasture and associated scrub.

Woodland.

Roads, paths and railways.

19: THE ROTTINGDEAN AND SALTDEAN DOWNS

THESE are the Downs that the famous folk singing Copper family have lived and sung in for generations. And they are the same Downs that Jim Copper said made him "prostrate with dismal" at the sight of their ancient emptiness covered with the slack urbanisations of the past ninety years.

Not far from the spot where Bob Copper scattered his father Jim's ashes you can sit on the steep slope of High Hill amongst the moss and flowers. All around is silence. A Kestrel feeds her young. *"Whee, whee, whee"*, they cry, like all hungry babies.

Some of the old Downs lives on. Enough to fight for.

Rottingdean old village. TQ 369 026.
ROTTINGDEAN old village marks the sole gap in the nearly nine miles of cliffs between Brighton's Old Steine and Newhaven. Probably for that reason French raiders landed there in 1377, during the Hundred Years War, and pillaged the place. The tower in the Norman church of St Margaret's has reddish, deeply cracked stonework inside, perhaps from the effects of its firing by that raiding party.

The centre of the original village lies round a large Green a quarter mile north of the shore. Much of the Green has long been 'privatised' by the building upon it of two big houses — The Elms, once Kipling's home, and The Dene — but its original rectangular shape is plain to see from the street plan. Was the village built up the dean to give some protection from raiders? And was the Green made its centre for the safety of the people's animals from such marauding raids?

All its farm buildings have long been converted into homes, but the great barn of Court Farm (up by the Bazehill Road turn off) is still impressive. At the north end of the Green are the gentry houses of the big farmers who dominated the parish — Challoners, Down House, Court House and Hillside.

Younsmere Pit and its slope. TQ 365 044.
A LONG grassy slope where horses graze overlooks the southern end of Woodingdean. It is not ancient Down pasture but it has regained many flowers, though the horses prevent much of a blossoming. Just inside the fence-line, half way up the crest of the spur, there is **a grassy pit**, large enough for a group of folk to lounge in, but small enough for them to be able to chat easily to each other.

Is this the Younsmere Pit where the officials of the Hundredal Court met in medieval times? We cannot know for certain, but that is what is conjectured.

'Hundreds' were a Saxon unit of government and brought together a number of manorial settlements. From later Norman times the villages of Ovingdean, Rottingdean, Falmer, Stanmer and Kingston were organized in the Younsmere Hundred. Their courts were held out on the open Downs, and the place was chosen for its rough centrality for all the communities. They are said to have met here right up till around two centuries ago.

The Bostle barrow field. TQ 371 054.

J U S T east of Woodingdean, on the top of the hill just south of the bridleway fenceline, there is a cluster of low grassy mounds. They're not much to look at, and the barrow field is a bit scruffy — a 'precious fragment' surrounded by huge plough lands. There's a lot of graves, though. In that small area you could, with care, count 27 small mounds, which are probably Saxon, and three larger, probably Bronze Age barrows. And that's not all of it, for thc bridleway you walked down crosses the flattened remains of more barrows and graves, and its very likely there are more all around.

The plough had recently clipped the edge of a couple of the barrows when we last went there on a November day. A Hare started up at our approach. A family of Badgers were obviously conducting their own excavations in several of the mounds. We looked at their excavated chalk rubble and I picked up a piece of rough pottery, with simple impressed decorative lines upon it. When I got home I looked at it under better light. My fingertip fitted neatly into each of the impressed marks. My finger was sitting in the thumb marks left by a potter who had made this piece perhaps 3,600 years ago. That is really something.

In 1997 archaeologists excavated the flattened part of the cemetery on the bridlepath alignment.[1] They found Saxon ring ditches with the skeletons of folk who must have been settlers at the very end of the pagan period. They found an unusual number of infant burials. In the Bronze Age the farming peoples may have set this place aside for the graves of their little children. They found cremations. One knotty bit of charcoal was tentatively identified as a species of *Daphne* shrub. There are two native species of *Daphne*: the sweet smelling Mezereon, *Daphne mezereon*, which is a vernal shrub that only recently went extinct on these Downs, and the evergreen Spurge Laurel, *D. laureola,* which is still found on our Downs, for instance in Coombe Plantation. Both species must always have been scarce, and are slight in size, so they wouldn't have been used as fuel. Perhaps they were cast on the pyre for their beauty, and if evergreen Spurge Laurel was used, because it symbolized the everlasting after-life.

The Bostle combe slope. TQ 371 048.

T H E R E is a delightful ancient Down pasture slope with thc softest Sheep's Fescue turf, just south of the barrow field. It is the sort of place you could sit all day, with a picnic and a drink. From it you can see only sky, the green valley, and the sea. It is silent, save for the gulls and perhaps a distant aeroplane. In spring there are Cowslips and Violets. In summer the Thyme is everywhere, and in autumn the Gorse comes back into bloom.

In the valley bottom down to New Barn, on the Falmer Road, you will notice small earth dams. They are there because in October 1987, heavy rains on these winter ploughed valley side soils caused muddy flood waters to rush down into many Ovingdean homes.

High Hill. TQ 378 041.

I T is the **north slope of the Hill, TQ 380 043,** that still retains the magic of old Downland. I love that place. I rate it as amongst the best on our Brighton Downs.

The old drove known as Bazehill Road takes you up to High Hill from Rottingdean.

High Hill's north slope: amongst the best of the Brighton Downs. Deeply threatened by dereliction.

Bazehill is a modern changing of the hill's old name: Bay's Hill. On the top is Balsdean farmstead, re-located there after the last world war destroyed the ancient hamlet of that name in the valley beyond. The views are breathtaking.

On an August day the slope is a tapestry of colour: blues, reds, oranges, whites, purples, yellows and all the myriad shades of green. There are orchids and so many flowers and butterflies. Silver-spotted Skipper has re-colonised and Chalkhill Blues are there, of course. In late summer the russet Robin's Pin-cushion can be seen on many a wild Rose bush. The slope's coolness brings a great variety of subtly hued mosses on the huge old anthills. It's a lovely place even in winter, when the bleached stalks are white with frost, and haws the birds have not yet taken are still crimson.

For all its beauty and peace, though, this slope is thoroughly neglected and almost all the upper half has disappeared under thorn scrub. Access is better from the bottom. I know one man who goes there on his own to cut down the invading thorn. The place needs so much more than that heroic effort.

If you look north from this slope you will see a derelict brick barn half a mile across the cornfields, near Harvey's Cross, TQ 385 052. Near there a barrow[2] was excavated around 1849 and a bronze hoard found with the skeleton. There were two 'Brighton loops' — our trademark Brighton Bronze Age artefact — and two other peculiar and presumably decorative objects.

Balsdean Pumping Station slope. TQ 376 045.

EARLY Spider Orchis occurs here, and Frog and Bee Orchids were present not so long ago, and may be still. There is Dodder — rare on Downland — and Horseshoe Vetch and many other old Down pasture specials, like Chalk Milkwort, Field Fleawort, and Chalk Waxcap.

This slope is a continuation to the west of the last site, yet the contrast makes the close affinity of the two sites difficult to recognize. If the last site is neglected and bosky, this site is grazed and clear of scrub. Yet a century ago there would have been no fence between them, though the flocks that grazed them had different owners.

The top of the slope is improved.

The Saltdean sites.

SALTDEAN feels a world away from its agricultural past, but there are a few fragments commemorating it. Three old (converted) flint barns survive along Saltdean Vale: the eighteenth century Saltdean Barn in Saltdean Park, the Newlands Barn on the corner with Lustrell's Crescent, and the Looes Barn at the edge of the open Downs. Near Looes Barn was a very large barrow made entirely of flint, which was pillaged for building work.

There are four old Down pasture sites around the edges of Saltdean, which are important for local people. All are in poor condition or are poorly managed.

Whiteway Lane, TQ 375 028, is a braided bostal which rises up the hillside from Rottingdean Green. It used to be the drove to Lustrell's Pasture, which was Rottingdean's eastern sheep common and the twin to Beacon Hill. Till recently you could find fragments of the old Down pasture wild flowers. Now it is lost to bushes and bits of rank grass and you find yourself watching out to avoid the dog's muck.

The Wivelsfield Road slope, TQ 381 034, is a peaceful, pleasant place. The southern end is 'improved' and the northern half is lost to dense scrub and new woodland. The middle section is beautiful old Down pasture, though, with Harebells and Rampion flower, Spring Sedge and Cowslips. The owner has cut it in two with fencing, however, so that the cattle cannot graze the northern part

of the old pasture. Eventually this means it will be lost to scrub unless this fence is removed.

The Coombe Farm bank, TQ 392 031, has many lovely flowers. June is the best time, when the Spotted Orchids are out, and the vetches and other small herbs, like Chalk Milkwort, are flowering. Many of the old Down pasture herbs are present, but at low abundance, for the ground is often muddy and poached by cattle and much is being lost to creeping scrub. The upper slope has rubble dumped on it and has been 'improved'.

The farmer sold two small fragments of this Access Land site to neighbouring residents, who extended their gardens by enclosing them with fences and planting their own stuff. At least that kind of damage doesn't happen on the Brighton Council owned farms.

The Greenbank Avenue quarry site, TQ 387 027, has lovely old Down pasture fragments around the little quarry. There is Burnet Rose at one of its few local sites, and bits of Cladonia lichen and nice mossy Sheep's Fescue turf on an old lynchet. There are Blue butterflies and much chirruping from grasshoppers in summer. Yet all around the edges of the site a mess of Bramble and Sycamore scrub encroaches and access is difficult, except from neighbouring back gardens. Some of those folk do bits of clearance on their own, as at High Hill, but they are fighting against the tide without a larger scale of help.

A scandalous mess.

Footnotes

1 'Archaeological investigations at The Bostle, Bronze Age and Anglo-Saxon barrow cemeteries, Balsdean, East Sussex, 1997' — Jacqueline I. McKinley. *Sussex Archaeological Collections*, Vol. 142, (2004), pages 25-44.

2 *Sussex Archaeological Collections*, Vol. 2, (1849), pages 265-6.

20: THE IFORD AND RODMELL DOWNS

A way from the South Downs Way few people, sadly, use these remote Downs. In prehistory it was not so. The Down between Highdole Hill and Fore Hill was a busy village in Iron Age and Roman times and many of the marks they left have survived.

There are many fine surviving Down pasture sites that deserve to be known better.

Unusually, the long and convoluted dry valley behind the scarp does not drain southwards to the sea, but easterly, then northerly to the Brooks and the Ouse. It used to be called 'Isenden', a Tolkienesque name, which sounds like it meant 'Ouse dean'.

A worker[1] at South Farm Rodmell has been recording the birds of these Downs for many years. He shows that patience can bring many special sights. Dotterel can be seen on passage on the flooded arable fields. Yellow Wagtail still clings on as a passage migrant. Both Barn Owl and Little Owl have regularly bred. Turtle Dove is still seen and breeds in the parish, and Sparrowhawk and Peregrine are common sights.

The villages between the Downs and the Brooks — Iford, Northease and Rodmell — have many beautiful flint buildings and two fine churches.

From Highdole Hill to Fore Hill

From Saltdean or Peacehaven you can walk to **Highdole Hill, TQ 397 045**, up the spine of Telscombe Tye. The views from the top are glorious, with lots of sea and distant glimpses of the Weald and white cliffs.

Yet the views are only half the pleasure here, for what strikes you, after some seconds standing so high, is the silence. When you walk the Brighton Downs a lot you get used to high places being noisy, for they so often overlook busy roads and suburbs. You get used to seeking silence in the valleys, not the Down tops. Here you can have both.

The huts of the Romano-British village on the hilltop seem to have been arranged around a banked roadway, with other roadways nearby and many small fields and several barrows, but modern ploughing has removed most of these remains.[2]

Towards Fore Hill, though, near the flint-walled **sheepfold, TQ 404 043**, the village remains are more obvious and the pasture has preserved a muddle of field lynchets and round barrows. We sat against one barrow topped with Gorse in flower, munching home-made cake and drinking tea. Just northeast on the skyline we could see well-preserved twin barrows beneath the palest pastel blue sky. The pasture

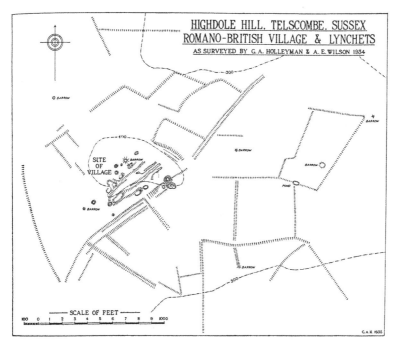

HIGHDOLE HILL, TELSCOMBE, SUSSEX
ROMANO-BRITISH VILLAGE & LYNCHETS
AS SURVEYED BY G.A. HOLLEYMAN & A.E. WILSON 1934

SITE OF VILLAGE

SCALE OF FEET

Isenden. From it you can see down to Seaford Bay and across to the long shoulder of Southease Hill.

You would assume that such a steep slope would have been safe from all 'improvement', but it is not so. Mill Hill was treated with agrochemicals and only at its base and along the old drove footpath on its northern edge does the old wildlife survive intact. Still, it is now well managed and the herbs and insects are returning.

Along the footpath edge you can still find Bastard Toadflax and Horseshoe Vetch. To the north of the footpath is a thicket of Gorse and thorn. If you look across at it from Fore Hill you can see that a tiny glade of chalk grassland survives in its middle. Till a decade ago you could walk to it from the footpath, and forty years ago the whole lower slope was Down pasture. Yet the owners on the hilltop (if it is they who own it) cannot be short of money for its management, judging by the size of their house and its electronic security system.

The arable field on the south east side of Mill Hill used to be called 'The Devil's Race' 160 years ago. What can that have commemorated? Did the name have any connection with the barrow field on the top of the Hill (now long ploughed flat)? There were at least 23 small mounds and two or three larger mounds. So many prehistoric moundings acquired such names — *Devil's Graves, Devil's Stairs, Devil's Shovelful,* and so on.

has been 'improved', but, still, there were carmine pink heads of Nodding Thistle and the yellow Gorse, like the *"old-gold common"* of AA Milne. The cattle around us in their woolly winter coats of many colours were placid and friendly and the western sun low behind them gave each one a golden halo.

These are democratic pleasures. You only need to walk to them.

Further north east the spur of **Fore Hill** drops into the dry valley. On its **steep northern slope, TQ 406 047**, the chalk grassland is well preserved, with lots of Cowslips, Harebells, Devil's-bit and Rampion. The steepest bit of its southeast facing slope, too, overlooking Cricketing Bottom, is good, with Marbled White and Common Blue, Dropwort, Thyme and Cowslips.

Mill Hill, Rodmell. TQ 412 052.

T H I S landscape is full of wonderful viewpoints. Standing on Mill Hill is almost like being on a cliff — which it must have been in Ice Age times, cut into by the rushing arctic torrent coming down from

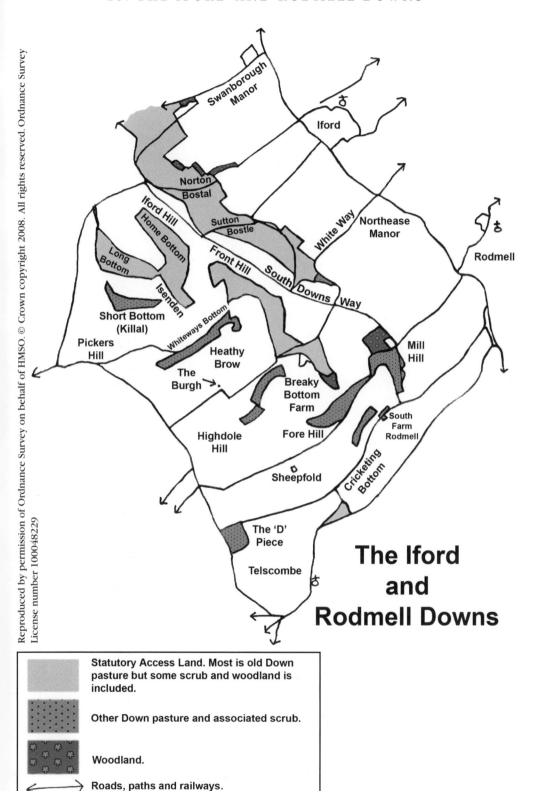

Swanborough Manor

Iford

Norton Bostal

Iford Hill

Home Bottom

Sutton Bostle

White Way

Northease Manor

Rodmell

Long Bottom

Front Hill

South Downs Way

Isenden

Short Bottom (Killal)

Whiteways Bottom

Pickers Hill

Heathy Brow

The Burgh

Mill Hill

Breaky Bottom Farm

South Farm Rodmell

Highdole Hill

Fore Hill

Sheepfold

Cricketing Bottom

The 'D' Piece

Telscombe

The Iford and Rodmell Downs

Statutory Access Land. Most is old Down pasture but some scrub and woodland is included.

Other Down pasture and associated scrub.

Woodland.

Roads, paths and railways.

The little farm of Breaky Bottom, now a vineyard.

Breaky Bottom. TQ 404 053.

THERE is a well known vineyard around this old flint farmstead on the sunny valley bottom. It is a delightful place.

They've had their troubles, though, for in October 1987 they were flooded 10 times by soil and water slurrying down from their neighbour's winter-ploughed fields. About 635 tonnes of soil was deposited there. It was only one of a whole series of such disasters coming with the widespread adoption of winter cultivation on the South Downs, which formed the nadir of Downland farmers' irresponsibility.

A steep Down pasture slope overlooks the vineyard, but it is in bad condition. Much of it has a rank Tor Grass cover, with rusty fallen fencing, which the desultory grazing does not address. Yet the old wildlife hangs on: Harebells, Small Copper, Moss Snail. It deserves better.

The **slope to the southwest of the vineyard, TQ 401 050**, has retained some of its old Down pasture flora. Above it on the spur is a **round barrow, TQ 401 049**.

The Burgh, TQ 397 050.

THE public footpath that runs northeast from the ridge between Pickers Hill and Highdole descends a spur. Just before it meets a fence you can see a large, very low mound. This is **The Burgh**, one of the few barrows on the Brighton Downs prominent enough to have acquired a name. You could be forgiven for missing it, now, for it was made of flint and most of it was removed for building material. The field has been pasture again for some years and there were Mushrooms and Parasols and Blackening Waxcap out when we visited.

The south slopes of Front Hill. TQ 402 056.

A DELIGHTFUL Down pasture slope two thirds of a mile long lies just to the south of the South Downs Way. All of it is sun-soaked and south facing. We approached from Breaky Bottom one July afternoon. The turf was spangled with Pyramidal Orchids, Rampion and Harebells.

Butterflies jigged about. The two parts of the site are grazed and well-managed, though the rather unremitting grazing of the northern half does not allow for flower displays.

Whiteway Bottom.

WHEN the sun is low you can see bold prehistoric field lynchets at the head of the Whiteway combe, TQ 391 052, and back towards Highdole, as well as up the dean around Long Bottom.

A path climbs up Whiteway Bottom to Pickers Hill and on the top there was a barrow field. It is ploughed out now.

The **south slope of Whiteway Bottom, TQ 396 054**, is a tranquil old Down pasture site. It was damaged by agro-chemicals at its western end, but the middle and eastern end is intact, with lots of butterflies, including Small Heath, Chalkhills, Common Blue and Marbled White, and lots of old Down pasture herbs. Once, forty years ago, I surprised a Hare there after a long hike. I sat down by some

Gorse and must have stayed there for a good hour, so peaceful and contented did it make me feel.

Killal, or Short Bottom. TQ 390 057.

WHITEWAY Bottom turns up the dean, where it used to be called Isenden, and splits into three combes. The first of these used to be called Short Bottom and is now Killal. There are Cowslips and Devil's-bit and Common Blue. A little copse has been planted and there are boney lynchets. It was a neglected place, but now it is grazed and well-managed.

Long Bottom. TQ 389 060.

A LOVELY place. Southwards from its steep slope you look across long ripples of hills, like the sea, and the cliffs of Seaford Head is where the view ends. There are tumps that could be barrows, and on the combe floor there used to be a large sarsen boulder. I cannot find it now. One June day I found Bee and Spotted Orchids, and sky blue Chalk Milkwort and Rockrose. Adonis

South slope of Front Hill — Whiteway Bottom slope — Seaford Head — Isenden — Short Bottom (Killal)

Blue butterfly and Yellow Belle moth were busy. In August there are Chalkhills and Wheatear start to return. There are Puffballs and the occasional Mushroom in autumn.

Home Bottom. TQ 392 063.

QUIET. The valley was damaged by agro-chemicals, but the old wildlife is returning.

The Line of the South Downs Way.

In this sub-landscape the Way runs for 1.75 miles along the scarp top and nowhere does it touch ancient Down pasture. The long views are gorgeous but you will not see the fairy flowers and insects that make Downland so special. There were three barrow clusters on Front Hill. They are ploughed out now.

The Iford and Northease scarp slope.

THE soft combes and spurs above the Vale of Brooks are elegant and heart-lifting. You can enjoy all the old Downland herbs and creatures there, amongst the sheep. There is very little Tor Grass invasion, so the walking is easy. There are no deep-cut bostals on the Iford Hill and Front Hill slopes, for there was no long distance traffic here of traders or herders. The gentle hill tracks only took the sheep back and forth at dawn and dusk to the farms in the Vale.

There are no ancient rew woodlands at the base of slope, probably because that land was so fine for cultivation that they were lost to the plough. There is little scrub on the slopes either, in this most treeless part of our Downs. Some woods were replanted along the base of slope in modern times, though, and some of their Beeches are already reaching a fine size.

At the southern end the Northease White Way cuts a more substantial bostal and there are two chalk pits by its side. The **Down pasture above the Whiteway, TQ 405 059**, is a lovely flowery spot. The Tor Grass, though, has more of a hold than further north along the scarp. Contented cattle are doing their best to eat it into submission!

The scarp foot villages.

IFORD, **TQ 408 073**, has many beautiful barns and cottages and nooks and crannies. Its Norman church is a fine building. **Old Northease, TQ 411 065**, has been taken over by a private school. It has a huge and beautiful old barn on its courtyard. The modern farm was built on the drove to the west. **Rodmell, TQ 420 063**, is a long village, running from the site of its old wharf by the Brooks to half way up the slope of Mill Hill. Like Iford, it is a place with many lovely flint built houses. The Norman church has carved stones taken from the pillaged Lewes Priory.

Footnotes

1   *Birds of Rodmell* — Michael Light (Third edition, 2005). I bought my copy in the church.

2   'An early British agricultural village site on Highdole Hill, near Telscombe' — G.A. Holleyman, *S.A.C.* 77 (1936), pages 202-21.

21: FROM TELSCOMBE CLIFFS TO SOUTHEASE

THIS is a landscape of opposites:
— the primeval ruggedness
of the seashore, free of coastal
engineering; the in-your-face cliff top
suburbs; and the unchanged seclusion of
the empty hills and their two little villages.

Telsombe and Southease villages must
once have been one community, with
Telscombe as an outlier of the mother
settlement of Southease. Telscombe
peasants always shared common rights
with Southease over their brooklands,
and the two manors were both owned
by Winchester's Hyde Abbey for nearly
600 years from Saxon times until the
Reformation.

When Telscombe's open fields were
enclosed in 1811 the Down pastures were
left as common land. They still are, and the
great Tye runs right down from the village
to the sea, forming a breathing space in the
suburban sprawl.

The cliffs of Telscombe Tye.
TQ 392 014.

THE cliffs below the Tye — apart from
the Portobello sewage outfall — are free of
breakwaters, cliff bevelling, and ramparted
undercliff walk. They are "the last clean,
wave-washed section"[1] of chalk cliff
between Brighton and Peacehaven, where
the natural processes of erosion still have
full play.

Take care, for the incoming tide can
easily cut off your return to the cliff steps
from the east round the Portobello groin.

This is a place of jagged, limpet-worn
rocks, draped in Bladder Wrack. The shrill
alarm calls of a pair of Rock Pipits echo.
Their dark grey-brown winter colours
make them almost invisible against the
shingle, till they move. There is a small
cave to the east of Portobello steps. You
can go there one day and walk upright
in it. You may go another day and find it
wholly filled with shingle. The forces that
batter these cliffs are awesome.

In the rocks of the chalk reef, below
the shingle, you may see the round or oval
shapes of large sea urchin fossils. These
will likely be one called *Echinocorys
scutata*. It is the same species you may
pick up on ploughed fields on the top of
the Downs, for the chalk strata tip upwards
to the north from the coast. You could
also find a little urchin, a bit smaller than
those marbles you played with as a kid,
called *Offaster pillula*. This is the best
place in Britain to find it. One of the urchin
fossils found here had evolved into a very
wacky pointed beastie that looks vaguely
like those chillums hash smokers burn

their throats with. It's called *Hagenowia rostrata*. Bizarre.

Stand back on the beach and look up at the white cliffs. The chalk you are looking at is hundreds of thousands of years younger than the chalk at the base of the Black Rock cliffs, for the strata rise as you go west. The chalk at the top of the cliffs east of Portobello, with its clear flint bands, is the highest and youngest in the geological strata of the Sussex coastal chalk.

When I went on a November afternoon there was a young couple with all their climbing gear drinking coffee. They told me they came about four times a week to practice for the Alps, for the climbing is similar, he said. She told me she had a collection of many fossils taken from these cliffs — dozens of the large sea urchins. When I left, I turned in the gathering gloom to see their progress. She was upside down in the ropes dangling from an overhang…

Telscombe Tye — the main part. TQ 392 017.

THE long ridge of Telscombe Tye rises for well over a mile northwards from the cliffs. Many a friendship is daily renewed on its green sward by walkers and their dogs.

It is not what it was, though, when, one October day 160 years ago, a huntsman[2] was inspired by the Tye to quote these lines from Cowper:

> The Common overgrown with fern, and rough
> With prickly gorse, that shapeless and deformed,
> And dangerous to the touch, has yet its bloom,
> And decks itself with ornament of gold.

His "odoriferous herbs and fungous fruits of earth" have not returned since the Tye lost its ancient Down pasture mantle to the plough during last century's wars.

Only two small areas of this main part of the Tye retain their aboriginal vegetation. One is the cliff top edge, with its maritime Buck's-horn Plantain, *Plantago coronopus*,

and Sea Thrift, *Armeria maritime*. There is Sea Stock, *Matthiola incana*, on the cliff face. The other is the north end of the tall Bronze Age **cross dyke, TQ 402 030**, which marks the Tye's north-eastern boundary, where three paths intersect.

Pedlersburgh, TQ 396 026, is a large round barrow, complete with 'pillage dimple' in its top. It marks the point on the Tye where you escape the urban and enter wild open Downland.

Telscombe Tye — The E Piece and The D Piece.

TELSCOMBE Tye has two separate parts which did escape the plough. The D Piece lies to the north west of Telscombe village and the E Piece lies to its north east. They are named for their shapes on the map.

The E Piece, TQ 409 037, is a strange and evocative place. Its Blackthorn thickets have a sleek look as though they have been 'Brylcreamed', for the salt wind from off the sea has relentlessly bent and flattened them away from its coming. Yet on a hot, still August day the place can feel like some Sicilian hillside: dusty, tracked, and hard-bitten by its hungry Rabbits. Many annual and biennial herbs love it, like Centaury, Field Pennycress, *Thlaspi arvense*, Yellow-wort, Carline Thistle, Autumn Gentian and Ploughman's Spikenard. The Small Bloody-nosed Beetle is there, with Small Heath and Common Blue.

The thickets are a sign of its long-neglect, but they also have their own secrets. There is the Thimblecap morel, and Twayblade Orchis. At spring time the turf has many Cowslips and Violets, too.

In autumn refugee Pheasants from the neighbouring game farm clatter everywhere, and the dead stalks of Devil's-bit are rough on your ankles. The tendrilous green and olive fronds of a Weld bush wave in the breeze like sea anemone arms.

The northern prong of The E Piece is separated from the rest by the Southease

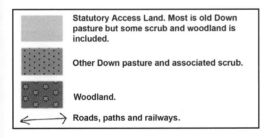

From Telscombe Cliffs to Southease

Rail Station

Iford Farm

Hostel

Southease

River Ouse

South Downs Way

Cricketing Bottom

The 'D' Piece

Southease Hill

Hill Buildings

Money Burgh

Telscombe

The 'E' Piece

Broadgreen Bottom

Dean's Farm

The Lydds

Bullock Down

The Lookout

Cross Dyke

The Valley

Halcombe

Piddinghoe

Pedlersburgh

Heathy Brow

Hoddern Farm

Saltdean

Peacehaven

Telscombe Tye

Telscombe Cliffs

Natural un-engineered cliffs

Portobello steps

Natural un-engineered cliffs

Statutory Access Land. Most is old Down pasture but some scrub and woodland is included.

Other Down pasture and associated scrub.

Woodland.

Roads, paths and railways.

Road and is sheep grazed. I have seen Adonis Blue there and Sussex Rampion.

The D Piece, TQ 399 037, lies a half mile west of that northern prong of The E Piece Both these bits are only separated from the field in between by slight banks, typical of boundaries on the old Downs, but very rare as boundary features in this age of barbed wire. The steep part of The D Piece still has old Down pasture, but upslope it has been improved.

Telscombe village, TQ 405 034.

B E A U T I F U L L Y placed. It has many interesting houses. The Norman church walls are full of sarsen stone fragments — up to two foot long — like currants in a cake.

The flint Youth Hostel cottages are the most welcoming place. You're not likely to find the lovely church or village club or National Trust manor house and gardens open, though most of the farmland around the village and part of the village itself are in public ownership (by the Ambrose Gorham Trust, a charity that Brighton City Council co-governs, and the National Trust).

The north slope of Southease Hill. TQ 412 045.

BETWEEN the Southease Road and Cricketing Bottom is a broad-backed sheep-grazed slope, with scattered Gorse and thorn brakes. It's a beautiful place. From a distance it looks undamaged, but it had agro-chemicals applied decades ago and is still recovering. Two autumns ago I found Butter Waxcap, *Hygrocybe ceracea*, there, and you may find occasional Harebells and Cowslips. Things are definitely improving. One steep part of the slope, TQ 414 047, survived the chemical peril, and there the old Down pasture herbs and insects are intact.

Hill Buildings. TQ 420 042.

H I L L Buildings was a little Victorian farm built after the enclosure of Southease in

1845. It had two gaunt cottages straight out of Wuthering Heights. They were deserted not so many years ago and slowly became ruinous. I've got a large collection of Owl pellets full of rodent bones and fur that I once found on the cottage bedroom window sill looking over the Ouse valley. A grand view for hiccupping up your undigested bits of dinner. New cottages have now been built, though the old flint barn and yard survive.

To the north is a **bushy chalk grassland bank, TQ 420 044**, with Spotted Orchis and Cowslips, Rampion and Dropwort. It's grazed now, after long dereliction.

Broadgreen Bottom. TQ 420 038.

P R E T T Y much all of the Southease Downs were old Down pasture. Now the north slope of the Bottom is the best surviving fragment. The western end is scruffy and Rabbity, so you'll find Hound's Tongue and Basil Thyme and other open ground short-lived species. Downslope at the eastern end the sward is more closed and you will find more of the old Down pasture perennials, like Sussex Rampion, Horseshoe Vetch and Devil's-bit. Autumn Ladies Tresses orchis occurs.

The south slope of Broadgreen Bottom has a long Gorse bank that is used for game bird cover. It is periodically brashed in a grid of upslope lines, like some bizarre modern haircut. A mess.

A new barn-like house has been built at the top of The Lookout, north Peacehaven, TQ 415 033. It surveys the whole lonely valley all the way down. You can't get away from it. At night its lights blaze like a lighthouse busting up the darkness. How was it allowed to be built?

Money Burgh. TQ 424 036.

T H E Money Burgh is a Neolithic long barrow dominating the narrow strait of the Ouse valley. Maybe prehistoric people

Halcombe's south slope: looking across to the bushed-up north slope.

crossed the estuary here. A medieval ferry crossed at Stock Cottages, nearby.

The Burgh is large — 40 by 20 paces and six foot tall — though much pitted by treasure seekers. Maybe they found some, judging by the barrow's name. A skeleton was found in it, but this was probably a secondary burial. The Burgh still has Rampion and other old herbs upon it, though all around are the improved horse fields of Dean's Farm.

We last went there on Halloween, and, by accident, the night came upon us while we were there. We had forgotten the sharp effect of the clocks being turned back. The Plough and Cassiopeia hung above us, and a night bird called — perhaps a Barn Owl — as we walked the fields back to Piddinghoe. Sean the Sheep and his mates stood on the black skyline and watched us. His dumpy body and little stick legs made it difficult to see him as a spectral figure.

Next to Dean's Farm are many game bird rearing pens and the gamekeepers' cottages. This part of our Downs is crawling with Pheasant and Partridge.

Southease. TQ 423 052.

ONE of my favourite villages. It is just a few old houses round a green with the round towered Church. In spring the churchyard is white with Snowdrops, like a late snowfall. Unforgettable. The church may have been built on a prehistoric barrow "of considerable magnitude".[3] Where the mound rises, against the west churchyard wall, a barn was demolished in 1852 and five skeletons were found.

The church is shrunken from the time of its building, when Southease was the most prosperous by far of the Ouse valley villages. It has a fading but evocative cycle of medieval wall paintings.

The parish had its radicals. John Theccher, a peasant, was pardoned for taking part in Jack Cade's rebellion in 1450.

Halcombe

BETWEEN north Peacehaven and Piddinghoe lies the peaceful Halcombe valley. It has delightful chalk grassland on both its south and north slopes, and the lower valley has a finger of brook meadows, with old flint walls and reedy ditches. The south slope and the spur between Halcombe and Piddinghoe have very tall and steep medieval lynchets. Some of them are like mini cliffs! The spur's wooded slope overlooking the Newhaven Road is even steeper and must indeed be an ancient river cliff.

The **south slope of Halcombe, TQ 427 031**, is the best Down pasture site on the Peacehaven Downs. In July of 2005 it was dancing with Dark Green Fritillary, Marbled White, Chalkhill Blue, and many other butterflies. All sorts of moths, bees, and spiders love this varied place, with its old anthills, mossy turf and rich scrub fringe. In spring there is Early Purple Orchis.

In that year we had to fight a campaign against the farmer, who had placed a large Pheasant pen on these pastures. We won the removal of the pen from the majority of its footprint, though the Ministry refused to use the penalty powers they had, and the pen is still on a part of the site.

The **north slope of Halcombe, TQ 423 031**, has lost much of its old pasture to scrub, but the turf that remains is very rich. There is Dyer's Greenweed, and Basil, Rampion and Squinancywort. Common Gromwell and Hound's Tongue testify to the presence of a large rabbit population. Chalkhill Blue is present in high summer.

The site is at risk from scrub. A decade ago you could walk along much more of its lower slope.

Footnotes

1   *British Upper Cretaceous Stratigraphy* — R.N. Mortimore, C.J. Wood and R.W. Gallois. Geological Conservation Review Series (JNCC, 2001), page 218.

2   Quoted from notebook of the Brookside Harriers, 1848-9 in *Sport and Nature in Sussex Downs* — Frederick F. Wood (Duckworth, 1928), page 126.

3   *Sussex Archaeological Collections*, Vol. 5 (1852), pages 204-5.

22: THE NEWHAVEN AND PEACEHAVEN CLIFFS AND DOWNS

I HAVE visited this landscape more times than any others on the Brighton Downs except Benfield Hill, the Devil's Dyke and Whitehawk Hill. It has given me more intense pleasure than any other place mentioned in this book.

It is not a pristine landscape. The relics of plotland and the continuing built development in and around Newhaven and Peacehaven have made sure of that. But its core qualities as a rugged seaside playground and paradise for wildlife have just about survived what the chaos of capitalist development and neglect has so far thrown at them.

From Newhaven's Down and cliff the long scimitar curve of Seaford Bay sweeps away, whilst the huggle muggle of wharfs and industrial buildings fills the river mouth. Huge ferries plough under speed to and from the harbour entrance, whilst Gulls and Fulmars dip and glide.

There are so many layers of interest. It's a great place for children and family events. There's good rock pooling when the tide is out. . There are wild walks to be had under Old Nore Point. The cliffs are fossiliferous and have scarce minerals and fine crystals. There is a rich birdlife and good fishing. The cliffs are high and the cliff top paths are dramatic and sometimes scary. The under cliff and the cliff top have very many scarce insects and other small creatures and fine seaside flowers, whereas Hoathdown inland has a flora more like our Wealden heaths and meadows. The Downs behind look across the Vale of Brooks to Lewes and Mount Caburn.

Newhaven. TQ 44 01.

NEWHAVEN is not a seaside town. It is a river port with Downland and cliffs between it and the sea. This character is very threatened, but it can still be plainly seen. The Norman church, TQ 442 011, sits up on the spur of the Down, beside the old road that came from Brighton over Rushy Hill, before the turnpike (now the A259) was made in modern times. The church has a sister in Normandy at Yainville, perhaps designed by the same master mason, which sits above the River Seine, just as Newhaven (known as Meeching in earlier times) church sits above the Ouse.

Newhaven's undercliff and shore.

WE'VE sat picknicking in the spring sunshine of the undercliff, whilst the mournful mewing of nesting Kittiwakes echoes from the sea and the sheer cliffs, like something from the age of Beowulf. Afterwards we've scrambled up the rock paths to look for fossils on the slumped cliff top. You can find large crystals of Selenite — Gypsum — on the under cliff, with luck.

On a fine winter day I've picked up jellied eels from the fishermen's shop on the West Quay and strong tea from the chippie on Fort Road and sat with my old mum in the car looking over the harbour wall at the incoming tide. The Heath-Robinson-looking port dredger chugs out of the harbour. Lines of Black-headed Gulls perch on the railings. Such dainty birds, with their red legs and black-tipped red beaks. I mean to give them some bits of my eel, but it's so tasty they only get the bones.

In May and June the cliffs are beautiful with the gorgeous splashings of pink Thrift and yellow Bird's-foot Trefoil, followed by snowy white Stonecrop. Fulmars swing out from their cliff face nest sites on their stiff albatross wings, and male doves 'proop' to their mates.

Raven

I've picked my way for hours on end along the cliff base in spring and summer time fossiling or insect hunting, whilst all around me multitudes of pretty little solitary bees and wasps dig and provision their tiny nurseries. As you stand below the sandy cliff face you'll notice a fine dust of sand and clay falling from places where the little miners are at work. The silence is broken with the pitter-patter of falling sand grains. I've made a count of 100 species of bee and wasp here — and a proper expert would add many more. Don't worry. They are harmless. I don't ever remember being stung there. Afterwards there's been more strong tea and cake at the 'fifties

amusement café by the harbour beach wall.

The harbour has a lovely sandy beach, which is covered at high tide. The building of the western harbour wall has caused a wide shingle beach to form to its west, under Castle Hill, which stops the tide ever reaching the cliff bottom behind it, as it does beyond. That means that the sands and clays that have slumped to the beach from the thick 'cap' on top of the chalk cliffs have not been washed away. They form a rocky playground, with lots of half private places for sun bathing and picnicking — and hunting for insects.

There are several points both east and west of Burrow Head where you can scramble up to the cliff top.

There is a real danger of cliff falls, though, particularly in wet winter months. Occasionally things get kicked down the cliff face — bottles, stones, etc — by daft people on the cliff top. Take care.

Brighton's true wilderness: The undercliff from Newhaven Beach to Peacehaven Steps.

Y o u can continue walking westwards, when the tide is out, from **Newhaven beach, TQ 442 999**, all the way to the beginning of the undercliff walk at **Peacehaven Steps, TQ 424 003**. You need to know your tides, though, because it is a mile of difficult walking over slippery and sometimes jagged chalk rock and bits of wet shingle. Leave plenty of time. The waves hit the cliff hard at high tide and have created a wave-cut notch along the cliff base. Later the cliff above the notch will collapse.

Newhaven and Peacehaven Cliffs and Downs

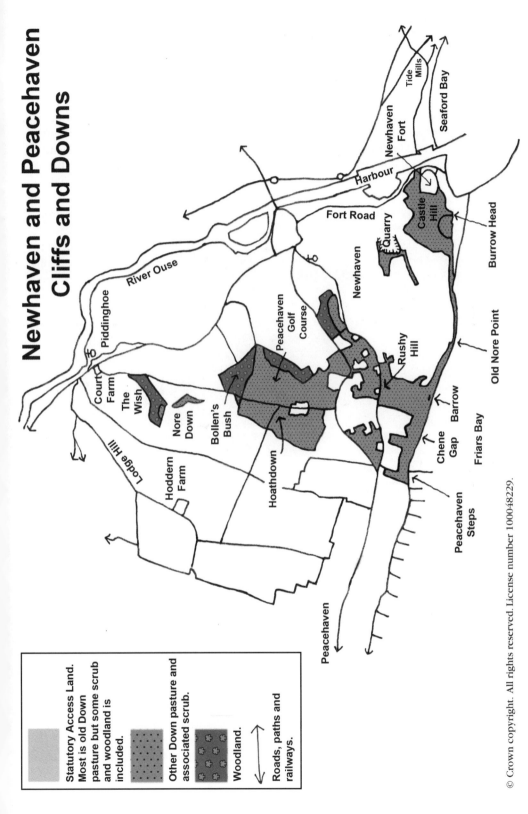

Tide Mills

Seaford Bay

Newhaven Fort

Harbour

Fort Road

Castle Hill

Burrow Head

Quarry

Newhaven

River Ouse

Piddinghoe

Peacehaven Golf Course

Rushy Hill

Old Nore Point

Court Farm

The Wish

Nore Down

Bollen's Bush

Barrow

Friars Bay

Lodge Hill

Hoddern Farm

Hoathdown

Chene Gap

Peacehaven Steps

Peacehaven

Statutory Access Land. Most is old Down pasture but some scrub and woodland is included.

Other Down pasture and associated scrub.

Woodland.

Roads, paths and railways.

It's worth it, though, for this is a spectacular place. You could be in any age of the early earth. Wild nature rules here. Many a wreck lies off shore and many lives have been lost.

The Peacehaven cliffs.

FROM Peacehaven Steps the cliffs rise sheer to around 200 feet tall in the sunlight eastwards. Descending the steps the dazzling white of the chalk makes me sneeze. Below, the sea is bottle green and through its glassy calmness you can see the chalk reef. From the under cliff walk the sun twinkles like Christmas lights on the ripples of the ocean. There is peace and silence — only the soft, liquid lullaby of the waves as they exhaust themselves on the strand line. Two Cormorants, or perhaps Shag, pass each other flying in opposite directions, like trains passing on different lines. Out at binocular distance two of their mates surface-dive-surface, like submarines with only their conning towers properly abreast the surface. Oystercatchers and Gannet are frequent visitors here.

I walk along the undercliff. Between groins 16 and 13 (the numbers are painted by the groin steps) I count the remains of the huge metre-and-more-wide Ammonites that lie on their sides on tall chalk reef plinths not far from the undercliff walk wall. At one point four or five of these octopoid monsters are held above the incoming tide as though being offered up by some Arthurian magic. Each year I visit the waves have eroded them further. Some are difficult to pick out from the surrounding Limpet and wave-worn rocks. But some display their elaborate suture patterns still.

Half way back up the steps I pass the shapes of worn Pill Sea Urchins, *Offaster pillula*, in the cliff face amongst a debris of other tiny fossil pieces.

The cliff top from Newhaven Fort to Peacehaven

THE partially restored **Fort, TQ 448 001**, was built in mid-Victorian times on the site of Tudor and Napoleonic precursors. It has good displays, but its opening is threatened by Council funding cutbacks. At the outbreak of World War Two it was the only coastal battery in use between Portsmouth and Dover. It played an important role in that war, being the base for the tragic

Newhaven's cliffs: The western harbour wall and Seaford Head on the horizon. On these cliffs be Kittiwakes a-nesting!

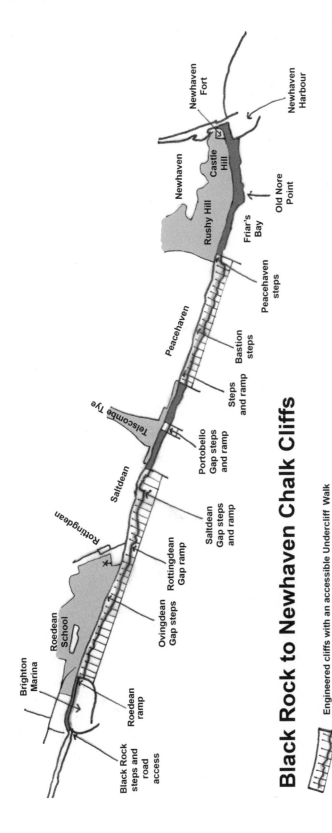

Black Rock to Newhaven Chalk Cliffs

Brighton Marina

Roedean School

Roedean ramp

Black Rock steps and road access

Rottingdean

Saltdean

Ovingdean Gap steps

Rottingdean Gap ramp

Saltdean Gap steps and ramp

Portobello Gap steps and ramp

Telscombe Tye

Steps and ramp

Bastion steps

Peacehaven

Peacehaven steps

Newhaven

Rushy Hill

Castle Hill

Friar's Bay

Old Nore Point

Newhaven Fort

Newhaven Harbour

Engineered cliffs with an accessible Undercliff Walk

Wholly natural cliffs and seashore

Open Downland to the cliff edge

335

Dieppe Raid in 1942 when thousands of soldiers lost their lives.

Some of its concrete defences have fallen down the eroding cliff face. Tunnels run down to the cliff base, where part of the buildings that constituted its first line of defence still stand.

To the west a short-worn lawn, rich in places with tiny clovers — Strawberry and Suckling Clovers, Shamrock and Fenugreek — marks the cliff edge, whilst behind, the bushy ground rises unevenly to the **gun emplacements and Coastguard tower on the top of Castle Hill, TQ 446 001**.

The names Castle Hill and Burrow Head, of the promontory to its seaward, may commemorate a far older defensive usage, however, than that of the gun batteries and Fort. Both must denote the **prehistoric camp, TQ 445 000**, whose northern earthworks lay around the lunette of high land behind the cliffs, now either massively slumped or buried beneath the hill top buildings. The southern earthworks have long been lost to the sea.

The trough of slumped land within the lunette of the ramparts is a delightful place, hot, still and peaceful in summer. Its meadowy grassland is being lost to scrub, but where it still exists it has abundant vetches, including the delectable Grass Vetchling, with Common Vetch, *Vicia sativa*, and Smooth and Hairy Tare, *V. tetrasperma* and *V. hirsuta*. There's

Teazel, too, and Fleabane, Knapweed, Hart's Tongue Fern and Carline Thistle. Where the earth is bare there may be a whitening of fossil shell fragments, including the characteristic fossil of this place, *Tympanotonos funatus*, scattered like primeval screws.

From the cliff edge in high summer you may see giant Hawk-moths — I've seen both Convolvulus, *Agrius convolvuli*, and Humming-bird — bumping into the cliff face at the end of their long sea crossing from France. Undeterred, they fly upwards, bumping the face until finally they clear the top, and are away. Peregrine Falcons live on these cliffs and can be seen daily, though they get harassed a bit by the stroppy Fulmars.

From the cliff top west of Castle Hill you can see the nesting Kittiwake on the sheer face in May and June, but the cliff edge is unstable, so it's not wise to go near the edge. Kittiwakes need to nest in these daft places, but there's no need for us to risk our lives.

Behind **Old Nore Point, TQ 436 999**, there is a narrow belt of farmland before Newhaven begins. Westwards a scatter of houses and rough tracks marks the site of the failed **Harbour Heights, TQ 433 003**, plotlands enterprise of the inter-war period.

West of that the ground rises to a **Bronze Age barrow, TQ 431 001**, on the

The cliff-top south of Rushy Hill. Surreal suburban street signs but no suburb: the failed plotlands speculation of Harbour Heights.

cliff edge, seawards of a sweep of golden Gorse. It is a glorious exposed site. Cliff erosion will likely destroy the barrow in the next decade or so.

Between the barrow and the edge of Peacehaven the half mile of cliffs have retained a fine maritime Downland turf at their edge, close cropped by Rabbits and dwarfed by salty sea winds. Low Gorse thickets are dotted around. You could see both Small and Large Bloody-nosed Beetles meandering about in their tortoise-like way. Be careful not to harm them. They are rounded and of a polished blue-black, with flat wide feet. They are scarce and special, nowadays. This cliff top has many peculiar and rare insects. Walking here I once just missed seeing a Hobby catch a Swallow in mid-air. Swallows used to nest in the old radar station buildings, now demolished.

On your way you will cross the little cleft called Chene Gap, TQ 428 002, perhaps a modification of 'Chain' Gap, where smugglers may have hauled up their wares from the beach by long chains. There used to be many rare mosses and lichens around the Gap. One or two were still there a few years ago.

Rushy Hill, TQ 430 007.
B E H I N D this clifftop turf the slopes rise to the crown of **Rushy Hill**. Most of these slopes are covered with the peculiar half-development of the failed **Peacehaven Heights plotland**. Nowadays, vegetable patches and chicken runs are giving way to dressage arenas, and the ramshackle plotlanders' dwellings are growing to look more like Mediterranean villas.

East of Rushy Hill there is an area of dense scrub woodland with an amenity meadow above known as **Meeching Down, TQ 438 010**.

From Rushy Hill you can look west across the flat plateau upon which Peacehaven is built to the rising ground of Whitehawk Hill and the Raceground stadium. It must have been a lonely stretch before the plotlands came in the 1920s.

Hoathdown: Friars Bay Gorse and Peacehaven Golf Course

T H E high ground of Rushy Hill continues north of the coast road as a wide ridge, whose old and sensible name is Hoathdown, that is 'heath down'. Small fragments of the heather still survive in one — possibly two — places, but much of the Down lay derelict for over a century. The northern end, known as Bollen's Bush, has long grown over into woodland. The western half is made up of pony paddocks at its southern end and a great mass of Gorse covering most of the rest. The eastern half is occupied by Peacehaven Golf Course, which has been there since the 1880s. Despite this recent history Hoathdown retains a most peculiar flora unlike anything else to be found on the Brighton Downs, and many special small creatures. It is a unique place.

Peacehaven Golf Course. TQ 432 014.
T H E golf course has sharp dips, little wet stream runnels and many rumples and bumps, which make it very different from the smooth, even slopes of the other courses on the Brighton Downs. That's because the geology of the course is very different. The whole of Hoathdown is made up of the same heathy sands and gravels that form the conspicuous 'cap' on the top of the Castle Hill chalk cliffs. You can find Pepper Saxifrage in summer and Green-winged Orchis in spring, both characteristic of Wealden meadows. You could find bits that have rushes and sedges and Fleabane marking their impeded drainage. At the southern end **the little valleyside, TQ 433 010**, has a good relic of true heath, with Bell Heather and Tormentil and many other heathy species. In the autumn the roughs and even the fairways have a rich Waxcap flora. In October of 2004 we found 20 species of Waxcap, Pink Gill and Fairy Club there, as well as many other old meadow fungi.

In summer there are many special mini beasts more typical of old heathland, including scarce solitary bees and wasps, flies and spiders. In the past the place has benefitted from a management which has been sympathetic to wildlife.

From the top of the course, at its northern end, there is a grand view over much of Newhaven. Its history can be scoped in a glance — wharves and port side, Victorian terraces, post war council housing, ancient Newhaven (Meeching) church, and the Poor Law Union Workhouse, TQ 440 010, behind it, looking like some Georgian manor. The view eastwards sweeps all over the Seaford Downs as far as Friston Forest, over the Cuckmere.

The Gorse Thickets. TQ 430 015.

THE western side of Hoathdown is a glorious coconut-smelling wilderness of very prickly Gorse in autumn. There are several grassy glades surviving, including one which was opened up to make a new golf fairway — never completed. The bigger glades have abundant Fleabane and Hairy Sedge, *Carex hirta*, and their edges are good for Blackberries and Dewberries. One tiny glade has retained a rich cluster of old heathland wildlife, including the scarce and handsome solitary wasp, *Astata boops* and its jewel-like cuckoo wasp species, *Hedychridium roseum*. There is a complex mat of lichens and mosses, and Waxcaps and Fairy Clubs hang on. Ling Heather was there a year or so ago. This minute wildlife 'hotspot' — now only a few metres in radius — has gradually been disappearing under encroaching Gorse. Yet it is owned by Lewes District Council.

On the north side of Hoathdown there is the Lewes District Council-owned amenity woodland of **Bollen's Bush, TQ 432 018**. Lewes District Council also own the **amenity woodland on the eastern side of the golf course, TQ 434 014**, where there are Bluebells in spring.

Old Hoddern Farm. TQ 422 022.

OLD Hoddern Farm is more like a small hamlet than a single farm. It has a gigantic barn, with a huge russet tiled south-facing roof. It's now converted into dwellings. There is a large old farmhouse and many other cottages and converted barns. It had its own chalkpit, complete with an old barn in the bottom. Stone-walled sandy fields surround it, and old apple trees hang over the hedges. A nice place.

Nore Down. TQ 431 023.

IT has the rumpled top that marks the presence of the Tertiary sands and clays underneath. On its west flank there are large medieval lynchets.

You won't notice these much, though, for the valley has been turned over to game shooting, and there's cover crops and a giant rearing pen covering part of a slope that used to have gorgeous old chalk grassland. From late summer onwards the valley is a giant poultry farm for pheasants. Horrible.

Court Farm, Piddinghoe. TQ 433 030

THIS Downland used to be farmed from Court Farm, Piddinghoe, but the farm buildings and meadows were sold off and are now a delightful small holding with the friendliest pigs. The house goes back to late medieval times and the derelict flint barns are old, too. The little wildfowl lake below was a Victorian brickfield.

Piddinghoe village, TQ 435 030, is on the bank of the River Ouse two miles inland from the sea. It must once have been a similar place to pre-modern Newhaven. The Norman church has a round tower, like those of Southease and St Michael's, Lewes, and may be built upon a large prehistoric burial mound, again like Southease upstream. There is a bottle-shaped brick firing kiln, commemorating the village's once-busy industrial past, and many old flint cottages.

APPENDICES

THE LEGAL POSITION
ON ACCESS TO THE
COUNTRYSIDE IN
ENGLAND

Trespass

SIMPLE **trespassing itself is not a criminal offence.** Trespass is almost entirely a **civil** matter. Notices proclaiming 'TRESPASSERS WILL BE PROSECUTED'are 'wooden lies'.[1]

However, walking on someone else's land without their consent is a civil trespass, whether or not you commit any damage, or realize that you are trespassing. You need commit no fault to be committing trespass (though, of course, if you commit damage you can be prosecuted for criminal damage).

The landowner can take you to a civil court, though cases brought against trespassers are extremely rare, and financial damages awarded against them tend to be almost nominal, since it is difficult to prove in simple trespass that any real loss has been caused to the landowner. Landowners risk having their civil litigation considered vexatious by the court if they take action after a simple civil trespass. Such civil action would be more likely if, for example, you persistently walked across one particular field and were in on-going dispute with the farmer about this.

Landowners or their agents have the right to remove you from land over which there is no public right of access. However, they can only do so after they have asked you to leave and you have refused. In removing you they can only use 'reasonable force'. Unless you act aggressively 'reasonable force' is unlikely to amount to very much. Anything more than gentle pushing should be considered questionable, and certainly if any actual injuries result, the landowner or their agent will have gone too far and very likely broken the law themselves.

The police will not want to be involved in simple civil trespass, and most landowners know that.

The Criminal Justice and Public Order Act of 1994, does make certain categories of trespass — usually en masse — criminal, but the Act should cause the ordinary right to roam walker no problems. The Act outlaws some categories of 'trespass with an intent to reside' (aimed at travellers); 'aggravated trespass' (aimed at hunt saboteurs); and 'trespassory assemblies' (aimed at raves and pagan gatherings).

The mass trespasses for the right to roam in 1998-9 were largely left alone by the police.

Rights of Way

YOU have the right to walk any public right of way (footpath, bridleway, or certain unpaved green roads), as well as to picnic or rest there (provided you do not obstruct the way). On the Brighton Downs rights of way are clearly marked on Ordnance Survey maps. On our Downs the standard of waymarking by signs and finger posts is high. Rights of way vary in their width according to historical circumstances, but should be a minimum width of 1m for footpaths and 2m for bridlepaths.[2]

The landowner cannot obstruct our access along a right of way and has a responsibility to maintain it in a usable condition, for instance with working stiles and access gates. If the landowner obstructs a right of way, for instance with barbed wire, the user has a right to remove a sufficient minimum of that obstacle to enable them to continue on their way. If the obstacle cannot be removed, the path user has the right to take the nearest usable route around the obstacle on that owner's land.

If a landowner ploughs over a path across a field (which they have a right to do) they must reinstate it within 24 hours, or a fortnight if it the first disturbance for a particular crop. You have the right to walk through the crops which may subsequently grow on the alignment of that path.

Cyclists and horse riders do not have the right to use footpaths (only bridleways and some green roads). Dogs must be kept under control.

Access Land

THE Countryside and Rights of Way Act of 2000 gives walkers the right to roam on designated Access Land on the Downs (as well as on heath, mountain, moor and common). This Access Land is marked on the Ordnance Survey Explorer maps with an orange tint. (However, in East Sussex commons — such as Telscombe Tye — are not yet shown as Access Land on the maps). Means of access, such as gates and stiles, should be provided by the landowner and local authority, and marked by signs. In some instances they are still not, or the access may be blocked. New access routes to access land sites across neighbouring land should be provided, if no existing right of way serves that purpose. Sometimes such access routes are not provided or are difficult to detect.

We have the right to roam statutory Access Land during the day or night. Camping and fires are not permitted, though. Dogs are restricted, and, in any case, must be kept on leads between March 1st and July 31st, as well as at any time in the vicinity of livestock. Cyclists and horse riders do not have a right of access, unless otherwise allowed by the landowner.

Landowners have the right to close Access Land for 28 days a year (which was conceded largely to mollify the grouse shooting lobby) and at other times if there are particular safety, management or wildlife protection considerations.

Landowners do not have a legal obligation to maintain all the ancient Down pasture on Access Land sites, unless they are otherwise statutorily protected as 'SSSI's' (Sites of Special Scientific Interest) or are protected as part of contractual agro-environmental agreements.

Some sites marked on the OS map as Access Land have parts which have been ploughed out (as at Broadgreen Bottom, Southease), and in such cases the landowner has no obligation to restore the land to its past character as species-rich Down pasture. We have no right of access to such ploughed out portions of a site.

Many wildlife-rich Down pasture sites were **not** designated as Access Land, and if we walk them we are committing a civil trespass.

There is much other land with full public access which is not at present shown on the OS maps. Thus, the council-owned Stanmer Park and woods, Hollingbury Hill and the Wild Park, Sheepcote Valley, and Castle Hill, Newhaven are not shown on the map. Some National Trust properties with public access, such as Ashcombe Bottom, are similarly not marked on the map. Some private landowners allow informal public access to parts of their properties and enjoy the presence of visitors. Some have done so for many years.

Footnotes

1   Special thanks to The Land Is Ours for use of their 'Trespassers Handbook' (unpublished) for this section.

2   I have used the Ramblers' Association's Handbook and Accommodation Guide, entitled *Walk Britain*, to help me précis the legal framework for rights of way.

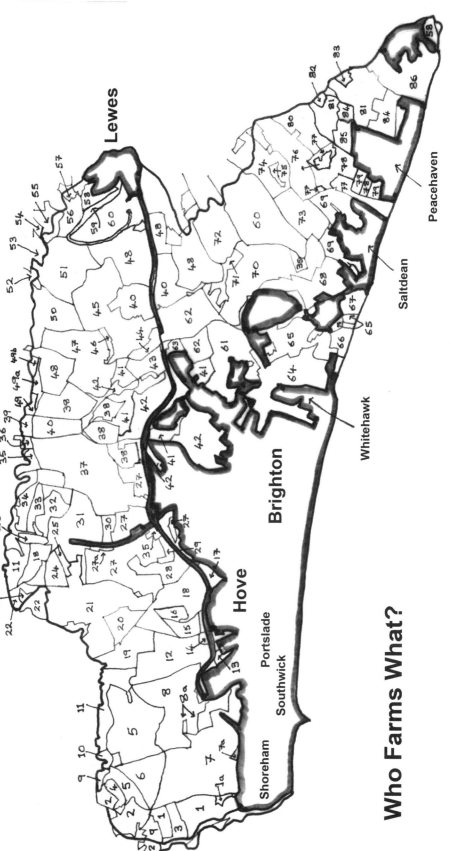

Who Farms What?

Lewes

Peacehaven

Saltdean

Whitehawk

Brighton

Hove

Portslade

Southwick

Shoreham

WHO FARMS WHAT?

THIS map shows the footprint of farms on the Brighton Downs to the best of my knowledge. Please accept my apologies if any information is wrong. Farm boundaries change — sometimes rapidly if farms are sold and split up or amalgamated.

Golf courses and amenity landscapes are included. Small parcels of land are mostly omitted.

The relevant farm houses often lie on the farms, but, nowadays, the farm house is often some distance away. You can mostly find the land manager with a bit of telephone detective work if you need to, for instance to report an injured or distressed farm animal.

Key

1. Old Erringham Farm.
1a. Mill Hill Local Nature Reserve. Managed by Adur District Council and South Downs Joint Committee.
2. Beeding Court Farm.
3. Beeding Quarry and Cement Works (derelict).
4. Golding Barn Industrial Estate. Also scrambler bike track in Room Bottom.
5. Paythorne Farm, incorporating Perching Manor, Aburton and Summersdeane Farms.
6. The Warren. Farmed from Wivelsden Farm, Wivelsfield Green.
7. New Erringham Farm.
7a. Slonk Hill Farm.
8. Mile Oak Farm.
8a. National Trust (Saddlescombe) with Mile Oak Farm as graziers.
9. Tottington Manor Farm.
10. Truleigh Manor Farm.
11. National Trust, Saddlescombe. Grazier is Wivelsden Farm, Wivelsfield Green.
12. New Barn Farm, Portslade.
13. East Hill Farm, Portslade. Managed by Mile Oak Farm.
14. Benfield Valley Pay and Play Golf Course.
15. West Hove Golf Course.
16. Brighton and Hove Golf Course.
17. Toad's Hole. Managed from Eastwood Farm, Shaves Wood Lane, Albourne.
18. Golf Farm, Devil's Dyke Road, with land at Pyecombe.
19. Devil's Dyke Farm.
20. Devil's Dyke Golf Course.
21. National Trust, Saddlescombe. Farmed by Plumpton Agricultural College.
22. Newtimber Place. Land farmed by Poynings Manor Farm.
23. Wolstonbury Limeworks.
24. Wayfield Farm.
25. Haresdean Riding Stables.
26. Rockrose Riding Stables.
27. Waterhall Farm. Farmed from Lower Wapses Farm, Twineham.
27a. Casterbridge. A smallholding.
28. Waterhall Golf Course.
29. Waterhall Sports Grounds. (Brighton and Hove City Council).

30. South Hill Farm.
31. Pangdean Farm. Split into several ownerships. Much of the land is now owned by a shooting business.
32. Pyecombe Golf Course.
33. New Barn Farm, Pyecombe.
34. Foxhole Farm, Clayton.
35. South East Water. The Keymer Post scarp site has various graziers. Part of the Balsdean site is managed by Balsdean Farm.
36. National Trust, East Sussex, Alfriston Clergy House. Grazier is Plumpton Agricultural College.
37. Standean Farm.
38. High Park Farm, Ditchling Road.
39. Sussex Wildlife Trust, Wood's Mill, near Henfield.
40. Housedean Farm, Falmer, which also owns part of the old Ditchling Tenantry Down.
41. Brighton and Hove City Council, with Northease Farm as graziers.
42. Brighton and Hove City Council.
43. Sussex University.
44. Three smallholdings and Falmer village.
45. Balmer Farm.
46. Mary Farmhouse and the north slope of Waterpit Hill.
47. Mary Farm.
48. Streathill, Ashcombe, and Kingston Farms.
49. Westmeston Farm, which is let to graziers.
49a. Old Middleton.
49b. The Gote.
50. Plumpton Agricultural College.
51. National Trust East Sussex, Alfriston Clergy House. Grazier is Plumpton Agricultural College.
52. Warningore Farm.
53. Court House Farm.
54. Mount Harry House.
55. Coombe Place.
56. Offham Farm.
57. The Forge, Offham.
58. Lewes District Council.

59. Old Lewes Race Course.
60. Iford Farm, which also owns Houndean Farm.
61. Upper Bevendean Farm.
62. Court Farm, Falmer.
63. Albion Football Stadium site.
64. Brighton Racecourse landscape. Principally owned by the City Council, plus the East Brighton Golf Club and the Racecourse.
65. Ovingdean Grange Farm. Let to Coombe Farm, Saltdean.
66. Roedean School. The farmland is managed by Ovingdean Grange Farm.
67. Beacon Hill. Principally owned by the City Council. St Dunstan's also there.
68. Challoners and New Barn Farm, Rottingdean.
69. Coombe Farm, Saltdean.
70. Balsdean Farm, Rottingdean.
71. Castle Hill National Nature Reserve. Natural England, Lewes.
72. Swanborough Manor Farm.
73. Pickershill Farm (with Tarring Neville Manor Farm and Cowlease Farm, Barcombe).
74. Northease Farm.
75. Breaky Bottom Farm, Rodmell.
76. South Farm, Rodmell.
77. Telscombe Tye. All three bits are owned by Telscombe Town Council. The Tye's main part is grazed by Stud Farm, Telscombe, and Coombe Farm, Saltdean.
78. Stud Farm, Telscombe.
79. Kirby Farm, Telscombe Cliffs.
80. Southease and Itford Farms.
81. Lower Hoddern Farm, Peacehaven.
82. Dean's Farm, Piddinghoe.
83. Court Farm, Piddinghoe. A smallholding.
84. Halcombe Farm, Peacehaven.
85. The Valley Road smallholdings, Peacehaven.
86. Hoddern Down and the Newhaven cliffs. Various owners including Peacehaven Golf Course, Lewes District Council and Lower Hoddern Farm.

THREATENED DOWN PASTURE SITES

Shoreham to Patcham Downs

— **Beeding Hill north west slope.**
Scrub encroachment and under-grazing.
— **Casterbridge slope, west of The
London Road Pylons.** Tor Grass
invasion, scrub encroachment and lack
of grazing.
— **Court Farm Barn fragment, Golf
Farm, off Devil's Dyke Road.**
Bulldozing. Lack of grazing.
— **Brighton and Hove Golf Course,
Devil's Dyke Road: Round Hill east
slope.** Lack of grazing or mowing and
scrub encroachment.
— **Cockroost Bottom lynchet and
mound.** Scrub encroachment and lack
of grazing.
— **Devil's Dyke Farm scarp.** Scrub
encroachment at base.
— **Mile Oak sites:**
    — **Whitelot Bottom head
    (Erringham Hole).** Scrub
    encroachment and under-grazing.
    — **Freshcombe, north-
    facing slope, north of
    Thundersbarrow Hill.** Scrub
    encroachment and under-grazing.
    — **Summers Deane west slope.**
    Scrub encroachment.
— **Mount Zion east slope, Portslade.**
Spraying with agro-chemicals.

— **Slonk Hill east slope, north west of
Holmbush.** Under-grazing and over-
grazing.
— **Toad's Hole valleyside, West
Blatchington.** Scrub encroachment
and lack of grazing or mowing.
— **Tottington Mount, head of Room
Bottom.** Tor Grass invasion and lack of
grazing.
— **Waterhall Golf Course.** Scrub
encroachment, lack of mowing or
grazing.
— **Waterhall Farm:**
    — **Valley north of North Heath
    Barn.** Scrub encroachment.
    Fragmentation for game keeping.
    — **Varncombe Hill south west
    slope.** Scrub encroachment.
— **West Hill combe, Pyecombe.** Tor
Grass invasion, under-grazing, and scrub
encroachment.
— **Wolstonbury Hill:**
    — **Sites on south slopes.** Tor Grass
    invasion, scrub encroachment and
    under-grazing / cattle poaching.
    — **Sites on east slope (Rockrose
    Riding school).** Over grazing.

Patcham to Lewes Downs

— **The Beeches slope, south of
Pyecombe Golf Course clubhouse.**

Tor Grass invasion, scrub encroachment and lack of grazing.
- **Big Bottom, Ditchling Beacon.** Tor Grass invasion, scrub encroachment and under-grazing.
- **Blackcap and Mount Harry scarp.** Scrub encroachment and under-grazing.
- **Clayton Mills scarp.** Tor Grass invasion, scrub encroachment and under-grazing.
- **Ditchling Beacon scarp.** Scrub encroachment and under-grazing.
- **Keymer Down scarp:** west slope of spur. Scrub encroachment and under-grazing.
- **Ladies Mile LNR Patcham, steep slope and west end.** Scrub encroachment and under-grazing.
- **Landport Fork, Lewes.** Lack of grazing.
- **Lewes Racecourse gallops and The Spital Down.** Scrub encroachment and lack of grazing.
- **Moulsecoomb Wild Park slopes.** Scrub encroachment and lack of mowing or grazing.
- **Offham chalk pits.** Scrub encroachment.
- **Pangdean Holt Bottom north slope.** Tor Grass invasion. Bush and game cover crop planting. Lack of grazing.
- **Pangdean South Hill west and north slopes.** Tor Grass invasion and under-grazing.
- **Pyecombe Golf Course.** Scrub encroachment, lack of mowing / grazing.
- **Stanmer Village: slope north east of The Street.** Scrub encroachment and under-grazing / cattle poaching.
- **Streat Hill bostal.** Scrub encroachment and lack of grazing.

Brighton to Newhaven Downs

- **Balsdean Bottom slope east of site of hamlet (above fenceline).** Tor Grass invasion and lack of grazing.
- **The Bostle, Woodingdean. Combe to south: west slope.** Scrub encroachment.
- **Breaky Bottom Farm slope.** Tor Grass invasion and under-grazing.
- **Castle Hill east side slope, Balsdean Bottom.** Tor Grass invasion, scrub encroachment and under-grazing.
- **Castle Hill north side valley / north slope.** Pheasant pen.
- **Cattle Hill slopes, Ovingdean.** Lack of grazing
- **Cold Coombes and Kingston Hill scarp.** Tor Grass invasion and under-grazing.
- **East Brighton Golf Course east slope.** Lack of grazing.
- **Halcombe north slope, Piddinghoe.** Scrub encroachment and lack of grazing.
- **Halcombe south slope, Piddinghoe.** Game farming and scrub encroachment.
- **High Hill north slope, Balsdean.** Scrub encroachment and lack of grazing.
- **Hoddern Down and Peacehaven Golf Course, Newhaven.** Scrub encroachment and possible golf course development.
- **Loose Bottom slopes and 'deer park entrenchment', Falmer.** Tor Grass invasion and scrub encroachment.
- **Mount Pleasant west slope, Ovingdean.** Lack of grazing and scrub encroachment.
- **Newhaven Cliffs and undercliff.** Scrub encroachment and building development.
- **Saltdean Coombe Farm sites:**
    - **Coombe Farm slope:** piecemeal enclosure, improvement, cattle poaching, scrub encroachment.
    - **Greenbank Avenue slope:** scrub encroachment and lack of grazing.
    - **Wivelsfield Road slope:** scrub encroachment.
- **Whitehawk Hill grasslands.** Lack of grazing and scrub encroachment. Wild fires.

THINGS I TAKE WHEN EXPLORING THE DOWNS

EVERYONE has different ideas of what's necessary to take to enjoy a good walk. Here's my own list.

— A good pair of walking boots. In winter, though, I often wear wellies even for longish walks.

— Enough clothing for likely weathers. If I'm in doubt about the weather I take slightly **more**. After all, if it turns out you've taken too much you can always put stuff in your bag, but if you've too little and get cold or wet then your walk is ruined.

— Ordnance Survey Explorer Map 122 (latest edition), covering Brighton and Hove, Lewes and Burgess Hill. This is **essential**. It covers all statutory Access Land and Rights of Way, and shows all fences and hedgerows.

— A cheap pair of lightweight wire cutters. I got mine from B&Q.

— A square of carpet about 18 inches by 18 inches to drape over the top of barbed wire fences when we're crossing them. It's very lightweight and saves our trousers and legs from snaring. It folds down small and goes in my shoulder bag.

— Lightweight bird watchers binoculars.

— A little x10 magnifying eyeglass on a string round my neck. You can order them from Watkins and Doncaster in Kent.

— Some plastic bags and small containers to put specimens in.

— A small notebook and pencil. Wildlife records are important.

— A bit to eat and drink — but nothing heavy.

— Sometimes a lightweight field guide to whatever kind of wildlife currently fascinates me — but the guide must be small and light.

— A tiny torch. In winter our walks always end in the dark and you may need the torch to read the map.

A FREEDOM TO ROAM
COUNTRYSIDE CODE

THE **countryside belongs to us all. The earth is a 'common treasury'.** Our collective ancestors tamed it and made it productive for us. We work it, make the machines that are used to manage it, process and consume its products, and provide services for countryside dwellers. **We have a natural right to roam it freely.**

— **Tread lightly. Leave nothing but your footprints.** No littering is acceptable — and that includes toilet paper and organic material like banana skins, apple cores, and orange peel. Make no fires except at recognized sites. They are not needed.

— **Do not unnecessarily damage standing crops or disturb livestock.** However, you do have the right to walk a public right of way even if it has been ploughed or planted with a crop.

— **Do not damage fences or hedges used to enclose livestock.** Close gates even when no livestock can be seen. However, many redundant wire fences are left to form hazards for the public. Do not let their presence deter your access. Additionally, land managers sometimes obstruct public rights of way and entry to statutory 'access land' sites. Such obstructions do not deserve our respect.

— **If possible, use soft words when a land manager attempts to exclude you.** A friendly relationship is rewarding and useful. Make an exact record of the conversation if there is a confrontation. If you are on land which has no right of public access, go round another way if they threaten force.

— **Report all new damage to wildlife habitat** (like unimproved chalk grassland, unimproved meadow, or hedgerows) **or to cultural features** (like burial mounds, old earthworks, or old flint walls) to your local Council Countryside Ranger Service, or to the SDJC (South Downs Joint Committee) or the future NPA (National Park Authority) Rangers. Do so **IMMEDIATELY**. Do not assume that other people have reported such abuses. That often does not happen. Anti-social land managers often rely on speed and secrecy to make damaging changes.

— **Immediately report all harm to farm livestock to the relevant** local farmstead. (See map of farm holdings on the Brighton Downs).

— **Immediately report all harm to wildlife** (such as Badger setts dug out, or signs of protected species killed, or protected plants dug out) to the Countryside Ranger Service and/ or to the police and RSPCA.

— **Keep dogs strictly under control.** Do not take them near livestock. Dogs can be a major threat to wildlife, too, such as ground nesting birds, reptiles and mammals, and a source of pollution. Do not let your dog approach other people or bark at them. If you yourself would not show another walker intrusive curiosity or aggression then do not let your dog do so.

— **Respect all laws protecting wildlife and cultural relics.**

— **To identify a species, therefore, "take the book to the specimen, not the specimen to the book"**, if possible.

— **But if you do need to take specimens** (for instance, of hard-to-identify small insects, like flies, beetles and bugs, or lower plants, like mosses, lichen and fungi) **take them very sparingly.** Try to take specimens only when the species seems plentiful and you have a legitimate on-going purpose (like recording local wildlife distribution, or doing on-going wildlife monitoring, or building up a reference collection).

— **Do not collect wild plants for decoration unless they are super-abundant.** Thus, no-one will mind if you collect some wild grasses or cow parsley, but the collection of cowslips or orchids is just not acceptable. Other people have a right to enjoy them in their wild state.

— **Only collect the very commonest wild foods, like blackberries, nettles, or hazelnuts.** Even most edible mushroom and other wild fungi are becoming much rarer and should not be collected for food except — occasionally — as 'tasters'. Leave them for other people to enjoy, and for the hosts of wild creatures — like beetles, flies and molluscs — that have evolved to depend upon them.

PLACE NAMES TELL STORIES

Tᴇʀᴇ's a fascinating layer of meaning in the history of place names, which you can tap into when you're on the Downs. The basic pattern of our place names was laid down by the Saxons, who first arrived around 400 AD and were dominant through into Norman times. There are only one or two local place names that may be earlier than that, going back to the ancient British people (such, possibly, as **Lewes** = *lexowias* = slope, or **Chiltington** = *ciltine* = precipice or steep slope).

The Saxons had a close and detailed interest in the features of the landscape. They had many more names for subtle features than us, just as the Inuit have many names for snow or the Bedouin have many names for desert.

Watch It!

Yᴏᴜ'ᴠᴇ got to be careful not to be fooled, though. Names can be messed up by one nudge of a map maker's elbow. **'Room' Bottom**, west of Truleigh Hill, was originally 'Broom' Bottom till someone dropped the 'B' by mistake on a Victorian map, and **'Rushey' Hill** above Newhaven was 'Brushey' Hill, till someone made the same mistake. **'Mossy' Bottom**, north of Shoreham, was 'Muster' Bottom on the seventeenth century map, which makes much more sense: the place where the wandering sheep flock was 'mustered' for the attention of the shepherd and farmer. Above Saddlescombe many walkers must have puzzled over the fact that the O/S map shows **East** and **West Hill** both marking what seems to be the same hilltop. In fact, West Hill is the western hill of (eastern) Pyecombe Parish and East Hill is the eastern hill of (western) Saddlescombe. West Hill *is* to the east of East Hill. Confused? The old name for West Hill — Constablewick Down — had far more poetry, anyway. **Swanborough Hill** above Iford, meant 'herders' hill': *swana-beorg*. Nothing to do with swans. And **Mount Harry** is not named after some bloke, but after a pagan sanctuary: a *hearg*, as is Harrow Hill north of Worthing (where lots of sacrificial ox skulls have been found) and Harrow Hill, where the school is, in Middlesex.

Loose Bottoms

Oʟᴅᴇʀ names were often very prosaic, though descriptive. The Downs are covered with **Round Hills, Mill Hills, New Barns** and **East, West, North and South Hills** (yawn), but we can have a cheap laugh at all the bottoms: **Loose Bottom, Big Bottom, Breaky Bottom, Long Bottom** (though none as good as the Scratchy Bottom at Lulworth, Dorset). 'Bottom' (from Saxon ***botm***) is actually quite a late term on the Downs, though the accompanying words can be much older. 'Loose', south east of Falmer (or 'Looes', north of Saltdean) comes from the Saxon word *blose*, for 'stock enclosure' (still to be seen as an earthwork at Loose Bottom), or perhaps, 'pigsty'. **'Breaky' Bottom**, west of Rodmell, perhaps refers to *'breaching'* that is ploughing up, the old sheep pasture.

Working the Land

W H A T , though, can we make of the several 'summer' place names: **Summer Down**, west of Saddlescombe, **Summersdeane**, north of Mile Oak and west of Breaky Bottom, or the lost **Soumer Brow**, above Mossy Bottom, Erringham? They surely connote a lost farming practice, as do the frequent 'Hogtrough' or 'Hog' names scattered around.

Only those working the land, too, would choose their names for the soil quality. *Clay*ton is self explanatory, as is **Red Hill** (marking the presence of reddish clay-with-flints deposits). There are two names based on the Saxon *horh*, meaning 'dirty': *Hor*ton, in Beeding, and *Hal*combe, Piddinghoe. Horton is next to marshy, messy ground and part of Halcombe's valley bottom is still wet land.

Most the names containing 'wick' mark the very old site of a specialist farm, *wic*, often of early, even Roman, date (from *'vicus'*) such as **East*wick*** up on the Downs east of Patcham, and ***Wick* Farm**, Woodingdean, perhaps both specialist sheep farms. **South*wick*, The *Wick*, Hove**, and **Esmere*wic*** (later Benfield), would have specialized in some of the rich produce of the coastal plain.

Valley Names

T H E R E were two important older local Saxon words for valley. One was *cumb* (modern combe) for a short bowl or trough shaped valley, like **Tels*combe*, Moulse*coomb*** (Wild Park) or **Well*combe*** (at Wolstonbury). The other was *denu* (modern 'dean') for a long, winding valley, like **Beven*dean*, Rotting*dean*** or **Summers*deane***. The 'wind gap' dry valley from Brighton to Pyecombe has multiple *denu* names along its length: **Raddyng*dean*** (lost), **Varn*dean*, Surren*den*, With*dean*, Patch*dean*** and **Pang*dean***. However, the dry valley from Brighton to Lewes doesn't seem to have any *dene* names surviving in use, though there are several for valleys going off it: **Holling*dean*, Houn*dean*,** and **Col*dean***. The latter is one of our oldest recorded Downland names — found in an 8th century Stanmer land grant. **House*dean*** and **Crane*dean***, east of Falmer, are corruptions of 'House *Down*' and 'Crane *Down*'.

Hill Names

T H E R E were at least five local Saxon words for hill and several other words for slope or bank. The most influential is *dun*, for a hill or an upland expanse, not surprisingly, for it has now become the name for all low, rounded hills: like the **South *Downs*** or **Ash*down* Forest**. The terms *ora* and *ofer* are much less well known. They both denote more or less the same hill formation: a flat topped ridge with a convex shoulder or shoulders. The difference between them is one of scale only. 'Oras' tend to be bigger ridges, like the scarp slope, whereas 'ofers' *may* be lower, like **South*over*** in Lewes (but think of Wind*over* Hill or High and *Over*). 'Ofers', again, may have settlements upon them, as Southover has, whereas 'oras' may have settlements at a distance. Sailors will be quite familiar with the term *ora* because many hills and cliffs (hills in cross section) seen by the Saxons from the sea were named *Ora* and used as navigational aids. Thus we have ***Nore* Point**, the southernmost point on the Newhaven cliffs. (*Atten ore* — at the hill — shortened to *'n ore*). There are several *ora* names on the scarp, and you can see from the map the appropriateness of the names. The eastern shoulder of Wolstonbury used to be called **The *Noor***, and old O/S editions mark the copse there as ***Newer* Copse**. The line of sub-hills under Kingston Hill marked by Scabby Brow, was called **Bread*nore* Laine** in the old days and Mill Hill, Rodmell was called **The *Noor***, too. It has a classic *ora* shape from below. Piddinghoe, too, has ***Nore* Down**.

Hoh as in **Pidding*hoe*** and **Balmer *Huff***, was a Saxon name for a hill that rose to a point, with a concave slope below it. In fact the name comes from the Saxon for heel, which, with a bit of imagination, it looks like. (The heel seen from sideways when someone's lying down, that is). In Piddinghoe three main Saxon hill terms come together in a single place: ***Nore Down*, Pidding*hoe***. Very droll.

Hyll for 'hill' seems to have been a later Saxon word and doesn't appear in the first wave of naming. The minor name *hlink*, for bank, ledge or terraced trackway turns up once or twice into modern times, though it doesn't appear anywhere on the modern O/S map. The south slope of Red Hill, just east of Sheepcote Valley, with its terraced bridleway, was called **The Link** into Victorian times, and there was another such name in Rodmell. The word is preserved in altered form in golf 'links'.

'Bostal' is the name lots of walkers of the Downs will know for the steep, often sunken paths down the scarp face (and, yes, it does sound like 'borstal', because the first such institution was named after a building outside Rochester at the top of such a path). It may come from the combination of *beorg stigel* (small steep hill path). *Beorg* is also the origin of the word 'barrow' for prehistoric burial mounds, because it denoted a small round, often artificial hill.

The name *cocc* for a hill (just surviving in hay*cock*) has one interesting possible usage in ***Cock*roost Hill**, north of Portslade. This was the home of the last group of Great Bustards in Sussex, till their demise about 1810. One Old English generic name for birds was 'cock', and it also seems possible that this hill is named after the Bustards' roost, which is always on high ground with good all round views. Maybe, then, the name refers to the birds or maybe it's an adaptation of the old hill name to fit the presence of the birds.

The old words for steep slope, *scora* or *shorve*, seem to be preserved in the names **Shore ham** and **Hods*hrove*** (Moulsecoombe), and Mill Hill, Shoreham certainly is steep — almost a cliff.

Port*slade* may derive from Port *slaed*, a name for a shallow sided, marshy valley, which it was at its south end. It may, however, be derived from Portes *lad*, meaning a channel or canal, which, again, it still has to its south.

Memories of Ancient Peoples

THE marks of the ancient peoples caused many evocative namings. ***Slonk* Hill**, west of Holmbush, must mark some forgotten Saxon act of slaughter (from *slog*, part of their verb *slean*, to slay or strike). **Money Burgh, Piddinghoe** (a Neolithic long barrow), and **Skeleton Hovel, Hangleton**, obviously commemorate the finds of some long-ago farm workers or antiquarian barrow robbers. **The Black Burgh** (a famous barrow — now lost) up on the Dyke Road at the very source of the Toad's Hole/Goldstone Valley, and the **Five Lord's *Burgh***, south of Plumpton Plain, must both be *beorg* (small hill) names, like **Pedlers*burgh*, Telscombe Tye**, and **Money *Burgh***. Both **Holling*bury*** and **Wolston*bury***, contain the Saxon word *burgh*, meaning fortified place. Hollingbury's camp is sometimes also called **Hollingbury 'Castle'** and we have several other Castle names: **Castle Hill** on the cliffs at Newhaven (marking the Bronze/Iron Age camp), **Castle Hill** north of Woodingdean (marking a much more peaceful early farming enclosure) and several mysterious **Scabes/Scabs Castles**. *What* do those 'scabby' names mean?

Woods and Ghost Woods

O U R Downs have been largely treeless for the last two millennia, so there are few wood names. Those there are tell an interesting story, though. *Holt* is the Saxon name for a single species wood, and there are three 'holts' surviving at Pangdean, Clayton, and Newtimber. All are ancient woods, rich in wildlife. All of them are at their core hazel woods, as we would expect on these wide sheep pastures where hazel hurdles were in such demand.

The lost name **'Bocholt'** for the ancient wood that used to sit in Ashcombe Bottom is fascinating. It means 'beech wood' (not box wood). The wood may have finally disappeared around 1800, though there's a chance that a small element provided continuity through to the present woodland, whose oldest part, however, is made up of old hazel coppice. So if the continuity does exist it is not of the presence of beech. The name **Ashcombe** refers to a Saxon bloke named Aecci, by the way, not ash trees.

The name **Hazelholt Bottom**, too, commemorates a lost holt at the far eastern boundary of Shoreham parish. The next combe to its north is called *Fresh*combe (although on the map the name is transferred to the farmstead on Truleigh Hill), which may just commemorate another old woodland name: *fyrhth*, now commonly changed to 'frith'. The 17th century spelling of Freshcombe was 'Frichcome', which is not impossibly far from 'frith'. The term *fyrhth* referred to scrubland, brushland areas, which Freshcombe still is, for its core is a very old Gorse thicket.

I know of two *hangra* names on our Downs. *Hangra* (later 'hanger') has the meaning of sloping wood, and **Hangle**ton's steep eastern slope is still crossed by the remains of an ancient hedge, which has a relict woodland/shady ground snail fauna. That's not definite evidence for past woodland, but still interesting. Mill Hill slope, Shoreham's, seventeenth century name was **'The Corne** (coney?) *Hanger'*, so even classic ancient chalk grassland sites may disguise a late woodland component.

Southease and **Northease**, have the second element *hese*, 'brushwood land', in them, which is surprising now in this tree-and-bush-less part of the Downs.

Withdean woods and **Stanmer woods** and the occasional woods between Stanmer and Lewes are all modern — a bit over a couple of centuries old at most — so the wood names are modern, too. Anything with 'plantation' in the name will be modern. **Waydown 'Copse'**, just north of Pyecombe Golf Clubhouse is several centuries old, but the 'copse' name gives it away as not ancient.

One term you won't find on the map is the old word *rew* for the slivers of woodland along the scarp bottom, where the steep sheep pastures meet the flat corn land. These linear woods very often contain relict ancient woodland wildlife hanging on by the skin of its teeth.

Windy Cricket

T H E R E are a couple of puzzling 'cricket' names right up on the Downs. One — **Cricketting Field** — (now lost) is right up on the windy top of Beeding Hill, and the other — **Cricketing Bottom** — lies between Telscombe and Southease. Early cricket was a game often played high up on Downs and wild commons. Broadhalfpenny Down above Hambledon in Hampshire, where the famous eighteenth century cricket pitch still survives, is in a similar windy, high place.

It's Us Who Name Things

P E O P L E keep on changing and renewing names. There's a whole crop of modern 'mood names' which tell their own stories. There must be many **'Happy Valleys'**. The valley just north of Offham Hill is one. The valley west of Woodingdean has been called **Happy Valley**, and the hill next to it called **Mount Pleasant**, since Victorian times. Previously they were called Wick Bottom and Round Hill respectively. **Peacehaven** and **Harbour Heights** are both modern 'mood names', as **Wonderhill Plantation** could be at Standean. **Mount Zion** north of Portslade must be a modernish name. (Further south the same ridge has the older name **Fore Down** and further south again it's called **East Hill**). People, especially children, invent names freely. We used to call the east slope of Benfield Hill **'the Adder patch'** (and it may still have Adders upon it). In Hangleton we called the old thicket in the valley south of Skeleton Hovel, **Foxes Wood**, and people still do. And local people call the wood in the combe behind Moulsecoomb Station **Dead Man's Wood.**

THE study of place names is very incomplete. There is lots of room for searching and speculation. Check out some of the books listed below.

The Place Names of Sussex, Parts One and Two — Mawer and Stenton (English Place-Name Society, Reprinted 2001)

Sussex Place-Names — Judith Glover (Countryside Books, 1997)

The Landscape of Place-Names — Gelling and Cole (Shaun Tyas, 2003)

The Guinness Book of British Place Names — McDonald and Cresswell (Guinness Publishing, 1993)

Place Names on the Brighton Downs

— **Aldrington.** Ealdhere's people's farm. (Saxon)
— **Anchor Bottom**, Beeding. An old anchorage on the River Adur. (Early modern?)
— **Ashcombe**, near Lewes. Aecci's combe. (Saxon)
— **Atlingworth Barn**, Portslade (now gone). Athel's people's enclosure. (Saxon. 'Athel' means 'Prince')
— **Balmer Farm**, Falmer. Hill pool. (Saxon)
— **Balmer Huff**, Falmer. Balmer Hill. (Saxon)
— **Balsdean**, Rottingdean. Beald's valley. (Saxon)
— **Beeding.** Beada's people's place. (Saxon)
— **Benfield**, Hangleton. Coarse grass field. (Recorded 1296. 'Esmerewic' in Domesday)
— **Bevendean**, Brighton. Beofa's valley. (Saxon)
— **The Bostle** (many). Steep road. (Saxon)
— **Bow Hill**, Stanmer. Curved like a bow.

— **Braypool**, Patcham. Bracken pool. (Recorded 1296)
— **Breach Road**, near Swanborough. Road to newly ploughed land. (Early modern?)
— **Breaky Bottom**, Rodmell. Newly ploughed valley. (Early modern?)
— **Brighton**. Beorhthelm's farm? (Saxon)
— **Buckingham**, Shoreham. Named after manorial steward's family. (Recorded 1230)
— **Bunkershill Plantation**, Ashcombe. After the battle in the American War of Independence?
— **Burnhouse Bostal**, Ditchling. There was a house by that name at the hill bottom. Presumably burnt, at some stage? (Modern?)
— **Clayton**. Farm on the clay. (Saxon)
— **Cockroost Hill**, Portslade. Bird roost hill or Bustard roost hill?
— **Coldean**, Stanmer. The cold valley. (Saxon)
— **Coldharbour**, Hurstpierpoint. (Modern)

— **Coney Hill**, Patcham. Rabbit hill? However, there was a Roger Cony in Patcham (1327).

— **Court Farm** (many places). The place where the manorial court was held. (Medieval)

— **The Cow Down**, Pyecombe. The cow common till 1872.

— **Cranedean**, Falmer. Crane Down (recorded 1609)

— **Danny**, Hurstpierpoint. Swine pasture on wet land? (Saxon)

— **Dean's Farm**, Piddinghoe. Valley farm. (Recorded 1279)

— **Dencher Road,** near Lewes. Road to the newly ploughed land. (Early modern?)

— **The Devil's Dyke**, Poynings. (Early modern?)

— **Ditchling**. Dicel's people's place. (Saxon)

— **Drove Road** (many). Road where stock daily driven to the pastures.

— **East Chiltington.** Place of the precipice or steep hill, i.e. the Downs scarp? (Celtic?)

— **Eastwick Barn**. Patcham's eastern farm. (Recorded 1296)

— **Edburton**. Eadburh's farm. Reputed grand daughter of King Alfred. (Saxon)

— **Erringham**, Shoreham. Erra's people's homestead. (Saxon)

— **Falmer**. Dark pool (Saxon)

— **Four Lord's Burgh**, Balmer. Named after the four lords of the manor whose land and parishes joined at this point. (Late medieval?)

— **Friar's Bay**, Newhaven. After William Fryer of Deans, Piddinghoe? (1693)

— **Fulking**, Edburton. Folca's people's place. (Saxon)

— **Golding Barn**, Beeding. Named after the Goldyng family. (Recorded 1296)

— **The Gote**, Streat. The stream. (Recorded 1332)

— **Halcombe Farm**, Piddinghoe. Dirty hollow. (Recorded 1261)

— **Hamsey**. Meadow village owned by the de Say family. (Hamm is Saxon. De Say is Norman)

— **Hangleton**. Hanger (sloping wood) farm. (Saxon)

— **Harvey's Cross,** Pickers Hill. Where gent died in hunting accident (1821)

— **Hazelholt Bottom**, Southwick. Hazel wood. (Recorded 1249)

— **Hoddern Farm**, Piddinghoe. Heath Down. (Recorded 1693)

— **Hodshrove**, Moulsecoomb. Heathy steep slope. (Recorded 1296)

— **Hogtrough Bottom**, Ditchling, Patcham and Falmer. (Modern?)

— **Holmbush**, Kingston Buci. At the holly tree. (Recorded 1296)

— **Horsehoe Plantation**, Streat. Mis-spelling of Horseshoe Plantation. (Modern)

— **Horton**, Beeding. Dirty farm. (Saxon)

— **Houndean Bottom**, near Lewes. Hounds valley or Hunda's valley. (Recorded 1230)

— **Housedean**, Falmer. House Down. (Recorded 1609)

— **Hove**. Hood — of fishermen's hut? (Saxon)

— **Hurstpierpoint**. Village of the wood. Owned by de Pierpoint family. (Saxon. Pierpoint is Norman)

— **Iford**. Yew tree ford, or ford by the marsh. (Saxon)

— **Jugg's Road**. Nickname for Brightonians — who brought their fish to Lewes market along this road. (Late medieval?)

— **Keymer**. Cow's pond. (Saxon)

— **Kingston Buci.** King's manor held by Bouce family. (Saxon. Bouce family are Norman)

— **Kingston near Lewes**. King's manor. (Recorded 1121)

— **Ladies Mile**, Patcham. An old Patcham drove road used by posh horse women. (Modern)

— **Landport Bottom,** near Lewes. Not known, but was a Medieval river crossing. (Recorded 1296)

— **Lewes**. Slope? (Celtic?)

— **Loose Bottom**, Falmer, Looes Barn, Saltdean. Stock enclosure. (Saxon)

— **Mary Farm**, Stanmer. Named after a member of the Pelham family. (Modern)

— **Meeching**, Newhaven. Sword men's place? (Saxon)

— **Middleton**. Farm between Streat and Westmeston. (Saxon)

— **Moon's Bottom**, Stanmer. Named after the farming family. (Early modern)

— **Mossy Bottom**, Shoreham. Was Muster Bottom. (Recorded 1693)

— **Moulsecoomb**, Patcham. Mul's hollow. (Saxon)

— **Moustone**, Balmer. Mul's stone. (Saxon)

— **Mount Harry**, Offham. Pagan temple hill? (Saxon? but first recorded 1610)

— **Mount Zion**, Portslade. (Sounds early modern?)

— **Nan Kemp's Grave**, Kingston near Lewes. Where that murderess is buried. (Modern)

— **New Barn**, Portslade. (Recorded 1577)

— **Newers Copse**, Pyecombe. Hill (ora) copse. (Saxon)

— **Newhaven**. New harbour. (Recorded 1587)

— **Newmarket**, Falmer. Was 'Newe Markett' (Recorded 1580)

— **Newtimber**. New timber (Saxon)

— **Nore Down**, Piddinghoe. Hill (ora) Down. (Saxon)

— **Northease Farm**. The northern brushwood land. (Saxon)

— **Northlane Barn**, Hangleton. North field. (Saxon?)

— **Novington**, East Chiltington. Ofa's people's farm? (Saxon)

— **Offham**. The crooked meadows. The Ouse bends here. (Saxon)

— **Ovingdean**, Brighton. Ofa's people's valley. (Saxon)

— **Pangdean**, Pyecombe. Pinca's valley. (Saxon)

— **Patcham**. Pecca's homestead. (Saxon)

— **Patchway**, Stanmer. Peccel's pagan temple. (Saxon)

— **Paythorne**, Edburton. Paga's thorn bush. (Saxon)

— **Peacehaven**. (Named 1919)

— **Perching**, Edburton. People of the enclosure. (Saxon)

— **Piddinghoe**. Pyda's people's hill. (Saxon)

— **Piddingworth**, Ditchling. Pydel's people's enclosure. (Saxon)

— **Plumpton**. Plum farm. (Saxon)

— **Portslade**. Someone called Port's shallow valley, or Port's dodgy river crossing. (Saxon)

— **Poynings**. Puna's people's place. (Saxon)

— **Preston**. Priests' farm. (Saxon)

— **Pyecombe**. The combe of the pointed hill, as in 'pike'? (Saxon)

— **Radynden**, Preston (lost). Radda's people's valley. (Saxon)

— **Rest and be Thankful stone**, Southwick. (Early modern?)

— **Rodmell**. Red earth place, i.e. clay-with-flints. (Saxon)

— **Roedean**, Brighton. Rough valley. (Recorded 1724)

— **Room Bottom**, Beeding. Was 'Broom'. The 'B' got lost. (Early modern?)

— **Rottingdean**. Rota's people's valley. (Saxon)

— **Rushy Hill**, Newhaven. Mis-spelling of Brushey Hill. (Early modern?)

— **Saddlescombe**, Newtimber. The hamlet stands on a 'saddle' of land. (Saxon)

— **Saltdean**, Rottingdean. Very salty sea winds. (Recorded 1740)

— **Scabes Castle**, Portslade; Scabby Brow, near Ashcombe, and others. Could refer to sheep scab? (Early modern?)

— **Sheepcote valley**, Brighton. Sheep sheds. (Early modern?)

— **Shoreham**. Homestead by the steep cliff. (Saxon).

— **Skeleton Hovel**, Hangleton. Was a prehistoric burial unearthed here? (Early modern?)

— **Slonk Hill**, Kingston Buci. Slaughter hill, after some battle. (Saxon)

— **Southease**. The southern brushwood land. (Saxon)

— **Southover**, Lewes. South hill (ofer). (Saxon)

— **Southwick**. Southern farm of Kingston. (See Wick). (Saxon)

— **Standean**, Ditchling and Balsdean. Valley of the sarsen stones. (Saxon)

— **Stanmer**. Stony pool. (Saxon)

— **Streat**. After the Roman road now called the Greensand Way. (Saxon)

— **Summersdean**, Edburton. Summer valley (Recorded 1296)

— **Summer Down**, Newtimber. Used for summer pasturage?

— **Swanborough**, Iford. Herders' hill. (Saxon)

— **Tegdown**, Patcham. Tegs are one or two year old sheep. (Early modern?)

— **Telscombe**. Tytel's hollow. (Saxon)

— **Telscombe Tye**. Telscombe common. (Saxon)

— **Tenant Hill** (several). Downland common. (Medieval?)

— **Thundersbarrow**, Southwick. After the pagan god Thor? (Saxon?)

— **Tottington Farm**, Beeding. Totta's farm. (Saxon)

— **Truleigh**, Edburton. Clearing with trees. (Saxon)

— **Varncombe**, Pyecombe. Bracken (fern) combe. 'F' became 'v' in Sussex dialect. (Recorded 1279)

— **Varndean**, Patcham. Bracken valley. (Recorded 1296)

— **Wales Farm**, Plumpton. From Walter de Westwales? (1332)

— **The Warenne**, Hurstpierpoint, The Warren, Beeding Hill. Warren Road, Woodingdean. Named after rabbit 'warrens', where rabbits were farmed from medieval to modern times.

— **Warningore**. Waenna's hill (ora). (Saxon)

— **Wayfield Farm**, Pyecombe. After Thomas de Wayvyle. (Recorded 1332)

— **West Blatchington**. Blaecca's people's farm. (Saxon)

— **Westmeston**. The most westerly farm (from Plumpton?). (Saxon)

— **Whitehawk Hill**, Brighton. White oak or white hawk? (Recorded 1587)

— **Whiteway Bottom**, Iford. Chalkland roads were often called whiteways.

— **Wick Farm** (several). Means specialist farm. (Possibly Roman in origin)

— **Wickhurst Barns**, Poynings. Possibly named after a local bloke: Bartholomew Wyker. (Recorded 1296)

— **Wish Bottom**, Pyecombe (and others). Marshy meadow. (Saxon)

— **Withdean**, Patcham. Wihta's valley. (Saxon)

— **Wolstonbury**, Pyecombe. Wulfstan's burgh? (Recorded 1740)

— **Woodingdean**, Brighton. (Early modern?)

CONTACTS

The Land Is Ours
c/o London Action Resource Centre,
62 Fieldgate Street,
London, E1 1ES
Email: mark@tlio.org.uk

The Open Spaces Society
25A Bell St.
Henley-on-Thames,
Oxon, RG9 2BA
Tel: 01491 573 535
Email: hq@oss.org.uk

The Ramblers Association
Tel: 0207 339 8500
Freedom to Roam team — Email:
freedom@ramblers.org.uk

Local site-based Downland conservation
groups:

— For Brighton groups contact:
Brighton Urban Wildlife Group
c/o The Booth Natural History Museum
(address below)
Tel: 01273 608 786
Email: brightonuwg@btconnect.com

— **The Lewes District Council
Community Ranger**
will have details of their local groups:
Tel: 01273 484 408

— **The South Downs Joint Committee
Rangers**
will have details of local groups
elsewhere on the Brighton Downs:
Tel: 01273 625 242

The Booth Museum of Natural History
194 Dyke Road,
Brighton, BN1 5AA
Tel: 01273 292 777
is an Aladdin's cave of collections. What
you see on public view is only a tiny
fraction of the treasures they have in their
crowded, under-funded space. Use them or
risk losing them!!

**The Brighton and Hove Archaeological
Society**
can be contacted via John Funnell:
Tel: 01273 607 127
Email: john.funnell@brightonarch.org.uk

**The Brighton and Hove Geological
Society**
c/o The Booth Museum (address above)
Enquiries to John Cooper, Chair:
Tel: 01273 292 780
Email: john.cooper@brighton-hove.gov.uk

RECOMMENDED BOOKS

For the South Downs Landscape

— *The South Downs* — Peter Brandon. (Phillimore, 1998)

— *The Natural History of Selborne* — Gilbert White (First published 1788)

— *Nature in Downland* — W. H. Hudson (First published 1900)

— *A South Down Farm in the Sixties* — Maude Robinson (First published 1938)

— *A Song for Every Season* — Bob Copper (Heinemann, First published 1971)

— *Sussex, Environment, Landscape and Society* (University of Sussex, 1983)

— *Prehistoric Sussex* — Miles Russell (Tempus, 2002)

— *The Archaeology of Sussex* — E. Cecil Curwen (Methuen, 1937)

— *The Downland Shepherds* — Barclay Wills, edited by Shaun Payne and Richard Pailthorpe (Alan Sutton, 1989)

For Field Identification

— *The Wild Flower Key* — Francis Rose (Warne, 1981)

— *Wild Orchids of Sussex* — David Lang (Pomegranate Press, 2001)

— *Wild Flowers of Chalk and Limestone* — J. E. Lousley (Collins, 1950)

— *Grasses, Sedges, Rushes and Ferns* — Francis Rose (Viking, 1989)

— *Mushrooms* — Roger Phillips (Macmillan, 2006)

— *Insects of Britain and Western Europe* — Michael Chinery (Collins, 1986)

— *Butterflies and Day-Flying Moths of Britain and Europe* — Michael Chinery (Collins, 1989)

— *Grasshoppers and Allied Insects of Great Britain and Northern Ireland* — Marshall, Haes and Ovenden (Harley Books, 1988)

— *The Land Snails of Britain and North-west Europe* — Kerney, Cameron and Riley (Collins, 1979)

— *Fossils of the Chalk* edited by Andrew Smith and David Batten (The Palaeontological Association, 2002)

— *Prehistoric Flintwork* — Chris Butler (Tempus, 2005)

For the Big Picture

— *This Land Is Ours* — Marion Shoard (Paladin, 1987)

— *A Right to Roam* — Marion Shoard (Oxford University Press, 1999)

— *Freedom to Roam* — Howard Hill (Moorland Publishing, 1980)

— *The Self-Managing Environment* — Alan Roberts (Alison and Busby, 1979)

— *Green Bans, Red Union* — Meredith and Verity Burgmann (UNSW Press, 1998)

GLOSSARY

Aboriginal (grassland): There from the beginning.

Arable: Ploughed cropland.

Agri-business: Modern capitalist farming industry. Far greater level of exploitation of the land than pre-modern agriculture.

Aquifer: Rock deposits (like chalk) containing water.

Argillaceous: Of rock made of fine-grained material, such as clay.

Barrow: Prehistoric burial mound. Comes from Saxon *beorg*, meaning round hill.

Bostal / Bostle: Steep road. (Saxon). Many on the escarpment.

Braided (paths): Several closely parallel tracks, mostly separated by banks.

Breccia: Rock made up of broken fragments embedded in a fine matrix.

Bridleway: Path open to horse riders and walkers, but not cars.

Bronze Age: Prehistoric period of bronze tool use. Roughly 4000 to 2700 years ago in Sussex.

Brookland: Flood plain of small streams (brooks) and fields.

Bungaroosh: Walling made of a mix of flint, chalk and brick rubble set in lime putty mortar made with sand and gravel.

Capitalism: Economic system based on private property, private profit, and production for the market (rather than directly for use).

Champion / 'Champaign' (country): Old landscape of strip-cultivated open fields and pastures with few hedges or trees.

Chrysalid: The hard cased transition stage between caterpillar and adult in moths and butterflies.

Clay-with-flints: Downland superficial deposit of clay with numerous, often yellowish, flints.

Common: Land traditionally subject to collective rights of usage (for pasture, wood, or turf, etc.) All commons now have a public right of access.

Coppice: A wood whose shrub layer (e.g. of hazel) is cut regularly for use.

Cornucopia: A 'horn of plenty' overflowing with fruit and vegetables.

Cross dyke / cross-ridge dyke / 'covered way': Prehistoric bank and ditch lines often across spurs or ridges. Probably boundaries.

Crustose: Forming a clinging crust, as some fungi and lichen do.

Desmesne: The medieval lord of the manor's home farm.

Dip slope: The gentle back slope of the Downs (running south).

Downs: Ranges of hills usually on chalk.

Drove: A road along which livestock were driven.

Escarpment: Continuous long steep slope at the edge of the plateau of the Downs (from Beeding Hill to Lewes, and from Kingston to Rodmell).

Fodder: Bulk livestock feed, like hay or vetches.

Fold: An enclosure or pen for sheep or other livestock. Usually moveable, but a few were built with flint walls.

Foliated (blue clay): Separable into thin layers.

Haywain: Wooden waggon for carrying hay and other crops.

Headings (of water works): Tunnels in the chalk carrying extracted water for human use.

Henge: Prehistoric, usually circular, ceremonial enclosure, usually with a perimeter bank and a ditch inside the bank.

Horsham slabs: Heavy sandstone slabs (from the Wealden Clay near Horsham) used for pre-modern roofing.

Jugg: Pre-modern nickname for Brighton fishermen.

Laines / Lanes: Old collectively managed, strip-cultivated open fields in our area. Big open fields.

Legumes: Plants of the pea family.

Lichen: Plants which are stable symbiotic combinations of fungi and algae.

Lignite: Carbon-loaded fossil plant remains in a softer condition than coal.

Liverwort: Small primitive plants often mistaken for mosses.

Lynchet: A ledge, terrace or bank. Usually refers to the remains of prehistoric or medieval field systems.

Manor: A medieval landed estate. The lord had judicial rights and kept the workers in servitude.

Mantra: A Hindu word or phrase holding spiritual power.

Marl (on the Downs): Rock layers within the chalk with a high clay content. Used for fertilizer.

Megalith: Great stones — used for prehistoric monuments.

Mesolithic: Middle Stone Age ('meso' = middle). Post-glacial gatherer-hunters with bows and arrows.

Mesotrophic (soils): With moderate amounts of nutrients present. Used here to describe plants that flourish in richer soils than Downland often provides.

Microliths: The tiny flint tools that Mesolithic people specialized in.

Moot (as at Balmer Down): An assembly place.

Mycorrhiza: The fused roots of a fungus and a higher plant, which exchange nourishment, usually to the mutual benefit of both species.

Neolithic: New Stone Age. The first farmers and herders.

Palaeolithic: Old Stone Age. When modern humans emerged during the Ice Age.

Pheromone: Chemical substances given out to affect other creatures (such as attractive sex pheromones).

Plotland: A modern landscape made up of makeshift homesteads, often without proper services.

Pollard: A tree retaining its trunk, but with its crown of branches periodically cut for use.

Prairie: Extensive grassy treeless plain, as in North America. (See 'Steppe').

Pylons (in this reference): Monumental towers or gateways. Used for the towers on the A23 London Road at Pangdean, which mark the start of Brighton's territory.

Puddingstone (as at Balmer Down): Rock made up of pebbles and a finer cementing matrix, like mixed fruit in a pudding.

Refugia: Places whose flora and fauna have remained unaltered by surrounding changes (of climate or human damage).

Rew: Thin strips of woodland used to mark boundaries. (See 'Shaw').

Roding: The male Woodcock's spring display, when they repeatedly fly round their woods, calling.

Sarsens: The sandstone rocks that littered the Downs in pre-modern times. Many of the big ones are now used ornamentally, often in parks. They're about 45 million years old.

Saxons: The Germanic people who came to England from around the Fourth Century AD, and dominated it till the Normans came in 1066 AD.

Scarp: The steep, outward-facing slope of the Downs.

Scrub: Bushy vegetation. The word is a variant of 'shrub'.

Shaw: A small linear woodland, often used as a boundary. (See 'Rew').

Spur: A hill or stumpy ridge projecting from the main range.

Steppe: Extensive grassy treeless plain, as in Russia. (See 'Prairie').

Tenantry Downs: Name of Downland commons, especially in Sussex. Common rights were held by the manorial ('copyhold') tenants in proportion to their open field strip holdings.

Terracettes: Small terraces on steep slopes caused by the repeated passing of sheep and, to a lesser degree, cattle. Characteristic of old grazed Down pasture and, from a distance, look a bit like thumb-prints.

Tertiary: Of the third order, the Age of Mammals.

Tillage: The working of land for crops

Tor Grass: A coarse, excluding, poorly digestible, mat-forming grass that is invasive on old Down pasture.

Traveller: Name used for all modern nomadic people in Britain of several cultures.

Trifoliate: Three-leaved, as in many clovers.

Tumulus: Archaeologists older name for a prehistoric burial mound.

Van dweller: Name for people who live in vans. Some would regard themselves as travellers and some would not.

Vermifuge: Vermin (especially insect) repellant.

Warren: Enclosure for the farming of rabbits.

Wildwood: The original woodland before humans altered and cleared it.